MEASUREMENT AND RESEARCH IN THE ACCOUNTABILITY ERA

Edited by

Carol Anne Dwyer
Educational Testing Service

 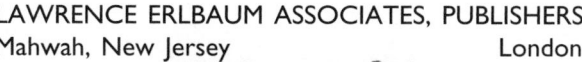

LAWRENCE ERLBAUM ASSOCIATES, PUBLISHERS

2005   Mahwah, New Jersey   London

Lawrence Erlbaum Associates, Inc., Publishers
10 Industrial Avenue
Mahwah, New Jersey 07430

Cover design by Kathryn Houghtaling Lacey

Library of Congress Cataloging-in-Publication Data

Measurement and research in the accountability era / edited by Carol Anne Dwyer.
   p. cm.
Includes bibliographical references and index.
"The chapters here were originally commissioned as part of the ETS 2003 Invitational
Conference . . . held in New York City in October 2003. The authors were invited to
expand on their conference presentations for publication"—Introd.
   ISBN 0-8058-5330-8 (alk. paper)
   1. Educational accountability—United States—Congresses. 2. Educational tests and
measurements—United States—Congresses. I. Dwyer, Carol Anne. II. ETS Invitational
Conference (2003 : New York, N.Y.)

LB2806.22.M43 2005
379.1′58—dc22   2004059125
                                                               CIP

Books published by Lawrence Erlbaum Associates are printed on acid-free paper,
and their bindings are chosen for strength and durability.

Printed in the United States of America
10 9 8 7 6 5 4 3 2 1

Contents

Preface   vii

Introduction   1

**PART I: THE SCIENCE OF EDUCATION
AND SCIENTIFIC EVIDENCE**

1   Toward a More Adequate Science of Education   7
    Ellen Condliffe Lagemann

2   Scientific Evidence and Inference in Educational Policy
and Practice: Implications for Evaluating Adequate
Yearly Progress   21
    Robert L. Linn

3   Issues Related to Disaggregating Data in a New
Accountability Era   31
    Sharon Lewis

4   Scientific Evidence and Inference in Educational
Policy and Practice: Defining and Implementing
"Scientifically Based Research"   41
    Lisa Towne

iii

PART II: CLOSING THE ACHIEVEMENT GAP

5   Prospects for School Reform and Closing
the Achievement Gap   59
Andrew C. Porter

PART III: IMPROVING TEACHER QUALITY

6   Accountability Testing and the Implications
for Teacher Professionalism   99
Caroline V. Gipps

7   The Persistent Problem of Out-of-Field Teaching   113
Richard M. Ingersoll

8   No Teacher Left Behind: Issues of Equity
and Teacher Quality   141
Gloria Ladson-Billings

**PART IV: TEST LINKING: TECHNICAL AND
CONCEPTUAL CHALLENGES**

9   *E Pluribus Unum:* Linking Tests and Democratic Education   165
Michael J. Feuer

10   Assessing the Validity of Test Linking: What Has
Happened Since *Uncommon Measures*?   185
Paul W. Holland

**PART V: ACCOUNTABILITY ISSUES
FOR ENGLISH-LANGUAGE LEARNERS**

11   ELLs Caught in the Crossfire Between Good Intentions
and Bad Instructional Choices   199
Lily Wong Fillmore

12   Report on an Informal Survey of ELL Educators
at the State and Local Levels   215
Julia Lara

PART VI: USING ECONOMETRIC MODES
IN SCHOOL ACCOUNTABILITY

13   Have Assessment-Based School Accountability Reforms
     Affected the Career Decisions of Teachers?   225
     Susanna Loeb and Felicia Estrada

14   Stricter Regulations or Additional Incentives?
     The Teacher Quality Policy Dilemma   257
     Steven G. Rivkin

15   Accounting for Schools: Econometric Issues
     in Measuring School Quality   275
     Cecilia Elena Rouse

PART VII: ALIGNING THE ELEMENTS OF
ACCOUNTABILITY SYSTEMS

16   Improving Preparation for Nonselective Postsecondary
     Education: Assessment and Accountability Issues   301
     Michael W. Kirst

17   Aligning Curriculum, Standards, and Assessments:
     Fulfilling the Promise of School Reform   315
     Eva L. Baker

Author Index   337

Subject Index   345

Preface

The 2003 Educational Testing Service Invitational Conference provided an opportunity to convene leading scholars and practitioners to deliberate on the important topic of measurement and accountability. This conference continues a longstanding ETS tradition of seeking to advance the science of measurement, to illuminate important research issues, and to inform policy. Since 1936, the education community has responded to our invitation to address the most pressing technical and policy issues associated with the evolving science of measurement. The 2003 conference was a sterling example of this tradition.

With the theme of "Measurement and Research Issues in the Accountability Era," our hope was to provide the occasion to look at where measurement and research have been and to identify the challenges to our field presented by standards-based reform and accountability policies. Presenters and participants were focused and candid in their analysis of the capacity to use valid data in the service of student learning. This balance and passion are quite apparent in these chapters, and serve to illustrate the professional standards and the sense of civic responsibility required in this age of high-stakes decisions based on measurement products.

As the tradition of the ETS Invitational Conference continues, so does our determination to serve learners. We are most grateful to the authors of these chapters for their support in this regard. We are confident that readers will find invaluable guidance in their efforts to improve learning outcomes for all students.

—*Sharon P. Robinson*

Introduction

The subject of accountability generates as much heat as light in the context of today's school reform efforts. Little can be accomplished, however, by rhetoric alone. The current focus on accountability creates an opportunity for unprecedented attention to the critical elements of an effective accountability system. These elements include careful specification of what students should learn, creation of realistic opportunities for all students to learn what is required, finding reliable and valid evidence of what learning has taken place, and creating appropriate incentives to improve the system.

This volume attempts to bring to bear the best thinking of leading scholars and experienced practitioners on measurement and research issues in the development and implementation of scientifically rigorous and educationally sound accountability systems. The chapters here were originally commissioned as part of ETS (Educational Testing Service) 2003 Invitational Conference, *Measurement and Research Issues in a New Accountability Era,* held in New York City in October 2003. The authors were invited to expand on their conference presentations for publication.

Accountability systems often appear simple on the surface. Unfortunately, however, as H. L. Mencken wrote, "For every complex problem there is an answer that is clear, simple, and wrong" (Mencken, 1990), and never was this more true than in the case of school reform and educational accountability systems. As the stakes associated with accountability and school reform have risen to unprecedented heights, the need for better scientific evidence on what works has become more and more apparent. Unfortunately, as this evidence emerges, new problems of interpretation are created: It becomes more and more difficult for policymakers, practitioners, and the general public to be sure what this evidence means to them.

It would be a mistake, however, to assume that adequate public awareness of the most basic accountability issues exists. In their 2002 survey commissioned by ETS, *A National Priority: Americans Speak on Teacher Quality,* the bipartisan pollsters Peter Hart and Robert Teeter document both the American public's general dissatisfaction with the state of public education and their lack of knowledge of important educational events. This dissatisfaction with schools is pervasive and of long duration, and there is little good news about progress over time in improving negative perceptions of our educational system. In Hart and Teeter's 2002 survey, over half of the general public felt that the American system of public education was deeply defective, and almost three quarters of the public are in favor of testing students and teachers, and of holding teachers and school administrators responsible for students' progress. From the point of view of the federal government and many states, great strides are being made to improve education through comprehensive (and expensive) accountability programs. Unfortunately, however, there is a tremendous gap between accountability efforts on the grand scale and even a minimal awareness of these efforts on the part of the public and among educators themselves. Interest in the topic clearly outpaces factual information. For example, Hart and Teeter found that only 12% of the public and 36% of teachers said they were aware that a major national school reform bill with bipartisan support and the approval of both houses of Congress, the No Child Left Behind Act (NCLB, 2002), had been signed into law in 2001. Although it is heartening that 63% of those identified as policymakers indicated awareness that NCLB exists, this figure is still far from the level of awareness that one might expect from educational policymakers concerning such a major piece of legislation as NCLB.

Findings such as those of Hart and Teeter make it clear that extraordinary efforts are needed if we are to fully inform the public and to marshal the political will required to meet the educational needs of all students, including those most at risk of being left behind: students living in poverty, English-language learners, and students with severe disabilities. Without effective intervention, the achievement gaps experienced by these students will continue to grow. Testing students is a necessary but not sufficient step to take to close these gaps; we need clear plans for effectively teaching those who have not learned up to standards, not just labels for these individuals and their schools. In addition to the ethical issue of taking collective responsibility for their education, we should also remember that all of these groups are growing in number, and will probably continue to do so.

The inevitable result will be that the practical and economic issues associated with the quality of their education will be greatly magnified in the future. If the promise of school reform for all children is to be realized at least in part by accountability systems, we must understand better how these systems can be made to work for the benefit of all students.

The authors in this book address the context in which educational reforms are taking place; present policy and technical analyses of the design and implementation of the NCLB and other major accountability systems currently in use; project trends for the future; and address the large framing questions of what works and how to bring all of the many elements of school reform and accountability into effective alignment.

We asked the authors to distill their research and measurement findings to provide guidance to the reader in understanding where we might find ways forward to educational improvements. For example, Andrew Porter's chapter focuses on achievement gaps. He first summarizes the enormous amount of research on current achievement gaps (how big they are, how stable over time, how stable over children's developmental span, and how important they are in practical terms), and then systematically evaluates the prospects for each of the major kinds of reform (preschool, teacher, instructional, standards based) that have been hypothesized to decrease these gaps. Eva Baker's chapter focuses on an equally large question, the alignment of components of educational accountability systems. She provides lucid guidance to understanding the nature of alignment itself, what we can reasonably expect of it, and how we might improve on the current state of widespread gaps in alignment.

Contributions such as these, and those of the other authors in this volume, help educational and measurement scholars, practitioners, policymakers, and others develop a deeper understanding of the data and the logic of accountability systems. In our new era of accountability, the importance of solid facts and empirically informed debate has never been more critical. As Ellen Lagemann reminds us in her chapter, it is a fundamental responsibility of the measurement and research community to provide reliable information that supports improved service to learners. This makes it a moral imperative as well as a technical challenge to improve the quality of measurement and research. Only then will we have the foundation needed to advance the learning of all students.

REFERENCES

Hart, P. D., & Teeter, R. M. (2002). *A national priority: Americans speak on teacher quality.* Princeton, NJ: Educational Testing Service. Retrieved April 7, 2004, from ftp://ftp.ets.org/pub/corp/survey2002.pdf

Mencken, H. L. (1990). *The vintage Mencken* (A. Cooke, Ed. Reissued ed.). New York: Vintage.

No Child Left Behind Act of 2001, Pub. L. No. 107-110, § 115 Stat. 1425 (2002).

THE SCIENCE OF EDUCATION
AND SCIENTIFIC EVIDENCE

1

Toward a More Adequate Science of Education

Ellen Condliffe Lagemann
Harvard Graduate School of Education

I am honored to be at this conference today. The ETS Invitational Conference has a long and proud history. There was a predecessor to the Conference held under the auspices of the American Council on Education and several other testing services beginning in 1936. That was discontinued during World War II, and, then, the Conference literally became the ETS Invitational Conference on Testing when ETS (Educational Testing Service) was founded in 1947 (Woods, 1956). By that time, it had shifted its focus from state educational testing to personality and educational testing of many different kinds. Subsequently in the 1960s and 1970s, it shifted focus again, now paying more attention to making testing useful and understandable to teachers (Anastasi, 1966). Today, ETS is reviving a Conference that has not been held in a number of years and, if the current gathering is consistent with the ever-broadening trend line of the Conference's history, I suspect our conversations will expand again, ranging even beyond matters of testing per se to more general questions concerning accountability in education.

As we all know, we are living today in a new era in education. It is an era of unprecedented accountability at the state, local, district, school, and even classroom level. It is an era when we are expecting more of students, teachers, and school leaders and when we are paying more and more—and perhaps too much—attention to "high stakes tests." We live in an era when, to a degree unprecedented in history, we are asking that education policies be buttressed by rigorous, "scientific" research. These new expectations are appropriate. We should provide an excellent and equal education to all children. We are the richest society in the history of the world and we owe it to all young people to guarantee that they will come of age ready to live meaningful and productive lives. That said, I also think we need to be realistic about the hurdles we will have to surmount to achieve this goal.

First of all, the economic downturn that is plaguing our country is undermining what progress there has been toward improving student achievement. State and local budget cuts will make it difficult to sustain professional development and tutoring programs. Financial stringency may also preclude the continuation and expansion of the after-school programs, mentoring, and summer internships that often make the difference between a student being able to finish school or dropping out. We continue to lose too many teachers and to see many of the best teachers leave high-poverty urban areas, where they are most needed, for higher paying suburban areas. Clearly, the opportunity side of the accountability equation is under strain, to say the least. That being the case, it is not clear that we will have the capacity to do what we hope in education.

Even without our current economic woes, however, meeting our expectations will be very, very difficult. We are just beginning to understand all that is involved in translating theory into practice in education. We now realize, for example, that, in addition to science, we need what I like to call "usable knowledge." Usable knowledge is knowledge derived from research that is then translated into the toys, texts, tests, and teaching materials that teachers and learners themselves can actually use to promote learning. Even though we are beginning to understand the importance of usable knowledge, there are relatively few researchers able to do this kind of work, there is little infrastructure to support it, and there are few opportunities for training.

What's to be done? Should we abandon our high hopes for education? Should we retreat from our commitment to educational equity? I think not. Rather, to create the knowledge and tools we need to meet our new expectations for education, I believe we need new standards of accountability for the education research community, new infrastructure for research, and new programs of research training. If we can create these things, I believe we will have gone a long way toward creating the conditions necessary to link educational theory and practice in powerful ways. I would like to talk about each of these in turn.

First, in this new era of ever-higher accountability, we need, I think, to ask more of ourselves as scholars of education. By tradition, most researchers have believed that they should be held accountable only for the significance of the questions they have asked and the appropriateness of the methods they have used to answer those questions. Although a number of researchers have focused their efforts on the consequences of testing, and the late Sam Messick and others have argued that those consequences should be considered an aspect of validity, matters of actual use have generally been seen as beyond a scholar's control or responsibility. Now, I would propose that we should change this and hold ourselves accountable for the applied value of our research. We should commit ourselves to generating new knowledge that will actually have a positive effect on policy and practice. We should commit ourselves not only to illuminating theories, but also to engineering products.

Though some scholars of education will continue to be concerned with what has traditionally been known as "basic research," others should now direct their attention to the actual day-to-day problems of learning and teaching in real-world educational settings. They should engage in what the late Donald Stokes called "use-oriented basic research" (Stokes, 1997). This means that they will do mission-oriented work, directed toward the need to understand practical problems. Some should also move even beyond that to engage in actual design work or engineering. To suggest that we need to supplement more traditional, theoretical work with more novel forms of research and engineering seems to me to be an appropriate new level of accountability for the field as a whole.

How do we achieve this new level of accountability? We do it by working to develop new methods for education research, all the while being careful to match our expectations and promises for research with clear understandings of what particular methods can yield (Shavelson & Towne, 2002).

At least since the 17th century, people have assumed that our understanding and mastery of the world has depended on slowly accumulating knowledge, piece by piece, and adding each new piece to what was already known about some given phenomenon. Physical, chemical, and biological phenomena were dissected in order to isolate, observe, and analyze all of the discrete molecules, gases, or genes of which they were composed. In a sense, the guiding principle of science was reductionism, the assumption being that if one understood all the various parts, one would be able to grasp the overall operation of whatever one was studying. For positivists, it was also important to move sequentially from the positing of assumptions based on theories to the testing of those assumptions with empirical evidence.

Today, this view is still held to be very important in some circles and it is being challenged in others. Much of the work currently being supported by the new Institute of Educational Sciences falls in line with a "hard" science view in which one intends to isolate and define cause-and-effect relationships. One example is the research going on under the auspices of the What Works Clearinghouse, which is generating research syntheses of studies of the same educational phenomena. The Campbell Collaboration located at the University of Pennsylvania is doing similar work.

The goal of efforts such as these is to produce tested generalizations that can inform educational policy and practice. Just as important, these projects seek constantly to refine methods that have been developing over nearly 30 years, which allow one to integrate the findings of different studies. As Harris Cooper and Larry Hedges (1994) put it in their introduction to *The Handbook of Research Synthesis,* synthesizers are analogous to "the bricklayers and hodcarriers of the science world" (p. 4). They are meant to "stack the bricks . . . and apply the mortar" (p. 4) that can hold the edifice together. The problem is that no two bricks—no two studies—are exactly alike. The synthesizer's task, then, is to identify how discrete studies are both similar and different and to account for the differences, especially if those differences pertain to the effects of a treatment.

Even though research synthesis is a technique that was pioneered by scholars of education, it has been less widely used in education than in medicine. This must change because research synthesis carries significant promise of helping to strengthen education research. Cooper and Hedges (1994) insist, for example, that primary research should not be included in a research synthesis unless the study's findings were subjected to some kind of a statistical test. No longer will it be sufficient to say: "I looked at the treatment and control scores and I find the treated group did better" (p. 7). Instead of such vague statements, Cooper and Hedges demand more rigorous, replicable evidence. Assuming one tempers one's expectations for such work with knowledge that "final," "sure" answers are impossible, our real hope lying in achieving better and better estimates, efforts to improve our understanding of causation in education should be important.

Especially in light of the current, often ideological, federal emphasis on methods that some see as providing "final" knowledge about cause-and-effect relationships, it is important to acknowledge the limitations of "what works" research. As Frederick Erickson and Kris Gutierrez (2002) noted in a recent article, "a logically and empirically prior question to 'Did it work?' is 'What was "it"?'—'What was the "treatment" as actually delivered?' " (p. 21). They rightly argue that an overemphasis on matters of causation can oversimplify the complexity of education and the myriad local variations that always creep into actual interventions. They insist, too, that in rushing to determine "what works," we need to be careful not to overlook the side effects that may emerge later on. Respecting calls for more rigor in education research should help us build an ever more reliable body of knowledge in education so long as those calls are tempered with well-informed cautions about what increased rigor can and cannot contribute to knowledge about education.

While people in education research debate the pros and cons of research syntheses, randomized trials, and other forms of "rigorous" research, across the sciences one finds more and more efforts to go beyond what some see as reductionist approaches to ones that are more complex. These may also be helpful to our thinking about methods in education research.

Some scholars are relying on graphing theory to study networks and discern the principles that organize them. Requiring what Duncan Watts, a Columbia sociologist who studies networks, has described as "the mathematical sophistication of the physicist, the insight of the sociologist, and experience of the entrepreneur," such efforts often involve teams of researchers (Watts, 2003, p. 304). That is also true of activities directed at developing a new science of "chaos." Scientists at the renowned Santa Fe Institute in New Mexico are leaders in this. As the science writer James Gleick (1987) observed in a book about this new field, chaos theory tries to make sense of "the irregular side of nature, the discontinuous and erratic side" (p. 3). It is concerned with the "puzzles," the "monstrosities," and the anomalies that science has traditionally left aside.

Efforts to develop new, more complex approaches to science are also appearing in education. Setting these within the context of more general changes in science should be helpful in matching expectations to methods. As I have argued in *An Elusive Science: The Troubling History of Education Research,* I believe that too often in the past, education research has proceeded in a vacuum, disconnected from developments in the arts and sciences. This is the historic legacy of the gender-related low status in which educational scholarship has been held (Lagemann, 2000). I believe this has weakened our field. If we want to develop the kind of knowledge we need to meet higher expectations for education, then I believe we need to be in conversation with people in other fields, who are on the cutting edge of thinking about problems of causation and scientific explanation.

I would like to give two examples of the kind of new work in education we need to discuss in that context. I believe that both have high potential to advance research in education. The first example has to do with new methods for describing changes in test scores over time. Judith Singer and John Willett (2003), two of my colleagues at the Harvard Graduate School of Education, have been developing these methods along with a number of other statisticians and they have now written a book designed to teach social investigators how to model and analyze change, relying on longitudinal data. Using multilevel statistical models, they have demonstrated both how one can describe within individual changes and analyze interindividual differences in change.

I am not a statistician, and I am not going to go into the details of Singer and Willett's (2003) work—for that, I would refer you to their new book, *Applied Longitudinal Data Analysis: Modeling Change and Event Occurrence.* In any case, the more important point for my argument is that Singer and Willett, among others, have developed a dynamic model that will enable scholars to describe and analyze multiple layers of change. This is crucial if one wants to understand human development, learning, or growth, not as single events, but as the multivariable, longitudinal processes they actually are. By collecting multiple waves of data over time, change becomes a discernible process that can be studied in systematic ways. Because understanding change is so essential to studying education, this represents more than incremental progress in the science of statistics. It represents a fundamental increase in our capacity to do education research and should be recognized as such.

If these new statistical methods provide one example of more dynamic, multifaceted approaches to education, the work Deborah Loewenberg Ball, David Cohen, Stephen Raudenbush, and Brian Rowan have been doing at the University of Michigan provides another. In a very large study of the relationship between resources and student outcomes, which was written up by Cohen, Raudenbush, and Ball (2002), the Michigan group found that to discern a relationship between resources and student outcomes researchers must, first, disaggregate the term *resources* to include "teachers' knowledge, skills, and strategic actions ... [as well as] students' experiences, knowledge, norms, and approaches to learning" (p. 85).[1] Then, they must examine how resources are used in instruction, which, in turn, depends on a wide range of variables—everything from parental attitudes toward the curriculum to school leadership.

The question the Michigan group asked has, of course, been contested among education researchers since even before publication, in 1966, of James Coleman's *Equality of Educational Opportunity*. And, now, using a much more complex and dynamic approach to its analysis, the Michigan researchers have addressed that question by posing a fundamental challenge to scholars of education. Finding that the value of resources for increased student outcomes depends on their use in instruction, they have observed that researchers will need to manage everything that is involved in shaping instruction. As the Michigan group itself did, researchers will have to step over the traditional question, which has been "how do the available resources affect learning," and instead ask: "What instructional approach, aimed at what instructional goals, is sufficient to ensure that students achieve those goals?" (Cohen et al., 2002, p. 109). Asking that question, they will, then, need deliberately to design and manage different programs of instruction. This will be necessary because understanding that the use of resources in instruction determines their value in terms of student achievement forces one to recognize that one must manage incentives for teachers to teach in particular ways and for students to learn. One also needs to

---

[1]Although he was not a coauthor of this particular essay, Brian Rowan is the study director for the Michigan group.

manage the educational environment, that is, the links between a school and surrounding institutions and between people working within a school.

Put most simply, if one accepts the findings of the Michigan group, one must acknowledge, as they do, that we need new, active approaches to the study of instruction. We need to develop specific and varied instructional programs—in their words "instructional regimes"—and then we need to experiment with different levels of resources to discern what the impact of these differing levels of resources will be on instruction (Cohen et al., 2002, p. 110). Again, using the language the Michigan group borrowed from medicine, scholars of education will have to run both efficacy trials, in which resources will be plentiful, and effectiveness trials, in which resources are constrained.

In the Cohen et al. (2002) write-up of the Michigan project, they acknowledge that there will continue to be important roles for other forms of research, ethnographies, surveys, and the like, that do not require large-scale active experimentation. Those kinds of research can offer important descriptive data. That said, the new approach they have modeled and described represents the boldest challenge of which I am aware to standard linear science in education. As they observe, taking up this challenge will be enormously expensive and especially difficult in the United States, owing to our highly diffuse systems of educational accountability and governance.

As part of our effort to develop new methods and to match those to realistic estimates of what they can yield, we need to concern ourselves with the norms of the education research community. Indeed, I believe we should face something that is widely known, but little discussed in public. Education is a very large field, with a great many different subspecialties, and a good deal of important research going on. Despite that, it seems clear that we do not have a strong research community for the field as a whole. To be sure, subfields have strong research communities, but these are not well linked to one another. That is the case because we do not have common norms and standards across the field to differentiate good from bad research and we do not have common standards for research training. There is not a body of knowledge that everyone engaged in education research needs to master and there are no skills that all need commonly to hold. In consequence, we have a cacophony of theories and methods, but lacking common norms, we cannot produce authoritative, warranted knowledge to offer to policymakers and practitioners.

More a community in name than as a result of powerful interdependencies, the education research community mirrors the diffuse systems of accountability and governance for public education that have grown up in the United States. These derive from long-established traditions of local control. Leaving room for local traditions, cultures, and values to play a role in the shaping of educational policies and practices is very important. Indeed, some would have it that most practical questions in education should be left to local decision making. The linguist David Olsen has recently argued, for example, that research should provide local educators with "an elaborated set of options," that they can then "combine with the accumulation of local experiences as to what works well and what works less well with their students and staff, in their school, in their community" (Olsen, 2003, p. 23). Even acknowledging the value of local influences, it is nonetheless clear that, to build a stronger research community in education, there will need to be concerted efforts to develop common standards and to gain support for them. This will be especially important as design and development work become increasingly significant alongside discipline-based studies. Disciplines are built around common standards. Newer styles of more applied research will need to develop them.

Design experiments are an example of this. According to Allan Collins, a leader in pioneering this work, design experiments are intended to introduce an innovation into a "real" educational setting and, then, through careful observation and quantitative comparison with control settings, to refine it and refine it again, all the while working at a practice site (Collins, Joseph, & Bielaczyc, 2002). In contrast to laboratory work, design work is located in "messy situations." It involves multiple rather than single dependent variables. One cannot hold variables constant, follow a fixed design, or test a hypothesis. One cannot even control the experiment. One is merely a coparticipant with others—notably, teachers, students, parents, and so on (Collins, 1999).

Design experiments represent very new, really emergent methods for simultaneously improving and studying education. Although they have gained credibility in the learning sciences community—one of the subcommunities of our field—they have not yet gained sufficient credibility in the wider world of educational scholarship. For that to happen, standards will need to be developed that, as Allan Collins, Diana Joseph, and Katerine Bielaczyc have argued, "make design experiments recognizable and accessible to other researchers" (Collins et al., electronic communication, Summer, 2003). The fact that proponents of design work are taking up this challenge bodes well for the emergence of explicit, shared norms for education research.

In combination, I believe that the continuing development of new methods coupled to realistic expectations and strengthened norms for research will slowly, over time, enable us to meet the heightened standards of accountability that, I believe, we, as education researchers, should now feel obligated to meet. In this way, we will provide the knowledge and tools we need to educate all children well. However, as I said at the start, I believe we also need new infrastructure for research and new models for research training.

The infrastructure that already exists at universities and other research centers is sufficient to support discipline-based research. It is not sufficient, however, to support more applied design and development work and explicit programs of research such as the one carried out by the researchers from the University of Michigan. To ensure that such work continues to advance, we will need to build new structures to facilitate research in multiple sites, to promote collaboration between and among researchers working on related problems, and to share data and works-in-progress even before they are ready for formal publication.

Recognizing this, the National Research Council has recently published the final report of the Committee on a Strategic Education Research Partnership (SERP). SERP is at once *"a program of use-inspired research and development," an organization* that will provide national and local infrastructure for research, and *a partnership* among researchers, practitioners, state policymakers, foundation officials, and other corporate, government, and nonprofit leaders. It is intended to provide opportunities for long-term, sustained research and development. Based on a careful analysis of current problems in the development and application of fundamental knowledge to educational problems, SERP is an expensive and ambitious plan for a major innovation in the way education research is mounted in the United States (Donovan, Wigdor, & Snow, 2003).

SERP proposes a research center, or "hub," with spokelike relationships between the center and networks of local researchers. Whether this structure will prove too cumbersome remains to be seen. It may turn out that we need instead to build confederations of smaller communities of practice (Wenger, 1998). Such communities would share conceptions of significance and method and offer opportunities for discussion and criticism. They could provide settings for concentrated work over extended periods of time, thereby helping to cumulate knowledge. They would be known for their expertise on the questions their members think most important and study. They would be linked to one another through collaborations born of necessity when the expertise of one community of practice could help another community with its ongoing research (Wenger, 1998).

Communities of practice already exist within some schools of education, within some departments within schools of education, and, in a virtual distributed sense, among colleagues at different locations, who share works-in-progress on a regular basis. At times, I am sure they have also existed within research institutes and think tanks. Given their importance, however, especially for researchers in training, I think schools of education should now make more deliberate efforts to build communities of practice.

Currently, faculty members in schools of education—as well as in other parts of research universities—carry out research in public schools, after-school settings, Head Start centers, and the like. Following principles of academic freedom and faculty autonomy, these research projects tend to be located wherever individual faculty members have personal connections. If faculty were instead willing to place some of their projects in locations where their university had a research/practice site, this would help aggregate interventions and perhaps increase their effects. In this way, particular school districts or neighborhoods could become laboratories for the design and evaluation of comprehensive educational services and the scholars, practitioners, and policymakers involved could develop into a community of practice with shared norms and standards. This should not in any way suggest that *all* research should be carried in local practice sites. There will, of course, be times when scholars need national data or data from several different locations. My suggestion is rather that we supplement existing research with studies that proceed within a local research/practice site.

Developing the infrastructure required to supplement basic work in disciplines with programs of more applied studies will be very expensive. It is estimated, for example, that the start-up costs of SERP will be approximately $500 million over the first 7 years. Clearly, therefore, the recognition that we must engage in this kind of work, if theory is to connect with practice in education, represents a challenge to funders of education research, both public and private. If funders believe that it is important to guarantee all children opportunities to learn to high levels, then, individually or in partnerships, they must dedicate the resources needed to build a strong infrastructure for education research. After publication of the Carnegie Foundation's famed *Flexner Report on Medical Education* in 1910, this was done in medicine. Now that must be done in education. Solo-practitioner research projects are fine and may yield very important new knowledge. Traditional research carried out in offices and libraries will always be necessary. But funders now need to go beyond the support of such projects to build the educational equivalent of teaching hospitals, which can invent and experiment with innovative solutions to educational problems.

That brings me to my third and last point, our need for new patterns of research training. I am convinced that there are three essential elements in the preparation of researchers who can work effectively in education. The first is a core curriculum that will promote students' capacity to be articulate about education. Students need to be able to articulate what purposes education can, does, and should serve. They need to understand and be able to describe what education is as a process; how learning is related to neuroscience, cognitive science, human development, and culture; why teaching is both an art and a science; and why educational problems should always be viewed through multiple lenses.

The second essential element of research training in education should, in my view, involve disciplinary study in a faculty of arts and science. Disciplines provide characteristic ways of asking questions, analyzing data, and presenting findings. They, quite literally, discipline one's thinking and, by doing so, deepen one's capacity to understand problems, albeit from a particular, disciplinary, perspective. Historians think about change over time. Time—when something happened—is always critical to their analyses. Anthropologists, by contrast, think about patterns in cultures via the analyses of language, gesture, and kinship relations, among other things. Time is not a dimension that has as much importance to them as it does to historians. In order to offer doctoral students the disciplinary work they need, faculties of education would do well, I believe, to partner with faculties of arts and sciences to create joint degree programs. In addition to strengthening the doctoral preparation of education researchers, this should help diminish the isolation that has traditionally kept schools of education at the margins of universities.

Finally, research training in education must involve practicum experiences in which students work as apprentices on a research team. Preferably, this experience will expose students to the complexity and importance of applied design and development work. It will help them realize that, although disciplinary thinking is important, interdisciplinary teams most effectively address educational problems. Recognizing that such experiences might prolong graduate study longer than is desirable, it might be that schools of education should develop significantly increased opportunities for postdoctoral fellowships that would enable young researchers to gain experience working in the field. As they do this, they will also have to negotiate with the powers that be in research universities concerning standards for tenure. Because tenure standards have traditionally placed a much higher value on original contributions to knowledge than on the applied value of one's research, they have often served as a disincentive, tending to prevent young scholars from engaging in design and development work. Perhaps following precedents for judging applied work in schools of engineering or architecture, faculties of education can begin to address this issue.

Of course, to sketch a general program of research preparation is much easier than designing curricula in detail. Designing actual curricula will be enormously difficult. And that is the point I would like to make in conclusion. To do all that I have suggested needs doing will present challenges to every person and every institution involved in education research. It will require that researchers rethink the ways they conceive and do research. It will necessitate even more deliberate efforts than exist today to articulate common norms and standards. It will demand that funders operate differently. It will make it necessary for schools of education to revamp their doctoral programs.

As a historian of education, I have sometimes toyed with the idea of writing a history of failed efforts to mobilize a Flexner-like revolution in education. These began in 1920 when the Carnegie Foundation published a bulletin entitled *The Professional Preparation of Teachers for American Public Schools.* Attempts to raise standards of training in education continued with J. B. Conant's *The Education of American Teachers,* which appeared in 1963. They were carried forward again by a study Charles E. Silberman did for the Carnegie Corporation of New York about "the education of educators," which was eventually published, in 1970, as *Crisis in the Classroom: The Remaking of American Education.* Representing only a very few of the high points of a continuing refrain, none of these works have had the desired effect. What, then, will it take to develop the research methods, norms, and standards, the infrastructure, and the research training we need to deliver instruction with sufficient power to help all children master the knowledge and skills they need to be productive workers, effective citizens, and satisfied human beings? I suspect that rather than a single dramatic report, it will take steady, determined work on the part of people like all of us in this room. We face huge challenges in education, but none so huge that they cannot be surmounted.

ACKNOWLEDGMENTS

I am grateful to Jen DeForest for help with the research on which this chapter is based. David Cohen, Michael Feuer, Daniel Koretz, Fritz Mosher, and Judith Singer provided very helpful comments.

REFERENCES

Anastasi, A. (1966). *Testing problems in perspective.* Washington, DC: American Council on Education.

Cohen, D. K., Raudenbush, S. W., & Ball, D. L. (2002). Resources, instruction, and research. In F. Mosteller & R. Boruch (Eds.), *Evidence matters: Randomized trials in education research* (pp. 80–119). Washington, DC: Brookings Institution.

Collins, A. (1999). The changing infrastructure of education. In E. C. Lagemann & L. S. Shulman (Eds.), *Issues in education research* (pp. 289–298). San Francisco: Jossey-Bass.

Collins, A., Joseph, D., & Bielaczyc, K. (2002). *Design research: Theoretical and methodological issues.* Retrieved from http://www.extension.harvard.edu/2002-03/programs/cte/ext02drt.pdf

Cooper, H., & Hedges, L. V. (1994). Research synthesis as a scientific enterprise. In H. Cooper & L. V. Hedges (Eds.), *The handbook of research synthesis* (pp. 4–14). New York: Russell Sage Foundation

Donovan, M. S., Wigdor, A. K, & Snow, C. E. (Eds.). (2003). *Strategic education research partnership.* Washington, DC: National Academies Press.

Erickson, F., & Gutierrez, K. (2002). Culture, rigor, and science in educational research. *Educational Researcher, 31*(8), 21–24.

Gleick, J. (1987). *Chaos: Making a new science.* London: Penguin.

Lagemann, E. C. (2000). *An elusive science: The troubling history of education research.* Chicago: University of Chicago Press.

Olsen, D. R. (2003). *Psychological theory and educational reform: How school remakes mind and society.* Cambridge, England: Cambridge University Press.

Shavelson, R. J., & Towne, L. (Eds.). (2002). *Scientific research in education.* Washington, DC: National Academies Press.

Silberman, C. E. (1970). *Crisis in the classroom: The remaking of American education.* New York: Random House.

Singer, J. D., & Willett, J. B. (2003). *Applied longitudinal data analysis: Modeling change and event occurrence.* New York: Oxford University Press.

Stokes, D. E. (1997). *Pasteur's quadrant: Basic science and technological innovation.* Washington, DC: Brookings Institution Press.

Watts, D. J. (2003). *Six degrees: The science of a connected age.* New York: Norton.

Wenger, E. (1998). *Communities of practice: Learning, meaning, and identity.* Cambridge, England: Cambridge University Press.

Woods, B. D. (1956). *Testing—Then and now: Invitational conference on testing problems.* Princeton: Educational Testing Service.

2

Scientific Evidence and Inference in Educational Policy and Practice: Implications for Evaluating Adequate Yearly Progress

Robert L. Linn
University of Colorado at Boulder
National Center for Research on Evaluation,
Standards, and Student Testing

The No Child Left Behind Act of 2001 (NCLB, 2002), which amends the Elementary and Secondary Act of 1965, is a law that provides billions of dollars in federal aid for a wide range of educational programs. As was noted by Feuer, Towne, and Shavelson (2002), NCLB "exalts scientific evidence as the key driver of education policy and practice" (p. 4). Indeed, "scientifically based research" is one of the dominant themes in the law. Provisions throughout the law require states and districts to demonstrate that funds obtained under the law will be spent on programs that are supported by scientifically based research. In the realm of education, this emphasis on scientific evidence is unprecedented.

Accountability also has a prominent role in NCLB: "The passage of the NCLB Act marked a significant shift in Federal educational policy from an emphasis on standards and assessments to an emphasis on accountability—school, district, and state accountability for students' academic achievement such that **all** students reach, at least a minimum, proficiency on the States academic achievement standards and the State academic assessments by 2013–14" (Marion et al., 2002, p. 5, emphasis in the original). The demonstration of adequate yearly progress (AYP) by schools and school districts is a key component of the accountability requirements in NCLB for schools and districts receiving Title I funds. States are required to define AYP for the state, school districts, and schools in a way that enables all students to meet the state's student achievement standards by 2013–2014.

In keeping with the stress on scientifically based research, NCLB requires states to develop accountability systems that are "valid and reliable." The AYP definitions must apply "the same high standards of academic achievement to all public elementary school and secondary school students in the State"; must be "statistically valid and reliable"; and must result in "continuous and substantial academic improvement for all students" (NCLB, § 1111(b)(2)(C)(ii–iii)). Furthermore:

> [The AYP definitions] must include separate annual measurable objectives for continuous and substantial improvement in both mathematics and reading/language arts for all students considered as a whole as well as for each of the following specific subgroups of students: students who are economically disadvantaged, students from major racial and ethnic groups, students with disabilities, and students with limited English proficiency. (Department of Education, 2002)

VALID AND RELIABLE

The terms *valid* and *reliable* are almost redundant in everyday usage and are interpreted to mean trustworthy or accurate. Distinctions are made in scientific uses of the two terms by measurement specialists, however. Reliability refers to the consistency or replicability of measurements. Validity, the more important of the two concepts, refers to the degree to which inferences and interpretations of measurement results are justified by supporting evidence. Thus to say that AYP definitions must be reliable implies that they should result in consistent classifications of schools as meeting or failing to meet AYP targets. Consistency of classification is highly dependent on the number of students that enter into the determination of AYP for a school. The reliability of AYP will be lower for small schools than for large schools (Hill & DePascale, 2003; Linn & Haug, 2002). Consequently, small schools will tend to show uneven results from year to year, so that a small school that meets its AYP target in one year may fail to do so the next, not because instruction has become less effective but because of the low reliability of the results due to the chance variation in the achievement level for small groups of students in a given grade from one year to the next.

The reliability will also be lower for schools where AYP must be reported for multiple subgroups of students than for schools with the same total number of students, but without subgroups for which results must be separately reported (Hill & DePascale, 2003; Kane, Staiger, & Geppert, 2002). Thus, the reliability of AYP results will be considerably lower for an integrated school with, say, 200 students in Grades 3 through 5 comprising roughly equal numbers of African American, Hispanic, and White students than for a school with the same total number of students that belong to a single racial/ethnic group. This is so because of the requirement that a school meet AYP targets not only for the total group of students, but for each of the subgroups for which separate reporting is required.

Unreliable determinations of the AYP status of a school certainly undermine the validity of the inferences that are based on AYP results. The inference that there was a decline in instructional quality in a small school that exceeded its AYP target by a comfortable margin in 2003, but failed to meet its goal in 2004 is not justified, and therefore invalid, if the result can be attributed to low reliability. In other words, reliability is a necessary condition for validity. A high level of reliability does not guarantee an adequate degree of validity, however. The reliability may be sufficiently high, for example, to be quite certain that the School A met its AYP target whereas School B did not. That is, the classification of the two schools as meeting and failing to meet AYP targets is dependable and would likely be replicated with another cohort of students in another year. Inferences about the two schools, however, may or may not be valid. Evidence may or may not support the inference that the instructional program in School A is good and that students are making good gains in achievement. Similarly, the inferences that the instructional program in School B needs improvement or that only small gains in achievement are being made by students in School B may or may not be justified. Some specific examples may help clarify the fact that reliable determination of the AYP status of schools is insufficient for assuring valid inferences about schools and student achievement.

DEFINITIONS OF AYP

Some additional details about the definition of AYP and AYP targets are needed in order to illustrate some of the features of AYP that affect the validity of inferences about schools based on AYP results. In order to track their AYP toward the goal of 100% proficient or above by 2013–2014, states have to define percentage proficient or above starting points. The starting point for each subject (reading/language arts and mathematics) is defined to be equal to the higher of the following two values: (a) the percentage of students in the lowest scoring subgroup who achieve at the proficient level or above; and (b) "the school at the 20th percentile in the State, based on enrollment, among all schools ranked by the percentage of students at the proficient level" (NCLB, § 1111 (b)(2)(E)(ii)). In most cases the latter value will be the higher one and will define the starting point.

Once a state has established an AYP starting point, it must then set intermediate goals for AYP that will ensure that all students meet the state's definition of proficient achievement by 2013–2014. The intermediate goals must "increase in equal increments over the period covered by the State's timeline, . . . provide for the first increase to occur in not more than 2 years, . . . [and] provide for each following increase to occur in not more than 3 years" (NCLB, § 1111 (b)(2)(H)). The equal-increments provision has been interpreted by the U.S. Department of Education (2002) in a way that allows states to vary the number of years between constant increments in the percentage of students at the proficient level or above. Thus, two states that have the same starting points and 2013–2014 goals may set different intermediate goals, as is illustrated in Fig. 2.1 for States X and Y. The straight-line definition of intermediate goals shown for State X is the pattern that was presented by the U.S. Department of Education to illustrate the setting of intermediate goals. It is more common, however, for a state to elect to adopt a pattern of AYP goals that is similar to that shown for State Y. That is, AYP growth functions are specified that have increments that occur every 3 years until 2010, after which increments are required every year, thereby postponing until later years gains that have to be realized every year.

There is considerable evidence that gains in student performance on the tests tend to be greatest in the first few years after they have been introduced as part of an accountability system and then taper off in later years. That is, the pattern of improvement in percentage of students scoring at the proficient level or above is a trend line that shows a decelerating rate of improvement over years rather than the accelerating curves that a number of states have adopted for the AYP intermediate goals between 2002 and 2014. Thus, it can be anticipated that the AYP goals, which are likely to be hard to meet in the early years, will become increasingly difficult to meet in the out years of the program.

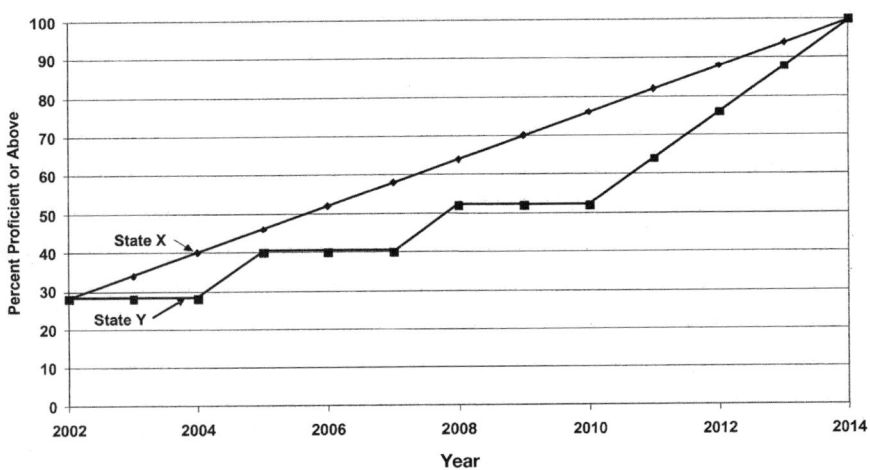

FIG. 2.1. Intermediate AYP percentage-proficient goals for two states with the same AYP starting points.

STATE-TO-STATE VARIABILITY IN AYP GOALS

Because states have their own assessments and establish their own definitions of proficient achievement, the starting points for states are radically different from state to state. Although some states have yet to define their starting points because they are in the process of introducing new assessments, starting points expressed as the percentage of students at the proficient level or above are available on state department of education Web sites for more than half the states. Starting points for Grade 4 mathematics assessments that are specified on the Web sites of 34 states range from a low (most stringent standard) of 8.3% proficient or above in Missouri to a high (most lenient standard) of 79.5% in Colorado. The corresponding range for mathematics assessments for the 34 states at Grade 8 is from 7% in Arizona to 74.6% in North Carolina (Linn, 2003b; Olson, 2003).

I doubt that anyone would believe that mathematics achievement is that much better in Colorado than in Missouri at Grade 4. Nor is the difference in starting point percentage proficient or above at Grade 8 a reflection of vastly better mathematics achievement in North Carolina than in Arizona. Instead, the huge differences in starting points reflect radically different definitions of proficient achievement in the different states. It is clear that valid inferences cannot be made about the relative proficiency of students in different states based on comparisons of percentage proficient statistics from state assessments employing such widely discrepant definitions of proficient achievement. Furthermore, the goals of 100% proficient by 2013–2014 lack comparability across states due to the different definitions of proficient student achievement.

The starting points and intermediate year percentage proficient or above AYP goals for the Grade 4 mathematics assessments for Colorado and Missouri are displayed in Fig. 2.2. A similar display is provided in Fig. 2.3 for the Grade 8 mathematics assessments for Arizona and North Carolina. As can be seen in the figures, all four states adopted a pattern of intermediate goals that follow a pattern similar to that shown in Fig. 2.1 for State Y. Because of the low percentage proficient or above starting points for Missouri and Arizona, the increments required in years with the big changes are necessarily quite large in comparison to the increments required for Colorado and North Carolina where the percentage proficient starting points are quite high.

From a comparison of the intermediate AYP goal lines for Colorado and Missouri in Fig. 2.2, and of Arizona and North Carolina in Fig. 2.3, it is evident that meeting AYP goals in any given year will mean quite different things for the two states involved in each comparison. Admittedly, the four states represent the extremes in terms of high and low percentage proficient AYP starting points at each grade level. Nonetheless, it seems clear that valid compari-

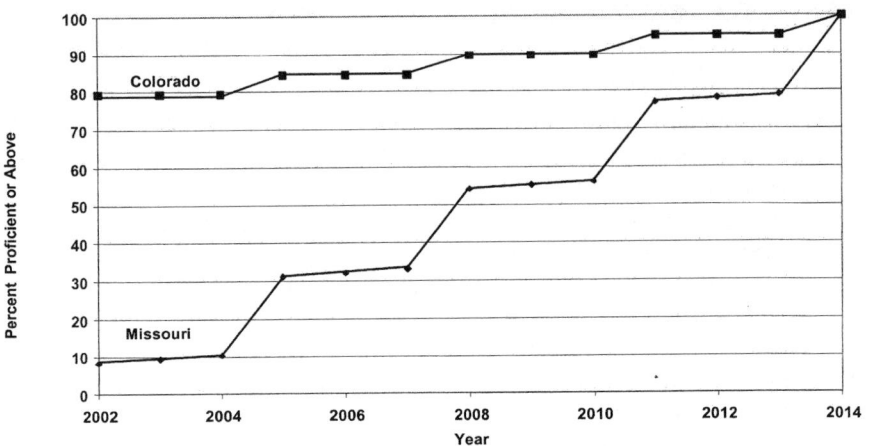

FIG. 2.2. Grade 4 mathematics percentage proficient or above AYP goals by year for Colorado and Missouri.

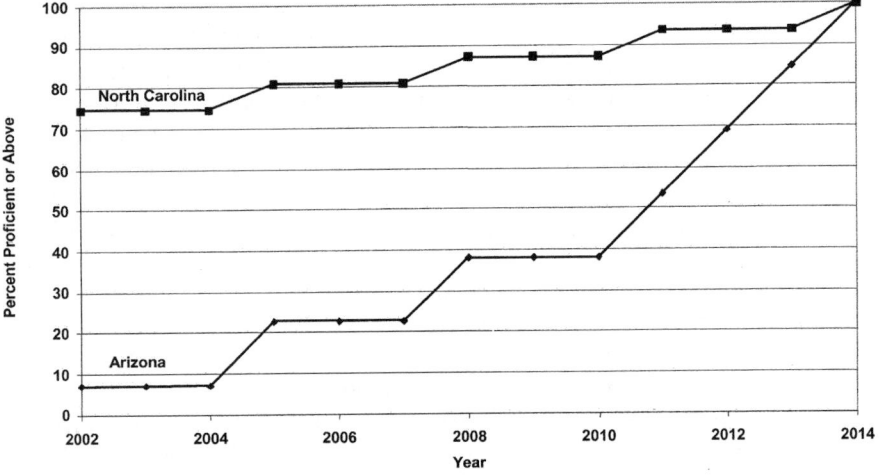

FIG. 2.3. Grade 8 mathematics percentage proficient or above AYP goals for Arizona and North Carolina.

sons across states will not be possible from the state assessment and percent proficient results reported under NCLB by each state.

NCLB does require states to participate in state administrations of the National Assessment of Educational Progress (NAEP) in reading and mathematics at Grades 4 and 8 in every other year starting in 2003. The law does not say what use will be made of the NAEP results, but there is some sense that they will be used to provide some kind of benchmark against which the state results can be compared. In other words, NAEP will provide an external check on the validity of the reported percentage proficient or above and on the changes in those percentages over the next few years.

Because Arizona and North Carolina both participated in the 2000 NAEP mathematics assessments, it is possible to get some foreshadowing of the use of NAEP results as a benchmark. At Grade 8 the percentage of students scoring at the proficient level or above on the 2000 NAEP mathematics assessment was somewhat higher in North Carolina (30%) than in Arizona (21%) (Braswell et al., 2001). The difference on NAEP is much smaller, however, than the difference in the Grade 8 mathematics starting points for NCLB for these two states. Arizona's starting point of 7% proficient or above is 14 points lower than the Arizona Grade 8 percentage proficient or above in mathematics on NAEP in 2000, whereas North Carolina's Grade 8 mathematics starting point of 74.6% is almost 45% higher than the percentage of students who were proficient or above on the 2000 Grade 8 NAEP mathematics assessment.

Colorado did not participate in the 2000 NAEP mathematics assessment so comparisons similar to those for Arizona and North Carolina are not possible for 2000. Both Colorado and Missouri did, however, participate in the Grade 4 NAEP mathematics in 1996. In 1996 the percentage of students scoring at the proficient level or higher in mathematics at Grade 4 was 22% in Colorado and 20% in Missouri—a difference of only 2%, which is tiny in comparison to the difference of 71% in their Grade 4 mathematics starting points for NCLB (Shaughnessy, Nelson, & Norris, 1997). It is also worth noting that the improvements in the percentage of students performing at the proficient level or above provides another sharp contrast with the increases that have been realized on NAEP. The percentage proficient or above AYP goal for Grade 4 mathematics increases from the 8.3% starting point in 2002 to an intermediate goal of 31.1% in 2006—an increase of 22.8 percentage points in 4 years. Missouri participated in the Grade 4 NAEP mathematics assessment in 2000 as well as in 1996. From 1996 to 2000 the percentage of Grade 4 students in Missouri who were at the proficient level or higher increased by 3 percentage points (from 20% to 23%) (Braswell et al., 2001). Rapid acceleration of the gains in percentage of students performing at the proficient level or above will clearly be needed for the goals to be met not only in Missouri, but in other states as well (Linn, 2003a). Changes in the percentage of students at the proficient level or above on NAEP will provide a check on the validity of the increases reported by states.

USING AYP RESULTS TO COMPARE SCHOOLS

It seems clear that it will be difficult to make valid comparisons of states based on their AYP results. But what about the validity of within-state comparisons of schools or school districts? Are valid inferences likely to be made about the quality of the instructional programs in schools? These questions are of fundamental importance to schools and districts that will face sanctions if they fail to meet AYP goals. Schools that fail to meet AYP goals for two consecutive years are placed in school improvement programs and the district must offer public school choice within the district. If the school fails to meet AYP goals the year after it is placed in school improvement, the district must provide supplemental services and technical assistance, which scientifically based research has shown to be effective. If the school still fails to meet AYP goals for the fourth consecutive year, it is subject to corrective action, which may include the replacement of staff. The school would be restructured in the following year if the school still did not meet AYP goals for a fifth consecutive year.

The solid line in Fig. 2.4 shows the percentage proficient or above AYP goal line that is similar to a fairly typical state. Also shown by the dashed lines are the percentage proficient or above results for three hypothetical schools. School A is a school where students have very low achievement with only 5% proficient or above in 2002, but where there is a steady and substantial increase in percentage of students who are proficient or above. Because School A has such a low starting point, it never reaches the AYP goals set by the state and would be subject to sanctions starting in 2004. Indeed, it would have to be reconstituted in 2007 despite the steady increase in the achievement of its students. School B just barely exceeds the state starting point in 2002 and has a steady, but more modest increase than School A in the percentage of students performing at the proficient level or

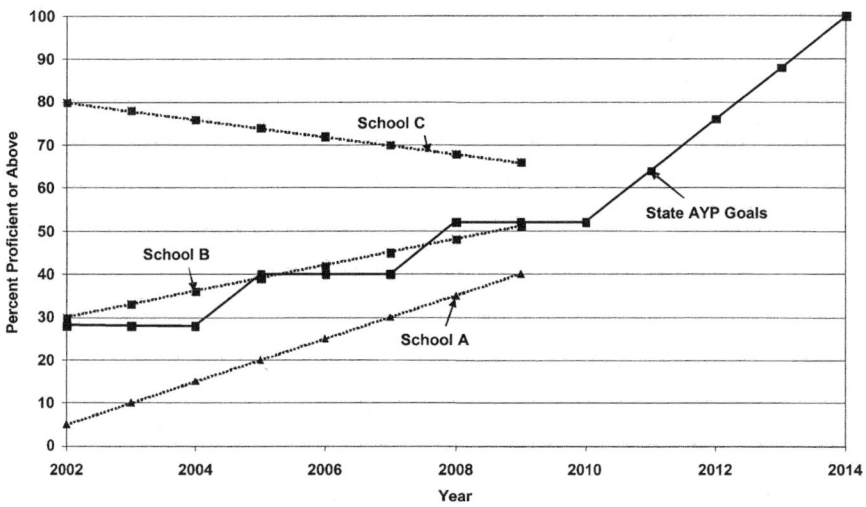

FIG. 2.4. Trends for three schools in comparison to state percentage proficient or above AYP goals.

above each year (3% a year compared to 5% a year in School A). Because students in School B had better achievement initially than their counterparts in School A, School B would meet the AYP goals in 2003 and 2004, fall slightly short of the goal in 2005, and then meet the goals again in 2006 and 2007. Based on the overall results, School B would not be placed in the school improvement category until 2009, which would be the first year that it failed to meet the AYP requirement for two consecutive years. Thus School B would not be subject to sanctions until 2009, despite the fact that its rate of improvement is more modest than that of School A.

An even sharper contrast is provided by School C, where a large majority of its students were at the proficient level or above in 2002. Despite a steady erosion of the percentage of students at the proficient level or above, School C would remain comfortably above the state AYP goal line for several years. Indeed, if the trend continued, School C would not fall below the AYP goal until 2011, despite the steady decline in its students' achievement. Overall, it seems clear that information about the standing of a school with respect to AYP requirements, by itself provides an insufficient basis for making valid inferences about school quality.

CONCLUSION

NCLB holds schools, districts, and states accountable for improving the academic achievement of students, particularly those who have been most likely to have poor achievement in the past. The accountability system is supposed to be based on reliable and valid indicators of adequate yearly progress, and decisions about instructional programs are supposed to be made on the basis of scientifically based research evidence. These are praiseworthy aspirations. In practice, however, there are several factors that threaten the validity of inferences that are likely to be made based on state assessments and AYP results.

Because the definition of proficient academic achievement and the choice of how achievement will be assessed are left to the states, there is no common meaning of proficient achievement. Consequently, valid inferences about the relative level of student achievement cannot be made from state assessment or AYP results alone. NAEP will provide a common basis for making comparisons across states, but it is not the primary basis for making judgments under NCLB.

Although the "P" in AYP stands for progress, whether a school meets or fails to meet AYP requirements does not depend on the gains in achievement that students have made. Rather, AYP depends only on the performance of students in a school in a given year. Consequently, schools where student achievement is actually improving a great deal may fail to meet their AYP goals because the students in that school had very low initial achievement. Conversely, a school that surpasses its AYP requirements by a comfortable margin may do so despite the fact that student achievement has shown little improvement because of the high initial achievement of the students. More than AYP determinations are needed to make valid inferences about the quality of instruction that is provided by different schools.

ACKNOWLEDGMENTS

Work on this chapter was partially supported under the Educational Research and Development Center Program PR/Award #R305B60002, as administered by the Institute of Education Sciences, U.S. Department of Education. The findings and opinions expressed in this chapter do not reflect the position or policies of the National Center for Education Research, the Institute of Education Sciences, or the U.S. Department of Education.

REFERENCES

Braswell, J. S., Lutkus, A. D., Grigg, W. S., Santapau, S. L., Tay-lim, B. S. H., & Johnson, M. S. (2001). *The nation's report card: Mathematics 2000.* Washington, DC: National Center for Education Statistics.

Feuer, M. J., Towne, L., & Shavelson, R. J. (2002). Scientific culture and educational research. *Educational Researcher, 31,* 4–14.

Hill, R. K., & DePascale, C. A. (2003, April). *Adequate yearly progress under NCLB: Reliability considerations.* Paper presented at the 2003 annual meeting of the National Council on Measurement in Education, Chicago. Retrieved April 1, 2004, from http://www.nciea.org/publications/NCMEconf_RHCD03.pdf

Kane, T. J., Staiger, D. O., & Geppert, J. (2002). *Randomly accountable.* Retrieved April 1, 2004, from http://www.educationnext.org/20021/56.html

Linn, R. L. (2003a). Accountability: Responsibility and reasonable expectations. *Educational Researcher, 32*(7), 3–13.

Linn, R. L. (2003b, September 1). Performance standards: Utility for different uses of assessment. *Education Policy Analysis Archives, 11*(31).

Linn, R. L., & Haug, C. (2002). Stability of school building scores and gains. *Educational Evaluation and Policy Analysis, 24*(1), 27–36.

Marion, S., White, C., Carlson, D., Erpenbach, W. J., Rabinowitz, S., & Sheinker, J. (2002). *Making valid and reliable decisions in determining adequate yearly progress.* Washington, DC: Council of Chief State School Officers.

No Child Left Behind Act of 2001, 20 U.S.C. § 6301 *et seq.* (2002).

Olson, L. (2003, August 6). "Approved" is relative term for Ed. Dep.: 11 states fully meet ESEA requirements. *Education Week, XXII*(43), 1, 34–36.

Shaughnessy, C. A., Nelson, J. E., & Norris, N. A. (1997). *NAEP 1996 mathematics cross-state data compendium for the grade 4 and grade 8 assessment: Findings from the state assessment in Mathematics of the National Assessment of Educational Progress.* Washington, DC: National Center for Education Statistics.

U.S. Department of Education. (2002). Title I—Improving the academic achievement of the disadvantaged: Proposed rules. *Federal Register, 67,* No. 151, August 6.

3

Issues Related to Disaggregating Data in a New Accountability Era

Sharon Lewis
Council of the Great City Schools

It is estimated that states and local governments administer 143 to nearly 400 million standardized tests yearly for education. Direct and indirect costs for these tests may be as high as $20 billion annually (Sacks, 1999). A short list of how the results of these tests might be used includes:

- Making promotion decisions.
- Identifying students eligible for special education, gifted and talented, and advanced-placement programs.
- Designing in-service programs for teachers.
- Making graduation decisions (27 states currently require or plan to require high school students to pass an exit exam to graduate; Education Commission of the States, 2002).
- Designing instructional programs for students.
- Monitoring school and district progress.
- Evaluating programs.

Those of us working with large, urban school systems may have a special interest in how assessment data are used, in that our students are probably tested more than any other group. The consequences of that testing may also have a greater influence on the lives of our students than on those of other students. The importance of using data to make decisions in schools and school districts cannot be overstated. And, of course, disaggregating data is paramount to using these data effectively.

The No Child Left Behind Act of 2001 (NCLB) requires state assessment data to be disaggregated for all students, major racial groups, gender, socioeconomic status, English-language learners, and students with disabilities (NCLB, 2002). If NCLB is to have a significant impact on student achievement, states and districts will have to be aware of several issues related to data disaggregation. I highlight seven critical issues related to disaggregating data by first providing a statement or overview of each, and then giving one or more illustrations of the issue. These illustrations are from widely varied sources: They are anecdotal, taken from newspaper articles, or cited from research that has been conducted by the Council of the Great City Schools (CGCS) or others.

DISAGGREGATING DATA AND STEREOTYPING STUDENTS

Unfortunately, many people view achievement gaps at the state and national levels as a confirmation that not all children can learn, and more specifically that African American and Latino children cannot learn at the same rate as their White peers. This interpretation of assessment results has fostered a long-standing debate within the African American community (and other communities as well) as to the validity and desirability of disaggregating data. Although there are plenty of examples to demonstrate the fallacy of interpreting test data in this way, this form of stereotyping continues and so, therefore, does the debate.

Illustration 1. *The Bell Curve* (Herrnstein & Murray, 1994) proposes a simple genetic explanation for the achievement gap: "Asians are smarter and blacks dumber than 'whites' (except for Jews, who are smarter than *anyone*)" (Blair, 2003).

Illustration 2. In a discussion about the implementation of NCLB in California, Orlando De Bruce said, "Too many [people] believe that California is simply too diverse to expect much of its kids. This sentiment is more than just collective apathy. It's bigotry. Period." He continues, "By saying that diversity is a liability, we suggest that low achievement is somehow inscribed on the DNA of poor, black, and brown kids" (Education Trust West, 2003).

DISAGGREGATING DATA ON MULTIPLE LEVELS—UNPACKING THE DATA

In general, the deeper the disaggregation, the more focused the information obtained. Unpacking data may help to identify areas of greatest need.

Illustration 1. In 1999 the average ACT (American College Test) composite score for the nation was 21.0; it was 18.9 for Great City School districts.[1] Students nationally outperformed those in large cities. Similarly in 1999, the average score for White students nationally was 21.7, and 21.9 for White students in Council member districts (ACT & CGCS, 2001). White students in urban schools thus outperformed those nationally. This is not a unique phenomenon: See also the results of the NAEP: Trial Urban District Assessment (National Council for Education Statistics [NCES], 2003).

Illustration 2. In urban schools the average score for African American students was 16.7, and 17.1 for African American students nationally. White students continued to score higher than African American students both nationally and in urban schools.

Illustration 3. The average score was 16.9 for urban African American females and 16.4 for urban African American males. Nationally, the average score for African American females was 17.3 and 16.7 for African American males. African American females nationally outperformed both African American males and African American females in Great City schools as well as African American males at the national level. African American males, particularly those in urban centers, consistently scored lower than any other group. Unpacking these data draws attention to the needs of this specific subgroup (ACT & CGCS, 2001).

---

[1]These districts include: Albuquerque Public Schools, Anchorage School District, Atlanta Public Schools, Austin Independent School District, Baltimore City Public Schools, Birmingham City Schools, Boston Public Schools, Broward County Public Schools, Buffalo City School District, Charlotte-Mecklenburg Schools, Chicago Public Schools, Clark County School District, Cleveland Municipal School District, Columbus Public Schools, Dallas Independent School District, Dayton Public Schools, Denver Public Schools, Des Moines Indep. Community School District, Detroit Public Schools, District of Columbia Public Schools, Duval County Public Schools, Fort Worth Independent School District, Fresno Unified School District, Greenville County School District, Guilford County Schools, Hillsborough County School District, Houston Independent School District, Indianapolis Public Schools, Jackson Public School District, Jefferson County Public Schools, Long Beach Unified School District, Los Angeles Unified School District, Memphis City Public Schools, Miami-Dade County Public Schools, Milwaukee Public Schools, Minneapolis Public Schools, Nashville-Davidson Metropolitan Public Schools, New Orleans Public Schools, New York City Department of Education, Newark Public Schools, Norfolk Public Schools, Oakland Unified School District, Oklahoma City Public Schools, Omaha Public Schools, Orange County Public Schools, Palm Beach County Public Schools, Philadelphia Public Schools, Pittsburgh Public Schools, Portland Public Schools, Providence Public Schools, Richmond Public Schools, Rochester City School District, Sacramento City Unified School District, Salt Lake City School District, San Diego Unified School District, San Francisco Unified School District, Seattle Public Schools, St. Louis Public Schools, St. Paul Public Schools, Toledo Public Schools, Tucson Unified School District.

DISAGGREGATING DATA TO MONITOR EQUITY ISSUES AND PROGRAM SUCCESS

Disaggregated data are critical when examining equity issues and program success. Superintendents and senior school district staffs need to monitor data to ensure that all students, particularly those students who have been historically disadvantaged by educational systems, have an "equal" opportunity to learn.

Illustration 1. The North Carolina End-of-Grade Test (EOG) is administered to all students in Charlotte-Mecklenburg Schools in Grades 6, 7, and 8. For two consecutive years, their superintendent reviewed the EOG math scores and course placements among White and African American students. After several unsuccessful conversations with staff about the racial disparities in course placements among students with the same EOG math scores, the superintendent required that African American students earning an EOG achievement level score at or above grade level (Levels III or IV) be placed in the same math classes as White students who had attained the same scores. This meant reorganizing classes during the fifth week of the semester, causing considerable movement and discontent. "In the end, teachers reported being pleasantly surprised by how well students performed in the more challenging classes. The result was that students landed on a course-taking path that included eighth-grade algebra and greater opportunities for more advanced courses in high school" (MDRC & CGCS, 2002).

Illustration 2. From *Education Daily* (Rubin, 2003): "The NAACP has filed a federal civil rights complaint charging that Florida's education system discriminates against black students, and calling for the suspension of the state's high-stakes testing program, among other recommendations" (p. 164). The article continues:

> Specifically, the NAACP says black students are under-represented in gifted and talented programs and Advanced Placement (AP) courses; over-represented in special education classes; and under-represented in dropout-prevention programs, despite having a higher dropout rate. Black students in Florida are also more likely to have unqualified teachers, and the state funding system penalizes low-income districts, the complaint says. (p. 164)

DISAGGREGATING DATA AND USING A COMPARISON, WHEN APPROPRIATE

To fully understand an event, good researchers use control groups for making comparisons. You often get an entirely different interpretation if you use a comparison group, and if you also disaggregate that comparison group.

Illustration. In 1998 the average ACT composite score for the nation was 21.0; it was 18.8 for students in CGCS districts. There was a 2.2-point difference between the nation and Great City School districts. However, when urban students took "core" academic courses their average increased to 19.7, thus reducing that difference to 1.3 points. One might be tempted to interpret these findings as indicating that the gap between urban students and the nation will begin to narrow when urban students take "core" courses. It is only fair, however, that we also disaggregate the national statistic for those students taking "core" courses. When making this more accurate comparison, the national average for students taking "core" courses increased to 22.1 and so the gap between urban students and the national group actually widened to 2.4 points (ACT & CGCS, 1999).

DISAGGREGATING MORE THAN THE OBVIOUS

As previously stated, the NCLB Act of 2001 requires that states and districts, for accountability purposes, disaggregate student assessment data by major racial/ethnic groups, English-language learners, students with special needs, and economically disadvantaged students. The obvious purpose of disaggregating data is to further refine the data-gathering process, thereby obtaining information that will be helpful to students and teachers. There are however, many other indicators that should be also examined if this is actually to happen.

Illustration 1. After several failed attempts to meet the academic standards required for high school entry, 1,600 over-age students in Chicago Public Schools were assigned to Academic Prep Centers. Students received "intensive academic care" as well as the services of nurses, social workers, psychologists, and counselors. In addition to reviewing academic data for this subgroup, vision screening was conducted. Four hundred students failed the first vision screening and at least half of these also failed a second confirming screening. For students who failed both vision screening tests the district then purchased two pairs of glasses: one to be taken home and one to remain in school. In an attempt to improve student achievement the Chicago schools had examined the customary assessment standards, but also atypical data as well (J. Bristol, personal communication, September 2003).

Illustration 2. NAEP disaggregates data into hundreds of nonassessment categories such as school factors, factors beyond school, instruction content and practice, teacher factors, community factors, and government factors. Results of the 2002 NAEP Trial Urban District Assessment (TUDA) for reading and writing indicated that Grade 4 students in New York City had lower scaled scores than students nationally, but outperformed their peers in Atlanta, Chicago, Los Angeles, and the District of Columbia. These data also showed that:

- New York City students who reported being asked to write long answers to questions on tests or who were given assignments that involved writing at least once a week outperformed those who reported that they were never asked to write long answers, and those who reported being asked to write long answers once or twice a year on TUDA Writing Grade 4.
- Students of New York City teachers holding a regular teaching certificate performed better on TUDA Reading Grade 4 than those whose teachers held only a provisional certificate (NCES, 2003).

DISAGGREGATING DATA WITHOUT POLITICS

The NCLB Act of 2001 heavily emphasizes data disaggregation. In general, I have supported the concept of NCLB and particularly its requirements for data disaggregation. NCLB's many unfavorable components are outweighed by the significance of having a strong national focus on providing a quality education for students who have been historically disadvantaged by educational systems. For the first time, schools would be held accountable for educating all students. For the first time, all schools, not just urban ones, would be held accountable for educating Black and Brown children. I held on to that belief for a long time, that is, until "political will" apparently lost out to the pressure to "look good." It seems as though the old saying, "the devil is in the details," is quite true in this case.

Illustration I. States were fairly consistent when identifying the minimum number of students in each data cell to be used for reporting purposes. The overwhelming majority of states indicated 10 students as the minimum number in any data cell to be reported, with a few states deciding on cell minimums of 5, 6, 9, 11, 16, 20, or 30. States were much more varied, however, when defining the minimum cell size necessary to determine adequate yearly progress (AYP) for a subgroup. For example, Texas requires a cell size of 40 for all students; 50 for a subgroup, assuming that the subgroup comprises at least 10% of the total group; or 200 if the subgroup comprises less than 10% of all students. Subgroup cell sizes for overall accountability are 30 for Washington; 40 for New York and North Carolina; and 50 for Virginia. California stipulates that its schools must have a minimum of 100 students with valid test scores for overall reporting; or 50 students in those cases in which a subgroup constitutes at least 15% of the students at the school who have valid test scores. Arkansas requires at least 25 students, over a 3-year period, to report scores. So in addition to each state administering a different test, each with a different level of difficulty, different accountability systems, and different definitions for proficient, we also have drastically different definitions for AYP (Erpenbach, Forte-Fast, & Potts, 2003).

Illustration 2. Hypothetically, a district with a small number of English-language learners or exceptional students and with an accountability cell size minimum requirement of 30 could legally assign their students in such a manner that no school had more than 30 of those students. Their curriculum may be limited, their instructional program might be minimal, and their teachers may be assigned to more than one school; because data on these students are not reported, however, their schools may still attain AYP.

DISAGGREGATING DATA AND FOLLOWING UP WITH APPROPRIATE ACTION

A critical component of testing for schools and school districts is reporting test results in a meaningful manner so that they can be used to influence instruction.

Illustration 1. The Council's research on three urban districts (Charlotte-Mecklenburg, Sacramento, and Houston) that are making overall improvements and narrowing the racial disparities showed that these districts used data to modify their instructional programs, shape professional-development programs, and monitor course placement, as well as to identify students' strengths and weaknesses (MDRC & CGCS, 2002).

Illustration 2. The following is an excerpt from the *Savannah Morning News*. The statements were made in response to the district's 2003 AYP results:

"I think that it's obvious our kids have not been exposed to the appropriate curriculum," said the district's director for exceptional children. "Do I think our kids are going to do better? Yeah. I know they're going to do better." She continued by saying that special education students will now be taught the same material as general education students. Special education students will be expected to achieve. "It's going to be a tough road and an uphill battle," she said. "But No Child Left Behind is the best thing to happen to special ed." (Richards, 2003)

In summary, disaggregated data can be very helpful to schools and school districts. It must, however, be used responsibly. Here are seven ways to do this:

1. **Stereotyping** may be minimized if disaggregated data are used to create special programs and interventions, which are designed to accelerate the learning of those students who are in greatest need.
2. **Unpacking** data will further refine the diagnostic phase of any systemic reform efforts.
3. **Monitoring** course enrollments in both lower and higher level courses is essential to ensuring that all children have an opportunity to learn, thus narrowing achievement gaps.
4. Using appropriate **comparisons** will help policymakers to fully understand the data and their implications.
5. Disaggregating data **not just by the traditional variables** but also by variables that are unique to a state's or district's specific situation is important.
6. Disaggregating data is **not for the "faint of heart."** You must be steadfast in your resolve to identify and educate students in the greatest need.
7. Doing nothing with test data is a waste of everyone's time. Collecting and analyzing data should lead directly to **systemic reform** of schools and school districts.

ACKNOWLEDGMENTS

The opinions expressed in this chapter do not reflect the position or policies of the Council of the Great City Schools (CGCS).

REFERENCES

ACT & Council of the Great City Schools. (1999, June). *Gateways to success: A report on urban student achievement and course-taking.* Retrieved September 2003 from http://www.cgcs.org/reports/gateway.html

ACT & Council of the Great City Schools. (2001, March). *A decade of ACT results in the nation's urban schools 1990–1999: A report on urban student achievement and course taking.* Retrieved April 1, 2004, from http://www.cgcs.org/pdfs/ACT_2000.PDF

Blair, J. (2003). How to improve education. *Big issue ground.* Retrieved September 18, 2003, from http://www.bigissueground.com/politics/blair-education.shtml

Education Commission of the States. (2002, December). *Assessment quick facts.* Retrieved April 1, 2004, from http://www.ecs.org/html/IssueSection.asp?issueid=%2012&s=Quick+Facts

Education Trust West. (2003, January 13). *Implementing NCLB in California: One step forward, three steps back? Confusion about the new law threatens advances for students.* Retrieved from http://www2.edtrust.org/edtrust/etw/one+step.htm

Erpenbach, W. J., Forte-Fast, E., & Potts, A. (2003, July). *Statewide educational accountability under NCLB: Central issues arising from an examination of state accountability workbooks and US Department of Education reviews under the No Child Left Behind Act of 2001.* Washington, DC: Council of Chief State School Officers.

Herrnstein, R. J., & Murray, C. (1994). *The bell curve: Intelligence and class structure in American life.* New York: The Free Press.

MDRC & Council of the Great City Schools. (2002, September). *Foundations for success: Case studies of how urban school systems improve student achievement.* Retrieved September 2003 from http://www.cgcs.org/reports/foundations.html

National Council for Education Statistics. (2003). *NAEP data tool.* Retrieved September 2003 from http://www.nces.ed.gov/nationsreportcard/naepdata

No Child Left Behind Act of 2001, Pub. L. No. 107-110, § 115 Stat. 1425 (2002).

Richards, J. S. (2003, August 24). Trivial data or a measure of success? *Savannah Morning News.* Retrieved April 1, 2004, from http://savannahnow.com/stories/082403/LOC_failingschools.shtml

Rubin, H. G. (2003, September 3). NAACP complaint alleges inequalities in Florida schools. *Education Daily, 36,* 164.

Sacks, P. (1999). *Standardized minds: The high price of America's testing culture and what we can do to change it.* Boulder, CO: Perseus.

4

Scientific Evidence and Inference in Educational Policy and Practice: Defining and Implementing "Scientifically Based Research"

Lisa Towne
National Research Council/National Academies

Evidence-based education is "the integration of professional wisdom with the best available empirical evidence in making decisions about how to deliver instruction" (Whitehurst, 2001). This idea of systematically linking research and reform in education is certainly not new. The passage of the No Child Left Behind Act of 2001 (NCLB, 2002), however, signaled a new era. The law, which authorizes nearly all of the major federal K–12 education programs, contains 111 references to using "scientifically based research" (SBR) to support instructional decisions. Although never labeled as such,[1] these SBR provisions effectively require the adoption of an evidence-based education framework for the use of federal funds. Similar language first appeared in the Reading Excellence Act and the Comprehensive School Reform Demonstration Act in the mid- to late-1990s.[2] They have also figured prominently in recent bills to reauthorize the U.S. Office of Educational Re-

---

[1] I use "evidence-based education" and "scientifically based research" interchangeably for ease of exposition and because the SBR provisions are the policy mechanism for promoting evidence-based education. They are not equivalent terms, however; I discuss the differences between them in a later section.

[2] Former U.S. Representative Bill Goodling (R-PA) introduced a reading bill in 1997 with references to "scientifically based research"; the Reading Excellence Act became law a year later. Guided by the leadership of U.S. Representative David Obey (D-WI) and former U.S. Representative John Porter (R-IL), the Comprehensive School Reform Demonstration (CSRD) program was created in the 1997 appropriations process under the federal Title I program, and also included language referencing "reliable, replicable research."

search and Improvement (OERI), including the Education Sciences Reform Act of 2002 (ESRA), which created the new Institute of Education Sciences (IES) and replaced OERI as the chief education research agency in the federal government. Bills pending to reauthorize both the Individuals with Disabilities Education Act and parts of the Higher Education Act also feature SBR provisions. When those bills become law, evidence-based education will be second only to accountability for student achievement as the key organizing principle for *all* of federal education policy.

HISTORICAL ROOTS

Evidence-based education is a young member of a growing family of evidence-based practice applications. One of the most influential early proponents of evidence-based practice was Professor Archibald Leman Cochrane, a British epidemiologist who wrote extensively in the 1950s and 1960s about improving the quality of evidence for use in medical practice (Institute of Medicine, 2001). In addition to the evidence-based medicine movement, similar efforts are under way in such areas as nursing (Melnyk, Fineout-Overholt, Stone, & Ackerman, 2000), social services (Gambrill, 1999), and occupational therapy (Law & Baum, 1998).

In education, a confluence of forces powers the evidence-based practice movement. A major development is the maturing base of research on early reading skill acquisition (see, e.g., National Reading Panel, 2000; National Research Council [NRC], 1998). These advances provided a compelling illustration of the potential of research to improve education by reaching policymakers with oversight of federal reading programs. Additional factors include the creation of the international Campbell Collaboration (see http://www.campbellcollaboration.org/), established to promote evidence-based practice in education, crime and justice, and social welfare; the continued development of research-based comprehensive school reform models; and the publication of results from a large-scale randomized study of class size reduction in Tennessee (see, e.g., Grissmer, 1999). Each of these efforts helped lay the groundwork for the now near ubiquitous calls for transforming education into an evidence-based field (see, e.g., NRC, 1999; U.S. Department of Education, 2002c).

THE UNIQUE NATURE OF SBR

The legal framework for this transformation—the SBR provisions—has two distinct purposes. Reflecting the peculiar public attitude toward the social and behavioral sciences (including education research), it is intended to simultaneously upgrade the quality of education research and to promote its use in driving policy and practice.

The primary purpose of SBR is, of course, to promote evidence-driven progress in education. This purpose is evident in NCLB and in other laws that fund service-based programs for schools, and is closely aligned with the broader goals of evidence-based education. Reflecting an enthusiasm for research as a tool to guide sound social policy, SBR is not unlike actions taken by legislators beginning in the 1960s, when set-asides for evaluating the effectiveness of social programs became the norm (Aaron, 1978).

On the other hand, a deep skepticism about the worth and quality of these endeavors (Kaestle, 1993; Pettigrew, 1985) underlies the second purpose of SBR: to improve the quality of education research. In ESRA, the definition of SBR effectively delineates the kind of research projects that can be funded by IES, setting a quality standard to guide the allocation of education research funds. Table 4.1 provides the definition of SBR from ESRA (2002).

Science policy has always been characterized by a struggle to balance the democratic principles of public accountability and the scientific principles of autonomy and self-regulation. This detailed delineation of scientific method, however, is unique in its reach. Crafting these definitions was an intentional effort on the part of congressional leaders to set a higher standard for education research, which they view as subpar (Robert Sweet, personal communication, July 16, 2003).

TABLE 4.1
Definition of "Scientifically Based Research Standards" in H.R. 3801

The term "scientifically based research standards" means research standards that—
   (i)   apply rigorous, systematic, and objective methodology to obtain reliable and valid knowledge relevant to education activities and programs; and
   (ii) present findings and make claims that are appropriate to and supported by the methods that have been employed.
The term includes, appropriate to the research being conducted—
   (i)   employing systematic, empirical methods that draw on observation or experiment;
   (ii) involving data analyses that are adequate to support the general findings;
   (iii) relying on measurements or observational methods that provide reliable data;
   (iv) making claims of causal relationships only in random assignment experiments or other designs (to the extent such designs substantially eliminate plausible competing explanations for the obtained results);
   (v)   ensuring that studies and methods are presented in sufficient detail and clarity to allow for replication or, at a minimum, to offer the opportunity to build systematically on the findings of the research;
   (vi) obtaining acceptance by a peer-reviewed journal or approval by a panel of independent experts through a comparably rigorous, objective, and scientific review; and
   (vii) using research designs and methods appropriate to the research question posed.

Note. This definition is not the same as the definitions that appear in NCLB. Specifically, the ESRA definition is more flexible than the NCLB definitions.

In sum, the SBR provisions are intended to simultaneously upgrade the quality of education research and to promote its use in driving policy and practice. Can they achieve both goals, and if so, how?

FACTORS INFLUENCING IMPLEMENTATION

There are few data on how the SBR provisions are being implemented at the federal, state, and local levels. What little evidence exists suggests that implementation thus far has been spotty, varying by jurisdiction and by program. This early experience does, however, point to some key issues that will influence its implementation and its long term success. I argue, with examples when they are available, that the main implementation challenges facing SBR and evidence-based education more broadly include defining and enforcing standards of research quality, crafting operational principles to guide implementation, acknowledging the professional judgment of educators, setting bold yet reachable expectations, and building the capacity of both researchers and practitioners.

Research Quality

The ways in which quality have been defined in the SBR provisions have raised both philosophical and practical questions. The appearance of definitions of "quantitative" and "qualitative" research standards in H.R. 4875, a bill introduced by Rep. Castle (R-DE) to reauthorize OERI in the summer of 2000, sparked a fierce debate among researchers about the philosophy of science and social science and the role of politics in research that continues today. Some have taken issue with what they see as a prescriptive and narrow emphasis on clinical trials, arguing that this method is appropriate only for certain kinds of questions (if at all) and that in many cases it is neither feasible nor ethical to implement in school settings (see, e.g., Howe, 2004). Near universal among the research communities is a distinct unease in the face of such a pointed attempt to dictate the parameters of their profession.

In this context, the NRC assembled an expert panel of researchers to offer their collective articulation of the nature of scientific research in education. In brief, the panel argued that all scientific inquiry shared a common set of principles, and that the specific ways in which those principles were applied in practice varied by field and discipline. These guiding principles are shown in Table 4.2.

The principles were not intended to replace the definitions of SBR in law, but in general terms they might be thought of as the scientific counterpart

TABLE 4.2
Guiding Principles for Scientific Inquiry

- Pose significant questions that can be investigated empirically.
- Link research to relevant theory.
- Use methods that permit direct investigation of the question.
- Provide a coherent and explicit chain of reasoning.
- Replicate and generalize across studies.
- Disclose research to encourage professional scrutiny and critique.

Note. From National Research Council (2002, p. 53).

to the politically devised definitions.[3] A comparison of Tables 4.1 and 4.2 reveals several common ideas between them: professional scrutiny and peer review, replication, and the use of methods best suited to address particular questions (see Eisenhart & Towne, 2003, for a description of the evolution of the SBR definitions and the role of the NRC committee's principles in shaping them). One important difference is in the relative weight given to method, particularly randomized designs. In the political definition, randomized designs are depicted as the "gold standard" (although the preferential language for trials is significantly toned down from early versions of the SBR definitions; again, see Eisenhart & Towne, 2003). The NRC panel did recommend that trials be conducted in education research more often than they have been historically, but made clear that there are other ways in which causal questions can be pursued rigorously and that methods do not themselves make inquiries scientific.

In practical terms, the magnitude of the difference between the political and scientific definitions will depend on how strictly the U.S. Department of Education interprets and enforces the SBR provisions. The statutory language in Table 4.1 leaves room for methods other than trials for addressing causal questions and for investigations that address descriptive or other types of researchable questions. Thus, it remains to be seen how they will be applied in practice. The input of the research communities will be crucial to ensuring that quality standards are upheld in ways that capitalize on the full range of methods, perspectives, and strengths in the field.

There are also practical barriers to using a narrowly interpreted SBR definition as the standard for research in evidence-based education. Precious few trials have been conducted in education to date (Boruch, DeMoya, & Snyder, 2001). In issuing its guidance on the comprehensive school reform program, the U.S. Department of Education (ED) acknowledges the lack of trials in the current literature: "In some cases, research that meets these criteria [in the law] is minimal or non-existent . . . In this case, school lead-

---

[3] I use the principles in *Scientific Research in Education* (NRC, 2002) as the best approximation of a scientific definition, recognizing that they are not universally accepted by the field.

ers will need to rely on the best available empirical evidence ... As the quantity, quality and availability of empirical, randomized studies increases, schools will be able to make a stronger connection between their design decisions and the evidence of 'what works' " (pp. 50–79).

Similar constraints will shape (at least in the short term) the multimillion-dollar IES-funded "What Works Clearinghouse" (WWC). The WWC is tasked with creating a registry of studies that address "what works" questions in education, rating the quality of each study in the registry, and developing "Evidence Reports" that synthesize findings from those studies that meet their quality standards. Although this quality threshold is not defined solely by the use of trials (see http://www.w-w-c.org/standards.html), it is set in such a way that few studies that employ alternative methods will pass muster. There is a real possibility that within some of the pressing areas in which evidence reports are being developed there will be little evidence to synthesize.

These examples illustrate that any effort to implement the SBR provisions will inevitably have to face the challenge posed by their dual purposes: Grantees of federal education dollars are required to use only high-quality research to make instructional decisions; yet much existing education research does not meet (legal) standards of quality.

Operational Principles

On the surface, moving from identifying high-quality studies to the research utilization process that evidence-based education calls for seems straightforward: After reviewing the results of high-quality research on a topic, school personnel would make choices consistent with the findings of available studies. But the existence or review of high-quality research does not lead directly to its appropriate and effective use in schools. In fact, the translation of research-based evidence into educational practice at the local level is a matter of some complexity.

At a broad level, the implementation of evidence-based education will be shaped by how social research affects decision making and decision makers (see, e.g., Feldman & March, 1981; Lindblom & Cohen, 1979; Weiss, 1991), how knowledge is diffused and ideas adopted in complex organizations (see, e.g., Rogers, 1995), and how such a framework fits into and supports existing reform efforts. These three strands can collectively give definition to the principles that will be needed to guide SBR implementation.

Operational principles derived from these framing ideas can assist practitioners in answering the myriad questions that are likely to arise in implementing the provisions: Where is the relevant research, and how can it be accessed? How can the jargon and technical language of research articles be translated into practical knowledge? What if one study suggests one course of action and another study seems to suggest the opposite? What if the research points in a direction that goes against an established approach that has proven successful? How can research findings be integrated with professional consensus, student and parent demands, and resource constraints? How does the relative strength of the knowledge base in different areas of education affect the decision calculus? What resources—time and money—are available to support research reviews and thoughtful action based on their results?

Although there are several definitions of SBR sprinkled throughout federal law, they do not define the practice of evidence-based education operationally (see Dunst et al. for an example of such a definition). They define what counts as high-quality evidence for use in that practice. Similarly, nonregulatory guidance issued by the U.S. Department of Education on the provisions in NCLB has also focused on research quality. In the Reading First (U.S. Department of Education, 2002a), Comprehensive School Reform (U.S. Department of Education, 2002b), and Title II (teacher quality) (U.S. Department of Education, 2004) programs—the three areas of NCLB in which guidance on the SBR provisions is specified—grantees are provided with a series of questions to use as a screen for what research studies should be consulted. Additionally, Reading First and Title II both include summary statements of the conclusions to be drawn from existing research in reading and teacher quality, respectively. The emphasis of nonfederal resource documents developed to assist schools and districts has also been on understanding the nature and quality of the research itself (e.g., Redfield & Sivin-Kachala, 2003; Stanovich & Stanovich, 2003).

Overall, there has been very little discussion that engages the "big picture" of what evidence-based education is and what it would look like in schools. As states and districts tackle the SBR provisions in more depth, there will be a premium on modeling how (high-quality) research can be used in schools. The NRC's Strategic Education Research Partnership is a notable exception; this initiative culminated in a comprehensive proposal for a fundamentally new infrastructure for education research that would feature strong collaborations between researchers and schools. The SERP plan envisions that such partnerships would not only improve the quality of education research but also its utilization (NRC, 2003).

SBR as Extending Standards-Based Reform

Integrating SBR into existing reform efforts—one of the major ideas for developing operating principles for implementation—can be accomplished by framing it in terms of the standards-based reform (the original SBR) models that pervade U.S. education policy. These models are systemic in nature, and supported by data-driven decision making. School personnel focus on the outcomes they are trying to improve, examine indicators of the extent to which they are achieving their goals, and alter the components of the education system to enable all students to meet high standards of excellence. Data-driven decision making becomes embedded in the day-to-day operations of schools, nurturing a culture that values data, analysis, and reflection.

Evidence-based education is a natural extension of data-driven decision making. More directly, evidence-based education assumes data-driven decision making. Educators and administrators with a solid grasp of local demographics, conditions, resources, gaps, and needs, have a framework for interpreting the implications of research results for their particular circumstances. Context is key—this localized knowledge provides the lens through which research can be understood and used to improve practice.

Recasting SBR in this way would also enable ED to circumvent potential problems associated with the local control of schools. For better or for worse, even the slightest hint of a mandate from the federal government—research based or not—on what programs or strategies should be used at the local level elicits quick and fierce opposition. Indeed, while negotiating with states on their Reading First applications, ED's intense scrutiny of state reading plans with respect to the SBR provisions ruffled the feathers of some who viewed it as an unwelcome encroachment on their sovereignty (Manzo, 2002a, 2002b). A framework for SBR that embeds the use of evidence into existing reform efforts and empowers school personnel to engage research as a standard part of their practice would ease some of these tensions and enable ED to be a more powerful advocate for evidence-based education.

Science vs. Professional Judgment

Another essential aspect of SBR that has yet to be fully articulated is how scientific knowledge relates to and supports other forms of knowledge in the practice of education. In the seminal publication defining evidence-based medicine (Sackett, Richardson, Rosenberg, & Haynes, 1997), this relationship is central: The practice is depicted as "a bottom-up approach that integrates the best external evidence with individual clinical expertise and patient choice" (p. 3). In such a conception, research-based knowledge is one important form of knowledge that feeds into the calculus of medical decision making and clinical practice. The critical judgment of health care professionals in assessing the unique needs of their patients is acknowledged explicitly.

The early implementation of SBR has tended to take a more top-down view that external evidence should uniquely drive practice.[4] For example, in

---

[4]The definition of evidence-based education in the opening sentence of this chapter is very similar to the Sackett et al. (1997) definition, and was taken from a presentation given by Grover (Russ) Whitehurst (2001), director of IES and a key figure in the implementation of the SBR provisions. However, Whitehurst's definition does not appear in any official document issued by the U.S. Department of Education related to SBR.

NCLB guidance, ED makes allowances for professional judgment only in the case that the current research base is scant. Comprehensive School Reform guidance states: "In some cases, research that meets these criteria is minimal or non-existent . . . In this case, school leaders will need to rely on . . . some degree of professional judgment in creating their programs" (U.S. Department of Education, 2002b). Further, the Department's strategic plan (U.S. Department of Education, 2002c), and annual report on the agency's progress (U.S. Department of Education, 2003) depict research-based knowledge as the preferable alternative to "professional consensus." Erickson and Gutierrez (2002), however, make the point that this dichotomy is unproductive.

Mandating such a hierarchy not only makes little sense in practical terms, but it is also unwise—it will only serve to insult and alienate the people most critical to the long-term viability of evidence-based education: front-line educators. The skillful melding of research findings, local information, and practical knowledge is the essence of this idea; explicitly acknowledging this fact will be crucial to its success.

Expectations

Because the real task of implementation has only just begun, the rhetoric surrounding SBR is carrying substantial weight. Some rhetorical claims, if taken as statements of expectations, could backfire: By promising too much, the long-term goals of evidence-based education may be compromised. Consider the following statement, issued by a nongovernmental advocacy organization pushing the use of randomized trials in education and other policy domains to support evidence-based practices: "Randomized controlled trials may offer a key to reversing decades of stagnation in American education, and sparking rapid, evidence-driven progress" (Coalition for Evidence-Based Policy, 2002). As a call to action issued by an advocacy group with an impressive board and staff, this is effective, compelling language. If it is taken to be a literal articulation of how to understand and promote the whole of evidence-based education, however, it could be problematic. Interpreted in the latter way, the claim suggests that trials themselves are the means by which education will improve. Again, although high-quality research (including, but not limited to, trials) is essential to the success of evidence-based education, it cannot itself quickly fix the ills—perceived or real—of our education system. Even if the phrase "randomized controlled trials" were replaced with "evidence-based education," the literal interpretation of the statement still likely overstates what can be expected of this trend, all else being equal.

History provides lessons of caution about making such claims. In a recent paper prepared for a U.S. Department of Education seminar on the SBR provisions, Steven Raudenbush (2002) quotes E. L. Thorndike in 1910, from the founding issue of the *Journal of Educational Psychology:*

> A complete science of psychology would tell every fact about everyone's intellect and character and behavior, would tell us the cause of every change in human nature, would tell us the result which every educational force—every act of every person that changed any other or the agent himself—would have. It would aid us to use human beings for the world's welfare with the same surety of the result that we now have when we use falling bodies or chemical elements. In proportion as we get such a science we shall become masters of our own souls as we are now masters of heat and light. Progress toward such a science is now being made.

These overinflated expectations of the field of educational psychology "overshadowed very real but slow progress in the study of education" and led to a decline in public support (Raudenbush, 2002). To avoid a similar fate, it will be important to set bold yet reachable expectations for SBR.

Capacity

Evidence-based education calls for a different way of doing business. Perhaps the most important and most difficult task in implementing SBR is to identify what kinds of capacity are needed to meet these demands on a large scale, to assess to what degree that capacity already exists, and to increase support where it is lacking. Sustainable, positive change can occur if key actors—both the users and producers of research—are engaged and supported to alter their practices.[5]

Users of Research: Practitioners

In a study that describes the first year of NCLB implementation at the state level (Center on Education Policy, 2003), state officials revealed that although most are aware of the SBR provisions, they have not made much progress implementing them. As they turn their attention to SBR, it is likely that many state and local education agencies will face difficulties because in the main, they lack research and evaluation capacity. And as state coffers continue to dwindle, it is not likely that this trend will reverse itself any time soon. In schools, principals and teachers sometimes have a methods course or two in their formal education, but they have rarely engaged in re-

---

[5]Here I touch on the capacity issues for researchers and practitioners separately. The Strategic Education Research Partnership (NRC, 2003) makes a compelling case for upgrading capacity simultaneously in a way that builds mutually reinforcing professional capabilities for generating and using high-quality education research.

search and are not typically trained to be discerning consumers of and contributors to research.

In addition to guidance issued by ED on the SBR provisions, several activities have been undertaken by other federal agencies, professional associations, advocacy organizations, and other such groups to help prepare these practitioners. For example, the Software Industry Information Association and the National Institute for Literacy have recently released documents (Redfield & Sivin-Kachala, 2003; Stanovich & Stanovich, 2003, respectively) with detailed descriptions of why SBR is important; instructions for how to understand, identify, and (for education developers) conduct high-quality research; and illustrations of the ways in which scientific thinking is reflected in educational practice. Additionally, the Education Commission of the States, in partnership with the Mid-Continent Regional Educational Laboratory, has taken a lead role in helping state policymakers understand and effectively implement SBR provisions. The North Central Regional Educational Laboratory has also developed several resources for their clients (see, e.g., North Central Regional Educational Laboratory, 2003).

Though unquestionably valuable, the bulk of this work—resource guides to help practitioners understand and identify high-quality education research—is only the very beginning of what is needed to enhance the capacity of practitioners. Or, more forcefully, this work should be thought of as a set of short-term measures; longer-term strategies should set out to make them unnecessary. Consider an excerpt from guidance issued by ED to help implement the SBR provisions for Comprehensive School Reform Demonstration (CSR) programs:

- Did the research test the stated hypotheses and justify the general conclusions drawn?
- Did the methods correspond to the nature and structure of the data? (U.S. Department of Education, 2002b, p. 8)

These are important questions to consider in assessing research quality. But is it reasonable to expect most educators and administrators to make sense of them? How could they tell if a study justified its conclusions without understanding of and experience with data, theoretical frameworks, rigorous reasoning, and how they are integrated to support inferences? How could educators relate the concepts of methodology and data without understanding and experience with analytic techniques?

As a general matter, researchers—not practitioners—ought to be doing the lion's share of this screening. Indeed, a key feature of the WWC is that it focuses the capacity of researchers to identify, screen, and synthesize a particular type of education research—tasks that require considerable time and technical skill—in the service of developing a decision-support tool for educators. In the longer term, these and other efforts should obviate the need for educators to conduct the equivalent of a literature review or research synthesis themselves.

Instead, capacity building for practitioners should focus on developing basic facility with research and its applications to practice, beginning with preservice training and extending throughout their careers. Additionally, careful consideration must be paid to ways in which these professionals can be supported to reflect on research evidence, to challenge their assumptions, and to consider implications as a standard part of their work and development.

Producers of Research: Investigators

Education researchers are trained in many disciplines, frame issues and questions with different epistemological paradigms, and work in a variety of university and other organizational settings. These differences are strong assets: They lend the field intellectual vibrancy and enable rich dialogue about the complex nature of education phenomena. But they also complicate efforts to develop a community of investigators with a strong, self-regulating culture (Lagemann, 2000; NRC, 2002) that can strengthen the research and its applications to practice.

The development of such a culture would entail stronger efforts to define and uphold quality standards in its products; to promote opportunities for sharing data and conducting secondary analyses and replications; to collaborate in cross-disciplinary investigations (especially those that integrate quantitative and qualitative methods); and to engage in rigorous, consistent efforts to take stock of what is known (Feuer, Towne, & Shavelson, 2002). In the context of promoting the goals of evidence-based education, attending to these issues more systematically would shift the burden of responsibility for making summary statements about the preponderance of evidence in important areas of education policy and practice from the consumers of research to the generators of research.

To engage in these sorts of activities on a large scale, structural and financial barriers will need to be surmounted. For example, the incentive structures within which researchers operate tend to devalue such efforts: Few grant-making organizations support syntheses or replications (preferring "new" investigations); major academic journals similarly discourage attempts to reanalyze data or otherwise extend previous work; cross-disciplinary projects require a considerable expenditure of energy that rarely "counts" toward faculty tenure or promotion; and delving into the tough work of understanding what the convergence of evidence might mean in local contexts is time not spent publishing or teaching.

With strong resolve and leadership, some of this work can be accomplished by shifting (scant) existing resources. However, additional financial supports will almost certainly be needed. The paltry federal investment in education research is well documented (although admittedly not very precisely: see Morrill, 1998; President's Committee of Advisors on Science and Technology, 1997) and widely bemoaned as an impediment to linking research and reform. It is hard to imagine that evidence-based education will succeed without funding increases to generate more and better research and to strengthen the community of investigators to be active participants. Indeed, the initial investment in the WWC—which involves developing a transparent process for judging and cataloguing existing studies, and providing a platform for building on existing work—will likely exceed $25 million, a substantial fraction of the IES budget for research.

There is some indication that the Bush administration and Congress recognize the need for more education research funding. In the FY04 budget year, the administration requested a $45 million increase for national topical research in the U.S. Department of Education (although overall cutting the IES budget by $26 million from FY03 levels through the proposed eliminations of programs like the Regional Educational Laboratory program—an effort intended to help states and districts utilize education research). The House passed a $56 million increase for IES whereas the Senate passed a $5 million increase (both rejecting the proposed cuts in the president's budget). It is yet to be seen how the final numbers will emerge from conference negotiations. At a time when our national budget is under severe strain, however, any increase for education research funding—a line item typically well under the radar screen of appropriators—must be viewed as a positive development.

A FIGHT WORTH FIGHTING

Few would argue with the basic premise that we ought to be doing a better job of using research to improve decision making in education. The SBR provisions offer an exciting opportunity to do that, but the implementation challenges are daunting. If indeed we are talking about transforming a system, however, this fact should not be surprising. What is needed is a frank conversation about the intellectual and financial resources required to achieve the exceedingly worthy goals of evidence-based education, and steadfast work to marshal them.

ACKNOWLEDGMENTS

The author is grateful to Michael J. Feuer, Richard Hershman, and Martin Orland for their critical comments and suggestions on an early draft of this chapter. All opinions, omissions, or errors are mine, and do not necessarily represent the views of the National Research Council/National Academies or Educational Testing Service.

REFERENCES

Aaron, H. J. (1978). *Politics and the professors: The great society in perspective*. Washington, DC: Brookings Institution Press.

Boruch, R., DeMoya, D., & Snyder, B. (2001). The importance of randomized field trials in education and related areas. In F. Mosteller & R. Boruch (Eds.), *Evidence matters: Randomized trials in education research* (pp. 50–79). Washington, DC: Brookings Institution Press.

Center on Education Policy. (2003). *From the capital to the classroom: State and federal efforts to implement the No Child Left Behind Act*. Washington, DC: Author.

Coalition for Evidence-Based Policy. (2002). *Bringing evidence-driven progress to education: A recommended strategy for the U.S. Department of Education*. Retrieved March 31, 2004, from http://www.excelgov.org/usermedia/images/uploads/PDFs/coalitionFinRpt.pdf

Dunst, C. J., Trivette, C. M., & Cutspec, P. A. (2002, September). Toward an operational definition of evidence-based practices. *Centerscope, 1*(1), 1–10.

Education Sciences Reform Act of 2002. (2002). Pub. L. No. 107-279. Retrieved December 2, 2003, from http://www.ed.gov/legislation/FedRegister/finrule/2002-4/122702a.html

Eisenhart, M., & Towne, L. (2003, October). Contestation and change in national policy on "scientifically-based" educational research. *Educational Researcher*. Retrieved March 31, 2004, from http://www.aera.net/pubs/er/toc/er3207.htm

Erickson, F., & Gutierrez, K. (2002). Culture, rigor, and science in educational research. *Educational Researcher, 31*(8), 21–24.

Feldman, M., & March, J. G. (1981). Information in organizations as signal and symbol. *Administrative Science Quarterly, 26,* 171–186.

Feuer, M J., Towne, L., & Shavelson, R. J. (2002). Scientific culture and educational research. *Educational Researcher, 31*(8), 4–14.

Gambrill, E. (1999). Evidence-based practice: An alternative to authority-based practice. *Families in Society: The Journal of Contemporary Human Services, 80,* 341–350.

Grissmer, D. (Ed.). (1999, Summer). Class size: Issues and new findings [Special issue]. *Educational Evaluation and Policy Analysis, 21*(2).

Howe, K. R. (2004, February). A critique of experimentalism. *Qualitative Inquiry, 10*(1), 42–61.

Institute of Medicine. (2001). *Crossing the quality chasm: A new health system for the 21st century.* Washington, DC: National Academies Press.

Kaestle, C. (1993). The awful reputation of educational research. *Educational Researcher, 22*(1), 26–31.

Lagemann, E. C. (2000). *An elusive science: The troubling history of education research.* Chicago: University of Chicago Press.

Law, M., & Baum, C. (1998). Evidence-based occupational therapy. *Canadian Journal of Occupational Therapy, 65,* 131–135.

Lindblom, C. E., & Cohen, D. K. (1979). *Usable knowledge: Social science and social problem-solving.* New Haven, CT: Yale University Press.

Manzo, K. K. (2002a, October 2). Majority of states told to revise reading plans. *Education Week.* Retrieved March 31, 2004, from http://www.edweek.net/ew/ewstory.cfm?slug=05read.h22&keywords=manzo

Manzo, K. K. (2002b, February 20). Some educators see reading rules as too restrictive. *Education Week.* Retrieved March 31, 2004, from http://www.edweek.net/ew/ewstory.cfm?slug=23read.h21&keywords=manzo

Melnyk, B. M., Fineout-Overholt, E., Stone, P., & Ackerman, M. (2000). Evidence-based practice: The past, the present, and recommendations for the millennium. *Pediatric Nursing, 26,* 77–80.

Morrill, W. (1998, October 6). *Shaping the future of educational research, development, and communication.* Working paper presented to the National Educational Research Policy and Priorities Board, U.S. Department of Education, Washington, DC.

National Reading Panel. (2000, April). *Teaching children to read: An evidence-based assessment of the scientific research literature on reading and its implications for reading instruction* (NIH Pub. No. 00-4769). Washington, DC: National Institute of Child Health and Human Development.

National Research Council. (1998). *Preventing reading difficulties in young children.* Committee on the prevention of reading difficulties in young children. C. E. Snow, M. S. Burns, & P. Griffin (Eds.), Division of Behavioral and Social Sciences and Education. Retrieved March 31, 2004, from http://books.nap.edu/html/prdyc/index.html

National Research Council. (1999). *Improving student learning: A strategic plan for education research and its utilization.* Committee on a Feasibility Study for a Strategic Education Research Program. Commission on Behavioral and Social Sciences and Education. Washington, DC: National Academy Press.

National Research Council. (2002). *Scientific research in education.* Committee on scientific principles in education research. R. J. Shavelson & L. Towne (Eds.), Center for Education, Division of Behavioral and Social Sciences and Education. Washington, DC: National Academies Press.

National Research Council. (2003). *Strategic education research partnership.* M. S. Donovan, A. K. Wigdor, & C. E. Snow (Eds.), Division of Behavioral and Social Sciences and Education. Washington, DC: National Academies Press.

No Child Left Behind Act of 2001, Pub. L. No. 107-110, § 115 Stat. 1425 (2002).

North Central Regional Educational Laboratory. (2003, Spring). A call for evidence: responding to the new emphasis on scientifically based research [Special issue]. *Learning Point, 5*(1).

Pettigrew, T. F. (1985). Can social scientists be effective actors in the policy arena? In R. L. Shotland & M. M. Mark (Eds.), *Social science and social policy* (pp. 123–124). Beverly Hills, CA: Sage.

President's Committee of Advisors on Science and Technology. (1997). *Report to the president on the use of technology to strengthen K–12 education in the United States.* Retrieved August 30, 2003, from http://www.ostp.gov/PCAST/k-12ed.html

Raudenbush, S. (2002, February 6). *The use of scientifically based research in education.* Paper presented at the meeting of the U.S. Department of Education, Washington, DC. Retrieved March 31, 2004, from http://www.ed.gov/nclb/methods/whatworks/research/index.html?exp=0

Redfield, D. L., & Sivin-Kachala, J. (2003). *Scientifically based research: A guide for education publishers and developers.* Washington, DC: Software & Information Industry Association.

Rogers, E. M. (1995). *Diffusion of innovations* (4th ed.). New York: The Free Press.

Sackett, D. L., Richardson, S. R., Rosenberg, W., & Haynes, R. B. (1997). *Evidence-based medicine: How to practice and teach EMB.* London: Churchill Livingstone.

Stanovich, P. J., & Stanovich, K. E. (2003). *Using research and reason in education: How teachers can use SBR to make curricular & instructional decisions.* National Institute for Literacy. Retrieved September 2002, from http://www.nifl.gov/partnershipforreading/publications/pdf/Stanovich_Color.pdf

U.S. Department of Education. (2002a). *Guidance for the Reading First program.* Retrieved September 2003, from at http://www.ed.gov/programs/readingfirst/guidance.pdf

U.S. Department of Education. (2002b). *Guidance on the Comprehensive School Reform Program.* Retrieved April 1, 2004, from http://www.ed.gov/programs/compreform/guidance/page_pg10.html?exp=0

U.S. Department of Education. (2002c). *Strategic plan, 2002–2007.* Retrieved September 2003, from http://www.ed.gov/about/reports/strat/plan2002-07/index.html

U.S. Department of Education. (2003). *Fiscal year 2002 performance and accountability report.* Retrieved April 1, 2004, from http://www.ed.gov/about/reports/annual/2002report/mda.pdf

U.S. Department of Education. (2004, January 16). *Improving teacher quality state grants, Title II, Part A: Non-regulatory guidance.* Retrieved April 1, 2004, from http://www.ed.gov/programs/teacherqual/guidance.doc

Weiss, C. H. (1991). Knowledge creep and decision accretion. In D. S. Anderson & B. J. Biddle (Eds.), *Knowledge for policy: Improving education through research* (pp. 183–192). London: Falmer Press.

Whitehurst, G. (2001). *Evidence-based education.* Retrieved September 2003, from http://www.ed.gov/admins/tchrqual/evidence/whitehurst.html

CLOSING THE ACHIEVEMENT GAP

5

Prospects for School Reform and Closing the Achievement Gap

Andrew C. Porter
Vanderbilt University

In the introduction to their comprehensive volume *The Black–White Test Score Gap,* Christopher Jencks and Meredith Phillips (1998) stated: "Reducing the test score gap is probably both necessary and sufficient for substantially reducing racial inequality in educational attainment and earnings. Changes in education and earnings would in turn help reduce racial differences in crime, health, and family structure, although we do not know how large these effects would be" (p. 4). Jencks and Phillips are not alone in their assessment of the importance of reducing, if not eliminating, the achievement gap. Reducing the gap, as well as raising the level of achievement for all students, has been the goal of education reform at least since the days of President Lyndon Johnson's war on poverty and the beginnings of Title I in 1965.

My purpose here is to describe the achievement gap—how big, how stable over time, how stable over age, and how important—and then to consider each of several reforms that have been hypothesized to decrease it. Analysis of the literature on reform success leads to tentative conclusions about what strategies are most promising for future reductions in the achievement gap.

The achievement gap has been the focus of so many reforms and so much research over such an extended period of time that I do not attempt an exhaustive treatment of the topic in this chapter. For example, the data I present on the achievement gap are intended to be illustrative rather than comprehensive. I have made a greater effort to be complete in considering interventions to close the achievement gap, but my review of the literature on the effectiveness of these interventions is again intended to be illustrative, not comprehensive. Hopefully, coverage is representative of what is known.

I do not address the nature–nurture controversy. Recognizing that there are great differences of opinion on the issue of nature–nurture—from Herrnstein and Murray (1994), at one end of the spectrum, to Nisbett (1998), at the other—most believe that even if there is a genetic component to the achievement gap, environment plays an enormously important role. Nisbett, in taking the extreme position on the importance of environment, stated, "The most relevant studies provide no evidence for the genetic superiority of either race, but strong evidence for a substantial environmental contribution to the IQ gap between blacks and whites" (p. 101). What follows is consistent with the importance of environment; evidence is assembled on the possibility of school reforms decreasing the achievement gap.

One difficulty in addressing the topic of the achievement gap and the efficacy of school reform is that the gap itself is defined in different ways—most frequently as a contrast between Black and White student achievement. Much less often, the gap is defined as a contrast between Hispanic and White student achievement. It is also commonly defined as a contrast between the achievement of students of lower and higher socioeconomic status (SES). In what follows, I move from one type of contrast to another, as the findings seem important. Allowing the definition of the achievement gap to vary from topic to topic and study to study was less than fully satisfying, but doing otherwise would have left out important results. Reducing the achievement gap between students of lower and higher SES may require different strategies than reducing the gap between Black and White or Hispanic and White students. Furthermore, it can be difficult to interpret the gap when it is defined in terms of SES because SES is measured in different ways. Sometimes, the SES contrasts are defined normatively (e.g., the top 10% vs. the bottom 10%), and sometimes they are defined against an external criterion. Interpretation of the achievement gap can also be difficult when it is defined in relation to race/ethnicity. For example, Hispanics are far from a homogeneous group, both because of differences in English-language facility and because of differences in origins (e.g., Chicano vs. Cuban). Even the definition and measurement of race/ethnicity is changing.

Reducing the achievement gap has not proven to be straightforward, either. Many initiatives to close the gap have actually widened it. This phenomenon first came to my attention with the evaluation of the *Sesame Street* television program for children. Cook et al. (1975) found that Black and White children who viewed *Sesame Street* for equal amounts of time had approximately equal gains in achievement. However, Black children watched the show less often than White children and were less likely to be involved with the educational toys and games derived from the show. Thus, *Sesame*

Street increased the achievement gap, despite the hope of its creators that the program would do just the opposite.

Another reason good instruction often increases the achievement gap is that, when all else is equal, higher achieving students generally gain more from good instruction than lower achieving students. Carroll's (1963) model of school learning explains such findings. Of course, the key is that everything else must be equal. In the *Sesame Street* example, everything else was not equal: Black children received less instruction than White children, an issue of *opportunity to learn* to which I return in the conclusions.

Before turning to the size and nature of the achievement gap, we must consider one final point. The achievement gap can be larger or smaller, depending on what is being measured and how. In what follows, I contrast reading to mathematics, and the findings are often different. Similarly, findings can differ when performance assessments are used to measure achievement rather than multiple-choice assessments. Several years ago, when performance assessment was being heavily promoted, many individuals hypothesized that the achievement gap would be smaller for performance assessments than for multiple-choice assessments (Feinberg, 1990; Linn, Baker, & Dunbar, 1991). These individuals believed that minority and low-income students actually knew more than multiple-choice tests revealed. Unfortunately, the opposite has proven to be true. Generally, the achievement gap is larger for performance assessments than for multiple-choice assessments. One explanation is that performance assessments are better measures of students' ability to apply and reason. The curriculum that minority and poor students receive provides less of an opportunity to learn applications and reasoning than that provided to White and more affluent students. Thus, multiple-choice tests may underestimate the achievement gap because they fail to measure content on which the achievement gap is especially large. Another explanation as to why the gap is greater for performance assessment is that low-achieving students appear less willing to put forth the effort necessary to complete performance assessment items (Routitsky & Turner, 2003).

HOW BIG IS THE ACHIEVEMENT GAP?

The best data for describing the achievement gap among racial/ethnic subgroups of students come from the National Assessment of Educational Progress (NAEP) long-term trend assessments in reading, mathematics, and science (National Center for Education Statistics [NCES], 2000). There are also long-term trend data for writing; but there may be some technical problems with these data, so they are not reported here.

NAEP long-term trend assessments have remained virtually unchanged since their first administrations over three decades ago. The design is a national probability sample of students at ages 9, 13, and 17. The test consists of rotated forms, so reporting at the student level is not appropriate. The scale is from 0 to 500, with performance levels established at intervals of 50 points, from 150 to 350. There have been 10 administrations in reading, 9 in mathematics, and 10 in science (NCES, 2000).

In the aggregate, scores increased between 1970 and 1999 in reading for students at ages 9 and 13 (but not age 17) and in mathematics for all three age groups. In science, the picture is more complex. Scores decreased from their 1970 baseline but by 1999 had regained the 1970 levels for 9- and 13-year-olds but not for 17-year-olds.

Of interest here, the NAEP data can be disaggregated by race/ethnicity into groups of White, Black, and Hispanic students (see Table 5.1 and Figs. 5.1–5.11). Generally, the data show the achievement gaps among these groups narrowing slightly over time, but not in all cases. As seen in Table 5.1 and Figs. 5.1–5.11, the Black–White gap for each subject and age is not clearly monotonically decreasing. Generally, the gap appears to narrow and to be at its smallest at a point sometime in the late 1980s. Since the late 1980s, the gap appears to be either stable or slightly increasing.

Table 5.2 shows changes in the achievement gap between Black and White students 1971–1999. In all but the contrast for 17-year-olds, the achievement gap has decreased significantly from the baseline year. Table 5.3 shows changes in the achievement gap between Hispanic and White students 1973–1999. For the Hispanic and White contrasts, the gap is reduced in mathematics for 13- and 17-year-olds, but only for 17-year-olds in reading and for none of the three age groups in science.

Kosters and Mast (2003) reached similar conclusions about changes in the achievement gap over time. In addition, they pointed out that there is substantial variation in the size of the achievement gap in different states, with the gap for Black versus White students only one third of a standard deviation in Maine and more than a standard deviation in Wisconsin, Connecticut, and several other states.

Even though the test and sampling procedure for long-term trend NAEP have remained unchanged for more than three decades, participation rates have changed, as illustrated in Table 5.4.

Clearly, participation rates have decreased over time, especially for 17-year-olds. Unfortunately, these data are not disaggregated by race/ethnicity or SES. However, if the decrease in participation rates is larger for schools serving high versus low concentrations of minority students, and if the same is true for students' participation rates within schools, it could be that over time the representativeness of the White sample is staying relatively constant, whereas the Black and Hispanic samples are becoming biased. If there is an increasing bias caused by shifts in participation rates, the bias is likely in a direction that favors higher participation by higher achieving stu-

TABLE 5.1
Reading Performance of 9-, 13-, and 17-Year-Olds

Reading	1971	1975	1980	1984	1988	1990	1992	1994	1996	1999
Age 9 White	214	217	221	218	218	217	218	218	220	221
Age 9 Black	170	181	189	186	189	182	185	185	191	186
Age 9 Hispanic		183	190	187	194	189	192	186	195	193
Age 13 White	261	262	264	263	261	262	266	265	266	267
Age 13 Black	222	226	233	236	243	241	238	234	234	238
Age 13 Hispanic		233	237	240	240	238	289	235	238	244
Age 17 White	291	293	293	295	295	297	297	296	295	295
Age 17 Black	239	241	243	264	274	267	261	266	266	264
Age 17 Hispanic		252	261	268	271	275	271	263	265	271

Mathematics	1973	1978	1982	1986	1990	1992	1994	1996	1999	
Age 9 White	225	224	224	227	235	235	237	237	239	
Age 9 Black	190	192	195	202	208	208	212	212	211	
Age 9 Hispanic	202	203	204	205	214	212	210	215	213	
Age 13 White	274	272	274	274	276	279	281	281	283	
Age 13 Black	228	230	240	249	249	250	252	252	251	
Age 13 Hispanic	239	238	252	254	255	259	256	256	259	
Age 17 White	310	306	304	308	309	312	312	313	315	
Age 17 Black	270	268	272	279	289	286	286	286	283	
Age 17 Hispanic	277	276	277	283	284	292	291	292	293	

Science	1970	1973	1977	1982	1986	1990	1992	1994	1996	1999
Age 9 White	236	231	230	229	232	237	239	240	239	240
Age 9 Black	179	177	175	187	196	196	200	201	202	199
Age 9 Hispanic			192	189	199	206	205	201	207	206
Age 13 White	263	259	256	257	259	264	267	267	266	266
Age 13 Black	215	205	208	217	222	226	224	224	226	227
Age 13 Hispanic			213	225	226	232	238	232	232	227
Age 17 White	312	304	298	293	298	301	304	306	307	306
Age 17 Black	258	250	240	235	253	253	256	257	260	254
Age 17 Hispanic			262	249	259	261	270	261	269	276

dents. Thus, over time the size of the achievement gap may be increasingly underestimated, especially for 17-year-olds.

Hedges and Nowell (1998) investigated whether the achievement gap is about the same throughout the entire distribution of Black and White 17-year-olds. They found that group differences are smallest toward the bottom of the two distributions, largest in the middle, and somewhat smaller near the top. The same pattern holds for reading, math, and science. Because there is less variance in the Black distribution, however, Black underrepresentation is greater for high scores than for low scores. For example, the proportion of Whites who score in the upper 5% is 10–20 times

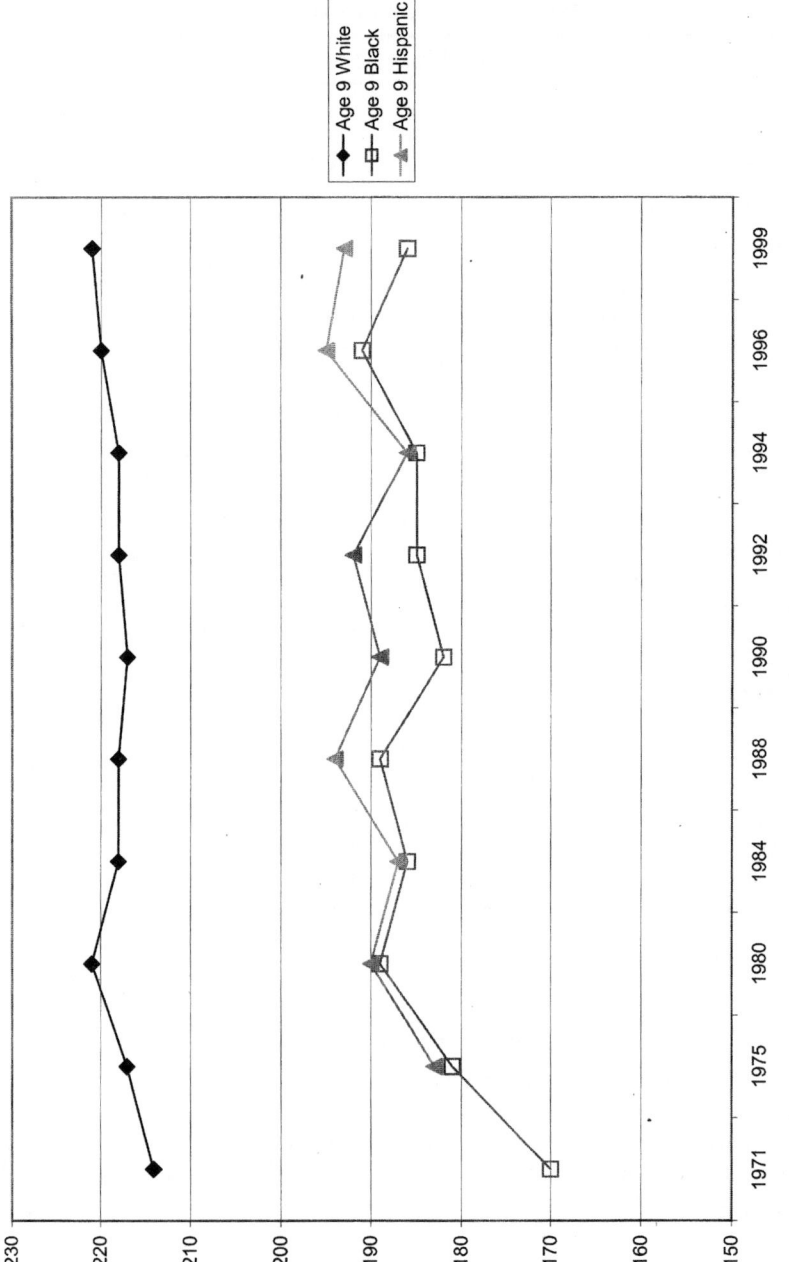

FIG. 5.1. Reading performance of 9-year-olds.

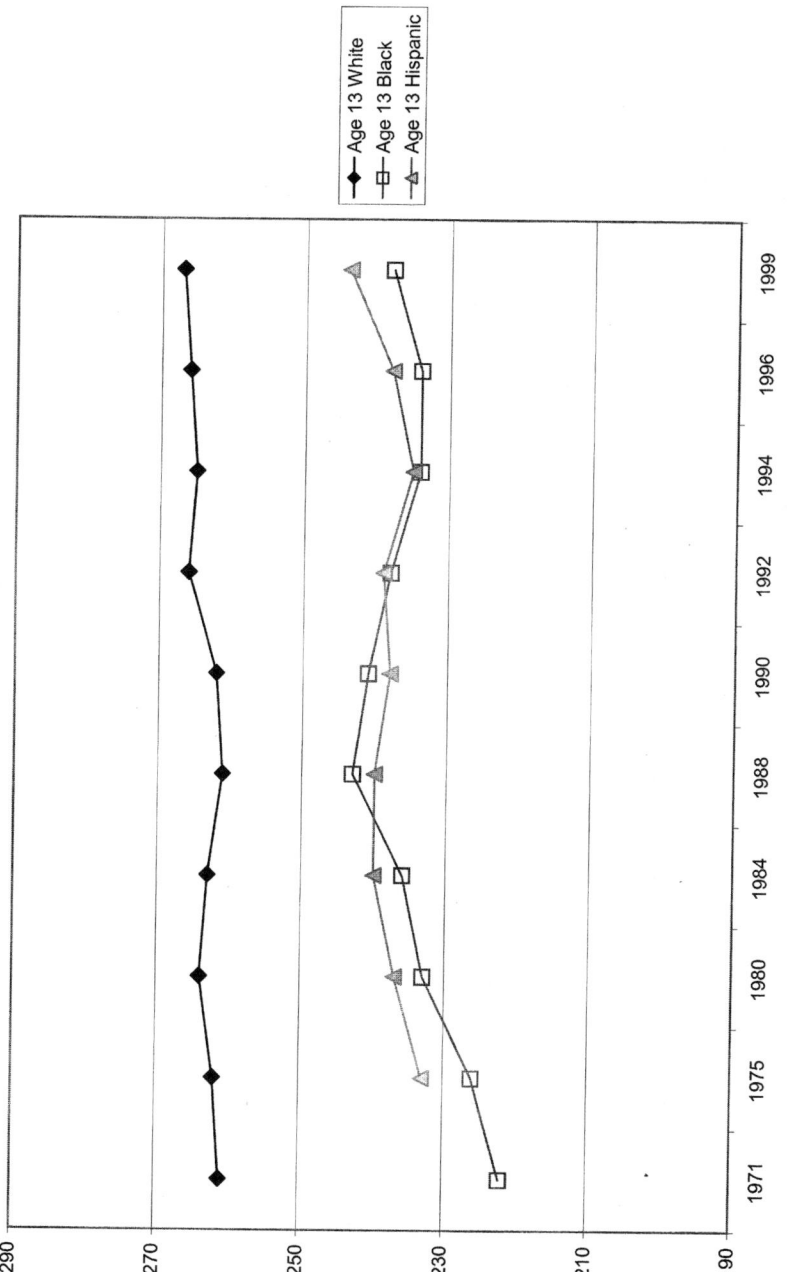

FIG. 5.2. Reading performance of 13-year-olds.

Legend:
- Age 13 White
- Age 13 Black
- Age 13 Hispanic

65

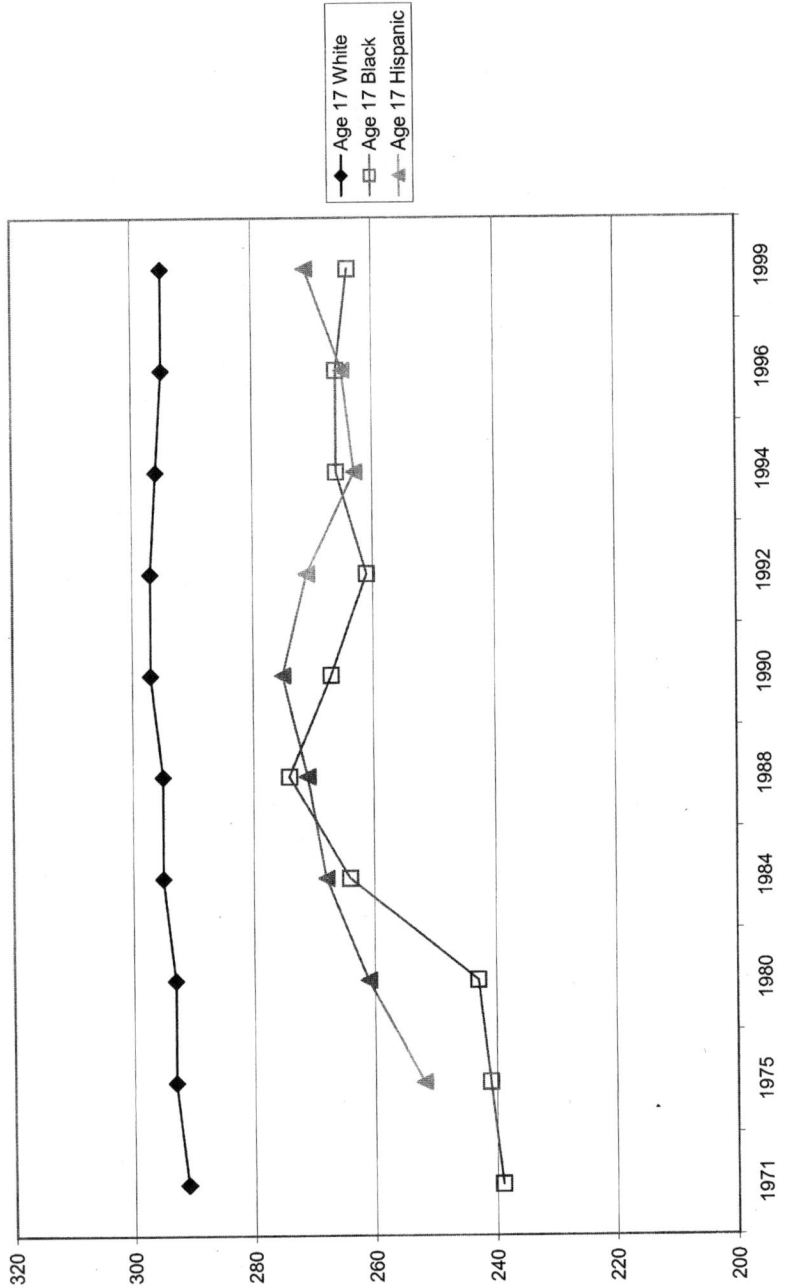

FIG. 5.3. Reading performance of 17-year-olds.

Legend:
Age 17 White
Age 17 Black
Age 17 Hispanic

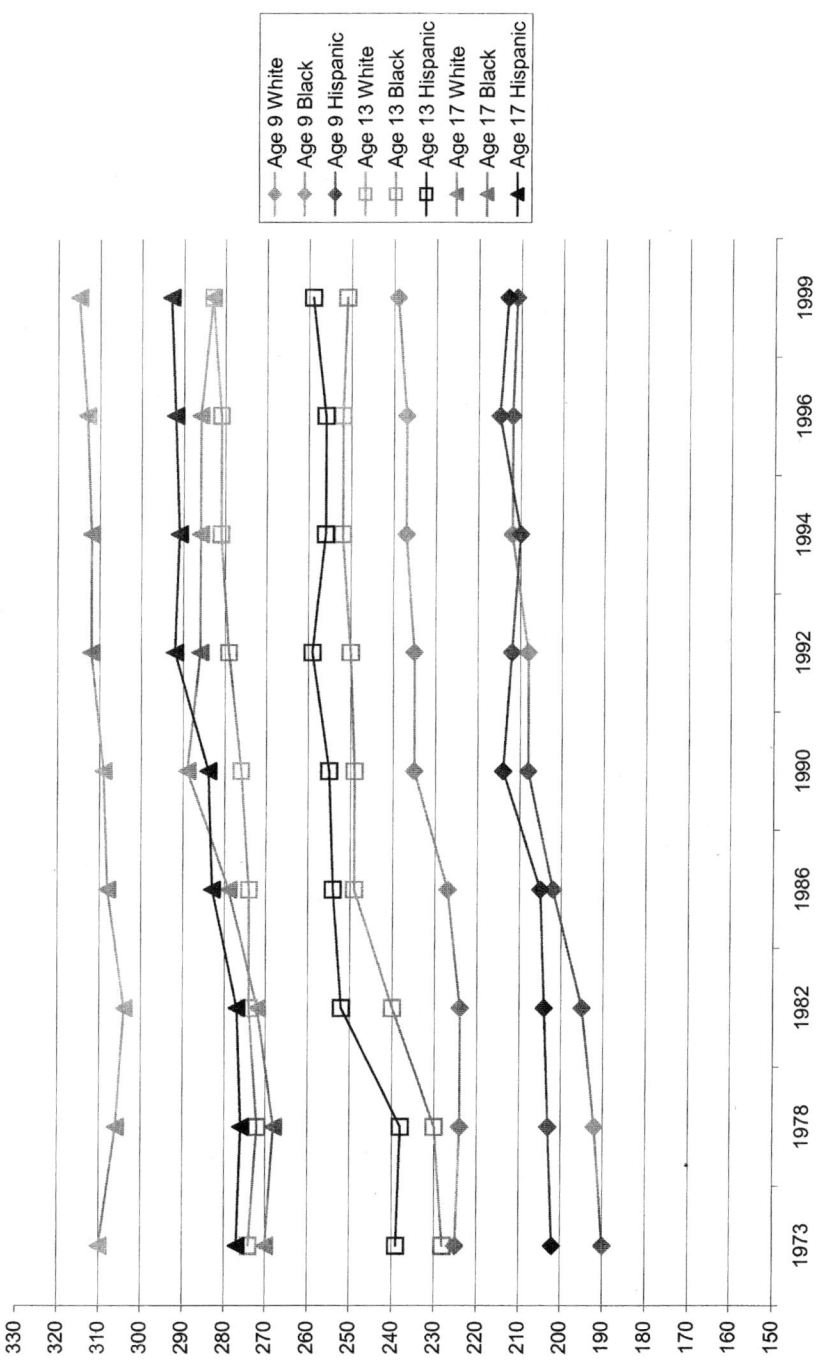

FIG. 5.4. Mathematics performance of 9, 13, and 17-year-olds.

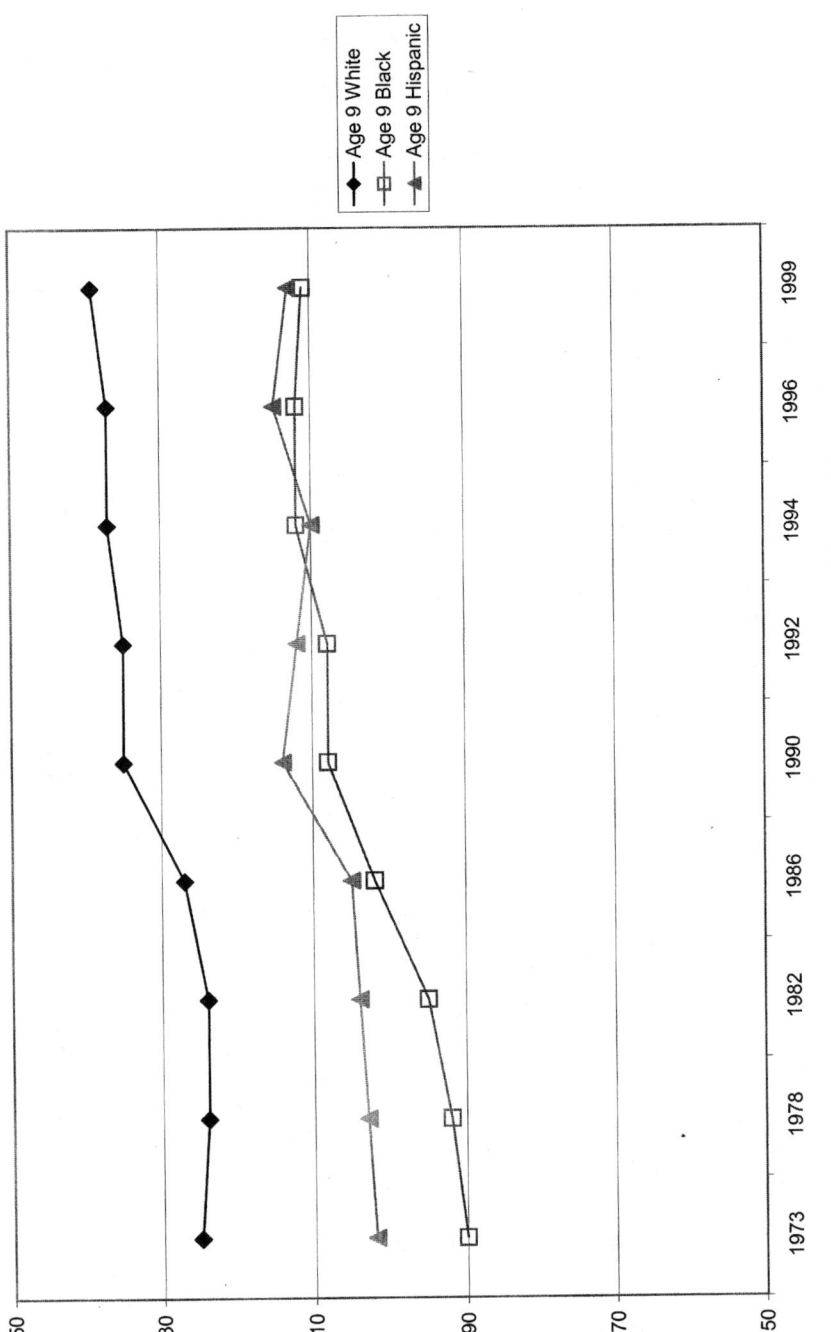

FIG. 5.5. Mathematics performance of 9-year-olds.

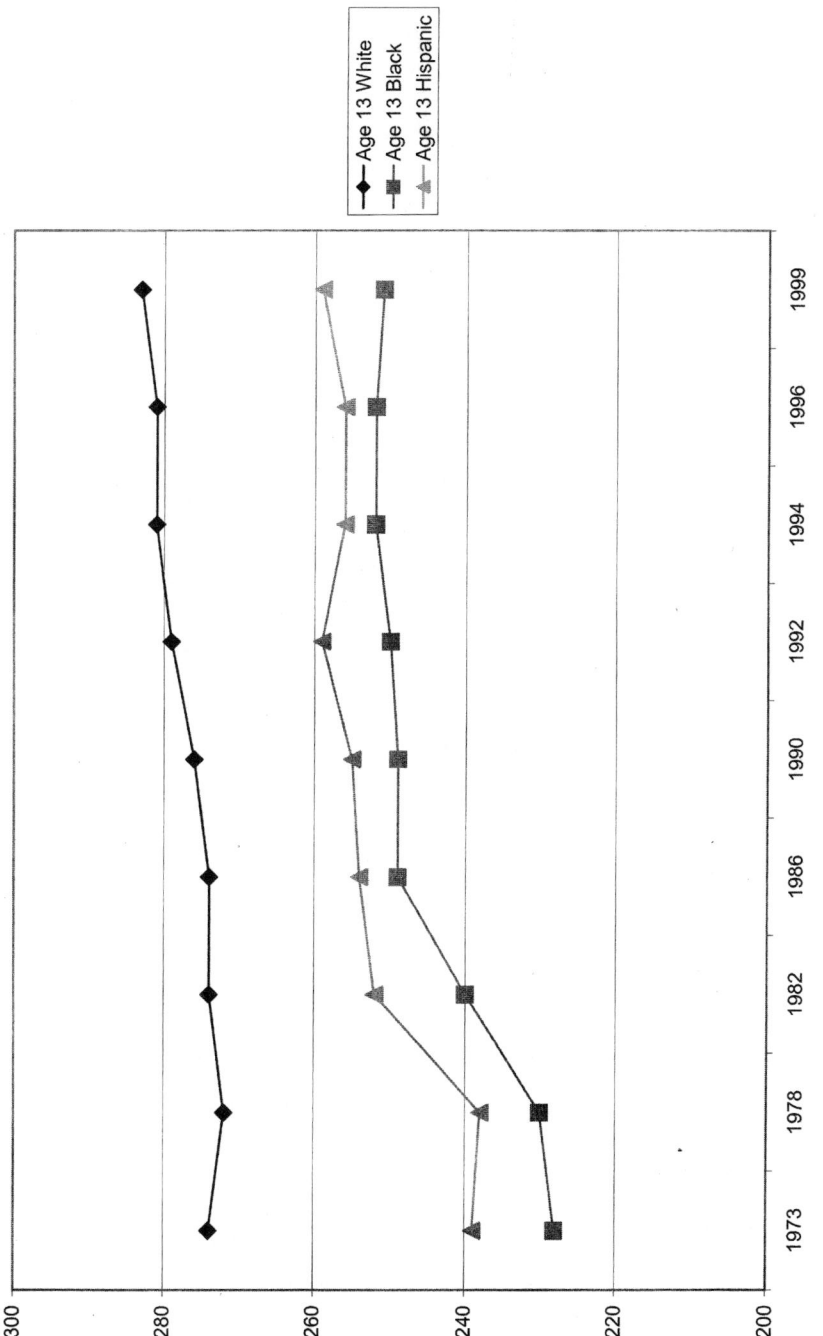

FIG. 5.6. Mathematics performance of 13-year-olds.

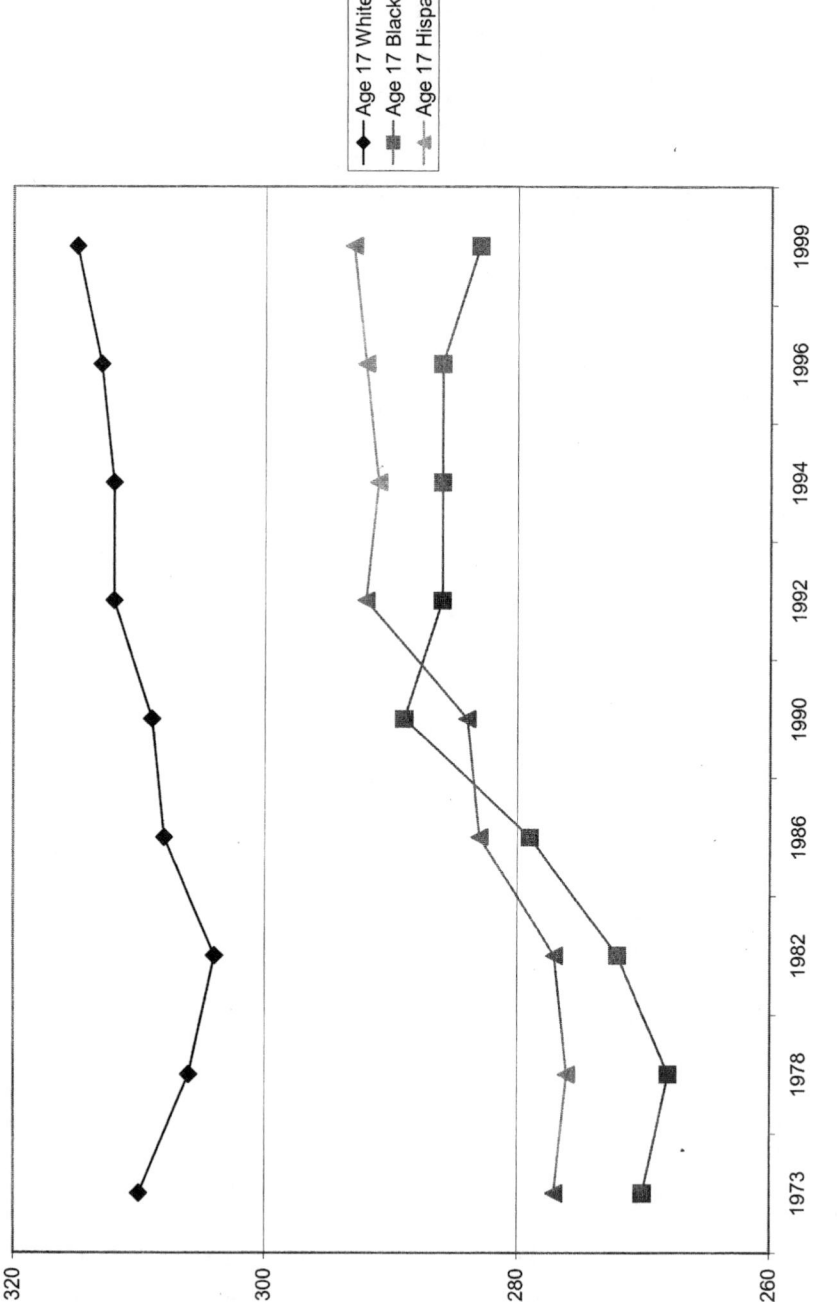

FIG. 5.7. Mathematics performance of 17-year-olds.

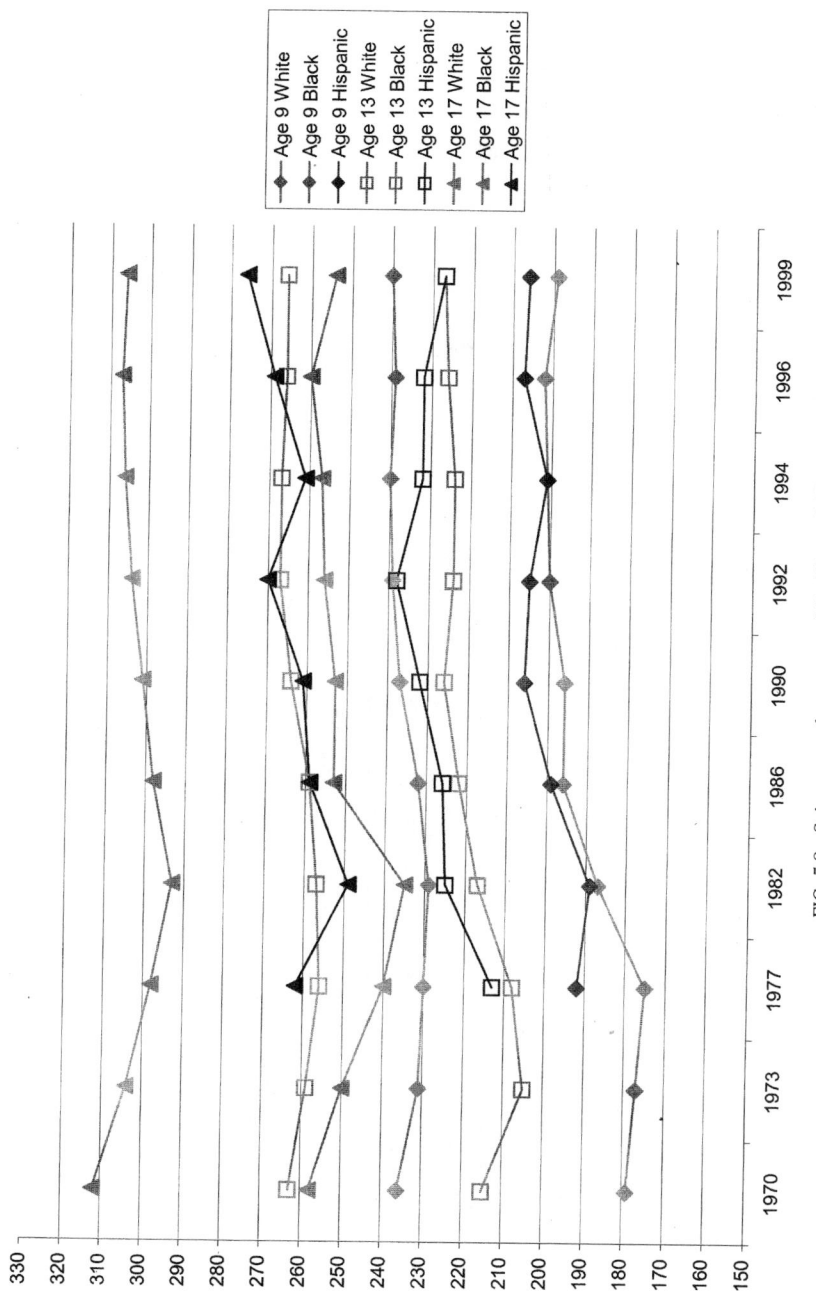

FIG. 5.8. Science performance of 9-, 13-, and 17-year-olds.

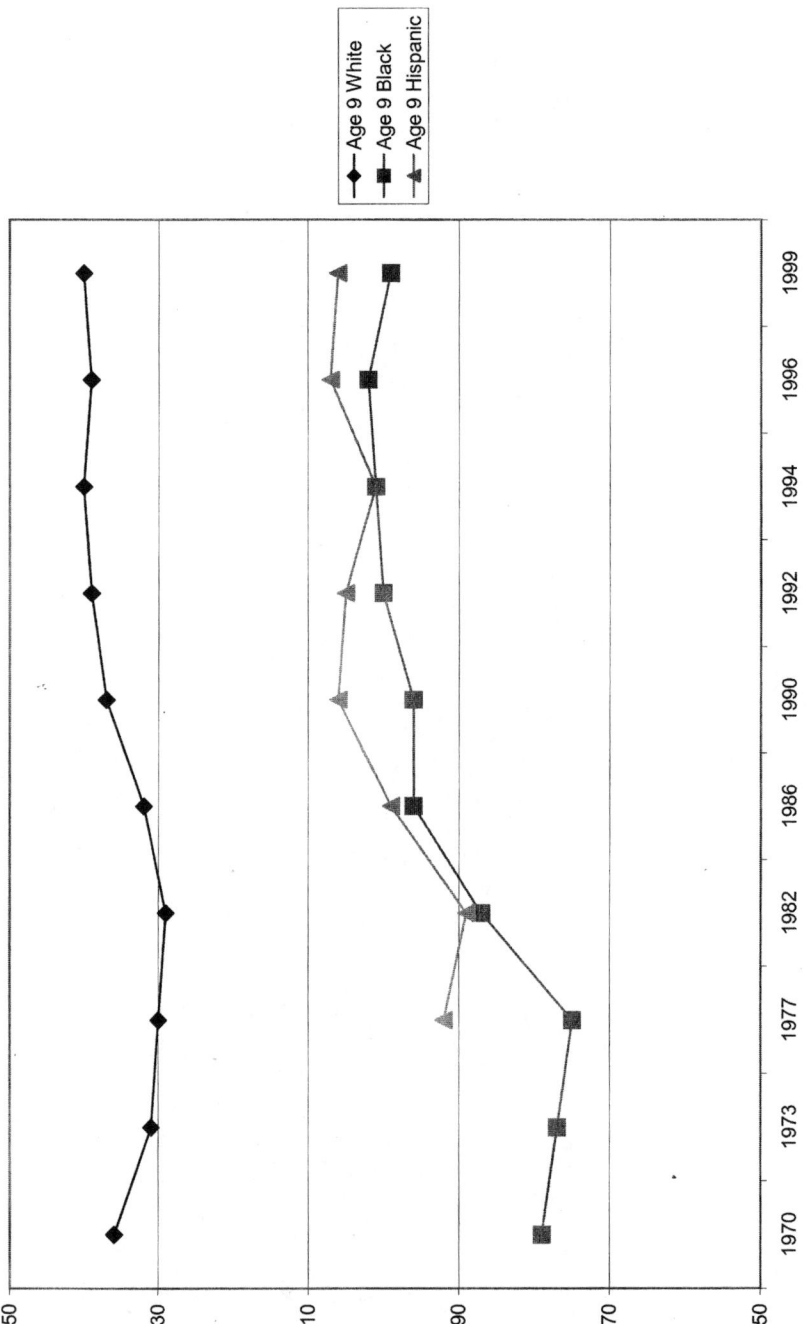

FIG. 5.9. Science performance of 9-year-olds.

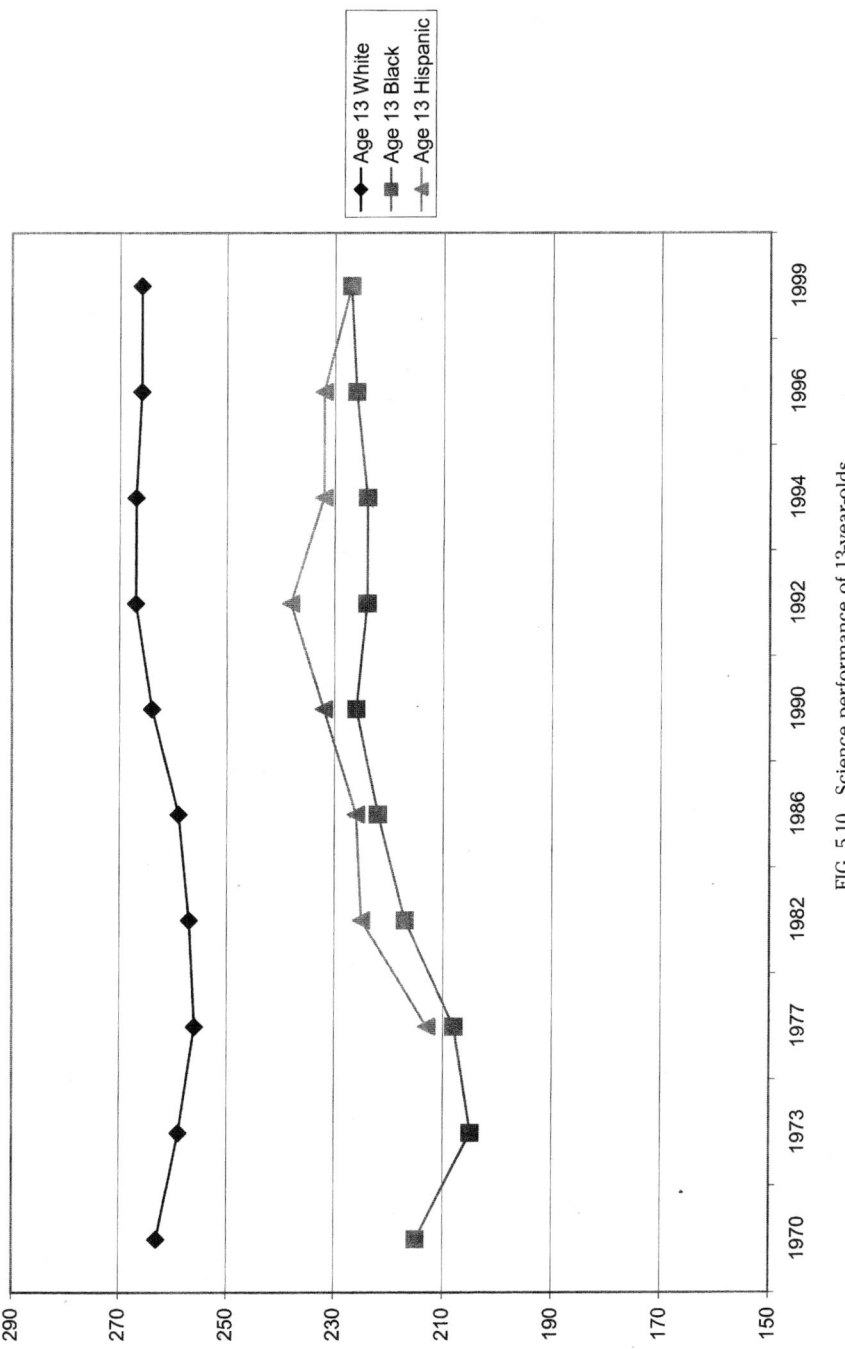

FIG. 5.10. Science performance of 13-year-olds.

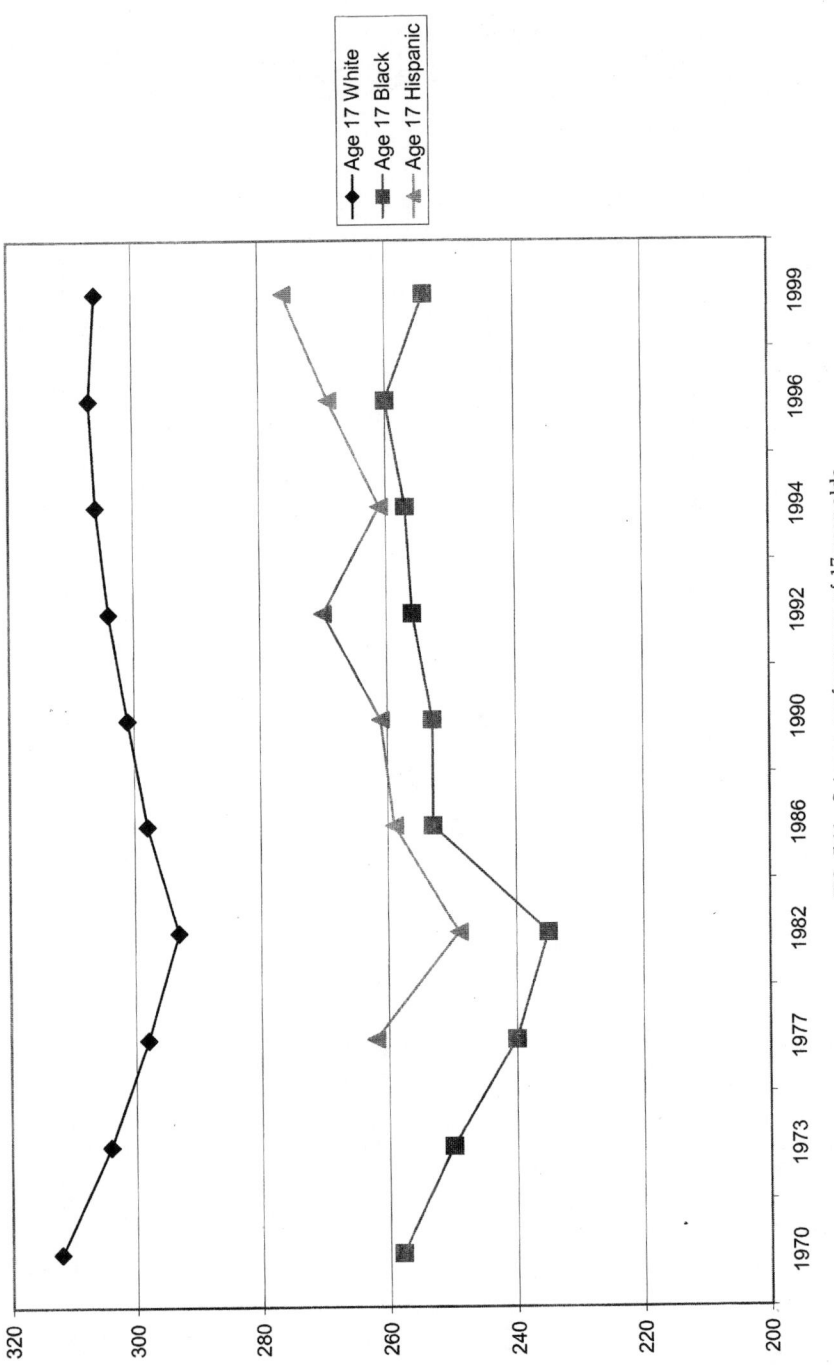

FIG. 5.11. Science performance of 17-year-olds.

TABLE 5.2
Changes in the Achievement Gap Between
Black and White Students, 1971–1999

	Reading		Mathematics		Science	
Age	1971	1999	1973	1999	1970	1999
9	44	35*	35	28*	57	41*
13	39	29*	46	32*	49	39*
17	53	31*	40	31*	54	52

Note. Values represent Black–White differences in score points. 1999 values with an asterisk indicate a significantly smaller gap than the 1971 value at the .01 level.

TABLE 5.3
Changes in the Achievement Gap Between
Hispanic and White Students, 1973–1999

	Reading		Mathematics		Science	
Age	1975	1999	1973	1999	1977	1999
9	34	28	23	26	38	34
13	30	23	35	24*	43	39
17	41	24*	33	22*	35	30

Note. Values represent Hispanic–White differences in score points. 1999 values with an asterisk indicate a significantly smaller gap than the value for the baseline year at the .01 level.

TABLE 5.4
Participation Rates in Long-Term Trend NAEP, 1971–1999

	Reading		Mathematics		Science	
Age	1971	1999	1973	1999	1973	1999
9	84%	80%	85%	78%	85%	78%
13	78%	74%	79%	73%	79%	73%
17	67%	59%	68%	59%	68%	59%

higher than the proportion of Blacks with such scores, and this order of difference has remained roughly unchanged in the last two decades.

There is of course a question of how race/ethnic identity is defined, and these definitions are changing with time. These changing definitions create great potential for confusion in studying changes in the achievement gap over time. Will we continue to have groups identified as Black, Hispanic, and White? Will the definitions of these groups remain stable? When self-identification is the method of measurement, will respondents' decision structures for identifying and reporting their race/ethnic identity remain constant over time? These are difficult questions to which the answers are not at present fully known.

One could, of course, study the achievement gap between groups of students of higher and lower SES. NAEP long-term trend reports data contrasting students by their parents' highest level of education (less than high school graduate, high school graduate, some education after high school) (NCES, 2000). Unfortunately, these data depend on students reporting their parents' highest level of education. In 1999, only 3% of 17-year-olds reported that they didn't know their parents' highest level of education; however, 11% of 13-year-olds and 34% of 9-year-olds reported lacking this knowledge. The score point differences between students reporting the highest and lowest levels of parental education ranged from the high 20 to the low 30 score points. These differences are roughly comparable to the achievement differences between Whites and Blacks, and perhaps slightly smaller than the achievement differences between Whites and Hispanics. K. R. White (1982) found that students from low SES score from .5 to .75 standard deviations (*SD*) lower than students from high SES. Clearly, SES and race/ethnicity are highly correlated; Hedges and Nowell (1998) reduce the Black–White achievement gap by one third when controlling for SES. But SES is a variable that is difficult to define and equally difficult to measure. Thus, interpreting SES effects is never straightforward.

HOW IMPORTANT IS THE ACHIEVEMENT GAP?

One way to think about the size of the achievement gap is in *standardized effect sizes*. Hedges and Nowell (1998) looked at the Black–White achievement gap for 17-year-olds. Included in their analyses were data from NAEP long-term trends. They report achievement gaps of something in excess of 1 *SD* in reading, mathematics, and science in the 1970s. By 1994, the reading gap had been reduced to .7 *SD,* and the mathematics gap to .9 *SD.* However, the science gap was still 1.1 standard deviations. One way to think about standardized effect size is to realize that for a normal distribution, a student going from the mean to 1 *SD* above the mean would move from the 50th to the 84th percentile.

Another way to think about the size of the achievement gap is in terms of *NAEP long-term trend performance levels,* which were set arbitrarily at 50-point intervals on the 500-point scale (NCES, 2000). For example, reading performance levels are summarized as follows:

- *Level 150:* Simple, discrete reading task.
- *Level 200:* Partially developed skills and understanding.
- *Level 250:* Interrelated ideas and make generalizations.

Although the performance levels were set arbitrarily, apparently content experts were able to distinguish between what students should know and be able to do when they score at one level versus another. With this in mind, we can once again examine some of the achievement gap data. In reading, for example, the Black–White student achievement gap at age 17 goes from 53 in 1971, roughly the difference between two adjacent perform-ance levels (i.e., 50 score points), to 31 in 1999, .6 of the difference between two adjacent performance levels. With the exception of science for 17-year-olds, the Black–White achievement gap in 1999 was from .6 to .8 of the differ-ence between a pair of immediately adjacent performance levels. The His-panic–White achievement gap was on average smaller, but still in the range of .6–.8 of the difference between a pair of immediately adjacent perform-ance levels.

In interpreting the achievement gap, there is another issue to consider. Over time, the percentage of the student body in the United States that is minority is increasing. For example, Scovronick and Hochschild (2003) re-port that, by the year 2015, in at least 15 states more than 40% of students in U.S. schools will be non-White. Currently, about 13% of U.S. citizens are Black and 13% are Hispanic. The percentage of Black citizens is expected to remain relatively constant, but the percentage of Hispanics is expected to double by the year 2025. Of course, the percentage of Black and Hispanic students is not evenly distributed geographically. Percentages of minority students are much larger in urban areas than elsewhere, and this is likely to remain at least as true in the near future as it is today. Thus, if the achieve-ment gap itself remains as large in the future as it is today, it will become even more profound in its impact on schools and the larger society.

AT WHAT AGE DOES THE ACHIEVEMENT GAP BEGIN, AND DOES THE GAP INCREASE WITH AGE?

For the NAEP long-term trend data, the earliest age is 9, an age when stu-dents are generally in Grade 4. But, is the gap already evident when stu-dents begin school? The answer is a clear yes. For example, the National Longitudinal Survey of Youth child data show that Black 3- and 4-year-olds fall at the 20th percentile of the national distribution on the Peabody Pic-ture Vocabulary Test (Jencks & Phillips, 1998), with a median difference of 1.2 *SD*s in favor of Whites. These effect sizes are comparable to the Black–White effect sizes for 9-year-olds shown in NAEP long-term trend data.

Conventional wisdom is that the achievement gap increases for students as they progress through grade levels of schooling. Phillips, Crouse, and Ralph (1998) took a careful look at what the data say concerning an increas-ing gap between racial/ethnic groups on achievement as students progress through school. First, the authors dismissed the value of using grade level as a metric for answering the question. An example illustrates the difficulties of using grade-level equivalents. Vocabulary scores for Black 6-year-olds match those of White 5-year-olds; in that sense, Black children are 1 year behind. Black 17-year-olds have vocabularies comparable to those of White 13-year-olds; in that sense, Black 17-year-olds are 4 years behind. In grade levels, Blacks are falling further behind. However, this result can occur even when the respective percentile ranks for Blacks and Whites remain stable over age. Thus, Phillips et al. focused their analyses on "age standardized" measures of the achievement gap, rather than on grade-level equivalents.

Examining cross-sectional results, Phillips et al. (1998) concluded that the standardized Black–White achievement gap (a) remains constant from 1st to 12th grade in reading and (b) widens by about .2 *SD* in math and vocabulary. But like the grade-equivalent results, these cross-sectional data can be misleading. Looking at students longitudinally, Phillips, Crouse, and Ralph concluded:

> All else equal, white students who start elementary school with test scores at the population mean can be expected to finish high school with test scores that are still at the mean. Black students who start elementary school with "true" test scores at the population mean can be expected to finish high school with math scores that lie .34 standard deviations below the mean and reading scores that lie .39 standard deviations below the mean. (p. 253)

These counterintuitive findings are due to the regression effect. Black students regress toward the Black student population mean, which is lower than the student population mean for Whites.

Thus, answering the question of whether the achievement gap increases during the school years is complicated. The gap does not increase as much as one might think if one studies grade equivalents, or as little as one might think if one studies cross-cohort comparisons. Nevertheless, the Black–White achievement gap does appear to increase from 1st to 12th grade. Whether the increase is due to schooling is another question altogether.

When considering the question of whether the achievement gap grows during the years of schooling, one finds an intriguing result related to summer effects. Cooper, Nye, Charlton, Lindsay, and Greathouse (1996) reviewed 39 studies, dating back to 1906, of the effects of summer recess on student achievement. They concluded that summer losses average about .1 of a standard deviation. The losses are greater (a) in math than in reading and (b) in the upper elementary grades than in the lower elementary grades. Most relevant here, summer losses are larger for students from lower SES families than for students from higher SES families. More recently, Alexander, Entwisle, and Olson (2001) reported results from studies of summer effects in Baltimore schools from 1982 to 1987. They found that lower SES students start out behind, keep up during each academic school year, but fall further behind each summer. Again, the summer losses are larger for math than reading. No significant effects were found for a Black–White contrast, but the lack of a Black–White effect should be interpreted with the understanding that SES was also a variable in the hierarchical linear models and may have eliminated the race/ethnicity effect.

Apparently, then, to the extent that there is an increasing achievement gap during the school years, the gap may be due to what happens outside, rather than inside, school. In that sense, the summer recess serves as a natural contrast. Perhaps not surprisingly, the very factors that lead to differences in student achievement in kindergarten or first grade continue to operate as students proceed through school. Perhaps surprisingly, students of varying SES gain at comparable rates while in school. But during the summer recess, the nonschool factors once again take over and the achievement gap increases.

SCHOOL REFORM FOR CLOSING
THE ACHIEVEMENT GAP

Ferguson (1998a) reviewed the evidence for six of the most popular strategies for reducing the Black–White achievement gap:

1. Preschool programs.
2. Student ability grouping.
3. Instructional interventions for students at risk of failure.
4. Matching of students and teachers by race.
5. Selection of teachers with strong test scores.
6. Smaller classes.

I start with Ferguson's six strategies and the evidence he provides, but I add to the evidence for the six with more recent literature, and I extend the strategies considered beyond Ferguson's six.

Preschool Reforms

Black, Hispanic, and low-SES students begin kindergarten already behind in student achievement. Many believe that greater participation of students from these groups in preschool programs would make them readier for kindergarten—less far behind and better able to take advantage of the learning opportunities of elementary schooling. Barnett (1992) found that students from low-income families participating in preschool programs gained 5–13 IQ points, equivalent to from one third to one full standard deviation effect size. Unfortunately, the studies reviewed by Barnett also found substantial declines in IQ, relative to comparison groups, by third grade.

One of the studies Barnett reviewed was the famous Perry Preschool study, which took place in the early 1960s using random assignment. One must be careful when inferring from this study. There are many different approaches to preschool, some academically more rigorous than others, and Perry Preschool may be one of the most rigorous. In any event, the Perry Preschool Project found substantial and continuing effects on student achievement—not only at the end of preschool, but as students progressed through regular school.

In addition to the methodologically rigorous studies reviewed by Barnett, there is a large body of evidence from nonexperimental studies. Currie and Thomas (1995) used the National Longitudinal Survey of Youth's child–mother file to estimate the effects of Head Start and other preschool programs. For the Peabody Picture Vocabulary Test, they found that Black and White 5-year-olds who attend Head Start score about 7 percentile points higher than their siblings who stay at home. Curiously, however, at age 10 the benefits for Whites persist, whereas the benefits for Blacks do not. Ferguson speculated that preschool effects for Black children may not be sustained because these children attend weaker schools than White children. In any event, fewer minority and poor students participate in strong preschool experiences; and although the evidence is not strong, the best preschool programs may be able to close the achievement gap in important and lasting ways.

Teacher Reforms

Teacher Achievement. Greenwald, Hedges, and Laine (1996) found, based on meta-analyses, that teachers who attend better colleges and/or score higher on standardized tests produce greater gains in student achievement. At the same time, such teachers are less likely to be teaching low-SES Black or Hispanic students. Thus, providing Black, Hispanic, or low-SES students with high-scoring teachers might reduce the achievement gap.

In a study of Texas teachers, Ferguson (1991) found that Black teachers scored one full standard deviation lower than White teachers on the Texas Examination of Current Administrators and Teachers. Grouping teachers into four groups, in a 2 × 2 table of high versus low teacher scores by high versus low student test scores, Ferguson found that, across grades from 1st to 11th, student test scores in districts with high teacher test scores converged to a level of high achievement (despite initial contrasts in student scores), and student test scores in districts with low teacher test scores converged to a low point. Ferguson estimated an effect size of 1.7 *SD*s across the span of 10 grade levels.

Ferguson also speculated that teacher certification testing might reduce the Black–White achievement gap. For example, in 1981 Alabama introduced certification testing, after which the test score gap between Black and White teachers fell sharply (Ferguson & Ladd, 1996). At the same time, Alabama districts with high concentrations of Black students had higher concentrations of Black teachers. To the degree that teachers with higher test scores produce greater student gains, certification in Alabama and other similar states may decrease the Black–White achievement gap.

Teacher Expectations. Ferguson (1998b) reviewed the literature on teacher expectations for Black and White students. If the standard is unconditional race neutrality—that is, teacher expectations that are the same for Black and White students despite differences in their past achievement—then clearly teachers have lower *expectations* for Black students than for White students. This result is found in study after study (Ferguson, 1998b). Teachers' *perceptions* of students are accurate and stable, however, and no better or worse as predictors of student test score performance for Blacks than for Whites (e.g., Haller, 1985). At the same time, studies that manipulate race/ethnic identity or other factors in order to manipulate teachers' perceptions of student achievement or ability do affect student achievement (about .5 *SD* for reading, but only .2 *SD* for mathematics). Intriguingly, Jussim, Eccles, and Madon (1996) found that the impact of teachers' perceptions on student test scores is greater for Blacks than for Whites.

Interventions designed to alter teacher perceptions have been tested for effects on student achievement. For example, Guskey (1982) investigated an intervention called Responsive Teaching, and Ferguson (1998b) investigated an intervention called Great Expectations. Neither of these interventions was uniformly effective in changing teachers' perceptions and practices, but each worked with some teachers. The studies suggest that interventions to change teachers' perceptions about what Black students are capable of achieving might decrease the Black–White achievement gap.

Black Teachers Teaching Black Students. There is considerable research on whether Black teachers teaching Black students produces greater gains in student achievement. The results are mixed but lean toward an affirmative answer. Murnane (1975) found that Black teachers had .25 to .5 *SD* greater effect than White teachers on Black students' achievement. In contrast, Ehrenberg and Brewer (1995) did not find significant effects of teachers' race on scores of White, Black, or Hispanic students. Alexander, Entwisle, and Thompson (1987) found that low-SES Black teachers produced higher gains for Black students than for White students, but only in mathematics. High-SES Black teachers, in contrast, produced the largest gains for White students.

Instructional Reforms

Instructional Interventions. Many instructional interventions focus on Black students (Levine, 1994) or, more generally, on students at risk (Slavin, Karweit, & Madden, 1989; Slavin & Madden, 1989). Ferguson (1998b) noted that this research shows many promising results, but he questioned whether the interventions are fragile special cases (i.e., not replicable). Thus, Ferguson focused on Success for All, which has been implemented in hundreds of schools across the nation (Slavin et al., 1996). Beginning in kindergarten and extending through at least the early elementary grades, Success for All is designed to ensure that every student succeeds. In analyses that compare gains achieved by the top 75% of students versus the bottom 25% of students on pretests, effect sizes are generally larger for the bottom 25%, ranging from .3 to slightly in excess of 1 *SD*. Thus, Success for All and similar programs may hold potential for reducing the achievement gap.

The teaching of metacognitive strategies in the context of specific academic subjects holds potential for reducing the achievement gap, especially at the elementary and middle school grades. Metacognitive strategies reflect cultural norms and methods of inquiry (Brice-Heath, 1983; Hutchins, 1995) and so cannot be assumed to develop without explicit instruction. Research shows that children can be taught strategies such as predicting outcomes, monitoring their own comprehension, learning to activate background knowledge, and planning ahead (National Research Council, 2000). Students from affluent families often acquire these metacognitive strategies, without explicit instruction, through their interactions outside school; but minority students and students from low-income families do not always acquire metacognitive skills without explicit instruction.

Boykin, Allen, Davis, and Senior (1997) found that students in early elementary school achieve better when instruction mixes and switches back and forth among tasks, rather than focusing on one task for a long period. Furthermore, gains for Black students are larger than those for Whites. Similarly, Boykin found that Black children from low-income families do better when classes include physical movement, music is playing in the background, and students work in teams (Allen & Boykin, 1991). Ferguson (1998a) speculates that such classroom environments may better match low-income Black students' home environments.

Reduced Class Size. One of the most popular current interventions for improving student achievement is a reduction in class size. Obviously, teachers favor a reduction in class size, not only because they believe it results in increased student achievement, but also because it makes their work more manageable. But reductions in class size are expensive. Furthermore, when done on a systemic basis, reductions in class size can have unanticipated negative consequences. For example, California undertook a statewide reduction in class size, which resulted in shortages of qualified teachers and classrooms for the increased number of classes. At the high school level, these problems were compounded by other shortages of resources, such as lab space for science classes. Nevertheless, reductions in class size remain a popular policy solution for increasing student achievement.

Ferguson (1998a) tentatively concluded that reducing class size not only improves student achievement in the aggregate, but also has a larger positive effect for Black students than for White students. First, he considered the results from the Tennessee Project STAR study, conducted in the second half of the 1980s. In that experiment, kindergarten students were randomly assigned to small classes (13–17 students), larger classes (22–26 students), or larger classes with a full-time classroom aide. Teachers were also randomly assigned to classes of different types. The assignments of students and teachers to class type were maintained from kindergarten through third grade. All analyses of this data set have concluded that small class size resulted in improved student achievement, primarily in the first year; but those early gains were maintained through the third grade. Furthermore, the effects for both reading and mathematics were approximately twice as large for Blacks as for Whites (Mosteller, 1995; Nye, Achilles, Zaharias, Fulton, & Wallenhorst, 1993; Nye, Boyd-Zaharias, & Fulton, 1994; Word et al., 1990). Ferguson also noted that class size decreased by about 25% from 1970 to 1990. He showed that the drop in class size over that period mirrored a decrease in the test score gap between Blacks and Whites for both mathematics and reading.

Ferguson (1998a) did not see these analyses as definitive, but he concluded that reducing class size may be a promising way to reduce the Black–White achievement gap. One possibility is to reduce class sizes for classes in which there are high concentrations of Black students—though this may be politically unacceptable in the long run, because White parents may want the same benefits for their children. Another possibility is to reduce class size for all students, relying on the differential positive effect in favor of Black students to reduce the Black–White achievement gap.

More recently, Nye, Hedges, and Konstantopoulos (2002) reanalyzed the Project STAR data, searching for differential effects for high- versus low-achieving students. They did not look for interactions between race/ethnicity and reductions in class size. In any event, somewhat in contradiction to the Ferguson conclusions, Nye et al. found no statistically significant differential effects of class size for low- versus high-achieving students. The sample mean differences did not even favor low-achieving students for math, although they did for reading.

Because achievement is clearly correlated with race/ethnicity, as well as SES, the lack of an interaction between reduction in class size and achievement level suggests that the differential effects for Black versus White students may not be as robust and large as one would hope. There is one important caveat to this conclusion, however. Because there was no pretest at the kindergarten level, Nye et al. (2002) focused their analyses on Grades 1 through 3, using a kindergarten posttest to identify low- versus high-achieving students. They did find an aggregate effect for reducing class size, even though they did not find any differential effect for low- versus high-achieving students. Still, their analyses did not include the kindergarten effect, which other analyses have shown to be larger than the outyear effects of class size on increasing student achievement in math and reading.

Ability Grouping and Tracking. Ability grouping is common in elementary school classrooms, and tracking is common in high schools, despite many efforts to decrease such practices. Controlling for SES, Blacks are not differentially placed in low-ability groups or tracks (Gamoran & Mare, 1989). Still, because Blacks on average are of lower SES than Whites, more Blacks are in low-ability groups and tracks than Whites. C. L. Kulik and J. A. Kulik (1987, 1989) concluded, based on meta-analytic reviews of the impact of ability grouping, that students assigned to separate classes based primarily on IQ or achievement test scores do not achieve less than they otherwise would (mean effect sizes of .03). In contrast, J. A. Kulik (1992) reported an effect size of .4 for students placed in enrichment classes and .8 for students placed in accelerated classes. Although these may well be overestimates of effect sizes, high-scoring students do appear to profit from tailored instruction (regardless of ethnicity or SES). Studies of grouping for reading instruction in elementary school are not very useful, because of lack of comparison groups. Grouping for reading is systemic.

Ferguson (1998a) concluded that the research on tracking at the high school level is "very incomplete" (p. 338). Oakes (1985) did find that teachers of higher track classes tend to be better teachers than teachers of lower track classes. But the differences in these data are surprisingly small, which may explain why C. L. Kulik and J. A. Kulik (1987, 1989) found no effects for grouping.

Perhaps the elimination of tracking will not serve to markedly decrease the achievement gap, unless as Ferguson (1998a) noted, "there are substantial differences in curriculum and courses taken" (p. 340). There is good reason to believe, however, that many students are experiencing such changes. For example, between 1982 and 1994, the proportion of Blacks completing chemistry doubled to 44%, and the proportion of Hispanics tripled to 46%. Similar gains were made in the proportions of Black and Hispanic students taking physics (National Science Board, 2002). In math, the proportion of Black students taking geometry doubled to 58%, and the proportion of Hispanics nearly tripled to 69%. Nevertheless, substantial differences remain between the proportions of Whites, Blacks, and Hispanics taking advanced courses in mathematics and science. For example, in 1998 64% of White high school graduates completed some advanced coursework in science, as compared with 55% of Black students and 49% of Hispanic students; in mathematics, 45% of White students, 30% of Black students, and 26% of Hispanic students completed some advanced courses (NCES, 2002).

The report *A Nation at Risk* (National Commission on Excellence in Education, 1983) called for a more rigorous school curriculum. By the mid- to late 1980s, most states had responded by increasing the number of academic credits required to graduate from high school. Some hypothesized that, as a consequence, high school graduation rates would decrease and dropout rates would increase, and that these negative results would inflict the greatest harm on minority and poor students. That hypothesis has not proven to be true; statistics show no signs of a decrease in student persistence (NCES, 2002).

When the retention problem did not materialize, some hypothesized that the response to higher graduation requirements would be increased enrollment in remedial and basic courses. Using transcript data, Clune and P. A. White (1992) found that credits completed in academic subjects increased by a substantial amount, with the largest increases in science, but substantial increases in mathematics as well. For example, in science, more students completed Biology 1, and in mathematics, Algebra 1, than had previously been the case.

These results led to a third hypothesis. Perhaps the academic courses showing higher enrollments than ever before were being dumbed down to accommodate the influx of weaker students. My research team and I (Porter, Kirst, Osthoff, Smithson, & Schneider, 1993) conducted a study in 18 high schools in 12 districts in six states to determine if teachers of courses experiencing large influxes of weaker students were in fact changing their curriculum in ways that weakened the content to accommodate the new students. Using daily teacher logs over the course of a full school year, teacher questionnaires, and observations, we concluded that there was no evidence that either math or science college preparatory courses were being dumbed down. We hypothesized that the law of inertia was at work: Teachers continued doing what they had always done.

In a subsequent study (P. A. White, Gamoran, Smithson, & Porter, 1996), we investigated the effects on students' completion of college prep math courses of participation in transition math classes or direct participation in college prep math classes. The transition math courses were Math A in California and Stretch Regents in New York. Both of these courses were designed for students who, it was believed, were not ready for college prep mathematics, but might make the transition to college prep mathematics with participation in a special course. Math A offered a unique curriculum, blending geometry and algebra. Stretch Regents was simply the New York State Regents college prep math program at a slower pace. The study involved two high schools in each of two districts in each of two states.

Using transcript data, we set two criteria for judging whether students completed appropriate amounts of mathematics:

1. Completion of three or more credits of mathematics (as required for high school graduation in two of the four districts); or
2. Completion of two or more college prep mathematics courses.

The three-credits criterion was met by 60% of students starting out in general math, 61% of those starting out in a transition math, and 84% of those starting out in college prep math. In contrast, the second criterion—completion of two or more college prep math courses—was met by 15% of students starting out in general math, 50% of those starting out in transition math, and 88% of those starting out in college prep math (P. A. White et al., 1996). Controlling for eighth-grade course grades or eighth-grade standardized test results when they were available, the value of transition and college prep courses was seen as even more substantial. For example, of students with a C in eighth-grade mathematics, two or more credits of college prep mathematics were completed by 1% of those enrolling initially in general math, 18% of those enrolling in transition math, and 88% of those enrolling directly into college prep math. We found similar results when controlling for eighth-grade standardized mathematics achievement.

In the same study, we administered an achievement test in the fall, winter, and spring of the 1992–1993 school year. The achievement test was taken from public release NAEP items selected to be consistent with the National Council of Teachers of Mathematics *Standards* (1989). With fall achievement as a control variable, students in general math gained the least in achievement, and students in college prep math gained the most, with students in transition math midway between (Gamoran, Porter, Smithson, & P. A. White, 1997). Based on these results, we concluded that general-track math classes should be eliminated. Although students did benefit from transition math classes in comparison to general math, it was participation in college prep math that benefited student achievement the most. Coupled with the earlier findings that enrolling more students in college prep math did not result in a dumbed-down curriculum and did result in more completion of college prep credits, these results suggest that the increasingly popular policy of requiring all students to take college prep mathematics (and perhaps science) will serve to reduce the achievement gap.

Promotion and Retention Policies. There has been a great deal of research and debate about the positive and negative effects of programs that tie student promotion to performance on standardized tests. Advocates believe that such programs end social promotion and motivate teachers and students to work harder and better. Critics cite the research that concludes that retention in grade hurts students, making them more likely to drop out and have negative self-esteem (Gampert, 1987; Gottfredson, Fink, & Graham, 1994; Grissom & Shepard, 1989; Reynolds, 1992; Roderick, 1994).

But not all policies of tying grade-to-grade promotion to performance on tests are the same. Some give students second and third chances. Others provide instructional support to students, and still others provide greater resources to schools and teachers. So, there is considerable room for variability among programs, and this variability might result in differential effects on students. It is also true that most of the research on the effects of retention have looked at only first-cohort effects. Although these studies have generally found negative effects of retention, it may be that subsequent cohorts receive better instruction and try harder than otherwise would have been the case. In short, when increasing percentages of students are retained, teachers, schools, and students may try harder in subsequent years.

Roderick, Jacob, and Bryk (2002) provided results from their study of Chicago's policy of tying student promotion to performance on the Iowa Test of Basic Skills (ITBS). The Chicago program is especially interesting for several reasons. First, it focuses on raising the performance of the lowest achieving students and the lowest achieving schools. Second, it began both school- and student-level accountability programs simultaneously. For example, to be promoted to fourth grade, students must be no more than 1 year below grade level. To be promoted to seventh grade, students must be no more than 1.5 years below grade level. And to be promoted to ninth grade, students must be no more than 1.8 years below grade level. These three cuts correspond roughly to the 20th percentile in the national distribution of achievement. At the same time, schools with less than 15% of their students exceeding the 50th percentile on the ITBS are placed on probation. Schools not making progress could be reconstituted.

Student accountability and school accountability in Chicago have real teeth. For example, in the first year of accountability, over half the high schools were placed on probation, and 71 out of 475 elementary schools were placed on probation. As for students in the early years, 20% of third graders were retained, and approximately 10% of sixth and eighth graders were retained (Roderick, Bryk, Jacob, Easton, & Allensworth, 1999).

A third interesting aspect of the Chicago program is that it has implemented a Summer Bridge Program and a Lighthouse After-School Program as extra support for low-achieving students. Students who do not meet the test score criterion for promotion are required to attend the Summer Bridge Program—3 hours a day, 5 days a week, for 6 weeks for third and sixth graders, and 4 hours a day, 5 days a week, for 7 weeks for eighth graders. There is a district-prescribed program of work.

The Lighthouse After-School Program is now in over 350 elementary schools. Lighthouse operates for 20 weeks, with 1 hour of instruction and 1 hour of recreation time, 3 to 4 days a week.

Roderick et al. (2002) analyzed data from 1993 to 1999 for students in Grades 3, 6, and 8. Analyses used as a control variable trajectories in student achievement prior to the year at which promotion decisions were made. Roderick et al. found that student achievement on the ITBS did increase substantially following the introduction of high-stakes testing in both reading and math and at all three grade levels. These effects were estimated on the grade levels just prior to the promotion decisions, where one might expect the greatest increase in effort by students and teachers. There was also evidence that students in the lowest performing schools, particularly those with high concentrations of Black students, gained the most. However, findings of interactions with levels of student prior achievement are not as straightforward. In reading, the lowest achieving students from previous years were the ones to gain the most. In fact, there was evidence that some of the highest achievers actually gained less following implementation of the policy for reading. In math, the pattern was just the opposite. The highest achieving students showed the greatest gains. Thus, at least from this one study of this one particular implementation of high-stakes testing, the conclusion is that the within-school achievement gap might be closed for reading but exacerbated for mathematics. At the same time, the overall achievement gap might be reduced in both subjects, because the policy appears to have its largest effect on low-performing schools, particularly those with high concentrations of Black students.

Standards-Based Reform

Although there are always several types of education reforms taking place at any one point in time, during the 1990s and extending to today the major education reform can be labeled *standards-based* or *systemic*. The key idea is to have a coherent state policy environment, at least in regard to what content is to be taught in core academic subjects. Reform leadership has come from the federal government, with substantial input from the education research community. Some might track standards-based reform to the report *A Nation at Risk* (National Commission on Excellence in Education, 1983). Others might say the beginning was the National Education Summit convened by President George H. W. Bush, in 1989, which resulted in national educational goals (U.S. Department of Education, 1990). A revised version of these goals was written into law by President Bill Clinton in 1994 in the Goals 2000: Educate America Act. The concept of standards-based reform was also written into the reauthorization of Title I in 1994 in the Improving America's Schools Act. Systemic reform can be dated to a National Science Foundation solicitation (1990) for statewide systemic initiatives in science, mathematics, and engineering education, and is more fully described by Smith and O'Day (1990).

At the core of both standards-based and systemic reform is the goal of high standards for all students. Standards are expressed in content standards for academic subjects. Student progress against the content standards is to be measured through aligned assessments. The entire content system is to be coherent, having aligned curriculum materials and aligned professional development as well. Increasingly, accountability for both schools and students has become an integral part of standards-based reform. At least in the beginning years of the reform, and especially for systemic reform, there was to be a restructured governance system. States were to provide leadership in the form of standards, assessments, and technical assistance. Schools were to create learning environments that produced the desired student achievement consistent with the state standards.

The standards-based reform movement received considerable additional weight with the passage of the No Child Left Behind Act (2002), signed into law by President George W. Bush, in 2001. No Child Left Behind is a comprehensive and prescriptive statement about federal requirements states must meet if they are to receive Title I funds. For our purposes here, it suffices to say that challenging state content standards, aligned assessments used for school and student accountability, and performance standards indicating what levels of student achievement are "proficient" are all mandated. Schools are given 12 years to bring 100% of their students to a level of proficiency—not only in the aggregate, but for groups disaggregated by race and ethnicity, students with disabilities, and students of limited English proficiency. Accountability does not wait for the 12 years to pass but proceeds annually against standards of "adequate yearly progress."

The goal of standards-based reform is challenging and ambitious academic content to be mastered by all students. The No Child Left Behind Act makes the focus on all students more salient than ever before by requiring disaggregated data. Because standards-based reform has been in progress for over a decade, the question might be asked whether it is decreasing the achievement gap. Kosters and Mast (2003) reviewed the literature and conducted additional analyses, concluding that the answer is no. In fact, as noted previously, the achievement gap has remained relatively stable in the 10 years or so of standards-based reform.

Does this mean that standards-based reform is incapable of decreasing the achievement gap? Not necessarily. First, standards-based reform has

never been fully implemented. Content standards are not as specific and focused as would probably be desirable, and assessments are not well
aligned to these standards (Porter, 2002). Neither is professional development well aligned to the content standards, or as high quality as would be
needed (Garet, Porter, Desimone, Birman, & Yoon, 2001). And accountability focused on disaggregated data is a new requirement. Perhaps if standards-based reform were more fully implemented, it might reduce the
achievement gap.

CONCLUSIONS

Clearly, the achievement gap continues to be large, whether defined by
race/ethnicity or SES. It is large for all ages and all academic content areas.
Although the gap narrowed during the 1970s and early 1980s, since then it
has been relatively stable. In fact, changes in participation rates in NAEP
may be causing an increasing underestimate of the gap in recent years. If
this is the case, the achievement gap may actually be increasing slightly in
the last decade.

The achievement gap is important. It is large, and it may account for
many other inequalities in our society. It may become even more important
in the not too distant future, as the percentage of minorities in our society
increases, especially for Hispanics.

Schooling appears to decrease the gap, at least in the sense that (a) the
gap is already present and substantial before school and (b) during the
K–12 school years, the gap does not increase during the academic year (although it does increase during the summer recess). Moreover, school reform may be a mechanism for further reducing the size of the gap. Toward
this end, several school reform initiatives were reviewed.

School reforms with potential for reducing the achievement gap were
clustered into four categories: preschool, teacher, instructional, and standards-based reform. The most promising strategies for reducing the achievement gap appear to share the ability to address inequalities in opportunity
to learn. Teacher quality appears to be an especially promising avenue.
Currently, Black, Hispanic, and low-income students are less likely to be
taught by high-quality teachers than are White and more affluent students.
A reform that redistributes teacher quality to be more equitable would undoubtedly decrease the achievement gap. Similarly, removing inequalities
in the content students study is an especially promising reform for reducing the achievement gap. One possibility is to eliminate basic and remedial
courses in high school, requiring instead that all students take college preparatory courses in core academic subjects. Such a strategy is more focused than policies that simply eliminate ability groups and tracking, but it

could be pursued through such reforms. Another possibility is to explicitly teach low-income and minority students metacognitive strategies. Pre-school reform could also be consistent with the theme of eliminating in-equalities in student opportunity to learn. Currently, Black, Hispanic, and low-income students are less likely to participate in high-quality preschool programs that focus on academic content.

Other reform strategies that do not directly address inequalities in stu-dent opportunity to learn appear to have less clear promise for reducing the achievement gap. Reduced class size may have greater benefits for stu-dent achievement for Black and low-income students than for White and af-fluent students, but the results are inconsistent. Data from a study of Chi-cago school reform suggest that promotion and retention policies, coupled with additional resources and targeted programs, may reduce the achieve-ment gap. Standards-based reform, today's most visible and well-funded ed-ucation reform, does not yet appear to have reduced the achievement gap, but perhaps this is because standards-based reform has yet to be anywhere near fully implemented.

The achievement gap is not the same across academic subjects. It is smaller for reading than for mathematics or science. It appears to increase less with age for reading than it does for math. Further, summer loss is greater in math than in reading. In the Chicago promotion and retention study, there were bigger gains for low-achieving students in reading, but the opposite was true in math. In the interventions that attempted to ma-nipulate teacher expectations, there were bigger effects in reading than in math. Thus, at least the reform strategies considered here are more promis-ing for reducing the achievement gap in reading than in mathematics.

One final comment is necessary to put these conclusions in context. Clearly, many factors affect the size and nature of the achievement gap, most of them outside school walls. For example, Tilly (1998) said, "The cru-cial causal mechanisms behind categorical inequality operate in the do-main of collective experience and social interaction" (p. 24).

Ogbu (2003) argued that minority children are socialized into different styles before they enter public schools. He found that Black students want to succeed in school, but they do not put forth the effort necessary to do so. He attributed Black students' limited effort to their inability to see school success as preparation for the job market, noting that Black stu-dents' role models are athletes and entertainers, not individuals successful in business and the professions. Ogbu concluded, "The academic achieve-ment gap is not likely to be closed by restructuring the educational system" (p. 274). I am inclined to agree. Because the gap is not caused by schools, it is unlikely that it could be fully closed by schools. At the same time, my analysis leads me to conclude that there are several promising strategies that, if vigorously pursued, could lead to substantial decreases in the achievement gap, and that decreases in the achievement gap would greatly benefit our society.

REFERENCES

Alexander, K. L., Entwisle, D. R., & Olson, L. S. (2001). Schools, achievement, and inequality: A seasonal perspective. *Educational Evaluation and Policy Analysis, 25*(2), 171–191.

Alexander, K. L., Entwisle, D. R., & Thompson, M. S. (1987). School performance, status relations, and the structure of sentiment: Bringing the teachers back in. *American Sociology Review, 52,* 665–682.

Allen, B. A., & Boykin, A. W. (1991). The influence of contextual factors on Afro-American and Euro-American children's performance: Effects of movement opportunity and music. *International Journal of Psychology, 26,* 373–387.

Barnett, W. S. (1992). Benefits of compensatory preschool education. *Journal of Human Behavior, 27*(2), 279–312.

Boykin, A. W., Allen, B., Davis, L. H., & Senior, A. M. (1997). Task performance of black and white children across levels of presentation variability. *Journal of Psychology, 131*(4), 427–437.

Brice-Heath, S. (1983). *Ways with words: Language, life and work in communities and classrooms.* Cambridge, England: Cambridge University Press.

Carroll, J. B. (1963). A model of school learning. *Teachers College Record, 64,* 723–733.

Clune, W. H., & White, P. A. (1992). Education reform in the trenches: Increased academic course taking in high schools with lower achieving students in states with higher graduation requirements. *Educational Evaluation and Policy Analysis, 14,* 2–20.

Cook, T. D., Appleton, H., Connor, R., Shaffer, A., Tamkin, G., & Weber, S. J. (1975). *"Sesame Street" revisited.* New York: Russell Sage Foundation.

Cooper, H., Nye, B., Charlton, K., Lindsay, J., & Greathouse, S. (1996). The effects of summer vacation on achievement test scores: A narrative and meta-analytic review. *Review of Educational Research, 66,* 227–268.

Currie, J., & Thomas, D. (1995). Does Head Start make a difference? *American Economic Review, 85*(3), 341–364.

Ehrenberg, R. G., & Brewer, D. J. (1995). Did teachers' verbal ability and race matter in the 1960s? Coleman revisited. *Economics of Education Review, 14,* 1–21.

Feinberg, L. (1990, Fall). Multiple-choice and its critics. *The College Board Review, 157,* 13–17, 30–31.

Ferguson, R. F. (1991). Paying for public education: New evidence on how and why money matters. *Harvard Journal on Legislation, 28*(2), 465–498.

Ferguson, R. F. (1998a). Can schools narrow the black–white test score gap? In C. Jencks & M. Phillips (Eds.), *The black–white test score gap* (pp. 318–374). Washington, DC: Brookings Institution Press.

Ferguson, R. F. (1998b). Teachers' perceptions and expectations and the black–white test score gap. In C. Jencks & M. Phillips (Eds.), *The black–white test score gap* (pp. 273–317). Washington, DC: Brookings Institution Press.

Ferguson, R. F., & Ladd, H. F. (1996). How and why money matters: An analysis of Alabama schools. In H. F. Ladd (Ed.), *Holding schools accountable.* Washington, DC: Brookings Institution Press.

Gamoran, A., & Mare, R. G. (1989). Secondary school tracking and educational inequality: Compensation, reinforcement, or neutrality? *American Journal of Sociology, 94,* 1146–1183.

Gamoran, A., Porter, A. C., Smithson, J., & White, P. A. (1997). Upgrading high school mathematics instruction: Improving learning opportunities for low-achieving, low-income youth. *Educational Evaluation and Policy Analysis, 19*(4), 325–338.

Gampert, R. A. (1987). *A follow-up study of the 1982–83 promotional gates students.* New York: New York City Public Schools, Office of Educational Assessment.

Garet, M. S., Porter, A. C., Desimone, L., Birman, B. F., & Yoon, K. (2001). What makes professional development effective? Results from a national sample of teachers. *American Educational Research Journal, 38*(4), 915–945.

Gottfredson, D. C., Fink, C. M., & Graham, N. (1994). Grade retention and problem behavior. *American Educational Research Journal, 31*(4), 761–784.

Greenwald, R., Hedges, L. V., & Laine, R. D. (1996). The effect of school resources on student achievement. *Review of Educational Research, 66,* 361–396.

Grissom, J. B., & Shepard, L. A. (1989). Repeating and dropping out of school. In L. A. Shepard & M. L. Smith (Eds.), *Flunking grades: Research and policies on retention* (pp. 34–63). London: Falmer Press.

Guskey, T. R. (1982). The effects of change in instructional effectiveness on the relationship of teacher expectations and student achievement. *Journal of Educational Research, 75,* 345–348.

Haller, E. J. (1985). Pupil race and elementary school ability grouping: Are teachers biased against black children? *American Educational Research Journal, 22*(4), 465–483.

Hedges, L. V., & Nowell, A. (1998). Black–white test score convergence since 1965. In C. Jencks & M. Phillips (Eds.), *The black–white test score gap* (pp. 149–181). Washington, DC: Brookings Institution Press.

Herrnstein, R. J., & Murray, C. (1994). *The bell curve: Intelligence and class structure in American life.* New York: The Free Press.

Hutchins, E. (1995). *Cognition in the wild.* Cambridge, MA: MIT Press.

Jencks, C., & Phillips, M. (Eds.). (1998). *The black–white test score gap.* Washington, DC: Brookings Institution Press.

Jussim, L., Eccles, J., & Madon, S. (1996). Social perceptions, social stereotypes, and teacher expectations: Accuracy and the quest for the powerful self-fulfilling prophecy. *Advances in Experimental Social Psychology, 28,* 281–387.

Kosters, M. H., & Mast, B. D. (2003). *Closing the education achievement gap: Is Title I working?* Washington, DC: AEI Press.

Kulik, C. L., & Kulik, J. A. (1987). Effects of ability grouping on student achievement. *Equity and Excellence, 23,* 22–30.

Kulik, C. L., & Kulik, J. A. (1989). Meta-analysis in educational research. *International Journal of Educational Research, 13,* 221–340.

Kulik, J. A. (1992). *An analysis of the research on ability grouping: Historical and contemporary perspectives.* Storrs: University of Connecticut, National Center on the Gifted and Talented.

Levine, D. L. (1994). Instructional approaches and interventions that can improve the academic performance of African American students. *Journal of Negro Education, 63,* 46–63.

Linn, R. L., Baker, E. L., & Dunbar, S. B. (1991). Complex, performance-based assessment: Expectations and validation criteria. *Educational Researcher, 20*(8), 15–21.

Mosteller, F. (1995). The Tennessee study of class size in the early school grades. *Future of Children, 5*(2), 113–127.

Murnane, R. (1975). *The impact of school resources on the learning of inner city children.* Cambridge, MA: Ballinger.

National Center for Education Statistics. (2000). *NAEP 1999 trends in academic progress: Three decades of student performance* (NCES 2000-469). Retrieved August 7, 2003, from http://nces.ed.gov/nationsreportcard/pdf/main1999/2000469.pdf

National Center for Education Statistics. (2002). *The condition of education 2002* (NCES 2002-025). Retrieved August 7, 2003, from http://nces.ed.gov/pubs2002/2002025.pdf

National Commission on Excellence in Education. (1983). *A nation at risk: The imperative for educational reform.* Washington, DC: U.S. Government Printing Office.

National Council of Teachers of Mathematics. (1989). *Curriculum and evaluation standards for school mathematics.* Reston, VA: Author.

National Research Council, Committee on Learning Research and Educational Practice. (2000). *How people learn: Brain, mind, experience, and school.* Washington, DC: National Academy Press.

National Science Board. (2002). *Science and engineering indicators 2000* (NSB-00-1). Retrieved August 7, 2003, from http://www.nsf.gov/sbe/srs/seind00/pdfstart.htm

National Science Foundation. (1990). *Statewide systemic initiatives in science, mathematics, and engineering education—Program solicitation 90-47.* Washington, DC: Author.

Nisbett, R. E. (1998). Race, genetics, and IQ. In C. Jencks & M. Phillips, *The black–white test score gap* (pp. 86–102). Washington, DC: Brookings Institution Press.

No Child Left Behind Act of 2001, Pub. L. No. 107-110, §. 115 Stat 1425 (2002). Retrieved August 7, 2003, from http://www.ed.gov/legislation/ESEA02/107-110.pdf

Nye, B. A., Achilles, C. M., Zaharias, J. B., Fulton, B. D., & Wallenhorst, M. P. (1993). Tennessee's bold experiment: Using research to inform policy and practice. *Tennessee Education, 22*(3), 10–20.

Nye, B. A., Boyd-Zaharias, J., & Fulton, B. D. (1994). *The lasting benefits study: A continuing analysis of the effect of small class size in kindergarten through third grade on student achievement test scores in subsequent grade levels: Seventh grade, 1992–1993, technical report.* Nashville: Tennessee State University, Center of Excellence for Research in Basic Skills.

Nye, B. A., Hedges, L. V., & Konstantopoulos, S. (2002). Do low-achieving students benefit more from small classes? Evidence from the Tennessee class size experiment. *Educational Evaluation and Policy Analysis, 24*(3), 201–217.

Oakes, J. (1985). *Keeping track: How schools structure inequality.* New Haven, CT: Yale University Press.

Ogbu, J. U. (2003). *Black American students in an affluent suburb: A study of academic disengagement.* Mahwah, NJ: Lawrence Erlbaum Associates.

Phillips, M., Crouse, J., & Ralph, J. (1998). Does the black–white test score gap widen after children enter school? In C. Jencks & M. Phillips (Eds.), *The black–white test score gap* (pp. 229–272). Washington, DC: Brookings Institution Press.

Porter, A. C. (2002). Measuring the content of instruction: Uses in research and practice. *Educational Researcher, 31*(7), 3–14.

Porter, A. C., Kirst, M. W., Osthoff, E. J., Smithson, J. S., & Schneider, S. A. (1993). *Reform up close: An analysis of high school mathematics and science classrooms* (Final Report to the National Science Foundation on Grant No. SPA-8953446 to the Consortium for Policy Research in Education). Madison: University of Wisconsin–Madison, Wisconsin Center for Education Research.

Reynolds, A. J. (1992). Grade retention and school adjustment: An explanatory analysis. *Educational Evaluation and Policy Analysis, 14*(2), 101–121.

Roderick, M. (1994). Grade retention and school dropout: Investigating the association. *American Educational Research Journal, 31*(4), 729–759.

Roderick, M., Bryk, A. S., Jacob, B. A., Easton, J. Q., & Allensworth, E. (1999). *Ending social promotion in Chicago: Results from the first two years.* Chicago: Consortium on Chicago School Research.

Roderick, M., Jacob, B. A., & Bryk, A. S. (2002). The impact of high-stakes testing in Chicago on student achievement in promotional gate grades. *Educational Evaluation and Policy Analysis, 24*(4), 333–357.

Routitsky, A., & Turner, R. (2003, April). *Item format types and their influence on cross-national comparisons of student learning.* Paper presented at the annual meeting of the American Educational Research Association, Chicago.

Scovronick, N., & Hochschild, J. L. (2003). *The American dream and the public schools.* New York: Oxford University Press.

Slavin, R. E., Karweit, N. L., & Madden, N. A. (1989). *Effective programs for students at risk.* Boston: Allyn & Bacon.

Slavin, R. E., & Madden, N. A. (1989, February). What works for students at risk: A research synthesis. *Educational Leadership, 46,* 4–13.

Slavin, R. E., Madden, N. A., Dolan, L. J., Wasik, B. A., Ross, S., Smith, L., & Dianda, M. (1996). Success for all: A summary of research. *Journal of Education for Students Placed at Risk, 1*(1), 41–76.

Smith, M. S., & O'Day, J. (1990). Systemic school reform. In S. H. Fuhrman & B. Malen (Eds.), *The politics of curriculum and testing: The 1990 yearbook of the politics of Education Association* (pp. 233–267). Bristol, PA: Falmer Press.

Tilly, C. (1998). *Durable inequality.* Berkeley: University of California Press.

U.S. Department of Education. (1990). *National goals for education.* Washington, DC: Author.

White, K. R. (1982). The relation between socioeconomic status and academic achievement. *Psychological Bulletin, 91,* 461–481.

White, P. A., Gamoran, A., Smithson, J., & Porter, A. C. (1996). Upgrading the high school math curriculum: Math course-taking patterns in seven high schools in California and New York. *Educational Evaluation and Policy Analysis, 18*(4), 285–307.

Word, E., Johnston, J., Bain, H. P., Fulton, B. D., Zaharias, J. B., Achilles, C. M., Lintz, M. N., Folger, J., & Breda, C. (1990). *Student/Teacher Achievement Ratio (STAR): Tennessee's K–3 class size study, final summary report, 1985–1990.* Nashville: Tennessee State Department of Education.

IMPROVING TEACHER QUALITY

6

Accountability Testing and the Implications for Teacher Professionalism

Caroline V. Gipps
Kingston University, London

In this chapter I sketch out the current state of play in accountability testing in England and look at the history, clarifying the reasons for its development. I then look at a major unintended consequence: the effect on teachers and their professionalism. My aim is to raise issues around the definition of "teacher quality" and whether it is reasonable to expect to have quality teachers if teachers feel de-skilled and de-professionalized.

SETTING THE SCENE

The current accountability movement in education in England began more than 25 years ago when the then Labour Prime Minister, James Callaghan, gave a speech at Ruskin College, Oxford. In this he argued that the key features of state education—the curriculum, standards of pupil performance, and the accountability of schools—being issues of national importance should be open to public debate. The Green Paper published the following year, Education in Schools: A Consultative Document (Williams & Morris, 1977), argued for a system of assessment for pupils, schools, and the education system, while rejecting regular testing of all pupils and publication of performance tables of schools, both of which we now have.

In the early 1980s there was no national curriculum in the UK, although in practice the syllabi of the school-leaving exams at age 16 determined the upper secondary school curriculum. There were no primary school exams

99

at age 11 any longer, although the majority of school districts required primary schools to test pupils at the ages of 8 and 11 with standardized tests of reading and mathematics. In the terms that we understand now, however, these were not accountability tests because no public use was made of the results (Gipps, Steadman, Blackstone, & Stierer, 1983). Schools used them to identify pupils who needed extra help and local school inspectors used them to support the management of schools in their district.

In 1980 the Conservative government introduced national criteria for the 16-year-old school-leaving examinations (the first direct intervention by a UK government in the content of the curriculum in the 20th century) and in 1982 schools were required to publish the results of exams at ages 16 and 18 so that parents could make informed choices about schooling. There was also a fairly common view that schools should be more accountable to the communities they serve. By 1992 the format in which these results were to be presented was laid down so that league tables could be produced locally, and the government produced annual league tables at the national level. Thus the formal use of school results to create a market in education began (Whitty, 1989).

The Education Reform Act of 1988 saw the introduction of a blueprint for a national assessment program and the enshrinement in law of a national curriculum (Gipps, Brown, McCallum, & McAlister, 1995). The assessment framework had many forward-looking and professionally supportive features, for example, a strong role for teacher assessment of pupils, criterion referencing, and an emphasis on performance assessment. All three of these features had, however, been significantly eroded 10 years on.

The national curriculum assessment program began in 1991 with assessment of 7-year-olds in English, mathematics, and science. By 1995 11-year-olds were also assessed on the same subjects, and by 1996 14-year-olds were included. At the start, performance tables of school results were to be published for 7-, 11-, and 14-year-old results annually. But tables for the 7-year-olds' results (and 14-year-olds') were dropped after teacher action and a boycott of national assessment in 1991 and 1992.

The growing national and governmental interest in, and control of, schooling is not unique to the UK, of course. Nor is the focus on assessment as the key tool of accountability. Standards setting, public performance monitoring, the introduction of markets into education—all of these are common trends across a number of countries, and they all require pupil assessment data. As the level of education of the population is seen as the key resource for many countries, with the role of physical and natural resources shifting at high speed in a global economy, so governments become ever more interested in the performance of schooling. This leads to more control, direction, and accountability, a trend from which the United States is certainly not exempt (Linn, 2000; Linn, Baker, & Betebenner, 2002).

THE CURRENT SITUATION IN ENGLAND

As explained earlier, a national curriculum was introduced in England and Wales in 1988. National assessment against the national curriculum was introduced progressively from 1990. Pupils are assessed at the end of the key stage (i.e., at ages 7, 11, and 14), using a combination of external tests and tasks, and by teachers' own assessment judgments. At age 16 assessment is through examinations set and marked by a number of Examination Boards under the regulation of the Qualifications and Curriculum Authority (QCA).

National Curriculum Assessment

The current arrangements for end-of-key-stage assessment are:

Key Stage 1 (Ages 5–7)

Tests:	English	reading; writing; spelling
	Mathematics	
Teacher Assessment:		English (reading and writing) mathematics; science

Key Stage 2 (Ages 7–11)

Tests:	English	reading; writing; spelling; handwriting
	Mathematics	with calculator; without calculator; mental arithmetic
	Science	two papers
Teacher Assessment:		English (reading and writing) mathematics; science

Key Stage 3 (Ages 11–14)

Tests:	English	reading and writing; Shakespeare
	Mathematics	with calculator; without calculator; mental arithmetic
	Science	two papers
Teacher Assessment:		conducted in all national curriculum subjects

Optional tests are available for years 3, 4, 5, 7, and 8, that is, in between key stages. These are very widely used.

Purposes.

- Reporting on the attainment of individual pupils.
- Monitoring national performance.

- Contributing to the improvement of teaching and learning.
- Contributing to monitoring the effectiveness of schools, alongside the school inspection system run by OfSTED—the Office for Standards in Education (formerly Her Majesty's Inspectorate, HMI).

Marking and Reporting. The national curriculum levels are broad bands, with each level representing, on average, progress over a 2-year period. The outcomes of both test and teacher assessment are expressed in terms of national curriculum levels. The dual reporting of a test level and a teacher assessment level for each pupil provides parents and pupils with two pieces of information: the externally validated summary of attainment and the longer-term overview of a range of performance based on teachers' judgments.

Key Stage 1 tests are marked by the pupils' own teachers. Key Stages 2 and 3 tests are marked externally. All results are collected centrally and, as well as being reported to individual pupils and their parents, are reported nationally. The results are used in school performance tables at Key stages 2 and 4 (although the Welsh Assembly has now stopped the publication of primary school results in Wales), for measuring added value, for benchmarking schools against one another, and for target setting.

General Certificate of Secondary Education (GCSE)

These exams are taken at age 16, the end of compulsory schooling. They are available in a wide range of subjects and pupils/schools choose which any individual will take beyond the core national curriculum. They include vocational subjects, for example, engineering (Vocational GCSEs), and pupils can also take General National Vocational Qualifications (GNVQ) at Level 1. This gave a total of 5.9 million exam entries at age 16 in 2002 (Boston, 2003). All subjects include some coursework element (a project supervised and marked in school), and all exam scripts are marked centrally.

There are plans to increase the number of vocational GCSE subjects available. Currently under discussion are strategies to streamline and clarify vocational examinations in the 14–19 age group, with the possible removal of the GNVQ exam.

General Certificate of Education: Advanced Level (GCE A-level)

The academic exam for 18-year-olds taken 2 years after the GCSE as the main qualifier for university entrance, the A-level, was changed 3 years ago. Curriculum 2000 was the overhaul of post-16 education introduced in September 2000. It followed ministers' complaints that the curriculum was too narrow and inflexible, preventing students from competing with European peers.

The main change was the "split" into AS-level and A2 exams, each of which count for 50% of the marks of the full A-level. Pupils are encouraged to take at least four AS exams in Year 12 and then at least three A2 exams the following year. Curriculum 2000 also introduced new vocational qualifications, "advanced extension" tests for more able students, and key skills qualifications in communication, number application, and computing.

However, as Chief Inspector David Bell said: "Despite the added burdens placed on schools, colleges and pupils, Curriculum 2000 has achieved much less than was intended. The range of subjects taken has not broadened significantly, and the scope of teaching within subjects has narrowed, as teachers have concentrated on course specifications" (Shaw, 2003, p. 3).

So, students now take major and significant exams at ages 16, 17, and 18. Evaluation evidence from the inspectors (OfSTED, 2003) is mixed: Stress levels are higher among students; they spend less time on sport, arts, and the like; the separate teaching and assessment of key skills has not been successful; and the increase in marking has overloaded the system, which came close to collapse in summer 2002.

IMPACT

So, is all this assessment making our schooling any better? Are standards rising? Does the country feel that schools are more accountable? What are the effects on teachers?

Scores on national tests and exams are rising; and performance on the latest international tests is high. Since 1988 (the first year of the new GCSE exam), the percentage of pupils gaining the top three grades has risen by around 10 percentage points in both maths and English.

National Curriculum Test scores at the primary school level did rise, but are now steady (see Table 6.1).

Recent assessments of 15-year-olds' reading, scientific, and mathematical literacy in the Programme for International Student Assessment (PISA; the newest of the international performance indicators, which emphasizes the use of knowledge) show that English youngsters score in the top group: fourth on science, seventh on reading, and eighth on mathematics (out of 32 countries). Only Korea scored higher in all three areas, whereas the English outperformed traditional rivals such as France and Germany (also the United States) (OECD, 2001). These assessments emphasize skills and the use of knowledge in real-world scenarios rather than knowledge content per se. Thus, the good news is that our youngsters have the ability to use higher order skills. But is this because of, or despite, regular testing? The

TABLE 6.1
Percentage of Pupils Gaining National Curriculum Assessment Level 2
or Above at KS1 (Age 7) and Level 4 or Above at KS2 (Age 11)

	KS1		KS2	
	English	Mathematics	English	Mathematics
1995	76	78	48	44
1996	80	80	58	54
2000	81/84	90	75	72
2001	84/86	91	75	71
2002	84/86	90	75	73

PISA studies show that our pupils have the most pressure on them, but that this has contributed little to higher standards. Other factors such as classroom climate and use of resources, however, have a greater effect. So, one could argue the effects of accountability testing in both ways: that our youngsters performed well in PISA because of regular testing (because the underlying basic skills were there), or despite it.

But at what cost have gains been made? Has the testing emphasis made schools less attractive to work in? There is evidence of widespread dissatisfaction with teaching as a potential or actual career. Recruitment to teacher training has been low in recent years and has only been "saved" recently by giving student teachers bursaries and loan repayments. The more worrying trend is teacher dropout. According to Slater and Thornton (2001), "A recent survey indicated that 12% of trainee teachers drop out of training before completion, 30% of newly qualified teachers never teach and a further 18% of new recruits leave the profession within three years" (p. 1). As Torrance (2003) observed, "Most explanations focus on overwork, linked to the pressure to meet targets, along with relatively low pay for an all-graduate profession" (p. 925).

If we could keep a fraction of this 48% of qualified teachers who leave the profession, we would have no teacher supply problem. There is currently a Parliamentary inquiry into teacher retention (Bassey, 2003); a report on the topic prepared for the OECD (Ross & Hutchings, 2003) trawled various studies and concluded that much of the research evidence suggests that teachers are leaving the profession (rather than leaving a post) because of frustrations about their professional autonomy and their ability to be creative in their work.

Another concern is that more pupils are being excluded from school, with a significant rise—up 11% from 2000 to 2001, including a 19% rise in primary school exclusions—after several years of reductions (BBC Education, 2002).

Not all of this can be laid at the door of accountability testing, of course, but unrealistic targets may well lower teacher morale. Michael Fullan and colleagues from the University of Toronto, who were brought in to evaluate the national literacy and numeracy strategies, concluded that national targets may no longer mobilize and motivate teachers, particularly if they are seen by schools and school districts to be unrealistic (Earl, Levin, Leithwood, Fullan, & Watson, 2001; Ward, 2003).

The chief inspector of schools has now admitted that national targets for school improvement are making teachers feel threatened and defeatist, and turning them into cynics. Furthermore, cheating is on the increase with a head teacher recently jailed for 3 months for altering pupils' test papers (PA News, 2003).

As QCA's own evaluations show, the drive to meet targets and the pressure of publication of league tables has a direct effect on what schools and teachers feel they can do:

> Whilst often wishing to innovate and/or encourage creativity within the curriculum, many schools are inhibited from doing so through anxiety over attaining and/or sustaining high levels of achievement. The factors most commonly identified as inhibitors are challenging targets and league tables. *(Key stages 1 and 2, 3 phase reports; mathematics, science and art and design reports.)*
>
> For schools and LEAs, the drive to improve standards and to meet challenging test targets is a crucial issue. For many schools at the key stage 1, 2 and 3 monitoring seminars, the nature of the curriculum is shaped by the need to improve performance in the core subjects, and particularly in English and mathematics. Some teachers report that formal assessment has reduced the amount of time available for teaching and is squeezing creativity from the curriculum. (QCA, 2002, p. 10)

A longitudinal study (McNess, Broadfoot, & Osborn, 2003) of the effects of the introduction of the national curriculum and assessment program, with related targets and league tables, on primary school pupils and teachers found that:

> Teachers in England were concerned that externally imposed educational change had not only increased their workload but also created a growing tension between the requirements of government and the needs of their pupils. A perceived demand for a delivery of "performance," for both themselves and their pupils, had created a policy focus that emphasised the managerially "effective," in the interests of accountability, while ignoring teachers' deeply rooted commitment to the affective aspects of teaching and learning. (p. 243)

The report went on to say:

> External accountability had increased, and although personal and moral responsibility was still seen as important, there was some evidence of a shift in climate from a covenant, based on trust, to a contract, based on delivery, of

education to meet external requirements and national economic goals. The pressure of time and a demand to plan, assess, and reach ever increasing, externally defined targets had resulted in an environment in which, for pupils as well as their teachers, the affective domain has been reduced in preference to the academic. (p. 249)

We found in our work with primary teachers, when probing their assessment practice in-depth, that it was not so much the imposition of assessment per se that teachers objected to but the type of assessment and the extent of its intrusion into the teachers' personal and professional classroom processes (Gipps et al., 1995).

One has to conclude, it seems, that the introduction of strong accountability measures—with external testing, targets, and monitoring (with punitive results)—acts to reduce teachers' feelings of professionalism and being valued.

WHAT CAN BE LEARNED FROM HISTORY?

We have been here before. In the late 19th century England had a curriculum and assessment system: The Revised Code and Payment by Results. This system, which stifled elementary education and profoundly affected the role of HMI (turning them from advisers to examiners), actually collapsed under its own administrative weight. Here is an extract from a book by Edmond Holmes, Chief Inspector for Elementary Schools, who published in 1911 a reflection on education over the previous 50 years, including Payment by Results:

> What the Department did to the teacher, it compelled him to do to the child. The teacher who is the slave of another's will cannot carry out his instructions except by making his pupils the slaves of his own will. The teacher who has been deprived by his superiors of freedom, initiative, and responsibility, cannot carry out his instructions except by depriving his pupils of the same vital qualities. . . .
>
> To be in bondage to a syllabus is a misfortune for a teacher, and a misfortune for the school that he teaches. To be in bondage to a syllabus which is binding on all schools alike, is a graver misfortune. To be in bondage to a bad syllabus is binding on all schools alike, is of all misfortunes the gravest.
>
> Of the evils that are inherent in the examination system as such—of its tendency to arrest growth, to deaden life, to paralyse the higher faculties, to externalise what is inward, to materialise what is spiritual, to involve education in an atmosphere to unreality and self-deception—I have already spoken at some length. In the days of payment by results various circumstances conspired to raise those evil tendencies to the highest imaginable "power." When inspectors ceased to examine (in the stricter sense of the word) they realised what infinite mischief the yearly examination had done. . . .

Not a thought was given, except in a small minority of the schools, to the real training of the child, to the fostering of his mental (and other) growth. To get him through the yearly examination by hook or by crook was the one concern of the teacher. As profound distrust of the teacher was the basis of the policy of the Department, so profound distrust of the child was the basis of the policy of the teacher. To leave the child to find out anything for himself, to work out anything for himself, would have been regarded as a proof of incapacity, not to say insanity, on the part of the teacher, and would have led to results which, from the "percentage" point of view, would probably have been disastrous. (pp. 103–109)

What about American history? John Nisbet (2000), the first President of British Educational Research Association (BERA), reminded us in the UK that the publication of results for individual schools in the form of league tables began in Boston in 1845, only to be abandoned as a "waste of time" 2 years later:

The State of Massachusetts set up a Board of Education in 1837 and appointed Horace Mann as its first Secretary. He had annoyed the Boston schoolteachers by criticising the standard of education in their schools. The Boston School Committee set about showing that Boston did not need supervision by the State authority. They decided to do this in 1845 by a systematic survey of schools using printed tests in a range of subjects: Grammar, Definitions, History, Natural Philosophy (or general science), Astronomy, Rhetoric, Writing and Arithmetic. Sampling was used to select about 500 scholars in the 13–14 age-range, and each test lasted one hour, with questions drawn from the textbooks in use in the schools. . . . Rules were laid down for scoring the tests which gave the scholars the benefit of doubt. Nevertheless, the results according to the Board's report, were "discouraging," averaging between 24 and 39%:

A large proportion of . . . boys and girls of fourteen or fifteen years of age . . . cannot write without such errors in grammar, in spelling and in punctuation, as we should blush to see in a letter from a son or daughter of their age. (Travers, 1983, p. 91)

Noting that some schools had better results than others, the Board published a "table of rank" for individual schools. The school which had the largest proportion of non-European immigrants was severely criticised, on the grounds that the master in charge lacked faith in the children's ability to learn and so taught them nothing. However, the commissioners of 150 years ago had the sense to observe:

We do not recommend the table of rank . . . as affording a precise estimate of the merits of the schools. . . . Even if it were a perfect demonstration . . . still we would not have it considered as an absolute test of the merits of the schools. . . . Let us look to the cultivation of religious sense, the supremacy of conscience, the duty of self-culture, the love of knowledge, the respect for order . . . before we say which school is first or which is last. (Travers, 1983, pp. 91–92)

The tests were repeated in 1846, but not in 1847. The Committee's 1849 Report gives the reason: it was because "no use had been made of the results given in 1845 and 1846, and the further giving of tests was clearly a waste of time." (pp. 16–17)

CONCLUSION

What we are seeing—certainly in England and I would tentatively suggest in the United States as well—is a shift from a situation in which the teachers' major responsibility is to their pupils, to one in which their major responsibility is to performance and accountability measures. The vastly increased central direction and control from our Labour Government has been met with mixed reactions: admiration from many onlookers and pragmatists; astonishment and dismay by the many teachers who had voted them in. There would, however, be little disagreement that the raft of targets, performance measures, strategies, and increased emphasis on testing and examination constitutes very much stronger control and external accountability, with a parallel reduction in teachers' professionalism.

Does/did the education system deserve this? If the "secret garden of the curriculum" had been opened up earlier than 1988, could the worst of this current testing-and-targets regime have been avoided? Would the English education system have been seen as more accountable and productive when the national (and international) moves to measure, control, and improve education swept in? Who knows? If there is a global trend, most self-respecting administrations want to be part of it. Certainly, as my colleague Alison Wolf argued, there is an increasing preoccupation among governments with monitoring and regulating the education process on which they spend so much money, and that concerns so many of their citizens. As politicians become more concerned to control education they turn increasingly to testing to monitor, control, and change the education system, strong in the belief that educational performance translates directly into economic growth (Wolf, 2002).

There are some signs of a softening, however, with concern over teacher retention and morale. Hargreaves (once head of the QCA) now argues within the Think Tank Demos, that performance indicators and coercion have not worked to raise standards, partly because the social context is very complex, but also because of the role assigned to teachers. In order to transform schooling, what is needed is the active consent of teachers: Rather than downgrade them to a technician role we need to engage them in the reform (Hargreaves, 2003).

As a caveat to government, let me just point out that in the PISA/OECD survey referred to previously, Finland's 15-year-olds were easily top in reading. Both the OECD analysis and Finnish academics attribute this in part to the status and autonomy of teachers. According to the OECD (2001) report, countries that perform best educate all children well, regardless of background and allow schools freedom from central control. And as Slater (2003) observed, "The OECD praises Finland for its comprehensive system and for giving teachers a high degree of responsibility and autonomy." Seppänen (2003) reported:

> "It is difficult to pinpoint the underlying reasons for Finland's extraordinary success to a single cause, it is more likely to be a combination of factors" said Pirjo Linakylä, professor at the educational research institute at Jyväskylä University. However, she sees the role of the teacher as crucial. "The teaching profession is very respected, with the best graduates routinely opting for a career in it." (p. 14)

Teacher Professionalism and Reengagement

Is high-quality teaching simply a matter of following given materials, activities, lesson structures, and formats? Is teaching as a profession going to be enhanced by the imposition of rigorous testing and targets regimes? When teachers' work is very publicly defined and monitored how do they retain a sense of professional responsibility and integrity? What I take from the English experience is that we need actively to plan how to help teachers to live with the dissonance that an accountability testing program brings.

In England we achieved professional reengagement, albeit unwittingly and only partially, through the Assessment for Learning initiative. The widespread push for, and uptake of, Assessment for Learning can be seen, I would argue, as a professional response to an overstructured testing regime that has led to a desire to use assessment in the classroom to enhance learning. Many of us in the assessment world have been encouraging teachers to go down this route (Gipps 1994, 2002) to develop their professional skills in classroom assessment and stop agonizing about national curriculum assessment about which they can do little. The response has been very encouraging. The review by Black and Wiliam (1998) did help by showing that, done appropriately, formative assessment with qualitative feedback does improve performance, and, what is more the gains are greater for the lower performing pupils. Faced with high-quality research evidence and teachers' engagement with the process, the Department of Education and Skills (DfES) and the Office for Standards in Education (OfSTED) have joined the bandwagon and are encouraging it too.

The result is that we have a nationwide move to enhance teachers' skills in formative assessment with feedback to the learner. Teachers have embraced these developments as they see an arena in which they can reassert their professional expertise and regain some autonomy and control over their assessment practice. There is solid evidence that this enhances student learning. I am not suggesting that the same initiative would work in the United States. I think you need to find your own initiative, but I do believe that it is an issue that needs to be addressed and planned for.

I am not against testing programs (if they are well designed and fit for the purpose), nor am I complacent about standards of performance in both basic and higher skills in the UK. My argument is that if we wish to have "teacher quality" alongside a punitive accountability testing regime, then we have to engage with the teaching profession. We need to develop a compact with teachers, to offer them support and professional development, so that they in turn can offer high-quality, professional teaching.

REFERENCES

Bassey, M. (2003). More advocacy: Give back autonomy to teachers. *Research Intelligence, 84,* 26–30.

BBC Education. (2002, March 23). Retrieved September 2003, from http://www.bbc.co.uk

Black, P., & Wiliam, D. (1998). Assessment and classroom learning. *Assessment in Education, 5*(1), 7–74.

Boston, K. (2003, March 21). Evolution not revolution. *Times Educational Supplement.*

Department for Education and Skills. (2001). *Education and training expenditure since 1991–92.* London: Author.

Earl, L., Levin, B., Leithwood, K., Fullan, M., & Watson, N. (2001). *Watching and learning 2: Evaluation of the implementation of the national literacy and numeracy strategies second annual report.* London: Department of Education and Employment.

Gipps, C. (1994). *Beyond testing: Towards a theory of educational assessment.* London: Falmer Press.

Gipps, C. (2002). Sociocultural perspectives on assessment. In G. Wells & G. Claxton (Eds.), *Learning for life in the 21st century: Sociocultural perspectives on the future of education* (pp. 73–83). London: Blackwell.

Gipps, C., Brown, M., McCallum, B., & McAlister, S. (1995). *Intuition or evidence? Teachers and national assessment of seven year olds.* Maidenhead, England: Open University Press.

Gipps, C., Steadman, S., Blackstone, T., & Stierer, B. (1983). *Testing children: Standardised testing in local education authorities and schools.* Portsmouth, NH: Heinemann Educational Books.

Hargreaves, D. H. (2003). *Education epidemic. Transforming secondary schools through innovation networks.* London: Demos.

Holmes, E. (1911). *What is and what might be.* London: Constable & Co.

Linn, R. (2000). Assessment and accountability. *Educational Researcher, 29*(2), 4–16.

Linn, R., Baker, E. L., & Betebenner, D. W. (2002). Accountability systems: Implications of require-ments of the No Child Left Behind Act of 2001. *Educational Researcher, 31*(6), 3–16.

Nisbet, J. (2000). League tables: Lessons from the past. *Research Intelligence.* Retrieved March 31, 2004, from http://www.bera.ac.uk/ri/no72/ri72nisbet.html

McNess, E., Broadfoot, P., & Osborn, M. (2003). Is the effective compromising the affective? *British Educational Research Journal, 29*(2), 243–257.

Office for Standards in Education. (2003). *Curriculum, 2000: Implementation* (HMI 993). London: Author.

Organisation for Economic Co-operation and Development. (2001). *Knowledge and skills for life: First results from PISA 2000.* Paris: Author.

PA News. (2003, July 3). Headteacher jailed for forging school tests. *Times Educational Supplement.*

Pollard, A., & Triggs, P. (2000). *What pupils say: Changing policy and practice in primary education.* London: Continuum.

Qualifications and Curriculum Authority. (2002, November). *Report on QCA's monitoring, evaluating and developing the curriculum 2001–2002.* London: Author.

Ross, A., & Hutchings, M. (2003). *Attracting, developing and retaining effective teachers in the United Kingdom of Great Britain and Northern Ireland.* Country Background Report for OECD. Retrieved September 2003, from http://www.oecd.org

Seppänen, R. (2003, April 7). Respect keeps scores on top. *Times Educational Supplement.*

Shaw, M. (2003, March 21). A-level shake-up fails to impress inspectors. *Times Educational Supplement.*

Slater, J. (2003, April 7). Class segregation holds back Britain. *Times Educational Supplement.*

Slater, J., & Thornton, K. (2001, November 2). Labour fails to stem exodus of teachers. *Times Educational Supplement.*

Torrance, H. (2003). Assessment of the national curriculum in England. In T. Kellaghan & D. Stufflebeam (Eds.), *International handbook of educational evaluation* (pp. 905–928). London: Kluwer Academic Press.

Travers, R. M. W. (1983). *How research has changed American schools: A history from 1840 to the present.* Kalamazoo, MI: Mythos Press.

Ward, Helen. (2003, January 24). Unrealistic targets lower staff morale. *Times Educational Supplement.*

Whitty, G. (1989). The new right and the national curriculum: State control or market forces? *Journal of Education Policy, 4,* 329–341.

Williams, S., & Morris, J. (1977). *Education in schools: A consultative document.* London: Her Majesty's Stationery Office.

Wolf, A. (2002). *Does education matter? Myths about education and economic growth.* London: Penguin.

7

The Persistent Problem of Out-of-Field Teaching

Richard M. Ingersoll
University of Pennsylvania
and
The Consortium for Policy Research in Education

The failure to ensure that the nation's classrooms are all staffed with qualified school teachers is one of the most important problems in contemporary American education. Over the past decade, numerous panels, commissions, and studies have focused attention on this problem and, in turn, numerous reforms have been initiated to upgrade the quality and quantity of the teaching force. This report focuses on the problem of underqualified teachers in the core academic fields at the 7th- to 12th-grade level. Using data from the nationally representative Schools and Staffing Survey, conducted by the National Center for Education Statistics, this analysis examined how many classes are not staffed by minimally qualified teachers, and to what extent these patterns have changed in recent years. The data show that although almost all teachers hold at least basic qualifications, there are large numbers of teachers assigned to teach subjects that do not match their qualifications—the phenomenon of out-of-field teaching. Moreover, the data show that out-of-field teaching has gotten slightly worse in recent years, despite a plethora of reforms targeted to improving teacher quality. The report discusses possible reasons for the failure of these reform efforts. My thesis is that, despite the unprecedented interest in, and awareness of, this problem, there remains little understanding of a key issue—the reasons for the prevalence of underqualified teaching in American schools—resulting thus far in a failure of teacher policy and reform. I conclude by drawing out the lessons and implications of these failures for the prospects of the No Child Left Behind Act to successfully address the problem of underqualified teachers in classrooms in the coming years.

Few educational problems have received more attention in recent times than the failure to ensure that our nation's elementary and secondary classrooms are all staffed with qualified teachers. Over the past decade, dozens of studies, commissions, and national reports have bemoaned the qualifications and quality of our teachers. Concern with the quality and qualifications of teachers is neither unique nor surprising. Elementary and secondary schooling are mandatory in the United States and it is into the custody of teachers that children are legally placed for a significant portion of their lives. The quality of teachers and teaching are undoubtedly among the most important factors shaping the learning and growth of students. Moreover, the largest single component of the cost of education in any country is teacher compensation.

However, although ensuring that our nation's classrooms are all staffed with qualified teachers is a perennially important issue in our schools, it is also among the least understood, especially in regard to the sources of the problem. One of the least recognized of these sources is the phenomenon known as out-of-field teaching—teachers assigned to teach subjects that do not match their training or education. This is a crucial factor because highly qualified teachers may actually become highly unqualified if they are assigned to teach subjects for which they have little background. Educators have, of course, long been aware of the existence of out-of-field teaching. James Conant, former President of Harvard University and father of the SAT, called attention to the widespread "misuse of teachers" through out-of-field assignments in his landmark 1963 study *The Education of American Teachers.* Albert Shanker, the former head of the American Federation of Teachers, condemned out-of-field teaching as education's "dirty little secret" in a 1985 opinion piece in the *New York Times.* But an absence of accurate statistics on out-of-field teaching has kept this problem largely unrecognized—a situation remedied with the release, beginning in the late 1980s, of the Schools and Staffing Survey (SASS), a major new survey of the nation's elementary and secondary teachers conducted by the National Center for Education Statistics (NCES) of the U.S. Department of Education.

In previous research using the SASS data I have shown that out-of-field teaching is a serious problem across the nation (Ingersoll, 1999, 2002b). These findings on out-of-field teaching have also been replicated. Several other researchers have also calculated levels of out-of-field teaching using the same, or similar, data sources and, although different analysts have focused an a wide range of different measures of out-of-field teaching, all have reached the same conclusion: that high levels of out-of-field teaching are a leading source of underqualified teaching in American schools (see, e.g., Bandeira de Mello & Broughman, 1996; Bobbitt & McMillen, 1995; Lewis et al., 1999; McMillen, Gruber, Henke, McGrath, & Cohen, 2002).

The findings of this research have captured widespread interest, have been featured in a number of major education reports (e.g., Education

Trust, 1996, 1998; Education Week, 1997, 1998, 2000, 2003; National Commission on Teaching and America's Future (NCTAF), 1996, 1997), and have been widely reported in the national media. As a result, over the past several years the problem of underqualified teachers has become a major concern in the realm of educational policy and its elimination a prominent target of reform legislation.

Most recent federal and state teacher policies and initiatives have focused on two general approaches to addressing these problems: upgrading the qualifications of teachers and increasing the quantity of teachers supplied. To address the quality issue, many states have pushed for more rigorous preservice and in-service teacher education, training, and licensing standards (licenses for teachers are known as teaching certificates and are issued by states). In response to the quantity issue, a host of initiatives and programs have been implemented that attempt to increase the supply of available teachers by recruiting new candidates into teaching. A wide range of alternative licensing programs has been implemented to ease entry into teaching. Programs such as Troops-to-Teachers are designed to entice professionals into midcareer changes to teaching. Other programs, such as Teach for America, seek to lure the "best and brightest" into the profession. Finally, financial incentives such as signing bonuses, student loan forgiveness, housing assistance, and tuition reimbursement have all been instituted to aid teacher recruitment (Hirsch, Koppich, & Knapp, 2001). These initiatives culminated in the reauthorization in January 2002 of the Elementary and Secondary Education Act, titled the No Child Left Behind Act of 2001 (NCLB). This legislation set a new, unprecedented, and laudable goal, to ensure that the nation's public elementary and secondary students are all taught by highly qualified teachers by the end of the 2005–2006 school year. In short, this legislation seeks to eliminate the problem of out-of-field teaching.

In general, NCLB defines a "highly qualified" teacher as someone who has a bachelor's degree, who holds a regular or full state-approved teaching certificate or license, and who is competent in each of the academic subjects they teach. There are several means by which teachers can establish "competency" in a subject. They can hold an undergraduate or graduate major or its equivalent in the subject, pass a test on the subject, hold an advanced teaching certificate in the subject, or meet some other state-approved method of evaluation for the subject. In order to assess how well schools are doing in regard to the new requirements and to hold them accountable if they do not meet them, NCLB requires three things of states and school districts: annual report cards, plans for improvement, and disclosure to parents of students taught by underqualified teachers.

The analysis in this report seeks to build on, and update with more recent data, earlier work on out-of-field teaching. It specifically examines the past decade's trends in out-of-field teaching for both the nation and the 50 states. The next section describes the SASS database and measures of out-of-field teaching in more detail. I then present data from the period 1987 to 2000 showing how much out-of-field teaching has existed, and to what extent it varies across different subjects and across different kinds of schools. One question of interest here is, have any of these reforms had an impact on the problem of ensuring that our nation's elementary and secondary classrooms are all staffed with qualified teachers?

The data show that although almost all teachers hold at least basic qualifications (i.e., a bachelor's degree and a full teaching certificate), there are large numbers of teachers assigned to teach subjects out of their fields of training. Moreover, perhaps surprisingly, the data show that there was little decrease in the amount of out-of-field teaching during this period, despite the implementation of numerous policy reform efforts. The following section turns to a discussion of possible reasons for the failure of teacher quality reform. My thesis is that, despite the unprecedented interest in, and awareness of, this problem, there remains little understanding of a key issue, the reasons for the prevalence of out-of-field teaching in American schools, and this lack of understanding has undermined recent reform efforts. I conclude by drawing out the lessons and implications of these failures for the prospects of current and future legislation, such as NCLB, to successfully address the problem of underqualified teachers in classrooms in the coming years.

DATA AND METHODS

Data

As mentioned earlier, the data for this analysis come from NCES' Schools and Staffing Survey. This is the largest and most comprehensive data set available on the staffing, occupational, and organizational characteristics of elementary and secondary schools. This survey was specifically designed to remedy the lack of nationally representative and comprehensive data on these issues (Haggstrom, Darling-Hammond, & Grissmer, 1988).

The U.S. Census Bureau collects the SASS data for NCES from random samples stratified by state, sector, and school level. To date, four independent cycles of SASS have been completed: 1987–1988, 1990–1991, 1993–1994, and 1999–2000 (for information on SASS, see Choy et al., 1993, or Henke, Choy, Chen, Geis, & Alt, 1997). Each cycle of SASS includes several sets of separate, but linked, questionnaires for school administrators and for a random sample of teachers within each school. The response rate has been relatively high: about 85% for teachers and 95% for administrators.

SASS is a large survey; in each cycle, the sample sizes are about 5,000 school districts, 11,000 schools, and 53,000 teachers. It is also a comprehensive survey; it provides accurate data for all 50 states (and Washington, DC) and all types of schools. Throughout, this analysis uses data weighted to compensate for the over- and undersampling of the complex stratified survey design. Each observation is weighted by the inverse of its probability of selection in order to obtain unbiased estimates of population parameters.

Measuring Out-of-Field Teaching

Empirical research on the extent of underqualified and out-of-field teaching has faced serious problems surrounding the validity of both data and methods; these issues warrant some extended discussion here. First, out-of-field teaching is politically sensitive—something that will most likely increase with the new requirements of NCLB. Hence, researchers have often been skeptical of data on out-of-field assignments obtained from local or state school officials (Haggstrom et al., 1988; Robinson, 1985).[1] One of the strengths of SASS in providing data on out-of-field teaching is that the data are not obtained from school officials, nor are they obtained by asking teachers themselves if they are assigned to teach out of their fields. SASS collects extensive information on both teachers' daily course schedules and their education, training, and certification from its very large nationally representative sample of teachers. From these data I independently calculate the extent of out-of-field teaching.

Empirical measurement of the extent of underqualified teaching is also difficult because there is little consensus, and much debate, over how to define a "qualified teacher." Although there is almost universal agreement that teachers do matter and that student learning is affected by the quality of teaching, there is a great deal of controversy concerning which kind of courses, training experiences, and credentials teachers ought to have to be considered adequately qualified.

One of the key areas of difference concerns the relative value of teachers' subject matter knowledge and pedagogical knowledge. On one end of this continuum are those who argue that content or subject knowledge—knowing what to teach—is of primary importance for a qualified teacher. At its extreme, this viewpoint assumes that training in teaching methods is unnecessary, and that having an academic degree in a subject is sufficient to be a qualified teacher in that subject. On the other end of this con-

---

[1]An example of where the SASS data on out-of-field assignments run counter to information obtained by school officials has arisen in the state of Maine. My research shows that high school teachers in Maine are often assigned to teach subjects for which they do not have certification, even though out-of-field assignments are prohibited by the Maine Department of Education. Researchers in that state have simply denied that a problem exists and have concluded that the SASS data "do not present a true picture of Maine's teachers" (Townsend, Cobb, Moirs, & McIntire, 1997, pp. 34–35, 71). For an excellent earlier report on the rules and regulations different states have concerning out-of-field assignments, see Robinson (1985).

tinuum are those who argue that pedagogical or methodological knowledge—knowing how to teach—is of primary importance to be qualified. In this view, in-depth knowledge of a subject is less important than in-depth skill in teaching. At its extreme, this viewpoint holds that "a good teacher can teach anything."

Teaching does have an extensive body of empirical research, going back decades, devoted to assessing the effects of various teacher qualifications on teacher and student performance. For measures of qualifications, researchers typically examine teachers' test scores or teachers' credentials, such as degree or teaching certificates, reflecting a variety of types of teacher education and training. Moreover, a number of these studies have found teacher education or training, of one sort or another, to be significantly related to increases in student achievement. For example, in a review of 60 empirical studies on the effects of teacher education, Greenwald, Hedges, and Laine (1996) concluded that teachers' degree levels consistently showed "very strong relations with student achievement . . . [in] a wide variety of studies over a three decade period" (pp. 284–285). Some studies look closely at the amount of subject-specific teacher education. For example, in a multilevel analysis of 1992 NAEP data, Raudenbush, Fotiu, and Cheong (1999) found teacher education in mathematics (as measured by a major in math or in math education) to be "consistently positively and highly significantly related to math proficiency" in eighth-grade students. Similarly, a recent analysis of 2000 NAEP data found that eighth-grade students whose math teachers had a regular teaching certificate in math or had a major or minor in math or math education scored significantly higher on the eighth-grade math test (Greenberg, Rhodes, Ye, & Stancavage, 2004).

The results from this literature are, however, often contradictory. There are also studies showing no positive effects for various measures of teacher qualifications. Given the inherent difficulties in accurately isolating and capturing the effects of teacher's qualifications on their students' achievement, and the weaknesses of much of the extant data and empirical research, this is not surprising. More and better teacher effects research is warranted to clarify some of the resulting uncertainties and many have called for more empirical study. Others have argued, however, that in the absence of solid documentation of their value, teacher training and licensing are unnecessary and burdensome barriers to the entry of willing candidates into the occupation of teaching. Proponents of this viewpoint often call for the elimination of one aspect or another of teaching training and certification requirements.

This stands in stark contrast to the situation in a number of other developed nations; recent cross-national data indicate that the entry requirements to becoming a teacher in the United States are less rigorous, less arduous, and less lengthy than those in many other countries (Wang, Coleman, Coley, & Phelps, 2003). It is also important to recognize that the argument that teacher training is an undue barrier to occupational entry stands in contrast to the perspective long held by organization theorists and among those who study work, organizations, and occupations in general. From a cross-occupational perspective, teaching has long been characterized as an easy-in/easy-out occupation. Compared to many other occupations and, in particular compared to the traditional professions, teaching has a relatively low entry bar, and a relatively wide entry gate. Becoming a professor, lawyer, accountant, architect, or engineer, for instance, generally involves more rigorous preparation and licensure requirements than does becoming an elementary- or secondary-level teacher. The ostensible rationale for their relatively low entry requirements is that teaching is assumed to be less complex and to require less ability and training than many other occupations and professions. But, analysts of work and occupations have traditionally classified teaching as a relatively complex form of work, characterized by uncertainty, intangibility, and ambiguity; and requiring as high a degree of initiative, thought, judgment, and skill as some of the traditional professions (e.g., Bidwell, 1965; Kohn & Schooler, 1983; Lortie, 1975).

Ironically, although the training and licensing requirements are lower for entering teaching than for many other occupations and lower than the requirements in some other nations, there appears to have been relatively greater effort expended to evaluate and scrutinize whether teaching requirements are useful or necessary. In a preliminary search I have been unable to find analogous evaluative and effects literatures for other occupations and professions. To be sure, there does appear to be interest in determining the best form of preparation of, for example, veterinarians, accountants, or lawyers. But, I have failed to find much debate over whether advanced training and education are themselves necessary for these jobs. For example, there does not appear to be a "professor effects" literature that examines whether professors' qualifications have a positive effect on student achievement or on research productivity (for a review of this literature, see Pascarella & Terenzini, 1991). Nevertheless almost all universities require a doctorate for academic positions.

This lack of consensus on how to define a qualified teacher has implications for research on out-of-field teaching; that is, how to define whether someone is qualified in the actual fields and subjects they are assigned to teach. Just as a qualified/unqualified teacher can be defined and measured in a number of ways, so can an in-field/out-of-field teacher. And just as all of the definitions of a qualified/unqualified teacher have weaknesses and are the source of much contention, the same applies to measures of in-field/out-of-field teaching. Those of us who do this research have developed over a dozen different measures of out-of-field teaching. They vary according to how high a standard they set. Some include anyone with an undergraduate minor in the field; others count only those with both a full degree and a certificate in the field. Measures also vary depending on whether they focus on the numbers of teachers doing it, or the numbers of students exposed to it, according to which fields and subjects they examine, and according to which school grade levels are included. These choices are consequential; each of the many different measures has its own advantages and disadvantages, strengths and weaknesses. (For detailed discussion and comparison, see Ingersoll, 2002a.)

One of the standard methods by which school officials attempt to assess teachers' educational and/or pedagogic qualifications in specific fields is to screen teachers' scores in field-specific examinations, such as the Praxis series of exams. The use of teachers' test scores could be a valuable means of assessing out-of-field teaching. But as of yet, there is no national database with data on both teachers' course loads and teacher test scores in all of the subjects they teach. With the passage of the NCLB, such data may hopefully become available.

Another possible method of assessing teachers' educational preparation in a field is to count the actual number of undergraduate or graduate courses completed in that field. Counting courses is, however, problematic. Analysts at NCES have found that, absent an analysis of actual course transcripts, teachers find it very difficult to accurately recollect the exact number of credits they have previously completed in different subjects (Chaney, 1994).

Perhaps a less precise but more reliable indicator of qualified teachers than test scores or course counts is whether teachers have a credential, such as a college degree or teaching certificate, in the fields they teach. School officials decide whether a candidate is qualified to teach a particular subject by examining whether a teacher has a teaching certificate or license in the fields they teach. Such data are available in SASS and I use this measure here. It is necessary to recognize, however, that the value of certification as an indicator of a qualified teacher is one of the issues most hotly debated. The kinds of certification provided, the rigor of teacher certification requirements, and the quality of teacher-training programs all vary widely across states (Tryneski, 1997). There is, for instance, heated controversy over whether teacher certification should or should not require a major or a minor in an academic discipline, rather than simply an education degree.

My primary focus here, a credential-type measure that has been widely used in this kind of research, is whether teachers have an undergraduate or graduate major or minor in the fields they teach. As defined here, this measure counts both academic *and* education majors and minors (e.g., a math teacher with a minor or major in either math *or* in math education is counted as in-field). Hence, it captures a mix of both subject and pedagogical knowledge in its definition of an in-field teacher—something often missed by observers who often have wrongly assumed that this measure of out-of-field teaching refers solely to a lack of subject knowledge in a field.

For these measures of out-of-field teaching I focus on departmentalized, that is, subject-area teachers, in the four core academic subjects—math, English, science, and social studies. Table 7.1 shows which certification, major, or minor fields I count as qualified for each assignment field. Parallel to the standard set by NCLB, I focus upon an expanded definition of *secondary* to include all core academic teachers in 7th through 12th grades, regardless of whether they were employed in middle schools, junior high schools, senior high schools, secondary schools, or combined-level schools.

As mentioned previously, measures of out-of-field teaching also vary depending on whether they focus on the numbers of individuals teaching out of their fields, or by the numbers of students or classes taught by an out-of-field teacher. The first of these choices, teachers who are out of field, has been the most frequently used because interest in out-of-field teaching has arisen in a context of research and policy focused on problems of teacher supply, demand, and quality. This type of measure is also useful to those concerned with the characteristics of the teaching force and those who want to know what portion of the teaching force is not qualified in their assigned fields. But it does not distinguish, nor weight, the amount of out-of-field teaching each teacher does. This type of measure counts teachers as out-of-field whether they teach only one class out of field or five classes out of field. Because the data show that the former is more likely the case than the latter, counting all teachers overestimates the overall amount of under-qualified teaching in classrooms.

For this reason, a second type of measure is useful, the percentage of teachers' total classes taught for which they do not have a particular credential. This measure indicates the proportion of classes offered in schools that are taught by out-of-field teachers. Here I use both types of measures.

Measures of out-of-field teaching that focus upon teachers' credentials are based on several related assumptions and it is useful to recognize these explicitly. The assumption underlying this research is that adequately qualified teachers, especially at the secondary school level and especially in the core academic fields, ought to have, as a minimum prerequisite, at least a college minor or a certificate in the subjects they teach. Of course, not all individuals need such a credential to be a quality teacher. There are, no doubt, some gifted individuals able to teach anything well, regardless of their educational background and preparation. On the other hand, having such a credential does not, of course, guarantee quality teaching, nor even a qualified teacher. There are also, of course, no doubt some other individuals who are unable to teach anything well, regardless of how many credentials they have.

My assumption is that being adequately qualified at the secondary level requires, *at a minimum,* preparation in how to teach, preparation in the particular subjects one is assigned to teach, and also preparation in how to teach particular subjects—a form of subject-specific pedagogy, akin to what

TABLE 7.1
Matching Teaching Fields With Training Fields

I. Teaching Fields	II. Teachers' Course Assignment Fields	III. Teachers' Major or Minor Fields	IV. Teachers' Certification Fields
English	literature composition/journalism/creative writing reading other English/language arts courses	communications or journalism English English education/language arts education literature reading education	English or language arts journalism reading
Mathematics	general mathematics business math algebra, elementary algebra, intermediate algebra, advanced geometry, plane/solid trigonometry analytical geometry probability/statistics calculus other mathematics	engineering mathematics mathematics education physics statistics	mathematics
Social studies	social studies history world civilization political science/government geography economics civics sociology/social organization psychology other social science	psychology public administration social studies/social sciences education economics history political science sociology American Indian studies other social sciences other area or ethnic studies	social studies/social sciences history
History	history world civilization	history	social studies/social sciences history
Science	general science biology/life science chemistry physics geology/earth science/space science other physical science other natural science	science education biology/life science chemistry earth science/geology physics engineering other natural sciences	general science biology/life science chemistry earth science/geology physics physical science other natural sciences
Life science *Physical science*	biology/life science chemistry physics geology/earth science/space science other physical science	biology/life science earth science/geology physics chemistry engineering	biology/life science chemistry physics geology/earth science/space science physical science

Shulman (1986) has called pedagogical content knowledge. On the one hand, simply knowing a subject well is rarely enough to teach it effectively. One could, for example, have a PhD in math, but not have a clue as to how to effectively teach decimals to ninth graders. On the other hand, general pedagogical skill is rarely enough. It is very difficult, challenging, and time-consuming to teach subjects that one does not know very well—something I found in my former experiences as a secondary school teacher who was often assigned by my school principal to teach subjects for which I had very little background. Hence, my assumption is that for most teachers it is difficult, at best, to teach well what one does not know well. That is, I assume that education and training do impart knowledge, and that teachers trained, for example, in how to teach social studies are unlikely to have a solid understanding of how to teach physics. In short, I assume that few parents would expect their teenagers to be taught, for example, 11th-grade trigonometry by a teacher who did not have some background in math or a related subject, no matter how bright the teacher. The data show, however, that there are millions of teenagers so taught each year.

HOW WIDESPREAD IS OUT-OF-FIELD TEACHING?

As shown in Table 7.2, in the 1999–2000 school year 38% of all 7th- to 12th-grade school teachers who taught one or more *math* classes did not have either a major or a minor in math, math education, or related disciplines like engineering, statistics, or physics. About one third of all 7th- to 12th-grade teachers who taught one or more *English* classes had neither a major or minor in English or related subjects such as literature, communications, speech, journalism, English education, or reading education. In *science,* slightly lower levels, about 28% of all 7th- to 12th-grade teachers who taught one or more science classes, did not have at least a minor in one of the sciences or in science education. Finally, about a quarter of those who taught one or more *social studies* classes were without at least a minor in any of the social sciences, in public affairs, social studies education, or history.

Whether I examined teachers without a major or minor or examined teachers without certification in their assigned fields, the numbers were similar. I found, for example, that almost a third of public 7th- to 12th-grade math teachers did not have regular or full teaching certificates in math (see Fig. 7.1).[2] Focusing on those without certificates, however, can lead one to underestimate the amount of underqualified teaching within broad multi-

[2]In Fig. 7.1, regular certification refers to all those with regular, standard, full, advanced, or probationary certification. It does not include temporary, alternative, or provisional certificates. "Probationary" refers to the initial license issued after satisfying all requirements except completion of probationary period.

TABLE 7.2
Percentage of Grade 7–12 Teachers in the Core Academic
Fields Without A Major or Minor in the Field, 1999–2000

	English	Math	Science			Social	
				Life Science	*Physical Science*	Studies	*History*
U.S. total	34.5	37.9	27.6	45.2	59.9	25.6	57.5
Public total	33.1	35.8	26.5	42.7	59.1	25.0	58.5
School poverty							
Low poverty	24.0	30.0	20.3	40.4	51.4	16.9	50.0
High poverty	41.7	51.4	32.0	41.2	64.0	31.9	61.2
School size							
Small	33.6	41.4	30.2	48.8	64.3	26.5	63.9
Large	27.0	30.0	22.4	38.5	53.2	21.8	56.0
Grade level							
7–8	43.3	52.7	39.5	59.2	82.3	34.9	61.0
9–12	23.7	27.9	19.8	36.8	51.4	20.5	57.7
Private total	41.8	48.8	32.7	54.2	60.1	29.3	52.5
Orientation							
Catholic	39.8	42.5	31.2	54.3	51.6	30.5	47.7
Other religious	46.0	57.8	39.8	54.7	68.7	31.4	57.8
Nonsectarian	39.4	45.9	25.5	53.6	56.1	24.8	53.2
School size							
Small	56.7	60.1	39.4	61.1	66.2	41.3	66.5
Large	9.2	11.0	10.0	24.0	28.3	5.6	30.3
Grade level							
7–8	60.0	64.7	54.0	70.0	83.9	43.0	63.7
9–12	29.9	39.4	21.8	45.7	48.2	20.6	46.7

Note.

1. The teaching fields of English, math, science, and social studies include only departmentalized teachers in Grades 7–12 and it includes those employed in middle schools.

2. The estimates for life science, physical science, and history represent the percentage of teachers without at least a minor in those particular subfields. For example, in science, teachers who hold a minor in any one of the sciences are defined as in-field. On the other hand, in physical science, which includes physics, chemistry, space science, and geology, teachers must hold a minor in one of those physical sciences to be defined as in-field, rather than simply having a minor in any science.

3. Low poverty refers to schools where 15% or less of the students receive publicly funded free or reduced-price lunches. High poverty refers to schools where over 80% do so.

4. Small schools are those with fewer than 300 students. Large schools are those with 1,000 or more students.

5. Middle categories of poverty and size are not shown.

disciplinary fields, such as science and social studies. Teachers in these fields are routinely required to teach any of a wide array of subjects within the department. Simply having a certificate in these fields, however, may not mean teachers are qualified to teach all of the subjects within the field. For example, a teacher with a degree in biology and a certificate in science may

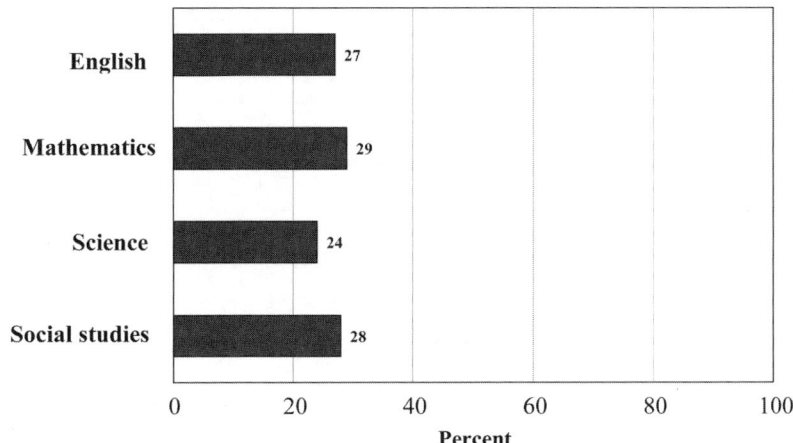

FIG. 7.1. Percentage of public Grade 7–12 teachers in the core academic fields without regular certification in the field 1999–2000.

not be qualified to teach physics. Indeed, when I raised the standard for a qualified teacher within science and social studies to a major or minor in the subfield taught, I found high levels of within-department but out-of-field teaching. For example, as shown in Table 7.2, 60% of those teaching physical science classes (chemistry, physics, earth, or space science) were without a major or minor in any of the physical sciences. Likewise, well over half of all those teaching history were without a major or minor in history itself.

Several points and limitations must be stressed concerning these measures and data. First, there is no doubt some of these out-of-field teachers may actually have been qualified, despite not having a minor, major, or certificate in the subject they taught. Some might have been qualified by virtue of knowledge gained through previous jobs, through life experiences, or through informal training. Others may have completed substantial college coursework in a field, but not have gotten a credential.

Moreover, out-of-field teaching is not the norm for most teachers, and the data show that almost none are teaching out of their fields for their entire course load. Most 7th- to 12th-grade subject-area teachers have a main field or a primary department in which they teach and most do have either a certificate or a degree in this main field. But many of these teachers are also assigned to teach some classes each day in other fields or departments. Mathematics teachers, for example, may not simply teach math; they may also be assigned to teach biology for part of the day. It is in these other assignments that teachers most often have little background.

But recall that my initial premise, as earlier outlined in the methods section, was that having a college minor is a *minimal* prerequisite. From this perspective, even a moderate number of teachers failing to meet such a low

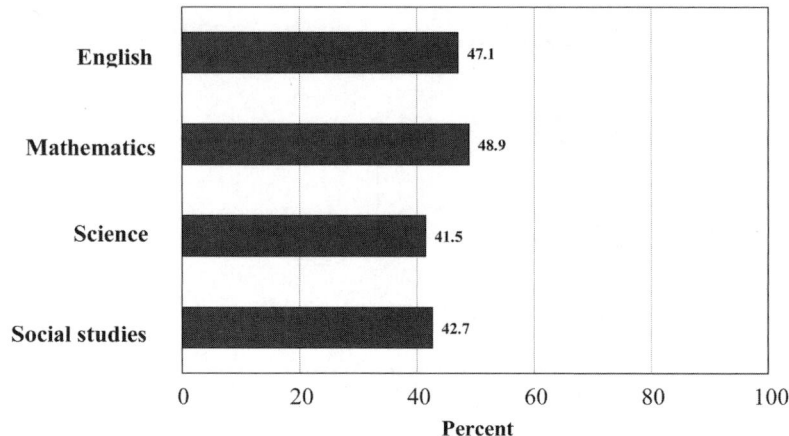

FIG. 7.2. Percentage of public Grade 7–12 teachers in the core academic fields who lack either a major or full certification or both in the field, 1999–2000.

bar signals the existence of serious problems in our schools. The data clearly indicate that this is the case. Different measures show different levels of this problem, but the data reveal that out-of-field teaching is widespread, no matter how it is defined. Indeed, when I upgraded the definition of a "qualified" teacher, for instance, to include only those who held *both* a college major and a teaching certificate in the field, the amount of out-of-field teaching substantially increased. As illustrated in Fig. 7.2, almost half of those who taught math did not have both a major and a full certificate in math. This is an important finding because it reflects the primary definition of "highly qualified" teachers embedded in NCLB. Finally, it is important to also note that the actual numbers of students affected is not trivial. For example in 1999–2000 in each of the fields of English, math, and history, well over 4 million 7th- to 12th-grade-level students were taught by teachers with neither a major nor a minor in the field taught.

DO SCHOOLS VARY IN THEIR LEVELS OF OUT-OF-FIELD TEACHING?

The data also show that there are striking differences in the amount of out-of-field teaching across different types of schools. It is widely believed that the most needy students in the United States, those from poor and low-income communities, are often taught by the least qualified teachers. This, of course, is held up as a major reason why such students often perform poorly in educational assessments (e.g., Darling-Hammond, 1987; Haycock, 1998, 2000; Kozol, 1991; Oakes, 1990). The data show that, indeed, school poverty levels were clearly associated with the amount of out-of-field teaching. That is, in most fields, teachers in high-poverty schools were more likely to be out-of-field than are teachers in more affluent schools. For example, almost a third of social studies teachers in high-poverty schools, as opposed to 17% in low-poverty schools, did not have at least a minor in social studies or related disciplines (see Table 7.2).

More affluent schools are by no means, however, free of out-of-field teaching and, interestingly, school poverty is not the only, nor even the most important, school characteristic related to the degree of out-of-field teaching. Other important sources of variation for out-of-field teaching are school sector and school size. Small schools (less than 300 students) have higher levels of out-of-field teaching in each of the core academic fields than do larger schools (1,000 or more). This gap is especially striking in the private sector. Private schools appear to have both the highest and lowest levels of out-of-field teaching. On the one hand, large private schools have unusually low overall levels of out-of-field teaching. On the other hand, small private schools have among the highest overall levels of out-of-field teaching. It must also be noted that large private schools account for less than 10% of 7th- to 12th-grade-level private school teachers, whereas small private schools account for 47% of these teachers, and 80% of these private schools. This suggests there is a large degree of diversity, at least in regard to teacher qualifications, in the private sector, something often overlooked in the ongoing debate over public versus private schooling. Moreover, the finding that school size is related to the extent of underqualified teaching raises questions for the "small is beautiful" notion that is currently popular among many education researchers and policymakers. In this view large schools are more impersonal, alienated, inflexible, and bureaucratic, and hence have less sense of cohesion, belongingness, and community. The conclusion, from this viewpoint, is that large schools are less effective places for students to learn and grow (for a review, see Bryk, Lee, & Smith, 1990). These data suggest, however, that one possible disadvantage of smaller schools, often overlooked in the debates over the relative merits of small and large, is a greater degree of underqualified teaching. Small schools may find it more difficult to allow staff specialization and, as a result, teachers in these schools are more often required to be generalists, regardless of their background and training (Monk, 1987).

The data also show that the problem of out-of-field teaching is worse in the seventh and eighth grades than in 9th–12th grades. This is probably due to the fact that many seventh- to eighth-grade teachers are employed in middle schools. Some states require middle school teachers to hold an elementary-school-type certificate that emphasizes a broad background and does not require substantial specialization in any one subject. This may be adequate preparation for those teaching in self-contained elementary classes, where the teacher teaches multiple subjects to the same class of students all or most of the day. But this is probably inadequate preparation in middle schools where such teachers are assigned to teach subject matter courses to classes of different students all of most of the day, as if they were departmentalized secondary-level teachers.

HAS OUT-OF-FIELD TEACHING INCREASED OR DECREASED IN RECENT YEARS?

Despite all the reform efforts reviewed earlier, out-of-field teaching does not appear to be decreasing. Overall for the nation, levels of out-of-field teaching changed little from 1987 to 2000 (see Fig. 7.3). Indeed, at the national level the overall amount of out-of-field teaching slightly increased in several of the core academic subjects in the last half of the 1990s (from 1993–1994 to 1999–2000.) During this period substantial teacher quality reform was being implemented, but notably, the NCLB act was not yet in effect.

However, the data also show substantial differences among states during this period. Table 7.3 more closely examines changes in out-of-field teaching for each state from 1993–1994 to the end of the decade. It presents data on the percentage of 7th- to 12th-grade *classes* in the four core academic fields (math, English, science, and social studies) taught by teachers who did not have a minor or major in the field taught. This is a different measure of out-of-field teaching than that used in Table 7.2, which focused on teachers instead of classes. Because most of those who teach out of their fields do so for only part of the day, the Table 7.3 estimates of the percentages of classes are lower than the Table 7.2 estimates of the percentages of teach-

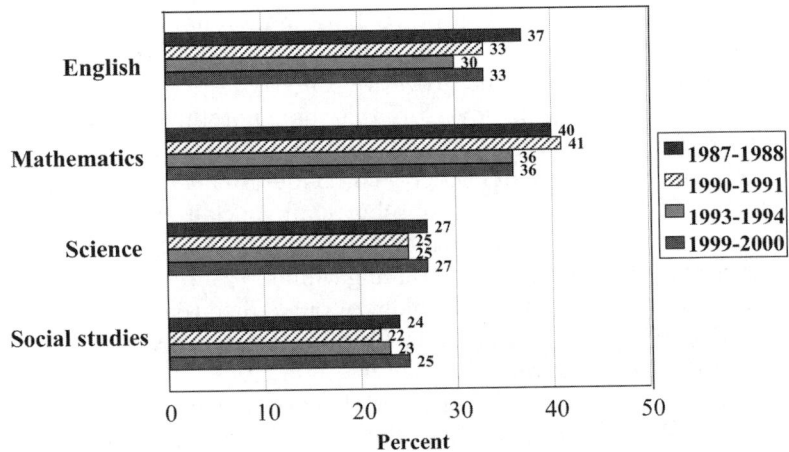

FIG. 7.3. Percentage of public school teachers in the core academic fields without a major or minor in the field, by year.

TABLE 7.3
Percentage of Public Grade 7–12 Classes in the Four Core Academic Fields
Taught by Teachers Without a Major or Minor in the Field, by Year and
State

	1993–1994	*1999–2000*
Nation	21.78	24.21*
Alabama	21.73	22.97
Alaska	30.80	29.44
Arizona	32.37	34.50
Arkansas	17.81	18.24
California	29.43	26.68
Colorado	19.11	20.05
Connecticut	13.49	27.31*
Delaware	29.01	37.45
District of Columbia	15.81	18.37
Florida	21.45	28.42*
Georgia	25.49	31.02
Hawaii	24.35	33.04
Idaho	21.82	26.22
Illinois	20.98	22.03
Indiana	17.23	12.99
Iowa	15.64	15.66
Kansas	22.12	19.51
Kentucky	29.47	31.68
Louisiana	29.63	40.15*
Maine	27.14	29.37
Maryland	20.71	22.33
Massachusetts	14.50	19.44
Michigan	19.66	20.44
Minnesota	10.01	7.28
Mississippi	26.71	30.03
Missouri	14.97	24.36*
Montana	19.96	20.47
Nebraska	15.46	15.49
Nevada	16.55	30.49*
New Hampshire	16.27	20.58
New Jersey	24.86	17.47*
New Mexico	23.15	35.17*
New York	13.12	18.11*
North Carolina	17.72	19.41
North Dakota	11.79	16.39
Ohio	25.30	30.08
Oklahoma	21.50	25.98
Oregon	28.51	26.05
Pennsylvania	20.82	22.22
Rhode Island	9.65	17.66
South Carolina	23.54	22.49

(Continued)

129

TABLE 7.3
(Continued)

	1993–1994	1999–2000
South Dakota	21.30	22.23
Tennessee	29.52	35.62
Texas	20.95	29.67*
Utah	17.16	19.37
Vermont	15.70	22.51
Virginia	26.60	28.37
Washington	26.94	26.03
West Virginia	21.54	30.38*
Wisconsin	27.14	13.68*
Wyoming	18.27	19.03

*Percentage differences from 1993–1994 to 1999–2000 were significant at $p < .05$.

ers. The classes measure is also the indicator that NCLB now requires states to report for schools.

Table 7.3 shows that in only 11 states did the proportion of out-of-field classes change over that period by a statistically significant amount (i.e., at a 95% level of confidence). For nine of those states, out-of-field teaching increased: Connecticut, Florida, Louisiana, Missouri, Nevada, New Mexico, New York, Texas, and West Virginia. For only two of those states did out-of-field teaching decrease: New Jersey and Wisconsin.

To be sure, there may have been improvements in states in the qualifications of teachers and teaching that are not captured by these data on out-of-field teaching. Moreover, the data in Table 7.3 do not separate the four core academic fields; small sample sizes made this determination difficult to assess with confidence. No doubt some states may have had improvements in some fields that are not captured here. But the data in Table 7.3 do indicate that most states during those years did not make any overall progress toward the goal of ensuring that our nation's 7th- to 12th-grade classrooms are all staffed with at least minimally qualified teachers, in this case defined as those staffed by teachers with at least a college minor in the subject taught. Note that this bar is lower than that sought by NCLB. This finding raises crucial questions: Why are so many teachers teaching subjects for which they have little background; why has contemporary education reform not alleviated this problem; and what are the prospects for NCLB doing so?

The next section turns to these questions. My objective is not to undertake a detailed look at why particular states fared better than others, but to examine the sources of out-of-field teaching and the limits of existing teacher policy.

WHY IS OUT-OF-FIELD TEACHING SO WIDESPREAD?

Typically, policymakers, commentators, and researchers have assumed two related explanations for the continuing problem of out-of-field teaching. One involves the adequacy of qualifications and preparation of teachers; the other involves the adequacy of the quantity of teachers produced. The first holds that out-of-field teaching is a problem of poorly prepared teachers. In this view, the preparation of teachers in college or university training programs, and as mandated by state certification standards, lacks adequate rigor, breadth, and depth, especially in academic and substantive coursework, resulting in high levels of out-of-field teaching (e.g., American Council on Education, 1999; Committee for Economic Development, 1996; Darling-Hammond, 1999; Soler, 1999; Toch, 1996). Proponents of this view often argue that the problem can be remedied by requiring prospective teachers to complete a "real" undergraduate major in an academic discipline. This view is certainly correct to point out serious shortcomings in many teacher preparation programs and in teacher certification standards, but these problems do not explain the practice of out-of-field teaching.

The SASS data indicate that most teachers do, in fact, hold college degrees and teaching certificates. Almost all public elementary and secondary school teachers in the United States have completed a 4-year college education. Ninety-nine percent of public school teachers hold at least a bachelor's degree and almost half hold a master's degree or higher. Moreover, as shown in Fig. 7.4, about 92% of public school teachers hold a regular or full

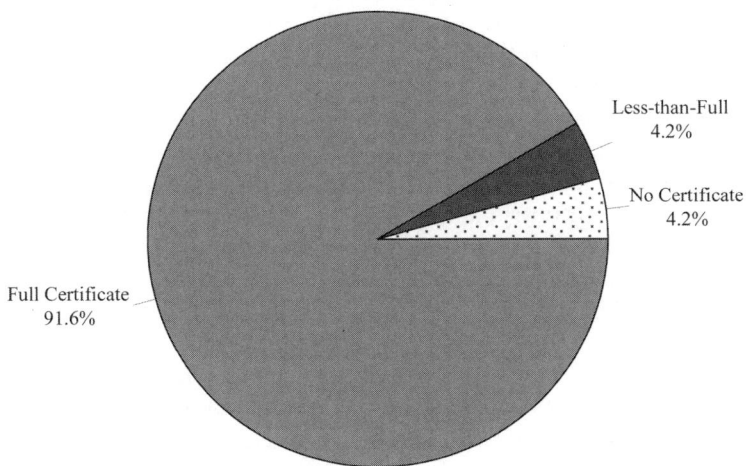

FIG. 7.4. Percentage of public school teachers, by type of certification, 1999–2000 (full includes advanced and probationary).

teaching certificate. Another 4% hold only a temporary, emergency, or provisional certificate. About 4% of public school teachers hold no teaching certificate of any type.

These latter data appear to conflict with conventional wisdom. In recent years, much attention has been focused on the plight of school districts, especially those serving low-income, urban communities, that have been forced to hire significant numbers of uncertified teachers to fill their teaching vacancies. The national data suggest, however, that the numbers of teachers without a full certificate actually represent only a small proportion of the K–12 public teaching force. In a workforce of almost 3 million, about 125,000 teachers have only a less-than-full certificate, and another 126,000 teachers have no certificate at all.

Many teachers, of course, have degrees in education, not academic degrees. Critics of teacher education have long argued that subject area education degrees, such as in math education, have tended to be overloaded with required courses in education to the neglect of coursework in the subject itself. Indeed, it is precisely because of such problems that many states have, over the past decade, upgraded teacher education by, among other things, requiring education majors to complete substantial coursework in an academic discipline (National Association of State Directors of Teacher Education and Certification, 1997). There is no question that the teaching force has benefited and can continue to benefit from higher standards of education and training.

However, this view confounds and confuses two different sources of the problem of underqualified teaching: teacher preservice education and teacher in-service assignment. The data show that those teaching out of field are typically veterans with an average of 14 years of teaching experience. About 45% of out-of-field teachers hold graduate degrees, but in disciplines other than the subjects in which they have been assigned to teach. At the secondary level, these misassignments typically involve one or two classes out of a normal daily schedule of five classes. Hence, out-of-field teachers are typically experienced and qualified individuals who have been assigned to teach part of their day in fields that do not match their training or education. This is a widespread and chronic phenomenon. The data show that each year some out-of-field teaching takes place in well over half of all U.S. secondary schools and each year over one fifth of the public 7th- to 12th-grade teaching force does some out-of-field teaching.

The key question thus becomes, why are so many teachers misassigned? In answer to this question, most observers and commentators have assumed that out-of-field teaching is a result of teacher shortages, the second of the two popular explanations of the source of out-of-field teaching. This view holds that shortfalls in the number of available qualified teachers, primarily due to increasing student enrollments and an aging teaching workforce, have forced many school systems to resort to lowering standards to fill teaching openings, the net effect of which is high levels of out-of-field teaching (see, e.g., NCTAF, 1996, 1997). This view seems to make sense, but the data show it is only partly true.

It is true that demand for teachers has increased in recent years. Since the mid-1980s, student enrollments have increased, the majority of schools have had job openings for teachers, and the size of the teacher workforce has increased. Most important, substantial numbers of schools do, indeed, report difficulties finding qualified candidates to fill their teaching openings (for a more detailed examination of the data on the teacher shortage, see Ingersoll, 2001, 2003a). These staffing difficulties are clearly a factor that contributes to out-of-field teaching.

There are, however, several problems with teacher shortages as an explanation for out-of-field teaching. First, shortages cannot explain the high levels of out-of-field teaching that exist in English and social studies, fields that have long been known to have teacher surpluses. Second, even when the rates of student enrollment increases were at their peak in the mid-1990s, not all schools experienced recruitment problems. The SASS data indicate that about half of all misassigned teachers in any given year were employed in schools that reported no difficulties whatsoever finding qualified candidates for their job openings that year. Indeed, in any given year much out-of-field teaching takes place in schools that did not even have any vacancies or openings for teachers in that year.

Some out-of-field teaching is no doubt unavoidable, but the data (see Table 7.2) also show that schools vary dramatically in how much out-of-field teaching they have. In a series of separate multivariate analyses designed to explore these school-to-school differences, I have found that the way schools are organized and teachers are managed accounts for as much of the problem of out-of-field teaching as do inadequacies in the supply of teachers. For example, I have found that, after controlling for school recruitment and hiring difficulties, and after controlling for school demographic characteristics, factors such as the quality of principal leadership, average class sizes, the character of the oversight of school hiring practices provided by the larger district, and the strategies schools use for teacher recruitment and hiring are all significantly related to the amount of out-of-field teaching in the school (Ingersoll, 2002b, 2004).

The data tell us that decisions concerning the hiring and selection of teachers and the allocation of teachers to course and program assignments are primarily the responsibility and prerogative of principals and other building-level school administrators (Ingersoll, 2003b). These administrators are charged with the often difficult task of providing an increasingly broad array of programs and courses with limited resources, limited time, a limited budget, and a limited teaching staff (Delany, 1991; Ruby, 1999). Some have argued that school managers have long faced a tension and gap between the expectations and demands placed on schools by state and federal governments and the time and resources provided to them (Kirst, 1984).

School principals not only have the responsibility for deciding who teaches which courses and programs, they also have an unusual degree of discretion in these decisions. Whereas teachers are subject to an elaborate array of state certification requirements designed to ensure their basic preparation and competence, there has been little regulation of how teachers are employed and utilized once on the job. Teacher employment regulations are weak or rarely enforced and most states routinely allow local school administrators to bypass even the limited requirements that do exist (*Education Week*, 2000, 2003; Robinson, 1985). In this context, assigning teachers to teach out of their fields is a useful and acceptable administrative practice.

Here are a few examples of decisions that principals may face. Rather than trying to find and hire a new science teacher to teach a newly state-mandated, but underfunded, science curriculum, a school principal may find it more convenient and cost-effective to assign a couple of English and social studies teachers to "cover" a section or two in science. If a teacher suddenly leaves in the middle of a semester, a principal may opt to hire a readily available, but not fully qualified and less expensive, substitute teacher, rather than to initiate a formal search for a new teacher. Similarly, when faced with the choice between hiring a fully qualified candidate for an English position and hiring a less-qualified candidate who is also willing to coach a major varsity sport, a principal may find it more expedient to do the latter. When faced with a tough choice between hiring an unqualified candidate for a science teacher position or doubling the class size of one of the fully qualified science teachers in the school, a principal might opt for the former. This results in a smaller class, but taught by a less-qualified teacher. If a full-time music teacher is under contract, but student enrollment is sufficient to fill only three music classes, the principal may find it both necessary and cost-effective in a given semester to assign the music teacher to teach two classes in English, in addition to the three classes in music, in order to employ the teacher for a regular full-time complement of five classes per semester. If a school has three full-time social studies teachers, but needs to offer 17 social studies courses, or the equivalent of 3.4 full-time positions, and also has four full-time English teachers, but needs to offer only 18 English courses, or the equivalent of 3.6 full-time positions, one solution would be to assign one of the English teachers to teach three English courses and two social studies courses.

All of these managerial choices to mis-assign teachers may save time and money for the school, and ultimately for the taxpayer, but they are not cost free and, moreover, with the advent of NCLB, they have become illegal.

WHAT ARE THE SOLUTIONS TO THE PROBLEM OF OUT-OF-FIELD TEACHING?

Understanding the reasons behind out-of-field teaching assignments is important because of their implications for solving the problem. As reviewed earlier, most recent federal, state, and local teacher policies and initiatives have focused on two general approaches to trying to ensure that all classrooms are staffed with qualified teachers: upgrading the qualifications of teachers and increasing the quantity of teachers. These kinds of initiatives are also emphasized in NCLB. The Title II portion of NCLB, for example, focuses on enhancing teacher in-service and preservice training and on teacher recruitment in its list of methods approved for funding.

Underlying these methods is what might be called a teacher deficit perspective. The assumption underlying this perspective is that the primary source of underqualified teachers in schools lies in deficits in teachers themselves: their numbers, preparation, knowledge, ability, licensing status, and so on. Upgrading teacher recruitment, preparation, and certification practices and requirements can, of course, be useful first steps. These methods do not, however, address the ways schools themselves contribute to the problem of underqualified teachers. The data tell us that solutions to the problem of out-of-field teaching must also look to how schools are managed and how teachers are utilized *once on the job.* In short, recruiting thousands of new candidates and providing them with rigorous preservice preparation or in-service professional development will not solve the problem if large numbers of such teachers continue to be assigned to teach subjects other than those for which they are well prepared. Indeed, if legislation such as NCLB results in increased accountability for teachers without commensurate changes in schools, it could lead to a classic problem of employees being blamed for things over which they have no control. This could end up exacerbating the very teacher quality and quantity problems that the legislation seeks to solve.

If assigning teachers to teach out of their fields has been a prevalent administrative practice for decades because it is more efficient and less expensive than the alternatives, then its elimination will not be easily accomplished simply by legislative fiat. In order to meet the goal of ensuring that all students are provided with qualified teachers, states will need to rethink how districts and schools go about managing their human resources.

One area that will need rethinking is how school staffing decisions are made and who makes them. The data tell us that teacher staffing decisions have traditionally followed a top-down command model: School principals make such decisions and teachers typically have little say over which courses they are assigned to teach (Ingersoll, 2003c). As the earlier examples illustrate, these staffing decisions often involve difficult trade-offs and sometimes lead to out-of-field teaching. In contrast, districts and schools could implement mechanisms of school-based management and distributed leadership where such decisions are shared with those who must live with, and may be held accountable for, the consequences: the faculty. Similarly, states could provide training and assistance to district and school administrators in how to better balance trade-offs among organizational, budgetary, *and* educational needs—the domain of instructional leadership.

Another area that will need rethinking concerns teacher employment practices. Meeting standards for qualified teachers will be more difficult in some settings than others. Rural school districts, for example, tend to have smaller secondary schools with smaller faculties. As a result, the data suggest, teachers in these schools are more often required to be generalists, teaching a variety of subjects regardless of their background. In these settings, states might consider the use of itinerant teachers, where schools could share the use of teachers with preparation in a specialty. This could include the employment of retired teachers. Similarly, states could fund technology in order to provide rural and hard-to-staff schools with electronic access to teachers with preparation in a specialty.

A third area that will need rethinking concerns the provision of administrative support for teachers. The data indicate that beginning teachers are more likely than veteran teachers to be given out-of-field assignments (Ingersoll, 1999). Disproportionately burdening newcomers probably contributes to the problem of high levels of beginning teacher attrition. Moreover, the data indicate that when teachers are mis-assigned they are largely left to their own devices. Where it is difficult to entirely eliminate out-of-field teaching, districts could prohibit out-of-field assignments for new teachers, provide funding for additional coursework for mis-assigned teachers, or provide funding for veteran teachers to mentor, assist, or team teach with mis-assigned teachers.

The aforementioned strategies can help states and districts ensure that all classes are staffed with qualified teachers. Ultimately, however, long-term solutions to these issues will require addressing the underlying systemic roots of the problem. Problems of teacher quality and quantity—inadequate preparation, low certification standards, teacher mis-assignment, teacher recruitment and retention difficulties—are not new to this occupation, and to some extent, can all be traced to a common root: the low stature and standing of the teaching occupation. Unlike many European and Asian nations, in this country elementary and secondary school teaching has been largely treated as semiskilled work since the development of public school system in the late 19th century (Etzioni, 1969; Lortie, 1975; Tyack, 1974).

The comparison with traditional professions is stark. Few would allow cardiologists to deliver babies, real estate lawyers to defend criminal cases, chemical engineers to design bridges, or sociology professors to teach English. This also applies for the high-skill blue-collar occupations as well; for example, few would hire an electrician to solve a plumbing problem. The commonly held assumption is that such traditional male-dominated occupations and professions require a great deal of expertise and that specialization is therefore necessary. In short, for well-paid, well-respected professions and occupations, it is rarely acceptable to lower standards as a coping mechanism.

In contrast, despite a wealth of research establishing that high-quality elementary and secondary teaching is highly complex work, the teaching occupation has never been granted commensurate stature and standing. Underlying out-of-field teaching, it appears, is the assumption that female-dominated, precollegiate school teaching requires far less skill, training, and expertise than traditional professions, and, that it is therefore appropriate to treat teachers like interchangeable blocks. The larger challenge is clear: Upgrading the quality of teaching in the long term requires that we begin now upgrading the quality of the teaching job and occupation.

ACKNOWLEDGMENTS

This chapter draws from research supported by a grant from the Center for the Study of Teaching and Policy under the Educational Research and Development Centers Program, PR/Award R308B970003, as administered by the National Institute on Educational Governance, Finance, Policymaking and Management, Office and Educational Research and Improvement, U.S. Department of Education. See Ingersoll (2003b) for an earlier report of this research. Opinions reflect those of the author and do not necessarily reflect those of the granting agencies. Thanks are due to Gema Barkanic for help with the data analysis. Thanks also are due to Mary Kennedy and Susanna Loeb for helpful comments on earlier versions of this analysis.

REFERENCES

American Council on Education. (1999). *To touch the future: Transforming the way teachers are taught.* Washington, DC: Author.

Bandeira de Mello, V., & Broughman, S. (1996). *SASS by state.* Washington, DC: U.S. Department of Education, National Center for Education Statistics.

Bidwell, C. (1965). The school as a formal organization. In J. March (Ed.), *Handbook of organizations* (pp. 973–1002). Chicago: Rand McNally.

Bobbitt, S., & McMillen, M. (1995). *Qualifications of the public school teacher workforce.* Washington, DC: National Center for Education Statistics.

Bryk, A., Lee, V., & Smith, J. (1990). High school organization and its effects on teachers and students: An interpretive summary of the research. In W. H. Clune & J. F. Witte (Eds.), *Choice and control in American education: Vol. 1. The theory of choice and control in education* (pp. 135–226). New York: Falmer Press.

Chaney, B. (1994). *The accuracy of teachers self reports on their postsecondary education.* Washington, DC: U.S. Department of Education, National Center for Education Statistics.

Choy, S., Bobbitt, S., Henke, R., Medrich, E., Horn, L., &. Lieberman, J. (1993). *Schools and staffing in the U.S.: A statistical profile, 1990–91.* Washington, DC: National Center for Education Statistics.

Committee for Economic Development. (1996). *American workers and economic change.* New York: Author.

Conant, J. (1963). *The education of American teachers.* New York: McGraw-Hill.

Darling-Hammond, L. (1987). Teacher quality and equality. In P. Keating & J. I. Goodlad (Eds.), *Access to knowledge* (pp. 237–258). New York: College Entrance Examination Board.

Darling-Hammond, L. (1999). *Teacher quality and student achievement: A review of state policy evidence.* Seattle: Center for the Study of Teaching and Policy, University of Washington.

Delany, B. (1991). Allocation, choice and stratification within high schools: How the sorting machine copes. *American Journal of Education, 99*(2), 181–207.

Education Trust. (1996, 1998). *Education watch.* Washington, DC: American Association for Higher Education.

Education Trust. (1998). *Education watch.* Washington, DC: American Association for Higher Education.

Education Week. (1997). *Quality counts: A report card on the condition of public education in the 50 states.* Washington, DC: Author.

Education Week. (1998). *Quality counts: A report card on the condition of public education in the 50 states.* Washington, DC: Author.

Education Week. (2000). *Quality counts: A report card on the condition of public education in the 50 states.* Washington, DC: Author.

Education Week. (2003, January). *Quality counts '03: "If I can't learn from you. . . ".* Washington, DC: Author.

Etzioni, A. (1969). *The semi-professions and their organization: Teachers, nurses and social workers.* New York: The Free Press.

Greenberg, E., Rhodes, D., Ye, Xioalan, & Stancavage, F. (2004). *Prepared to teach: Teacher preparation and student achievement in 8th grade mathematics.* Paper presented at the American Educational Research Association Annual Meeting, San Diego.

Greenwald, R., Hedges, L., & Laine, R. (1996). The effect of school resources on student achievement. *Review of Educational Research, 66,* 361–396.

Haggstrom, G. W., Darling-Hammond, L., & Grissmer, D. (1988). *Assessing teacher supply and demand.* Santa Monica, CA: RAND Corporation.

Haycock, K. (1998). Good teaching matters . . . a lot. *Thinking K–16: A Publication of the Education Trust, 3*(2), 3–14.

Haycock, K. (2000). No more settling for less. *Thinking K–16: A Publication of the Education Trust, 4*(1), 3–12.

Henke, R., Choy, S., Chen, X., Geis, S., & Alt, M. (1997). *America's teachers: Profile of a profession, 1993–94.* Washington, DC: National Center for Education Statistics.

Hirsch, E, Koppich, J., & Knapp, M. (2001). *Revisiting what states are doing to improve the quality of teaching: An update on patterns and trends.* Seattle: Center for the Study of Teaching and Policy, University of Washington.

Ingersoll, R. (1999). The problem of underqualified teachers in American secondary schools. *Educational Researcher, 28*(2), 26–37.

Ingersoll, R. (2001). Teacher turnover and teacher shortages: An organizational analysis. *American Educational Research Journal, 38*(3), 499–534.

Ingersoll, R. (2002a). *Measuring out-of-field teaching.* Unpublished manuscript.

Ingersoll, R. (2002b). *Out-of-field teaching, educational inequality and the organization of schools: An exploratory analysis.* Seattle: Center for the Study of Teaching and Policy, University of Washington.

Ingersoll, R. (2003a). *Is there really a teacher shortage?* Seattle: Center for the Study of Teaching and Policy, University of Washington.

Ingersoll, R. (2003b). *Out-of-field teaching and the limits of teacher policy.* Seattle: Center for the Study of Teaching and Policy, University of Washington.

Ingersoll, R. (2003c). *Who controls teachers' work?: Power and accountability in America's schools.* Cambridge, MA: Harvard University Press.

Ingersoll, R. (2004). Why some schools have more underqualified teachers than others. In D. Ravitch (Ed.), *Brookings papers on education policy* (pp. 45–88). Washington, DC: Brookings Institution.

Kirst, M. (1984). *Who controls our schools?: American values in conflict.* New York: Freeman.

Kohn, M., & Schooler. C. (1983). *Work and personality.* Norwood, NJ: Ablex.

Kozol, J. (1991). *Savage inequalities.* New York: HarperCollins.

Lewis, L., Parsad, B., Carey, N., Bartfai, N., Farris, E., Smerdon, B., & Greene, B. (1999). *Teacher quality: A report on the preparation and qualifications of public school teachers.* Washington, DC: National Center for Education Statistics.

Lortie, D. (1975). *School teacher.* Chicago: University of Chicago Press.

McMillen, M,. Gruber, K., Henke, R., McGrath, D., &. Cohen, B. A. (2002, August). *Qualifications of the public school teacher workforce: Prevalence of out-of-field teaching 1987–88 to 1999–2000.* Washington, DC: National Center for Education Statistics.

Monk, D. (1987). Secondary school size and curriculum comprehensiveness. *Economics of Education Review, 6*(2), 137–150.

National Association of State Directors of Teacher Education and Certification. (1997). *Manual on certification and preparation of educational personnel in the United States and Canada.* Centralia, WA: Author.

National Commission on Teaching and America's Future. (1996). *What matters most: Teaching for America's future.* New York: Author

National Commission on Teaching and America's Future. (1997). *Doing what matters most: Investing in quality teaching.* New York: Author.

Oakes, J. (1990). *Multiplying inequalities: The effects of race, social class, and tracking on opportunities to learn mathematics and science.* Santa Monica, CA: RAND Corporation.

Pascarella, E., & Terenzini, P. (1991). *How college affects students: Findings and insights from twenty years of research.* San Francisco: Jossey-Bass.

Raudenbush, S., Fotiu, R., & Cheong, Y. (1999). Synthesizing results from the trial state assessment. *Journal of Educational and Behavioral Statistics, 24*(4), 413–438.

Robinson, V. (1985). *Making do in the classroom: A report on the misassignment of teachers.* Washington, DC: Council for Basic Education and American Federation of Teachers.

Ruby, A. (1999, April). *An implementable curriculum approach in improving science instruction in urban schools.* Paper presented at the annual meeting of the American Educational Research Association, Montreal.

Shanker, A. (1985, October 27). Education's dirty little secret. *New York Times,* p. E9.

Shulman, L. (1986). Those who understand: Knowledge growth in teaching. *Educational Researcher, 15,* 4–14.

Soler, S. (1999). *Teacher quality is job one: Why states need to revamp teacher certification.* Washington DC: Progressive Policy Institute.

Toch, T. (1996, February 26). Why teachers don't teach: How teacher unions are wrecking our schools. *U.S. News and World Report,* pp. 62–71.

Townsend, R., Cobb, C., Moirs, K., & McIntire, W. (1997). *The status of teaching in Maine: A policy inventory.* Orono: Education Policy Research Institute, University of Maine.

Tryneski, J. (1997). *Requirements for certification of teachers, counselors, librarians, administrators for elementary and secondary schools.* Chicago: University of Chicago Press.

Tyack, D. (1974). *The one best system.* Cambridge, MA: Harvard University Press.

Wang, A., Coleman, A., Coley, R., & Phelps, R. (2003). *Preparing teachers around the world.* Princeton, NJ: Educational Testing Service.

8

No Teacher Left Behind: Issues of Equity and Teacher Quality

Gloria Ladson-Billings

University of Wisconsin–Madison

As the President and Congress promise to "Leave No Child Behind," many young people across LA County lack access to the most fundamental precondition of learning—a quality teacher. In 448 LA County schools, at least 30% of the teachers are uncredentialed. At some schools, the figures are far worse: 52% uncredentialed at 116th St in LAUSD, 65% uncredentialed at Abbott Elementary in Lynwood and 85% uncredentialed at Francis Willard Elementary in Compton. It is no coincidence, that these four schools serve low-income communities of color. Schools with high levels of uncredentialed teachers are concentrated in LA County's poorest communities.

—John Rogers, Associate Director of IDEA

EAST LANSING, Mich. — While Michigan has a high-quality teaching force, high-quality teachers are not equally available in all schools, especially those in urban areas or with high percentages of poor and minority students, according to a report released today by the Education Policy Center at Michigan State University.

ARLINGTON, VA, MARCH 27, 2003 — More than 11 million children—one in four students—attend urban schools in which many of their teachers need help providing high-quality science instruction.

—NSTA Pressroom

Jenny Stockard[1] *is a young woman teaching mathematics in an urban middle school. In her former job Jenny was a program analyst for a high-technology company. Unfortunately, the rapid downturn in the industry and subsequent economic recession made it difficult for Jenny to find an equivalent job in either her area or at other companies. As her severance package and unemployment benefits became depleted, one of Jenny's friends suggested that she apply for a job in the city's public schools. "But I'm not qualified to teach," she insisted. "So what," remarked her friend. "These urban schools are so desperate that anybody with a pulse can get a job. Besides how much do you have to know to teach a bunch of city kids? As long as you keep them quiet and don't allow them to kill each other no one will really hassle you. The pay's not that great but at least you'll have health insurance, short workdays, a long summer, and you won't lose your condo."*

Jenny's friend was right about how easy it was to get hired at her local school district. When she indicated that she was a computer science major with a minor in mathematics she was immediately offered a position as a mathematics teacher at one of the middle schools. However her friend was wrong about the nature of the work. The school principal expected her to teach the students well enough to successfully pass a high-stakes mathematics test. Most of her students came to her with huge skills deficits in mathematics and Jenny had no idea of where to begin. She relied heavily on the textbook and tried to teach the students the way she remembered her middle school math classes. She lectured (although few students paid attention), worked a few problems, and assigned homework. Within a week Jenny recognized that most of the students were not doing the homework. In several of her classes students spent the entire hour with their heads down on the desk sleeping. Others talked with their friends or listened to their Walkmen (which was against school rules). Jenny could not imagine how it would be possible to ensure that all of the students passed the district's mathematics test.

The "Jenny Stockard" story replicates itself throughout the nation, particularly in those schools serving poor students, students of color, and immigrant students. Thus teacher quality becomes an equity issue. Which students have access to quality teachers? What are some of the factors that predict teacher quality? How do we make sense of school reform designed for all students but realistically achievable by some?

The reauthorization of the Elementary and Secondary Education Act (ESEA) has been titled the No Child Left Behind Act of 2001 (NCLB). Provisions of the act call for increased accountability, school choice, state and local flexibility in funding and resource allocation, and increased emphasis on reading. Some of the other provision changes include class-size reduction and improving teacher quality. The provision on teacher quality is the focus of this discussion.

---

[1]This is a pseudonym.

According to the Executive Summary of the legislation, the U.S. Department of Education (2002) seeks to improve teacher quality through state grants "that focus on using practices grounded in scientifically based research to prepare, train, and recruit high-quality teachers." Furthermore, this portion of the legislation "gives States and LEAs flexibility to select the strategies that best meet their particular needs for improved teaching that will help them raise achievement in the core academic subjects." I would argue that this legislation allows space for educators to entertain a perspective that leaves no *teacher* behind. No matter how much effort we say we are putting into raising student achievement and improving the academic lives of students, if we ignore the salient role that teachers play in educating students, we cannot claim to be serious about educational reform.

In its 1996 report, *What Matters Most: Teaching for America's Future,* the National Commission on Teaching and America's Future (NCTAF) argued that there exist several barriers to ensuring that every public school student be in a classroom with a highly qualified teacher. These barriers include:

- Low expectations for student performance.
- Unenforced standards for teachers.
- Major flaws in teacher preparation.
- Slipshod teacher recruitment.
- Inadequate induction for beginning teachers.
- Lack of professional development and reward for knowledge and skill.
- Schools structured for failure rather than success.

In this chapter I use the NCTAF stated barriers as a template to discuss how each raises equity questions about teacher quality. For the purposes of this chapter, equity refers to "equality of access to and opportunities for meaningful, authentic learning experiences, which are inclusive of learners from diverse background, which are relevant to learners" (Grant & Ladson-Billings, 1997, p. 103).

LOW EXPECTATION FOR STUDENT PERFORMANCE

According to Good and Brophy (2000), teacher expectation effects are the result of differential interactions with students according to beliefs held about the students. Several researchers (Pajares, 1992; Wigfield, Galper, Denton, & Seefeldt, 1999) argue that teachers' beliefs about students influence how they ultimately behave toward them. These expectations color the interactions teachers have with students and determine instructional outcomes. When teachers' expectations toward students are low, these expectations negatively impact achievement (Brophy, 1985). One might assume that low teacher expectations are randomly distributed throughout the teaching population. Unfortunately, the evidence from 16 studies suggests that teachers regularly had higher expectations for White students than for African American students (Baron, Tom, & Cooper, 1985). Thus, status characteristics such as race, class, gender, and language impact teachers' expectations toward students.

Good and Brophy (1990) assert that:

> Expectations tend to be self-sustaining. They affect both *perception,* by causing teachers to be alert for what they expect and less likely to notice what they do not expect, and *interpretation,* by causing teachers to interpret (and perhaps distort) what they see so that it is consistent with their expectations. Some expectations persist even though they do not coincide with the facts. (p. 441)

In his classic study, Rist (1970) reported that without any objective data a kindergarten teacher made decisions about ability grouping for her students within days of their arrival in her class. Rist observed that all of the children in the lowest group were from single-parent households and received Aid to Families of Dependent Children (AFDC, or welfare). Ray surmised that assignment to ability groups was made based solely on the teacher's assessment of the children's economic resources. This assignment to ability groups would not be so pernicious if the teacher did not subsequently act as if the students belonged in the groups. Rist reported that the teacher seated the low group farther away from her and spent much less time instructing them. By the end of the year, this lack of instruction resulted in lower performance that validated the teacher's initial expectation for the students.

Students' sense of their own knowledge and abilities is tied to their perception of how capable they think teachers and other significant adults believe them to be. Do they have teachers who fail to push them intellectually and who attempt to keep them busy with mindless worksheets and activities? Or, do they have teachers who understand that students are learners who come to school with knowledge and that knowledge must be challenged, extended, and incorporated into the classroom?

Generally speaking, teachers who teach in communities serving middle- to upper-middle-class students come to their work believing that their students are capable of learning whatever they have to teach them. When the students struggle, these teachers assume that there is something wrong with the material or the way they are teaching it. They do not assume that the students cannot learn or are not "ready" to learn (Graue, 1993). Their teachers, their parents, and their peers communicate high expectations for these students. "Gifted and talented," advanced-placement, and honors programs are good examples of programs where high expectations are implicit.

Cohen's (1994) research indicated that student status characteristics (e.g., race, class, gender) created a sense of expectations that became a generalized set of expectations concerning students' academic abilities and behavior. Middle-class, White female students are expected to be docile, compliant, and good readers; working-class and poor African American male students are expected to be aggressive, belligerent, and low performers. In an incident in my local community, a middle-class White middle school male student was suspended for bringing a knife to school. The student argued that the knife was a part of his science project, but the school district's strict "zero tolerance" policy did not make exceptions for educational uses for anything designated as a weapon. The student's parents took the school district to court, which permitted the news media to present aspects of the case to the public. Repeatedly, the student was referred to as an "honor student" although his academic record was irrelevant to the weapons policy. Ultimately, the boy was reinstated and a number of parents of children of color who were suspended for the same infraction had their children's suspensions overturned. The minority parents' argument was that the White student's academic excellence could not be the mitigating factor in his suspension. This is an extreme example of the way expectations shape possibilities for students. We could not possibly expect an honor student to have a sinister motive in bringing a weapon to school, but our expectations lead us to surmise that the poor students of color who bring weapons create a clear and present danger.

UNENFORCED TEACHER STANDARDS

Despite all of the recent attention and efforts toward standards-based school reform, the place where the standards movement falls flat is in regulating teacher performance, particularly regulating it in schools serving poor children of color and immigrant children. A number of structural issues are responsible for the problem of unenforced teacher standards. Individual states define standards for teachers in their jurisdictions. Thus, what the standards are depend on where you are. Unlike medicine, which is governed by the American Medical Association, or law, which is governed by the American Bar Association, state legislatures and/or state departments of public instruction regulate teacher certification. What it means to be a teacher in a particular state may reflect the specific needs and idiosyncrasies of a state or local educational agency. The pattern is that in poor school districts teacher standards tend to be relaxed because of the difficulty in finding enough teachers.

According to *Education Week*'s Ansell and McCabe (2003), "students in high-poverty, high-minority, and low-performing schools are less likely than other pupils to be taught by teachers trained in their subjects, and few states and districts have designed specific policy strategies to close the gap." They point out that although many states and districts have instituted efforts to attract and retained skilled teachers, few of these efforts focus on matching well-qualified teachers with high-need schools.

Although states and school districts are demanding that students meet higher academic standards, they do not always demand those same standards for teachers. In the most recent Schools and Staffing Survey (SASS) data that were released by the U.S. Department of Education on May 31, 2002, during the 1999–2000 school year 58% of middle school students were learning English from teachers without a major or credential in that subject, and 57% were learning science from similarly underqualified teachers. Seventy-one percent of the middle school teachers teaching history, 61% of foreign-language teachers, and 69% of the mathematics teachers in the middle school were also underqualified. Out-of-field teaching also occurs at the high school but the problem is not as acute as it is in the middle school (Gewertz, 2002).

The data suggest that schools in urban districts are twice as likely to hire teachers who have no license or only an emergency or temporary license (*Education Week,* 1998). These same schools have a *teacher* absentee rate that is twice that of their nonurban counterparts. Secondary schools in urban districts have teaching vacancy rates in mathematics, physical sciences, and biology of 44%, 35%, and 32%, respectively. Urban districts with a poverty rate of 50% or greater have 45% of their mathematics teachers who do not have a college major or minor in mathematics. Urban eighth graders are about twice as likely as nonurban eighth graders to attend schools where at least one teacher leaves before the end of the school year (*Education Week,* 1998).

This lack of teacher quality control makes it nearly impossible for states and school districts to hold teachers to rigorous standards. The fact that unqualified and underqualified teachers are overrepresented in schools serving poor children of color and immigrant children clearly make unenforced teacher standards an equity issue.

MAJOR FLAWS IN TEACHER PREPARATION

One of the first access points for improving teaching quality is in the initial preparation of teachers. The majority of teachers are prepared in the 1,300 colleges and universities across the nation. Here schools, colleges, and departments of education take responsibility for recruiting, preparing, and recommending candidates for state certification and/or licensure. With these many programs, one might expect there to be tremendous variation between and among teacher preparation programs. Surprisingly, there is not. When I work with school districts I often show them a slide that outlines teacher preparation. The slide includes the following data:

- General education (30+ liberal studies course credits).
- Major (30+ upper-division courses in a field of study).
- Minor (20+ upper-division courses in another field of study).
- Professional-education coursework.
  - Foundation courses.
  - Methods courses.
  - Field experiences (practica, student teaching).

I then ask the audience members if this pattern of preparation seems familiar. Typically most of the teachers and administrators nod in agreement. Then I share with them that the course-taking pattern is taken directly from my own transcript and I began teaching in 1968! My point, of course, is that we have failed to make substantive changes in the way we prepare teachers, yet we assume this preparation is adequate and appropriate for school students of the 21st century.

Teacher education has at least three leverage points that can and should be considered to improve teacher quality—admissions, pre–student teaching, and certification. I discuss each briefly to explain how they might serve as quality monitors.

Admissions. Both the Holmes Group report (1990) and the Carnegie Forum report (1986) lamented the poor academic quality of people choosing to go into teaching. These reports indicated that teaching as a profession failed to draw the best and the brightest minds and without better (i.e., brighter) people entering the field, it was impossible to improve our schools. I want to argue that this focus on the so-called best and brightest is limited, at least from the perspective of ensuring high-quality teachers in schools serving the nation's poor, children of color, and immigrant children. If we are using test scores and grade point averages as proxies or evidence of teacher quality, we are likely to miss the opportunity to draw from a deep reservoir of experience and wisdom that potential candidates without the highest test scores (and grades) may have. For instance, at one top school of education, the elementary teacher education candidates have extremely high grade point averages. They earn those grade point averages by failing to challenge themselves intellectually. They regularly select those courses that will help them boost their grade point averages while shunning more academically rigorous courses. Although the school can boast of its students' high grade points, there is no evidence that these students are any better prepared to teach in urban classrooms than students with lower grade point averages.

Schools, colleges, and departments of education can develop a different admissions rubric to "construct a class" similar to the ways selective colleges and universities construct a freshman class. Admissions committees might argue that they do not want a teacher education program composed solely of female, monolingual English, geographically local, White students. In building their teacher education programs, teacher educators can begin to look for students with experiences in the communities they hope their graduates will serve. Whereas teacher education reforms such as the Interstate New Teacher Assessment and Support Consortium (INTASC) argue that we must assess teachers' dispositions (which assumes that teacher education programs foster such dispositions), it is more reasonable that teacher education programs should screen and select for candidates who already possess the dispositions they seek.

Unfortunately, in far too many of the colleges and universities that serve large numbers of working-class students and students of color (i.e., state and regional colleges, historically Black colleges and universities, Latino-serving institutions, Tribal colleges), fewer students are showing an interest in becoming teachers. Thus, many of the teacher education programs in these schools are struggling to survive. In a political economy that favors high technology and science, smaller and more regionally based schools garner additional dollars by showcasing academic programs such as engineering, computer sciences, natural sciences, and life sciences. Teacher education programs rarely attract large external grants and are wholly dependent on student tuition (especially from full-time students) to survive. College students from poor and working-class backgrounds often choose more financially lucrative professions—medicine, law, and business—over teaching.

Clearly, there have been alternative programs developed to address the equity issues inherent in program admissions. These programs tend to be small and funded on soft money—grants or gifts. Some of these programs recruit current paraprofessionals, instructional aides, or community members to finish college degrees and earn teacher certification. Others seek to encourage career changers to choose teaching and still others offer loan and tuition forgiveness to those who will agree to teach in urban schools serving poor and working-class students. Each of these approaches is admirable, but none reflects a comprehensive strategy to the teacher education admissions problem.

Pre–Student Teaching. Just prior to teacher education students' completing their certification program, there is an opportunity to evaluate how ready they might be for the final phase of preparation. Most teacher education programs include earlier opportunities for field experiences but student teaching is a legal designation somewhat akin to an internship. In most cases, students who have successfully passed the prerequisite courses are given an opportunity to do student teaching. This could, however, be a more rigorously monitored transition in which teacher educators and practicing teachers make assessments as to how prepared students are to continue toward certification. The difficulty of this process is compounded by the fact that chronic teacher shortages in urban (and rural) schools mean that teacher education programs cannot afford to deny many candidates the opportunity to do student teaching and to proceed to certification.

In an ideal situation, however, this junction of the preparation program would be an important place to make a judgment about the worthiness of a teacher education candidate to continue on to certification and licensure. The fact that preservice teachers have successfully mastered coursework does not necessarily indicate that they are ready for the responsibility of classroom teaching. Most teacher education programs include some form of modified field experience prior to student teaching and these field experiences should be carefully evaluated to determine whether or not students can handle the added responsibility that student teaching brings.

One useful analogy to the student teaching experience is the medical internship. Medical schools accept a select group of students; after a rigorous training, medical students compete for internships. Placing student teachers is much less rigorous and systematic. Teacher education staffs attempt to match students with appropriate teachers and classrooms according to the certification they are seeking. Some programs insist that at least one of the field experiences take place in a classroom serving diverse groups of students. How that "diversity" is defined varies greatly across programs. It can refer to race, class, language, and/or disability. Student teachers often operate in a "sellers' market" in which cooperating teachers can decide whether to participate in the preparation program and the quality of those cooperating teachers is not guaranteed. The need for field experience placements can be so great that any available classroom becomes a place where several preservice teachers compete to practice. If teacher educators could assure cooperating teachers that all students designated as student teachers were indeed ready to student teach, perhaps programs could be more selective in their placement.

Certification. The culmination of the teacher education preparation program is certification. This process typically means that a teacher education program is prepared to recommend a student to the state's credentialing authority where the candidate applies for her license. Students who master their coursework and student teaching can expect to receive their certification. This process is typically *pro forma*. After completing all course and program requirements, students work with teacher education staff and state personnel to complete the paperwork and apply for their license. This process should also be more carefully monitored and controlled. Teacher educators could make assessments about the totality of the teacher education experience and decide whether teacher candidates were ready for certification and licensure.

A number of teacher education programs have migrated to standards-based programs in which students must demonstrate mastery of program competencies or standards. This demonstration often takes the form of a performance or portfolio (actual or electronic) where teacher education students can showcase their knowledge and skills. Teacher educators can use the portfolio evidence to support their decisions about certification. It is also possible for teacher educators to depart from the usual pass–fail rubric to a more graduated assessment that provides a tiered certificate (e.g., full certificate, partial certificate, limited certificate, not certified). New teachers hired with less than a full certificate could be hired at a lower salary and guaranteed up to 2 years of support to bring their certificates up to full certification.

I have offered these monitoring points (admissions, student teaching, and certification) to suggest that teacher education programs could do a much better job of deciding who is qualified to teach. We could move away from factory-like preparation programs that take in a cohort of students, move them lockstep through courses and field experiences, and in the end declare them all certified to teach. The point of increasing the monitoring is to stem the tide of increased attrition among new teachers (Ingersoll, 2002).

The equity issue that emerges from inadequate teacher preparation is that schools serving poor and immigrant students and students of color often must accept those teachers who may have performed marginally in their preparation programs. New teachers who "barely made it" through a teacher education program are unlikely to be prepared to serve the nation's neediest students, yet these are exactly the teachers who end up in urban (and rural) classrooms. Suburban schools serving middle- and upper-middle-class students can be much more selective in their hiring and can siphon off the best teacher candidates from the most prestigious teacher education programs.

SLIPSHOD TEACHER RECRUITMENT

When major corporations look to hire new professionals, they target colleges and universities they believe produce the kind of potential employee that will help them meet their corporate goals. They alert the placement offices, set up interview schedules, and meet with prospective recruits. Rarely do corporations hire people who have slipped a résumé over the transom. They know whom they want and they go out to search for them. As a part of their search, corporations lay out their mission and future direction. They are explicit about what they are looking for, and they are interested in what potential employees want to do with their careers. The newly hired corporate employee is likely to sit down with their manager or the human resources director to map out a 5-year plan and the corporation works with the employee to meet his or her goals. This strategy of recruiting and hiring virtually is unheard of in the hiring of teachers.

When teacher education graduates look for jobs they often go to job fairs or send letters of inquiry to school districts that interest them or to those that advertise job openings. No elaborate recruiting takes place at the university (except in cases where school districts are experiencing acute shortages). The typical new teacher has an interview with a personnel director in a big-city school district or with a principal in a smaller district. She is treated as if the job she accepts is the job she will remain in until retirement. There is no thought given to what her future plans may be and job advancement is left solely to the individual teacher.

A RAND Corporation study (Wise, Darling-Hammond, & Berry, 1987) found that many school districts do not hire the most qualified applicants for teaching positions because their own bureaucracies and procedures prevent them from doing so. Their recruitment is uncoordinated, the screening process is cumbersome, the applicants are treated unprofessionally, and the timing of the hiring decisions can be delayed until the school year begins (or later).

Three telling examples of recruitment suggest that schools are ill prepared to hire the teachers they need. In a well-regarded school district in the upper Midwest, the school district had an aggressive campaign to recruit African American teachers. The district sent a recruiter to historically Black colleges and universities throughout the South. The teachers who were recruited had a difficult time adjusting to the weather, the culture, and the customs of the community. Little or no thought was given to recruiting within major urban centers in the Midwest where many urban campuses also serve a number of African American teacher education students. In a California district, a superintendent who was desperate to recruit more Spanish-speaking teachers began a program to bring teachers from Spain. By the end of the first semester, more than half of the Spanish teachers had quit and returned to Spain. When the superintendent was asked why she recruited Spanish teachers over Mexican-American or Mexican (or other Latin American teachers) she replied that she had not considered that there were enough "educated" Mexicans to assume teaching positions. In New York City, one district decided to recruit teachers from Ireland. Like the California experiment with the teachers from Spain, many of these teachers gave up before the year's end.

To be sure, I am not indicting teachers from international contexts. Some of the most successful professional-development activities rely on cross-cultural teacher exchanges. However, these experiments are almost always tried in schools serving our neediest students. The students in these schools can ill afford time for a teacher to master the language, the culture, and the system before she can teach them. Such teachers should be recruited to teach in ideal settings where their pedagogical expertise is supported by stable communities and experienced colleagues.

INADEQUATE INDUCTION FOR BEGINNING TEACHERS

The statement I make to preservice teacher education students with whom I work is "No matter what we do with you in this program, when you finish, you will be a beginner." The concept of beginning is poorly understood in teaching. The failure to understand how to induct and support new professionals into teaching is one of the major shortcomings of the field. In its most recent report, *No Dream Denied,* the NCTAF (2003) asserts that, "the real school staffing problem is teacher retention. Our inability to support high quality teaching in many of our schools is driven not by too few teachers entering the profession, but by too many leaving for other jobs" (p. 6). The most prized jobs in education typically go to teachers who have the most seniority in the system. Thus, new teachers often are left to fend for themselves in some of the most difficult classroom situations. Although this may be a fairly common practice, the way this practice manifests itself results in inequities.

School districts serving middle- to upper-middle-class communities are more likely to have stable teaching and administrative staffs. Turnover in these schools results from predictable (and manageable) attrition—retirement, relocation, death. Thus, few upper-middle-class communities experience huge turnover in any one year, and they are less likely to have to provide extensive amounts of new-teacher support. The ability to work in an environment with many experienced professionals can also provide new teachers with ready support through the informal networks that evolve in a school (see Rosenholtz, 1990).

New teachers who begin careers in poorly resourced schools find themselves in environments where many of their colleagues are new or inexperienced. Thus, the pressure on the system to assist new teachers generally exceeds the ability of the system to respond. New teachers are expected to manage the classroom, learn a new curriculum, and assimilate a great deal of system-specific knowledge (e.g., attendance forms, rules, district policies, and many other particular norms and folkways). In an environment where many teachers are new there is a lack of institutional history and coherence in the programming.

During the 1980s many states instituted programs to support new teachers. Generally these initiatives, which initially set out to both mentor and evaluate, dropped the mentorship component and became programs focused on evaluation (NCTAF, 1996). In schools located in the poorest communities there are not enough experienced, high-quality teachers to serve as mentors. Equity issues thus surface once again. Schools serving poor students, immigrant students, and students of color have an inordinate proportion of inexperienced teachers and there are few mentors available to support and mentor them.

In an ideal setting, new teachers would be placed in schools where there were early-career, mid-career, and end-of-career colleagues with whom they could interact. Each new teacher would receive both a mentor and a buddy. The mentor's role would be to assist with the transition from preservice to in-service teaching. The mentor would be available to offer both praise and criticism and to help with the development of the new professional. The buddy would serve as a listener and shoulder to cry on. These two roles are important because mentors are unable to critique and evaluate if the relationship becomes too close and personal; and the buddy cannot be a professional friend if she or he is also expected to evaluate. Mentors may be people with whom a new professional has little in common outside the work environment. The buddy should be someone who shares some interests with the new professional. That common ground may come as a result of age, personal status (e.g., single, married, parent, regional, racial, linguistic, or school ties), or self-selection. The point is that new teachers need to have both of these roles filled in order to negotiate teaching successfully. Some fill these roles outside of the workplace with friends, former teacher education colleagues, and sympathetic family members. If schools are interested in supporting new teachers however, they need to be proactive in developing mentors and buddies for them.

LACK OF PROFESSIONAL DEVELOPMENT AND REWARDS FOR KNOWLEDGE AND SKILL

In addition to not understanding the concept of the beginner, schools also seem not to understand that teachers need help to improve their knowledge and skills. One of the challenges of improving teachers' knowledge and skills is the circular problem of professional development. Many people (administrators, teachers, parents, and community members) do not believe that professional development is needed and are concerned that that which is available to large numbers of teachers is of poor quality.

Administrators typically attempt to provide professional development in the most inexpensive and efficient manner, but that strategy results in the creation of one-shot, one-size-fits-all workshops or in-service days. This failure to tailor professional development to meet the specific needs of teachers reinforces the notion that professional development is of little or no value. Whereas most corporate and service sectors invest in the development of their employees to the tune of 5% to 10% of their operating budgets, schools in the United States invest as little as 1% to 3% of their budgets for professional development (NCTAF, 1996).

In addition to the limited resources available for professional development, teachers have virtually no time to meet, plan, and study with colleagues to develop curriculum, improve instruction, sharpen their assessment abilities, or conduct research—all vital for helping students meet the more rigorous standards that many states and school districts are demanding. In other industrial nations (e.g., Germany, Japan, China) teachers spend between 15 and 20 hours a week doing this kind of work. Projects like "lesson-study" where teachers meet to examine and reexamine a particular lesson to improve it and their pedagogical approach to such teaching are common in Japan and some parts of Latin America.

In schools serving poor children, immigrant children, and children of color, professional development is virtually nonexistent. Even if budgets do allow for professional development for individual teachers, the inability to recruit enough substitute teachers does not allow for regular classroom teachers to take advantage of these opportunities. New teachers in our nation's poorest urban (and rural) school districts find their work incredibly lonely. They are isolated and thus left to their own devices to attempt to teach their students.

Not only do schools underfund professional development, they fail to reward those teachers who do have special expertise. Schools offer the same remuneration to teachers based on seniority and accumulated credit hours. Those teachers who take their professional development seriously and enroll in graduate-level courses, attend professional conferences, and/or work with other professionals to improve, do so knowing that their schools will not fully acknowledge or reward their efforts. Not only do schools fail to reward teachers' expertise, some school cultures actively demean and disparage those teachers who attempt to improve their practice. In work with excellent teachers of African American students, Ladson-Billings (1994) found outstanding teachers who often were alienated from their peers. These teachers reported that they avoided their schools' faculty lounges because their colleagues participated in constant parent and student bashing and in activities that were unrelated to teaching (e.g., card playing, direct-sales marketing, gossiping). Indeed, one of the ancillary benefits of participating in the study, according to the teachers, was that they were able to form collegial relationships with other expert teachers who were interested in discussing curriculum, pedagogy, and assessment.

SCHOOLS STRUCTURED FOR FAILURE

It is hard to believe that some schools are literally organized for failure, but they are. They use time, staff, and money unproductively (NCTAF, 1996). It should come as no surprise that the schools most likely to be organized this way serve poor children, immigrant children, and children of color. In these schools evidence of "success" may be order and regimentation. Rather than focusing on teaching and learning, many of these schools focus on making sure that all students are seated, quiet, and busy at some task that may or may not be related to learning. Haberman (1991) asserts that in most urban schools teaching comprises of the following activities:

- Giving information.
- Asking questions.
- Giving directions.
- Making assignments.
- Monitoring seatwork.
- Receiving assignments.
- Giving tests.
- Reviewing tests.
- Assigning homework.
- Reviewing homework.
- Settling disputes.
- Punishing noncompliance.
- Marking papers.
- Giving grades.

Haberman suggests that, taken alone, any one of these activities could be considered a legitimate pedagogical activity. However, "taken together and performed to the systematic exclusion of other acts they have become the pedagogical coin of the realm in urban schools. They constitute the pedagogy of poverty—not merely what teachers do and what youngsters expect, but for different reasons what parents, the community, and the general public assume teaching to be" (p. 290). Haberman further asserts that the pedagogy of poverty appeals to several groups of people. It appeals to people who themselves did not do well in school, to those who rely on common sense rather than on thoughtful analysis, to those who fear children of color and the poor, to those who have low expectations for children of color and the poor, and to those who do not know the full range of available pedagogical options.

In this current high-stakes test environment, many students are suffering under a pedagogy of test prep and scripted lessons. To maintain order in these classrooms teachers often assume an authoritarian and directive teaching style. The focus is on control. So many students in poor communities have been subjected to this form of schooling (I purposely resist the inclination to call this "teaching" or "education") that they have come to expect this. Haberman (1991) says that in this environment students reward teachers by complying and they punish them by resisting. This misleads teachers into believing that some things they do "work" whereas others do not.

Imagine an enthusiastic beginning elementary teacher who attempts to try new things with her students. Instead of passing out worksheets and routine drills and activities she organizes her students into collaborative learning teams. She structures tasks that require students to contribute their different abilities and skills. She asks her students to maintain writing logs and to participate in planning of classroom learning activities. It is conceivable that in a school dominated by the "pedagogy of poverty" the students will balk at this pedagogical change. They may have become so accustomed to the predictability and mindlessness of the pedagogy of poverty that they resist real teaching. It is at this point that a new teacher either perseveres or conforms to the school norms.

In an earlier study Ladson-Billings (2001) described a new teacher who faced a similar dilemma. Fortunately for his students, this teacher resisted what I termed "permission to fail" and instead made demands to succeed. The teacher's third-grade students resisted writing assignments and even asked that he give them worksheets. Rather than accede to the students' demands, the teacher began to examine his pedagogy and explored what he felt were good motivational techniques for supporting students' writing. Ultimately, he was able to merge the students' love of music with writing. He taught them how to work in cooperative groups and encouraged them to explore writing in a new way. He was able to maintain his focus on authentic teaching by affiliating with a teachers' writing project in his area. In other words, this teacher found both mentors and buddies beyond the boundaries of a school that was structured for failure.

When urban high schools regularly report graduating classes that are about one fourth the size of their first-year classes we know that these schools are structured for failure instead of success. When 14-year-olds are permitted to make decisions that are not in their best interests (e.g., not taking algebra, foreign-language courses, or other prerequisite courses that will lead to tertiary education), schools cannot contend that they are structured for success. When urban schools regularly suspend and expel students because of draconian discipline codes (e.g., when hat wearing becomes a reason for exclusion), they are not structured for success. When certain subgroups (e.g., African Americans, Latinos, immigrants) regularly and almost predictably fail to experience success, we cannot believe that their schools are structured for success.

WHY CAN'T POOR CHILDREN GET GOOD TEACHERS

There are several elements of schooling in the United States that many reform discussions never engage. They include school funding, the legacy of racism, and the evacuation of the public sphere. The scope of these issues is overwhelming and thought to be beyond the purview of educators and education scholars. These issues also are beyond the scope of this discussion. They do, however, constitute the tableau upon which public schooling occurs and must be made visible for serious reform to take hold.

School Funding. Jonathan Kozol (1991) exposed the egregious inequities that exist in the way schools are funded. The United States is so wedded to the notion of funding schools via local property taxes that we forget that children throughout the nation start each morning pledging allegiance to the same flag and to "one nation indivisible." Our funding schemes suggest that they should be pledging allegiance to their neighborhoods because children living in wealthy neighborhoods have access to public schools with plenty of resources and children living in poor neighborhoods do not. No other industrialized nation treats its children as if they are tied solely to their local communities for their education. Instead, most nations understand that their children are citizens in the making and that their allegiance and productivity should accrue to the nation as a whole, not to local, particular neighborhoods or communities.

When we tell students that their quality of their education is tied to the quality of the homes in which they live, we condemn poor children to poor schools and we continue to privilege wealthy children. Homeless children are hardly entitled to schools at all. Until we take seriously the call to fund our schools more equitably, the tinkering we do with the discrete elements of schooling (e.g., curriculum, standards, assessment) will produce the same predictable results. School-funding problems speak to the structural inequity on which our entire education system rests. Unfortunately, equalizing school funding debates rarely progress beyond rhetoric. Rich people proudly insist that they moved to certain neighborhoods because of the schools and they have no intention of "diverting" their resources to "other people's children" (Delpit, 1988). Clearly there will be those schools that are poorly funded and yet the students perform at better than predicted levels. These are the exceptions, however, and they cannot be used as excuses to maintain inequity. Perhaps the only way around the school-funding issue is to differentially reward teachers who teach the neediest students as a way to induce high-quality teachers to work in poorly resourced schools.

Legacy of Racism. If school funding is a difficult issue to talk about, the legacy of racism is almost impossible to discuss. So ugly is our racial past that in polite society we would much rather ignore it. We think we should "get over it," but we have not yet figured out how to "get through it." It is no accident that the students who are not White (with the exception of some students of Asian descent) regularly perform at levels beneath their White counterparts. It is no accident that race and class are conflated and Black and Brown children receive substandard educations. Legal scholar Derrick Bell (1992) argues that racism is a permanent fixture of U.S. society. It is so endemic, he asserts, that it feels both normal and natural to us. Thus, the fact that poor Black and Brown children are not thriving in our schools makes sense to us. We certainly would not expect them to be doing better than White middle-class students.

What other evidence do we have that the legacy of racism persists in our schools? The *Christian Science Monitor* (Jonsson, 2003) reports a study conducted by Georgia State University that indicates that White teachers are fleeing Black schools. In 2001, 32% of Georgia's White teachers left schools serving Black students. The same trend is occurring in North Carolina, Texas, and California. Of course, one might argue that teachers flee schools that fail to provide them with adequate resources, instructional leadership, parent support, and opportunities for professional development. However, the fact that such schools so seamlessly align with racially oppressed groups is no coincidence. Rather it is a function of a highly racialized society that refuses to adequately address the institutional and structural racism that is designed to privilege Whites and those who conform to White norms.

Evacuation of the Public Sphere. Again I have identified an issue that is much larger than the scope of a chapter on teacher quality. Teacher quality is, however, symptomatic of this larger issue. Evacuation of the public sphere is one of the most dangerous threats to a democracy. Throughout the society there is a retreat from all things public. Public transportation, public health, public schools, and public life all seem to carry stigmas. What once were proud emblems of a democratic society are receding behind a discourse of markets and privatization. We now believe that the market should determine everything—the quality of our health, the quality of our communities, and the quality of our education.

My argument is not one against capitalism but rather one against losing our sense of the public good. There are some things we cannot leave to markets because there are some things to which we believe everyone should have access—clean air, fresh water, safety, health, and education. When we decide to live in gated communities, away from central cities, and fail to enter into public discussions, we sacrifice the essential components of democracy—engagement in the public sphere. Parker (2003) suggests that as citizens in a democracy we have access to two publics: the big public we know as citizens of a nation and the little publics that carry our particular concerns, be they circumscribed by race, class, gender, religion, region, language, age, and ability. The great challenge of developing unity out of diversity requires involvement in both publics simultaneously.

Each of these macro social issues makes our attempts to ensure quality teachers for all students seem like an insurmountable challenge. I have inserted these issues in this discussion to point toward the interconnected way that decisions made at one level ultimately impact possibilities at another level. The push for National Board for Professional Teaching Standards (NBPTS) certification for teachers is an attempt to address some of the teacher quality concerns facing many school districts. Again, the equity issue emerges. NBPTS certification is expensive in both time and money. Those states, districts, and schools best prepared to support their teachers through the certification process tend to be those serving middle- and upper-middle-class communities. The teacher "shortages" in urban and rural school districts overshadow any attempt to provide NBPTS certification for teachers serving these communities. The kind of teaching rewarded by NBPTS looks unlike the more structured, traditional pedagogy that predominates urban classrooms. In schools where teachers are under incredible pressure to have students perform on standardized tests, the curriculum and the pedagogy often are reduced to a "test-prep" approach. There is no time to try the innovative teaching strategies that NBPTS encourages. There is no time for reflective practice or authentic assessment. In addition to there being no time, there is no money for NBPTS certification in urban and rural schools. It costs between $1,000 and $1,500 for teachers to sit for NBPTS certification. Few urban and rural school districts can afford to subsidize teachers for this certification. Thus, the prospects for poor children getting quality teachers look very bleak.

EPILOGUE

As I look over this chapter, I realize that it is so pessimistic that one must wonder what, if anything, we can do. I am not convinced that I have to wrap this discussion up in a neat, "things will get better" discourse. I do, however, think I should offer some practical suggestions for improving our current situation. What I am suggesting are not new ideas and I have no assurance that they will ever be implemented, but they offer some possibilities:

- *Substantially increase the pay for urban and rural teachers:* We should be able to reward people for doing more difficult work.
- *Reduce class size in urban and rural classrooms:* Poor children come to school with greater needs. They often are what I term, "school dependent"; that is, all of their educational resources are provided by the school. To serve their increased needs, class size should be smaller.
- *Maintain a ratio of three times as many experienced teachers as inexperienced teachers in urban and rural schools:* Poor children need access to stability and experience in their schooling experiences. New teachers need the help of experienced colleagues.
- *Require year-round contracts for urban and rural teachers (and make the summer vacation a mandatory professional-development experience):* The public mistakenly sees teaching as easy because "teachers have the summer off." The truth is that teachers are paid only during the months they work. Many teachers work additional jobs to supplement their incomes. To keep urban and rural teachers focused on improving the education of their children, we should guarantee them contracts that help upgrade their skills and assure them an income.
- *Reward success:* Much of teaching is based on a punishment model. We place schools that are unsuccessful on probation. We retain students who do not pass high-stakes exams. We reassign teachers who do not produce expected results. What if we rewarded teachers for success much the way professional athletes have incentives built in their contracts?
- *Create stronger partnerships between urban and rural school districts and teacher education programs:* Teacher education programs find themselves trying to be all things to all schools. Every major urban and rural area should develop an exclusive relationship with one or more teacher education programs to prepare teachers for their districts. This partnership would involve collaborative relationship throughout the program from foundation courses through student teaching and first-year induction.

Each of these recommendations is a step that members of the education community can take. They do not eliminate the need to address the larger social issues of funding, ongoing racism, or abandonment of the public sphere. The problem of teacher quality for the nation's neediest students is both complicated and complex. It involves many steps and those steps are interconnected and intertwined. My recommendations are the necessary (but not sufficient) steps to take if we are to leave no teacher behind.

REFERENCES

Ansell, S. E., & McCabe, M. (2003, January). Off target. *Education Week* (pp. 57–72). Retrieved September 2003 from http://www.edweek.org/sreports/qc03/templates/article.cfm?slug=17target.h22&keywords=ansell

Baron, R. M., Tom, D. Y. H., & Cooper, H. M. (1985). Social class, race, and teacher expectations. In J. B. Dusek (Ed.), *Teacher expectancies* (pp. 251–269). Hillsdale, NJ: Lawrence Erlbaum Associates.

Bell, D. (1992). *Faces at the bottom of the well: The permanence of racism.* New York: Basic Books.

Brophy, J. E. (1985). Teacher–student interaction. In J. B. Dusek (Ed.), *Teacher expectancies* (pp. 303–328). Hillsdale, NJ: Lawrence Erlbaum Associates.

Carnegie Forum on Education and the Economy. (1986). *A nation prepared: Teachers for the 21st century.* New York: Carnegie Corporation.

Cohen, E. (1994). *Designing groupwork strategies for heterogeneous classrooms.* New York: Teachers College Press.

Delpit, L. (1988). The silenced dialogue: Power and pedagogy in educating other people's children. *Harvard Educational Review, 56,* 379–395.

Education Week. (1998, January). *Quality counts '98: The urban challenge: Public education in the 50 states.* Retrieved September 2003 from http://www.edweek.org/sreports/qc98/challenges/teach/te-n.htm

Gewertz, C. (2002, June 12). Qualifications of teachers falling short. *Education Week,* p. A2.

Good, T. L., & Brophy, J. E. (1990). *Educational psychology: A realistic approach* (4th ed.). New York: Longman.

Good, T. L., & Brophy, J. E. (2000). *Looking in classrooms* (8th ed.). New York: Addison-Wesley.

Grant, C. A., & Ladson-Billings, G. (Eds.). (1997). *Dictionary of multicultural education.* Phoenix, AZ: Oryx Press.

Graue, M. E. (1993). *Ready for what? Constructing meanings of readiness for kindergarten.* Albany: State University of New York Press.

Haberman, M. (1991). The pedagogy of poverty versus good teaching. *Phi Delta Kappan, 73,* 290–294.

Holmes Group. (1990). *Teachers for tomorrow's school.* East Lansing, MI: Author.

Ingersoll, R. (2002). The teacher shortage: A case of wrong diagnosis and wrong prescription. *NASSP Bulletin, 86,* 16–31.

Jonsson, P. (2003, January 21). White teachers flee black schools. *Christian Science Monitor.*

Kozol, J. (1991). *Savage inequalities: Children in America's schools.* New York: Crown.

Ladson-Billings, G. (1994). *The dreamkeepers: Successful teachers of African American children.* San Francisco: Jossey Bass.

Ladson-Billings, G. (2001). *Crossing over to Canaan: The journey of new teachers in diverse classrooms.* San Francisco: Jossey Bass.

National Commission on Teaching and America's Future. (1996). *What matter's most: Teaching and America's future.* New York: Teachers College Press.

National Commission on Teaching and America's Future. (2003). *No dream denied: A pledge to America's children.* Washington, DC: Author.

No Child Left Behind Act of 2001, Pub. L. No. 107–110 § 115 Stat. 1425 (2002).

Pajares, M. F. (1992). Teachers' beliefs and educational research: Cleaning up a messy contract. *Review of Educational Research, 62,* 307–332.

Parker, W. (2003). *Teaching democracy: Unity and diversity in public life.* New York: Teachers College Press.

Rist, R. (1970). Student social class and teacher expectations: The self-fulfilling prophecy in ghetto education. *Harvard Educational Review, 40,* 411–451.

Rosenholtz, S. (1990). Education reform strategies: Will they increase teacher commitment? In A. Lieberman (Ed.), *Schools as collaborative culture: Creating the future now* (pp. 79–101). New York: Falmer Press.

U.S. Department of Education. (2002). *Elementary & secondary education: Executive summary.* NCLB Legislation. Retrieved October 20, 2003, from http://www.ed.gov/ nclb/overview/intro/ execsumm.html

Wigfield, A., Galper, A., Denton, K., & Seefeldt, C. (1999). Teachers' beliefs about former Head Start and non–Head Start first-grade children's motivation, performance, and future educational prospects. *Journal of Educational Psychology, 91,* 98–104.

Wise, A., Darling-Hammond, L., & Berry, B. (1987). *Effective teacher selection, from recruitment to retention.* Santa Monica, CA: RAND Corporation.

TEST LINKING: TECHNICAL AND CONCEPTUAL CHALLENGES

E Pluribus Unum: Linking Tests and Democratic Education

Michael J. Feuer
The National Academies
National Research Council

> *State college football coach to his team: "You guys line up alphabetically by height."*
>
> —*Uncorroborated quotation*

CONSTANCY AND CHANGE IN SCHOOL REFORM

In his final oeuvre before his untimely death, the historian Lawrence Cremin outlined three "grand stories" that capture the debates over American education policy since the Second World War (Cremin, 1990).[1] The first is associated with James Conant, former President of Harvard and American statesman, for whom "popular education meant the extension of access to secondary and junior college education coupled with a narrowing and toughening of secondary school curricula, [and] the protection of higher education from the . . . threat of heterogeneity by contraction of enrollment and tightening of academic and professional standards . . ." (Cremin, 1990, p. 25). The second grand story has its origins in the upheavals of the 1960s, which led to the proliferation of free schools, alternative curricula, and restructuring of schooling at every level. According to a number of key policy reports of the 1970s, these reforms had failed miserably: "The American high school [had become] an institution victimized by its own success: the closer it came to

---

[1]Cremin credits Cohen and Garet (1975) with the concept of "grand story."

165

achieving universality, the larger, the less responsive, and the more isolated an institution it became . . ." (Cremin, 1990, p. 26).[2] The remedy proposed was to afford young people greater opportunities to pursue vocational and other interests, while safeguarding the goals of higher education—research, the transmission of high culture, and the preparation of elites.

The third grand story is associated most directly with *A Nation at Risk* (National Commission on Excellence in Education, 1983), the remarkable report that offered a scathing indictment of American education; proposed a series of recommendations designed to toughen standards and hold school systems accountable; paved the way for the standards-based reform movement of the late 1980s and 1990s; reinforced the concept of outcomes rather than inputs as the criterion to govern school policy; reintroduced international comparisons as a potent political spur to educational change; suggested at least implicitly that as long as *any* American students or schools were at risk then we were *all* at risk; and exerted sufficient rhetorical (if not empirically rigorous) clout to shape state and federal policy for the next two decades at least.

If there is a common strand in these stories, it might be summarized as the pursuit of two seemingly conflicting goals simultaneously—increased access *and* higher standards—a tension that has characterized American public education at least since the end of the 19th century (see, e.g., Cremin, 1990; Kaestle, 1983; Katz, 1968; Tyack & Cuban, 1995). It is perhaps most clearly manifest in Conant's dual concerns for expansion of the franchise and cultivation of the elite, but the idea is certainly there in prior and subsequent chapters of the radical drama of American education. Though every generation likes to see itself as pioneer—in terms either of suffering from a new or special educational problem or of coming up with a new or innovative solution to a familiar one—history suggests that late-20th-century efforts to promote greater equity and increased access while also raising standards of performance and protecting high culture and the highest achieving students, have roots in the common school reforms of the mid-19th century.[3] Popular education with quality standards was never an easy or obvious ideal: "[It is] as radical an idea as Americans have embraced" (Cremin, 1990, p. 30). And the reform movement of the 1980s and 1990s, pro-

---

[2]The reports to which Cremin refers are: *Youth: Transition to Adulthood* (Panel on Youth of the President's Science Advisory Committee, 1973); *The Reform of Secondary Education* (National Commission on the Reform of Secondary Education, 1973); and *The Education of Adolescents* (National Panel on High School and Adolescent Education, 1974).

[3]Whether the common school reformers were explicitly focused on protecting high-achieving students is of course debatable. I infer from Horace Mann's introduction of uniform written examinations an interest in academic knowledge as a principal expected outcome of schooling, and from his (and other reformers') use of the results of such exams to hold schoolmasters accountable for their children's performance a certain anxiety over the effects of enfranchising an increasingly heterogeneous student body on maintenance of academic standards.

pelled with slogans such as "high standards for all," or, as in today's context, "no child left behind," is a natural—if inordinately complicated—continuation of the radical tradition.

A second common strand is the reliance on public institutions—including the federal government, despite its constitutionally circumscribed role—to influence patterns of school finance and governance, promote and enforce norms of access, and hold public officials accountable. For a country with a proud history of decentralized education and, more generally, a moral and economic commitment to private markets as the default mode through which to arrange society's transactions, the increasing federal role during the last two decades has been extraordinary.[4] Nowhere was the irony more sublime than with the publication of *Nation at Risk*, which, after all, had been commissioned by an administration on record for advocating a *reduction* in the federal role in education (and eventual elimination of the federal Department of Education), but that wielded unprecedented influence on broad educational strategies at all levels and demonstrated, quite unintentionally, at least one enormously valuable role for the federal government in matters of national educational strategy. Having embraced the rhetoric of impending national catastrophe and capitulation to the combined economic and educational forces of foreign rivals, and the need, therefore, to harness our resources in our own national defense, even the Reagan administration could not easily declare the educational arena off-limits to federal policy. (There is another, less charitable, interpretation: Beneath the rhetorical veneer of improving public education there was lurking in *Nation at Risk* the intended elevation of standards and public expectations to impossible heights, a strategy designed to cause further erosion in support for public schools and the gradual acceptance of privatization [vouchers] and its variants. When the National Assessment of Educational Progress (NAEP) first set performance standards, its leaders were occasionally accused of a conspiracy to undermine public education via precisely the route of setting impossibly high standards [see, e.g., Berliner & Biddle, 1995]. Adjudicating these theories is clearly beyond the scope of this chapter.)

TENSIONS OF FEDERALISM IN EDUCATION POLICY

Reliance on government, and the forging of a new partnership between the federal and state governments implicit in the post–*Nation at Risk* era, brings

---

[4]On markets and bureaucracies generally, see Williamson (1975). It is worth noting that despite Milton Friedman's importation of the market metaphor to matters of education (Friedman, 1955), and the generation of research and advocacy about voucher systems that Friedman's proposal spawned (e.g., Chubb & Moe, 1990), Cremin did not include the debate over school choice and vouchers as one of the grand stories.

into sharp relief one of the thorniest predicaments of American education. Students of the history of federalism and the battles fought by that generation of radicals who founded the new republic will recognize in the tensions between national and local educational norms a broader political and cultural context. Simply put, *if there is a national ethos of education it is both enhanced and constrained by the diversity and variety of our schools and the systems by which they are governed.* The meta-story covering all the other grand stories is the complexity of aggregating individual and local educational values into an acceptable definition of national goals and standards.

Recall the data that summarize the American experiment in decentralized education: roughly 47 million pupils enrolled in 92,000 elementary and secondary schools, managed by local authorities in 15,000 districts spread across the 50 states and territories. But it is not just the size of the enterprise and its geographic dispersion. What matters more is the simultaneity of three ideals in American history and culture: (a) education is a reflection of beliefs in what constitutes "the good life" (in the Aristotelian sense: See Cremin (1990), Aristotle's *Politics* (350 BCE); (b) the good life is best defined and organized by individuals and communities rather than by large government bureaucracies miles away physically and culturally; and (c) our diversity notwithstanding, and our preservation of local grass-roots democracy notwithstanding, we are one nation undivided.

Indeed, Americans cherish their local control of schooling, and if asked explicitly they would most likely say that the diversity and variety across jurisdictions is a reflection of our democratic beginnings, an attribute of schooling that is, *in itself,* an indicator of success. At the very least it has helped distinguish us from European education philosophies and systems.[5] Parents in Dubuque take pride in knowing that their children's schooling does not necessarily resemble the schooling experienced by children in Juneau or New York.[6] Not that they would necessarily object if they discovered a high degree of commonality in curricula or pedagogical strategies; but what matters is that in each locale citizens believe that education bears

---

[5]Readers interested in comparisons between American and European philosophy of education should start with de Tocqueville, who spent only 9 months in the United States (in 1832) but who figured out much of the uniqueness of the new nation. On the American idealization of equality (in the sense of class, and obviously not, at that time, in the sense of skin color) as a root cause of our distinctive approach to education, de Tocqueville had this extraordinary insight: "If [an observer who is desirous of forming an opinion on the state of instruction among the Anglo-Americans] . . . singles out only the learned, he will be astonished to find how few they are; but if he counts the ignorant, the American people will appear to be the most enlightened in the world. The whole population . . . is situated between these two extremes" (de Tocqueville, 1840/1990, p. 315).

[6]I say this casually, and have no specific data to offer about parents in Dubuque, Juneau, or New York.

at least some of the imprint of their community.[7] If Americans are fundamentalist about anything, it is that our national character derives its identity from the aggregation of state, local, and individual preferences—and not the other way around.

It may be said, therefore, that in American politics—and education—the default system is local governance. If in the European democracies central authority is the "given" and community-based decision making the exception, the myth of American democracy, rooted in the distaste for authoritarian government that motivated the founders of the republic, is that "all politics is local." But it has been the peculiar genius of the American system to not confer too much power in *any* branch of government: We may admire and nurture our localism, but we also (increasingly) hold state and local authorities accountable to higher standards, whether through the Constitution or the courts or the Congress.

The importance of structural checks on localism cannot be overstated. There are obviously enough examples of how the preference for grassroots organizing has created a safe haven for the worst sorts of parochialism. Surely one of the sources of the extraordinary inequality in per-pupil expenditures is attributable to an education finance system that relies on local property taxes. And were it not for federal intervention, "states' rights" would have perpetuated racial segregation, gender bias, and the gradual encroachment of religious instruction in public classrooms.

As with many aspects of American public life, then, schools have found themselves in a tug-of-war between local and national forces, and the tensions have increased notably since the Second World War (Kaestle, 2003). And though the American system is based on tension—checks and balances—it also rewards compromise and moderation over intransigence and extremism. Yet, however appealing intuitively and philosophically is the idea that we can have a national ethos of education while preserving and nurturing state and local instincts, finding the balance has always required a good bit of operational compromise and linguistic deftness. The concept of "national" is tolerable—but only to a point: Those who confound "national" with "federal" do so at their own peril. And those who propose governmental policies that might be seen as threats to the federalist order need to tread very gingerly—a lesson learned and applied by both major political parties.

For example, it was not until 1994 that the Congress codified in federal law *(Goals 2000)* a set of eight "national educational goals," six of which were taken from the Charlottesville summit of 1989, a landmark political

---

[7]Without question, the effects of a large and complex textbook and testing industry have been profoundly "standardizing" even across the mosaic of America. For a chilling account of the downside risks of market-based provision of schoolbooks and tests, see Ravitch (2003).

event that brought together the National Governors Association (Chairman: Governor Bill Clinton) and the White House (President George H. W. Bush), with business and industry leaders, union heads, and other education statespersons. The result was the first-ever articulation of "national goals" for American education.[8] The passage of *Goals 2000* was accompanied by significant reforms in the Elementary and Secondary Education Act (in particular its Title 1); 3 years later, passage of the revised Americans with Disabilities Education Act further cemented the concept of standards-based federal policy. Historians rightly viewed these developments (along with the less successful attempt in *America 2000,* a bill introduced but defeated in 1992) as a historical breach in the contract that kept the feds at a safe distance from state and local education authorities.

But even the national goals did not simplify or clarify the question of authority. It was still up to the states and districts to shape the goals according to their own specific ideals, to develop their own "challenging" content and performance standards, and to implement the spirit of the newly articulated national educational ethos according to locally determined preferences. The question of whether and how the tremendous variety in state definitions of "challenging" would be aggregated into a measure of national progress was not directly tackled. And there were no obvious exemplars from which to borrow ideas for a blueprint: No other democracy values local prerogatives in education quite the way we do.

Guided by the consummate politician Bill Clinton, in his capacity as Chairman of the National Governors Association, the architects of the national goals understood the political and cultural significance of maintaining a conceptual firewall between national and federal. And they had recent experiences to guide them in this delicate dance. Codification of national standards in specific content areas, notably in mathematics and later in science, and the then-20-year-old example of the NAEP, offered ample evidence of the fundamental distaste for nationally authoritative (i.e., federal) decisions about the purposes and outcomes of education, the content and style of assessments, and the determination of acceptable levels of performance. NAEP's founders (in the mid-1960s) sought broad indications of the *nation's* trends in achievement, but built the indicator system around a complex apparatus that distilled regional and discipline-based definitions of content into acceptable national terms (National Research Council [NRC], 2000). Similarly, the early efforts to codify mathematics education standards (National Council of Teachers of Mathematics, 2000) relied on extensive and exhaustive (if not exhausting) consultations with teachers and others rather than on an authoritative top-down definition of what mattered in mathemat-

---

[8]I am indebted to Marty Orland for reminding me of the chronology of these various efforts. For a brief description of the Summit, see http://wvde.state.wv.us/ed1st/abouted1st.html.

ics learning. When the National Science Education Standards project was undertaken some years later (National Academy of Sciences, 1996), it involved one of the largest committees on record in the annals of the NRC and somewhere in the neighborhood of 18,000 reviewers!

These examples suffice to posit a rather obvious axiom: If there are to be national standards in American education, they will derive from the aggregation of state and local definitions and not from a top-down federal-level authority. A perhaps less obvious corollary, however, is that *any such aggregation will always be imperfect.*[9]

MULTIPLE TESTS, ONE NATION: PSYCHOMETRICS TO THE RESCUE?

Captivated by the zeitgeist of national standards as a defense against foreign competition and American educational decline, the first Bush administration put forth a plan for *America 2000,* which included provisions for federally sponsored but locally designed tests. The segue from national goals (Charlottesville) to measures that could indicate progress toward reaching those goals (tests) is, in retrospect, obvious. Again, though, the translation of a reasonable intuition—we need tests to gauge whether we are reaching our goals—into an operational system that meets criteria of psychometric validity, reliability, and fairness, encountered familiar and formidable obstacles of history, culture, and politics. (Alert political scientists noticed the irony of a Republican administration promoting *anything* national regarding education. By the time the No Child Left Behind Act of 2001 (NCLB, 2002) passed—with strong bipartisan support—in the first years of the second Bush administration, it was clear that conventional party dichotomies no longer applied.) In 1997, when President Clinton tried to advance the cause of national testing, he had to add the word *voluntary,* knowing full well that any plan to impose federally mandated tests on states and districts would run afoul of the prohibition against encroachment by Washington into the affairs of state and local governments. (In the end both efforts failed: Demo-

---

[9]The assertion that in the United States national standards can derive only from the accumulation, mixing, and blending of state and local definitions, is not just obvious, but probably quite banal, at least to anyone who has been watching the last 20 years of school reform. But the implications are worth contemplating through a different lens. Consider, for example, social choice theory as developed in economics and political science. Knowing of the difficulty, if not the impossibility, of devising a democratic system that aggregates individual preferences without violating certain basic principles might shed light on why school reform *options* always seem to be suboptimal; and why the field might be ready for a new approach to setting reform expectations, that is, in terms of "second-best" or even "third-best" options. See my later recommendation for "procedural rationality" as a paradigm for understanding—and shaping—education policy.

crats voted against the first Bush plan—*America 2000*—because it did not include enough in new federal funds for public schools; Republicans voted against the Clinton voluntary testing plan because it didn't allow for voucher experiments; and in neither case was the idea of national testing warmly embraced by teachers, education researchers, policy groups, or the general public.)

Not surprisingly, a major stumbling block to the Clinton voluntary national test (VNT) was the word *national* juxtaposed with the word *testing.* Standardized testing was always a flashpoint for controversy (Cronbach, 1975)[10] and now even more so given the allegation (from both the right and the left) that national tests were a national curriculum in disguise.[11]

This is how the otherwise arcane science of test score linkage and equating suddenly found its way into the halls of Congress and into federal education legislation. It was as if psychometrics had been asked for an operational solution to the ideal etched in our Great Seal and in our political culture: *e pluribus unum,*[12] has never been easy to translate into practice—and certainly not during the testing wars of the 1990s!

The proposed VNT, which was one of the more remarkable planks in President Clinton's 1997 State of the Union address, triggered a major national debate on a number of political and technical issues. At the core was the tension between standardization and diversity, stretched to its limits by the American public's apparently insatiable appetite for systematic information about student achievement. "Educators, parents, policy makers, and others want[ed] to know more than existing tests [could] show ... [and] in particular they want[ed] to know how students measure[d] up to national and international benchmarks" (NRC, 1999b, p. 9).

In Congress, the *pluribus* and *unum* problem was most stridently articulated by Representative William Goodling, a former schoolteacher who had risen to the chairmanship of the powerful House Education and Workforce Committee. A moderate Republican committed to improvement of school-

---

[10]See Cronbach, 1975. The three decades since Cronbach's paper chronicled five decades of controversy have not been witness to much abatement of the controversies. See also Feuer (1994).

[11]Chester Finn is credited with the wry observation that the voluntary national testing program had only two things going against it: Half the country hated the word *national,* and the other half hated the word *testing.* For more on the history of testing controversy, see U.S. Congress (1992). If the right was mostly worried about the specter of national curriculum, the left was mostly worried about the discriminatory effects of excessive reliance on tests. See National Research Council (1999a).

[12]"Out of many, one" is a clear reference to the 13 colonies united into one nation—symbolized by the shield on the eagle's breast. As explained in the official description of the Great Seal, the 13 vertical stripes "represent the several states all joined in one solid compact entire, supporting a Chief, which unites the whole & represents Congress. The Motto alludes to this union." See, for example, http://www.greatseal.com/mottoes/unum.html.

ing for American kids, Goodling embraced the idea of standards and test-based accountability; but he could not abide the notion that the federal bureaucracy would be in charge of decisions in all those 15,000 school districts and that the feds would in any way be charged with developing curriculum. He liked the idea of testing—most politicians, regardless of party, have discovered that test scores can be a powerful bludgeon[13]—and he liked that they would be voluntary. He warmed to the idea of providing Americans with information about their kids' achievement that showed them how we were doing as a nation competing in the world. But the thought of placing something this important in the hands of a federal agency drove even the usually mild-mannered Goodling to uncharacteristic anger.

Goodling's rebuttal came in the form of an intuitively appealing question: Would it not be possible to allow states and districts to continue using their own or commercially produced tests (the decentralization impulse), but to score all these different tests on the same scale (the national impulse)? In other words, couldn't psychometrics find a way to place the results from the dozens of different tests, devised with varying frameworks and compilations of content and using different formats and administrative procedures (a very healthy *pluribus*) on a single and easily understandable scale (the *unum*)? Could the disparate definitions and priorities for content and performance across the 50 states, as symbolized in the tests designed or used by those states, be distilled into a reporting system that allowed Americans wherever they live to see how their children are doing?

The Goodling challenge involved a collision between politics and science, and led to a congressional request to the NRC (the operating arm of the National Academies of Sciences and Engineering) for a scientific study.[14] For the psychometric community, and in particular for the small branch that specialized in the mathematics of test score linking, it must have felt like an Andy Warhol moment to see Public Law 105-78 call for a "feasibility study to determine if an equivalency scale can be developed that would allow test scores from commercially available standardized tests and State assessments to be compared with each other and the National Assessment of Educational Progress ... (Emergency Student Loan Consolidation Act, 1997, sec. 306)." As the 2003 Educational Testing Service (ETS) conference made clear, the linking idea has remained in the headlines well beyond the Warhol 15 minutes. . . .

The NRC's (1999b) report began with this summary:

---

[13]Today's politicians who embrace testing are perpetuating a tradition begun, ironically, by the champion of common schooling, Horace Mann, in the early 19th century. See Tyack (1974); also U.S. Congress (1992, chap. 4).

[14]From the other side of the aisle came the request for a study of the potentially discriminatory effects of the VNT, especially if used for promotion and graduation decisions. The result was *High Stakes* (NRC, 1999a).

Viewed through [the] lens of our unique experiment in pluralism and federalism, the question motivating this study is both predictable and sensible: Given the rich and increasingly diverse array of tests used by states and districts in pursuit of improved educational performance, can information be provided on a common scale? Can scores on one test be made interpretable in terms of scores on other tests? Can we have more uniform data about student performance from our healthy hodgepodge of state and local programs? Can linkage be the testing equivalent of "e pluribus unum?" (p. 10)

The committee's answer to these questions was, essentially, "no." Developing a new scale to link all the existing tests would not be feasible and would not make sense; and using the existing NAEP scale and achievement levels would not work either. The only glimmer of hope rested in a much-reduced formulation of the problem, that is, that under limited conditions links between *some* tests might be defensible for a limited set of inferences.

Without rehearsing here the details of the NRC committee's deliberations, its conclusions rested on a few key characteristics of the existing ecology of testing in the United States:

Test content: because tests inevitably cover only portions of a domain of interest, e.g., mathematics, test developers must make choices in what to cover and with what emphasis. Fourth-grade reading, notwithstanding the casual remarks offered by critics of psychometric precision—"after all, reading is reading . . ."—may not be defined and converted into test items in the same way in different places. In the end, "when content differences are significant, scores from one test provide poor estimates of scores on another test [and] any calculated linkage between them would have little practical meaning and would be misleading for many uses."

Test format: as state and local authority for education is strengthened, so too is the likelihood of increased variation and innovation in test design. State assessments had already begun to incorporate open-ended questions, constructed-response items, and even written essay questions, in addition to the more conventional multiple-choice items; computer-based testing was also becoming more popular. The effects of differences in test format on the validity of inferences from linked scores are difficult to predict.

Measurement error: because all test results are estimates of performance subject to some level of error, the question of whether score reliability is compromised by linking has important practical consequences. "If test A, with a large margin of error, is linked with test B, which is much more precise, the score of a person who took test A still has the margin of error of test A even when [the result] is reported in terms of the scale of test B."

Test uses and consequences. There is ample evidence on threats to test validity caused by differences in the uses to which test results are applied. Given the variability in the purposes of testing and the application of results to policy decisions in the states and districts, there is danger that simple test linking will be misleading and unstable over time. (NRC, 1999b, pp. 87–89)

PROCEDURAL RATIONALITY AND MOSTELLER'S QUERY

The pessimism in the NRC report was surprising, given the natural penchant of scientists to find technical solutions to complex problems.[15] Under the extraordinary leadership of chairman Paul Holland, the committee sought valiantly to find some way to give even a faintly positive answer to the question it had been posed: "We reached these conclusions despite our appreciation of the potential value of a technical solution to the dual challenges of maintaining diversity and innovation in testing while satisfying growing demands for nationally benchmarked data on individual student performance" (NRC, 1999b, p. 4).

In the end, the committee's answers seemed definitive, but were never couched in the glee one often encounters when social scientists catch a fundamental flaw in a policy proposal.[16] On the contrary, the final deliberations were much inspired by committee member Frederick Mosteller's insistence that merely pointing to potential flaws or compromises to validity and reliability was not enough: The question was *by how much would score meanings be compromised under various linkage schemes?*[17]

It was beyond the scope and resources of the original committee to collect and analyze the data needed to answer Mosteller's question, although it did open the door to a slight reinterpretation of the original charge and to the possibility that under some circumstances linkage of some tests might be feasible.[18]

Without revisiting the original conclusions, then, I would like here to return to Mosteller's question and consider some of its broader implications for future work on linking, testing, and—more generally—education research and policy. Let us review: The historical and political context of American education is a breeding ground for internally contradictory, at times intrac-

---

[15]Committee member Dan Koretz (personal communication, 1998) observed one of the big ironies in this line of work: Most people believe in "multiple measures," that is, that no single score should be sufficient to determine important outcomes for individuals or organizations—but many would like to see the multiple measures collapsed into a single number! On the principle of multiple measures, see American Educational Research Association, American Psychological Association, and National Council on Measurement in Education (1999).

[16]On the *schadenfreude* in social science, see Hirschman (1991). See also Feuer (2002).

[17]Don McLaughlin's recent work (1998) addresses the kind of issue raised by Mosteller.

[18]From the onset there were those who argued that the NRC committee had adopted an unnecessarily extreme formulation of the charge. Some reviewers of the report made the same point. See also Holland (2003).

table, challenges. The latest manifestation is, of course, the landmark NCLB legislation. Here test linking has not yet arisen explicitly, though one can certainly imagine that when some states appear to make better "adequate yearly progress" than others (e.g., Dillon, 2003), the cry will be heard for comparability.[19] If history is a guide, we can safely anticipate a congressional request for a scientific study of the validity of interstate comparisons . . . or for guidance on the establishment of a valid methodology to report the results on a single scale . . . or perhaps even for a voluntary program in which states would agree to use the same test. American politics is, after all, persistent, and questions about testing are not typically overburdened by memory.

Clearly, though, education is not the only arena of American public life where the combined pressures for national and local governance or the existence of multiple measurement systems create confusion. A digression to consider some other situations may be helpful. A recent *Wall Street Journal* article about economic indicators had this to say:

> Consumer confidence is down, but gross domestic product is up. Unemployment is relatively high, as are sales of new homes, but product prices are down. The budget deficit is up, which is bad, but interest rates are down, which is good. *With so much data giving such mixed signals, it's not surprising that many economists are waffling about the state of the US economy.* [italics added] (Crossen, 2003, p. B1)

Couldn't some of that waffling be cured by an econometric model that aggregated these various indicators into a single number, or at least placed

---

[19]Early drafts of NCLB provided for NAEP to serve as the "confirmatory" test, that is, the central benchmark against which to weigh the various states' individually tailored tests. This would have entailed a linkage of the sort envisioned by the Goodling alternative to the VNT. The more pressing dilemma inherent in NCLB is one of blunt incentives: If the law has an underlying theory of action, it is that schools, teachers, and students will respond to incentives for improved performance; holding them accountable, therefore, means measuring their progress against a defined expectation or standard. The problem, of course, is that setting the standard too low perpetuates the unacceptable status quo, whereas setting it too high leads to unacceptable failure rates, erosion of morale, frustration, and ultimately political backlash. In a word, what NCLB is missing is a fine-tuning knob—which has been missing throughout the long history of test-based accountability (see U.S. Congress, 1992). The potential disaster as states attempt to comply with NCLB has been well documented: In his presidential address to the American Educational Research Association earlier this year, Robert Linn showed that under reasonable assumptions it would take more than 100 years to achieve goals laid out in NCLB—not the 12 years allowed in the law! In his most recent paper on this subject, Linn (2003b) argues that "variability in the definitions of proficient academic achievement by states for purposes of the No Child Left Behind Act of 2001 is . . . so great that characterizing achievement is meaningless." See also Linn's paper prepared for the 2003 ETS conference (Linn, 2003c). For the effects of overzealous policy goals, see Mathews (2003).

the disparate scores from the various productivity and employment surveys on a single scale? Granted, the analogy with educational test score linking is not quite accurate—economic indicators used in the *Wall Street Journal* article are not derived from 50+ independent surveys based on disparate definitions and different intended uses—but the result is, similarly, a cacophony of information without a clear national signal.

Other examples, also from economics, provide analogies that shed light on the peculiarities of the test linkage problem. Consider cross-national estimation of poverty, which relies on statistics that are "dependent upon and as fluid as the definition of poverty, the particular circumstance, purpose, or intended use, as well as the choice of the producer-user" (David, 2002). In one economic analysis, there is direct reference to Paul Holland's work, though not to his work on linking and equating per se: "the problem [cross-population comparability of economic status indices] is similar to that faced by psychometricians in intelligence [*sic*] testing using question banks: even for the same level of intelligence some questions exhibit differential item functioning (DIF) . . . [and] we propose one way of making estimates of economic status comparable across countries which [assumes] that the entire set of consumer durables not exhibit DIF."[20] And perhaps the most obvious case of "linking" in economics is in converting currencies to a common numeraire: Having a basis for converting Italian lira to U.S. dollars improves on the otherwise misleading usage of the word *millionaire*. More generally, economists long ago developed "purchasing power parity" as the conceptual anchor for valid cross-national comparisons of money income.

Some international economic work does clearly rely on *ex ante* agreement about variables, survey design, and so on. The Luxembourg Income Study (2000), for example, is an ongoing project that seeks to "harmonize and standardize the micro-data from the different [country] surveys in order to facilitate comparative research" (LES section, para. 3). In this respect, the basic method is analogous to the "embedding" approach to test linking (Holland, 2003; NRC, 1999a). It is interesting to note that with respect to cross-national comparisons, some education researchers may be ahead of at least some of their friends who work in international economics. International comparisons of educational achievement no longer rely on *ex post* efforts to standardize existing data from whatever tests are used around the world; rather, the investment is made *ex ante* in the design of instruments that are administered under reasonably uniform conditions everywhere (NRC, 2003).

My aim with these examples is not to suggest a formulaic linkage between educational test equating and methods used in other domains plagued by disparate data streams and the quest for comparability. It is,

---

[20]Tandon, A., Gakidou, E., Sousa, A., and Murray, C. J. L., 2004.

rather, to suggest that implicit in all these methods is an acknowledgment that perfect comparability is most likely neither feasible nor desirable, and that rational policymakers need to satisfy themselves with results that provide *reasonable* estimates rather than conclusive answers. I borrow here from Herbert Simon's distinction between "substantive" and "procedural" rationality (e.g., Simon, 1978): When the complexity of a problem exceeds the bounds of human (and technological) information-processing capacity, or when inherent contradictions in assumptions or goals rule out a theoretical optimum, the rational approach is (or should be) to strive for *satisfactory* solutions based on *reasonable* deliberation.

Simon introduced the term *satisficing* to connote an alternative to the conventional assumption in economics that rational human beings seek optimal (substantively rational) solutions (i.e., he intended it not necessarily as a normative principle but rather as an axiom from which predictions about individual and organizational behavior could be improved). The constraints on U.S. educational testing—that national measures preserve state and local individuality, that test content be aligned to educational goals, that test outcomes be used in accountability even at the risk of compromises to the validity of the test measures—rule out "optimization" as the applicable paradigm.

What does a shift toward procedural rationality mean for test linking? It means new terms of engagement between the researcher and policy communities. First, researchers need to keep Professor Mosteller's question front and center in their work: Given the likely infeasibility of a scale that will accurately integrate multiple measures of educational performance, that is, that will *optimize* the equivalency problem, what are the methods that will produce minimal and acceptable threats to validity and reliability? What would constitute *satisfactory* levels of equivalency for specific intended uses of the results? What risks from potential misunderstanding of the linked scores might be tolerable in view of anticipated benefits? To answer these questions, researchers will need to be conscious of intended (and possibly unintended) uses of the results, and will need to explore both experimental and theoretical options (Holland, 2003).

A similar argument can be made for any test-based accountability system, whether it uses linked scores or not. Perhaps most important, researchers will need to accept the challenge of linkage (if it is posed again, in whatever guise) as a legitimate expression of deeply held American ideals and not as a silly question advanced by naive politicians or statistically challenged historians. This by no means discounts the importance of rigorous analysis and rejection of scientifically indefensible propositions; but it does suggest more leniency by researchers, less overt pleasure in announcing the inevitable failure of certain propositions and policies, and a more catholic attitude toward the possibility that some unforeseen consequences might be beneficial (Feuer, 2002; Hirschman, 1991).[21]

Indeed, the central challenge faced by researchers in this field is the delineation of boundaries to the validity of second-best (satisficing) solutions, explication of constraints imposed by the political or cultural context, and rigorous analyses of the plausibility, utility, benefits, and costs of alternative solutions to even the most apparently intractable questions. In this regard it is useful to recall other families of problems with inherent "impossibilities." For example, Kenneth Arrow's (1951) proof that no decision rule (such as majority voting) can be devised that fulfills five minimal conditions (e.g., transitivity of preferences) was not a *prima facie* case against democracy. Rather it opened the door to rethinking basic concepts of social welfare and political economy, and for models that could "alleviate the pessimism" engendered by Arrow's insight (Royal Swedish Academy of Sciences, 1998; Sen, 1970). The significance of understanding limits to democratic governance, possible compromises necessary for social and economic progress, and how the constraints on human information-processing capacity explain the emergence of political and organizational systems, was not lost on the world community. Arrow, Sen, and Simon all won Nobel Prizes.

The policy community needs to be conscious of its side of the bargain if procedural rationality is to become a useful paradigm. First, policymakers need to appreciate that scientific research is, by definition, an exercise in skepticism, and they should not mistake researchers' penchant for inquiry as apology for the status quo. Scientists (and engineers) are principally motivated by the search for valid descriptions and explanations of complex phenomena and solutions that are grounded in theory and experimentation (e.g., Feuer, Towne, & Shavelson, 2002; NRC, 2002). Granted, the occasionally excessive pessimism registered by some social scientists has not won favor among politicians and policymakers who seek at least incrementally better—if not optimal—solutions to complex social and educational phenomena. But the burden here is primarily on the policy community, where political instincts often trigger *ad hominem* rejection of some research and the insinuation that the researcher is politically motivated—just because he or she says "no" to some propositions.

Second, and perhaps most important, policymakers need to accept the warnings about intended and unintended uses of certain types of data, and be more vigilant in preventing information from being misused and harmful to individuals or groups. The clearest examples, perhaps not surprisingly,

---

[21]One of the unforeseen benefits of the linking debate was to stimulate advances in the statistical theory of equating, which has important applications in a variety of contexts. See Holland (2003).

come from the world of educational testing. The American educational policy landscape is littered with pollution from wanton disregard for the limitations of test scores as the basis for decisions that have significant consequences (see, e.g., Linn, 2003a; NRC, 1999a; U.S. Congress, 1992). If policymakers accept the concept embedded in procedural rationality, for example, that some testing programs produce group results that should not be the basis for decisions about specific individuals, or that some links across tests provide broad estimates rather than accurate conclusions about individuals, they might then be in a better position to resist the temptations of test misuse. (In this context it would be interesting to explore whether cross-national economic comparisons, such as those alluded to earlier, are or should be used for "high stakes" decisions by governments, and how such uses would be received.) Simply put, certain kinds of decisions require higher levels of validity and reliability than do other kinds (e.g., U.S. Congress, 1990). And the general public, already sufficiently confused by the incessant barrage of conflicting evidence from disparate assessment programs, might come to appreciate the value—and limitations—of measurement as a tool for reform.

There can be little doubt that the American educational policy community will continue to pose seemingly intractable technical problems. Perhaps the next "grand story" will be one of compromise, the substitution of procedural for substantive rationality in our education policy and research debates, and the gradual realization that American democracy—and democratic education—is a messy proposition that requires tolerance for ambiguity and for reasonable rather than pristine answers. Figuring out just how reasonable is reasonable—answering Mosteller's question—is no trivial matter. And until the optimal links are designed and tested, and until the ambiguities are removed, we would all be wise to remember the words of F. Scott Fitzgerald: *The test of a first-rate intelligence is the ability to hold two opposed ideas in the mind at the same time, and still retain the ability to function.*

ACKNOWLEDGMENTS

The opinions in this chapter do not necessarily represent the positions of the National Academies or any of its boards and committees, except where explicitly referenced. I have benefited from the helpful suggestions of Hanna Arzi, David Berliner, Sarah Feuer, Carl Kaestle, David Klahr, Ellen Lagemann, Robert Linn, Richard Murnane, Marty Orland, and Lisa Towne. Paula Melville provided superb editorial assistance. Alas I cannot hold anyone but myself responsible for remaining errors of fact or logic.

REFERENCES

American Educational Research Association, American Psychological Association, & National Council on Measurement in Education. (1999). *Standards for educational and psychological testing.* Washington, DC: American Educational Research Association.

Arrow, K. (1951). *Social choice and individual values.* New Haven, CT: Yale University Press.

Berliner, D., & Biddle, B. (1995). *The manufactured crisis: Myths, fraud, and the attack on America's public schools.* New York: Perseus.

Chubb, J., & Moe, T. (1990). *Politics, markets, and America's schools.* Washington, DC: Brookings Institution Press.

Cohen, D., & Garet, M. (1975, February). Reforming educational policy with applied social research. *Harvard Educational Review, 45,* 17–43.

Cremin, L. (1990). *Popular education and its discontents.* New York: Harper & Row.

Cronbach, L. (1975, January). Five decades of public controversy over mental testing. *The American Psychologist, 30,* 1–14.

Crossen, C. (2003, August 6). Before the depression, economic indicators forecast a rosy future. *The Wall Street Journal,* p. B1.

David, I. P. (2002, November 27–29). *On comparability of poverty statistics from different sources and disaggregation levels.* Paper presented at the meeting of UN-ESCAP Committee on Statistics. http://www.unescap.org/stat/cos13/cos13_7e.pdf

de Tocqueville, A. (1990). *Democracy in America* (Vol. 1). New York: Random House. (Original work published 1840)

Dillon, S. (2003, August 31). State cutbacks put schools and federal law to the test. *The New York Times,* p. A1.

Emergency Student Loan Consolidation Act, Pub. L. No. 105-78, § 111 Stat. 1467 (1997).

Feuer, M. J. (1994). Social policy, intelligence, and testing. In R. Sternberg (Ed.), *Encyclopedia of human intelligence* (Vol. 2, pp. 984–992). New York: Macmillan.

Feuer, M. (2002, October 24). *Accountability, testing, and unintended consequences.* Paper presented at the Brookings-Wharton Conference on Urban Affairs, Washington, DC.

Feuer, M. J., Towne, L., & Shavelson, R. J. (2002, November). Scientific culture and educational research. *Educational Researcher, 31*(8), 4–14.

Friedman, M. (1955). The role of government in education. In R. A. Solo (Ed.), *Economics and the public interest* (pp. 123–144). New Brunswick, NJ: Rutgers University Press.

Hirschman, A. (1991). *The rhetoric of reaction.* Cambridge, MA: Harvard University Press.

Holland, P. (2003, October 3). *Assessing the validity of test linking: What has happened since uncommon measures?* Paper presented at the ETS Invitational Conference: Measurement and Research Issues in a New Accountability Era, New York.

Holland, P., & Wainer, H. (1993). *Differential item functioning.* Hillsdale, NJ: Lawrence Erlbaum Associates.

Kaestle, C. (1983). *Pillars of the republic: Common schools and American society 1780–1860.* New York: Farrar, Straus & Giroux.

Kaestle, C. (2003, April 23). *Mobilizing school reform from above: Five decades of federal and national strategies.* AERA Distinguished Lecture, Chicago.

Katz, M. (1968). *Irony of early school reform: Educational innovation in mid-nineteenth century Massachusetts.* Boston: Beacon Press.

Linn, R. L. (2003a, July). Accountability: Responsibility and reasonable expectations. *Educational Researcher, 32*(7), 3–13.

Linn, R. L. (2003b, September 1). Performance standards: Utility for different uses of assessments. *Education Policy Analysis Archives, 11*(31). Retrieved September 2003 from http://epaa.asu.edu/epaa/v11n31/.

Linn, R. L. (2003c, October 3). *Scientific evidence in educational policy and practice: Implications for evaluating adequate yearly progress.* Paper presented at the ETS Invitational Conference: Measurement and Research Issues in a New Accountability Era, New York.

Luxembourg Income Study. (2000). Retrieved September 2003 from http://www.lisproject.org/introduction/history.htm

Mathews, J. (2003, September 16). To educators, "No Child" goals out of reach. *The Washington Post,* p. A12.

McLaughlin, D. (1998). *Study of the linkages of 1996 NAEP and state mathematics assessments in four states: Final report.* Washington, DC: American Institutes for Research.

National Academy of Sciences. (1996). *National science education standards.* Washington, DC: National Academy Press. Retrieved September 2003 from http://www.nap.edu/catalog/4962.html

National Commission on Excellence in Education. (1983). *A nation at risk: The imperative for educational reform.* Washington, DC: U.S. Government Printing Office.

National Commission on the Reform of Secondary Education. (1973). *The reform of secondary education: A report to the public and the profession.* New York: McGraw-Hill.

National Council of Teachers of Mathematics. (2000). *Principles and standards for school mathematics.* Reston, VA: Author. Retrieved September 2003 from http://www.nctm.org/standards/introducing.html

National Panel on High School and Adolescent Education. (1974). *The education of adolescents.* Washington, DC: U.S. Office of Education.

National Research Council. (1999a). *High stakes: Testing for tracking, promotion, and graduation.* Committee on Appropriate Test Use. J. P. Heubert & R. M. Hauser (Eds.), Board on Testing and Assessment, Commission on Behavioral and Social Sciences and Education, National Research Council. Washington, DC: National Academy Press.

National Research Council. (1999b). *Uncommon measures: Equivalence and linkage among educational tests.* Committee on Equivalency and Linkage of Educational Tests. M. J. Feuer, P. W. Holland, B. F. Green, M. W. Bertenthal, & F. C. Hemphill (Eds.), Board on Testing and Assessment, Commission on Behavioral and Social Sciences and Education, National Research Council. Washington, DC: National Academy Press.

National Research Council. (2000). *Grading the nation's report card: Research from the evaluation of NAEP.* Committee on the Evaluation of National and State Assessments of Educational Progress. N. S. Raju, J. W. Pellegrino, M. W. Bertenthal, K. J. Mitchell, & L. R. Jones (Eds.), Board on Testing and Assessment, Commission on Behavioral and Social Sciences and Education. Washington, DC: National Academy Press.

National Research Council. (2002). *Scientific research in education.* Committee on Scientific Principles for Education Research. R. J. Shavelson & L. Towne (Eds.), Center for Education, Division of Behavioral and Social Sciences and Education. Washington, DC: National Academy Press.

National Research Council. (2003). *Understanding others, educating ourselves: Getting more from international comparative studies in education.* Committee on a Framework and Long-Term Research Agenda for International Comparative Education Studies. C. C. Chabbott & E. J. Elliott (Eds.), Board on International Comparative Studies in Education, Board on Testing and Assessment, Center for Education, Division of Behavioral and Social Sciences and Education. Washington, DC: National Academy Press.

No Child Left Behind Act of 2001, Pub. L. No. 107-110, § 115 Stat. 1425 (2002).

Panel on Youth of the President's Science Advisory Committee. (1973). *Youth: Transition to adulthood.* Washington, DC: U.S. Government Printing Office.

Ravitch, D. (2003, April 15). *The language police: How pressure groups restrict what students learn* (A. Green, Ed.). New York: Knopf.

Royal Swedish Academy of Sciences. (1998, October 14). *The Sveriges Riksbank (Bank of Sweden) Prize in Economic Sciences in Memory of Alfred Nobel for 1998.* Retrieved September 2003 from http://www.nobel.se/economics/laureates/1998/press.html

Sen, A. K. (1970). *Collective choice and social welfare.* San Francisco: Holden Day.

Simon, H. (1978). Rationality as a process and as product of thought. *American Economic Review, 68*(2), 1–16.

Tandon, A., Gakidou, E., Sousa, A., & Murray, C. J. L. (2004). *Cross-population comparability and PPPs: Using micro-data on indicators of consumer durables.* Paper presented at the Population Association of America Annual Meeting, April 1–3, 2004, Boston, MA.

Tyack, D. (1974). *The one best system: A history of American urban education.* Cambridge, MA: Harvard University Press.

Tyack, D., & Cuban, L. (1995). *Tinkering toward utopia: A century of public school reform.* Cambridge, MA: Harvard University Press.

U.S. Congress, Office of Technology Assessment. (1990). *The use of integrity tests for pre-employment screening* (Report No. OTA-SET-442). Washington, DC: U.S. Government Printing Office.

U.S. Congress, Office of Technology Assessment. (1992). *Testing in American schools, asking the right questions* (Report No. OTA-SET-519). Washington, DC: U.S. Government Printing Office.

Williamson, O. (1975). *Markets and hierarchies: Analysis and antitrust implications.* New York: The Free Press.

10

Assessing the Validity of Test Linking: What Has Happened Since *Uncommon Measures?*

Paul W. Holland
Educational Testing Service

First you try to solve the problem that they ask you about. Then you try to formulate and solve their real problem.
—Advice from Frederick Mosteller to a young statistician (1966)

Can politics provide the impetus to advance the science of assessment? Feuer (2003) shows how the fundamental tension between the "*e pluribus*" and the "*unum*" of American society resulted in a "collision between politics and science" in the Voluntary National Testing (VNT) debate of the mid-1990s. Two distinct National Research Council (NRC) panels were commissioned by Congress to address the question of linking the scores on different tests (the "*e pluribus*") to a common scale (the "*unum*"). "Linking" the scores on two tests means that there is a formula that takes a score from one test, say X, and puts it on the scale of the other test, say Y, in such a way that *a score on X can be interpreted as if it were a score on Y.*

Each NRC panel wrote a report saying "no" to the request for a simple, mechanical, psychometric/statistical solution to this problem that would be satisfactory for the several uses that the committee envisioned. *Uncommon Measures* (Feuer, Holland, Green, Bertenthal, & Hemphill, 1999) addressed the general question of linking various distinct tests to a common scale; *Embedding Questions* (Koretz, Bertenthal, & Green, 1999) addressed the same issue but focused, as Congress requested, on a very specific method of doing the linking—that of using common items in both tests to make the link, rather than using common people taking both tests.

These NRC reports summarized, in my opinion, the accepted professional knowledge extant at the time of their writing. Their negative conclusions run counter to the usual helpful stance that statisticians provide when faced with subtle problems of data design and analysis. But their negative conclusions were, in my opinion, the proper conclusions to be drawn from years of practical work with many tests and their various uses.

As the chair of one of the NRC panels and a member of the other, I suppose my support for their conclusions goes without saying. I wish to emphasize, however, that it was the shared knowledge of professionals in the field that was the primary support for the conclusions. This is not the same type of knowledge that is available from a history of detailed quantitative studies of the effects and consequences of linking various types of tests to each other. There were few if any such studies to draw on, and so, in the end, professional judgment had to be our guide.

I was not entirely satisfied by this state of affairs, and a bit disappointed by our reliance on professional judgment. However, the field of psychometrics was not as mature as it needed to be to provide a careful quantitative discussion of how bad a link between two tests would be if they diverged significantly from being "equally reliable measures of the same construct." Nevertheless, I believed then and still believe that our professional knowledge was not based on myth, or was an unduly conservative point of view. As I continue to study this problem I see that what we concluded was proper and that our negative advice, as far as it went, was sound.

Of course, the problem of linking tests has a 100-year history and the problem of linking nonparallel tests has not gone unnoticed. The discussions of Linn (1993) and of Mislevy (1992) reflect analyses of test linking that go back many years, for example, Angoff (1971). What was missing was a serious quantitative assessment of what can go wrong. The NRC reports suggested that inappropriate test linking would cause the sky to fall, but common sense says that in some cases it could be merely a gentle rain or even a light fog. Without a quantitative assessment of the consequences, it is hard to know what to expect in any given case. And this is exactly what educational policymakers really need to know about linking. It is the "real problem" to which the quotation from Fred Mosteller refers.

Which all leads me back to my initial question: Can politics provide the impetus to advance the science of assessment? In my case, I have spent a great deal of time since the reports were written examining how to address the question of quantifying the effect of linking tests that were never designed to be linked in the first place. This chapter summarizes my efforts and those of my colleagues and indicates areas where I think fruitful work can be pursued. In this regard, I hope that graduate students and researchers will jump on this bandwagon and push the efforts indicated here in useful directions. As Feuer (2003) implies, the desire to link tests will never go away. It is a manifestation of a deep and fundamental tension in American society, and will continue to arise as a simple solution to a complex problem. Continuing to say "no" will not do as users become more sophisticated and demand more evidence of the consequences of suboptimal test linking in specific situations. I regard this as a serious but healthy challenge and one that can be the source of many interesting projects. It is something that can truly advance our knowledge of psychometrics. So, I conclude that yes, politics can provide the impetus to advance a science, even psychometrics!

SO, WHAT'S THE PROBLEM WITH LINKING THE UNLINKABLE?

There are many ways to look at a request to link the scores of tests that were never designed with this in mind. The NRC panels explicitly recognized that a test score is not simply the result of an examinee sitting down and answering a series of questions. Certainly an examinee has to do that, but there is a whole substructure underlying a test score that goes way beyond the simple formula of "examinee + test = score." This "substructure" is often not recognized, and the intuitive test theory that informs most lay understanding of tests and scores is oblivious to it. Mislevy and Braun (2003) describe several aspects of intuitive test theory and compare it to intuitive physics. Intuitive science is often useful for simple things but just as it cannot put a man on the moon, it cannot maintain a serious testing program for very long. Two of the basic "primitives" of intuitive test theory identified by Mislevy and Braun are: "Any two tests with the same title measure the same thing" and "Any two tests that measure the same thing can be made interchangeable, with a little equating magic." But of course, reality is never so intuitive.

Every test or assessment is designed to *sample* certain behaviors of an examinee. As with any other sample, a test is limited both by its *coverage* of some population of test content or "domain" of interest and by its *size*. (Note that here we are talking about samples of test questions not of people.) Sample coverage is all about what the test is intended to "measure." Sample size is all about the accuracy or "reliability" of this measurement. Two assessments with the same title, say two state assessments of fourth grade mathematics, can sample different aspects of this vast domain, and can do so with differing accuracy. In *Uncommon Measures,* both test content (sample coverage) and test reliability/accuracy (sample size) were mentioned as two important factors that would affect the validity of a link between the scores of two tests. In addition, *test formats* (multiple choice, constructed response, computer-based tests, performance-based assessments, etc.) and *test use and consequences* (ranking, cut scores, gains over past scores, etc.) were also identified as two factors that could affect the validity of a link. In *Embedding Questions,* the following "threats to obtaining a common measure" were identified and discussed: the degree of *standardization* of the test administration, *accommodations* to the test administration offered to examinees who need special treatment (LEP, SD, etc.), the *time of year* of the assessment with respect to schooling practices, provisions for *test security,* and the *stakes* that the results of the test will have for various participants in the testing enterprise (students, teachers, school administrators, state education departments, legislators, etc.).

All of the factors summarized in the two reports are part of the substructure underlying any testing program and the scores that emerge from it. In short, tests and assessments are complex cultural activities that are influenced by many factors. Ignoring this substructure can render the interpretation of a test score quite ambiguous. In particular, if two tests differ substantially in these several dimensions, the ability to provide a valid link between their scores may become mere wishful thinking, or at least so goes the professional wisdom gleaned from a century of the science of assessment, and I tend to believe it.

So the basic problem is that many things can influence a test score beyond the mere words in the questions and the examinee's ability. In view of this, *Uncommon Measures* made three recommendations for future research on test linking: (a) developing criteria for evaluating the quality of a link between tests, (b) determining the level of precision needed to make valid inferences about linked tests, and (c) improving the reporting of information from linked tests. The research I now turn to addresses aspects of the first two of these topics.

MEASURING THE "EQUATABILITY" OF TESTS

How can we evaluate the "quality" of a link between two tests? My colleague, Neil Dorans, and I, with others, have begun to formulate ways of quantifying the problems that arise when test scores are linked. We have focused on the most stringent form of test linking, which is called *test equating*. The goal of test equating is to make the scores on the two linked tests interchangeable for any purpose. We identified five "requirements" for test equating. These requirements have appeared in various forms throughout the literature on test equating. Verbatim from Dorans and Holland (2000) they are:

(a) **The Equal Construct Requirement:** tests that measure different constructs should not be equated.

(b) **The Equal Reliability Requirement:** tests that measure the same construct but which differ in reliability should not be equated.

(c) **The Symmetry Requirement:** the equating function for equating the scores of Y to those of X should be the *inverse* of the equating function for equating the scores of X to those of Y.

(d) **The Equity Requirement:** it ought to be a matter of indifference for an examinee to be tested by either one of two tests that have been equated.

(e) **Population Invariance Requirement:** the choice of (sub) population used to compute the equating function between the scores of tests X and Y should not matter—i.e., the equating function used to link the scores of X and Y should be *population invariant.* (pp. 282–283)

The first two requirements are continued recognition that linking is most satisfactory when the two tests measure the same thing with the same level of accuracy. They restate the first two factors from *Uncommon Measures,* mentioned earlier, that can affect the validity of test linking. The symmetry requirement is different. It limits certain aspects of the mathematical form that the formula for performing a linkage can take. It summarizes an 80-year-old debate in psychometrics regarding the acceptability of using certain regression-based methods to equate test scores.

The equity requirement can be viewed as a way to evaluate whether a proposed test equating is satisfactory. A very strong evaluation is required, however, to hold for *any* test taker and requires assessments of their indifference or preference. Finally, we come to the fifth requirement of *population invariance.* This is also an evaluation of a proposed test equating, and it requires that the same equating function be obtained no matter what subpopulation provides the data used for the computation.

Dorans and I found that population invariance provided the most direct method we could envision for evaluating the "validity of a link." Our reasoning was that if you got different equating functions depending on which subpopulation of examinees supplied the data for the computation then that was a sign of a problem. If the difference was small then it was a small problem, but if it were large then that was one measurable sense in which a link could be "invalid." Our reasoning was roughly that if you got a substantially different equating function when you used data from, say, the boys, as compared to when you used the data from the girls, then the link was unsatisfactory. In more concrete terms, if the link for boys transformed a 75 on X to a 78 on Y but for girls a 75 was transformed to a 73, then this was a clear case of both "population sensitivity" and "link invalidity." Who could justify linking X and Y in this situation? Perhaps you might require a bigger difference than 78 − 73 to convince you, but that is merely a matter of degree!

It is not enough, however, to notice a disparity between the equating functions; we wanted to produce a measure of how big this disparity was. In Dorans and Holland (2000) we proposed several related measures that can be used for this purpose. The simplest one results in a single number and it provides an index of how dissimilar the equating functions are for various subpopulations of examinees in a data set. More complicated measures show how the equating functions differ all along the score scale. To describe these measures we need to introduce some notation.

We let X and Y denote the two tests and let their scores be x and y, respectively. In this discussion we regard the direction of the equating to be from X to Y. In order to calculate an equating function between X and Y we need data and that will come from a *target population* of examinees, which we denote by **P**. In addition, there are several subpopulations of **P** that will play a role, and we denote them by $\mathbf{P}_j$. The subpopulations are viewed as partitions of **P** into mutually exclusive and exhaustive subsets such as males and females, or several racial/ethnic groups or even the fourth grade in 2002 versus the fourth grade in 2003.

An equating function that maps the scores on X to those of Y, computed using the data from **P**, is denoted by $e_\mathbf{P}(x)$. When the data are from $\mathbf{P}_j$ the equating function is denoted by $e_{\mathbf{P}_j}(x)$. Two very important equating functions are the linear and equipercentile equating functions. They may be denoted as

$$\text{Lin}_\mathbf{P}(x) = \mu_{Y\mathbf{P}} + (\sigma_{Y\mathbf{P}}/\sigma_{X\mathbf{P}})(x - \mu_{X\mathbf{P}}) \tag{1}$$

and

$$\text{Equi}_\mathbf{P}(x) = G_\mathbf{P}^{-1}(F_\mathbf{P}(x)), \tag{2}$$

where in Equation 1 $\mu_{X\mathbf{P}}$ and $\sigma_{X\mathbf{P}}$ denote the mean and standard deviation of X-scores over **P** whereas $\mu_{Y\mathbf{P}}$ and $\sigma_{Y\mathbf{P}}$ denote these moments for the distribution of Y-scores over **P**; and in Equation 2, $F_\mathbf{P}(x)$ is the cumulative distribution function (cdf) of X-scores over **P** whereas $G_\mathbf{P}^{-1}$ denotes the inverse of the cdf of Y-scores over **P**. It is easy and instructive to see that both Equations 1 and 2 satisfy the Symmetry Requirement indicated earlier. In my work, I tend to regard the equipercentile function, $\text{Equi}_\mathbf{P}(x)$, as the more basic equating function and the linear function, $\text{Lin}_\mathbf{P}(x)$, as a linear approximation to it. This relationship is discussed in detail in von Davier, Holland, and Thayer (2004).

In addition to a system of equating functions—an overall function, $e_\mathbf{P}(x)$, for all of **P** and separate functions, $e_{\mathbf{P}_j}(x)$, for each subpopulation of interest, $\mathbf{P}_j$—we also assume there are a set of weights, w_j, one for each subpopulation. The weights should be positive and sum to one over the set of subpopulations being considered. We originally thought that the weights might just be proportional to the size of each subpopulation, but this is not entirely satisfactory. I have come to think that equal weights are probably a good idea on the grounds that if you regard a subpopulation worth examining then it should be given equal weight with all the others under consideration. This is an area where consensus needs to be found because the choice of weights can affect the results, as we see next. I begin with the most general measure, called RMSD(x). It is defined by

$$RMSD(x) = \frac{\sqrt{\sum_j w_j (e_{P_j}(x) - e_P(x))^2}}{\sigma_{YP}}. \tag{3}$$

The RMSD(x) is based on the differences, $e_P(x) - e_{P_j}(x)$, between the equating function computed for the whole target population, $e_P(x)$, and the ones computed for each subpopulation, $e_{P_j}(x)$. These differences are combined into the root mean square and then divided by the standard deviation of Y over the population **P** in order to remove the effect of scale differences to allow data from different equatings to be more easily compared. This is the proper standard deviation because $e_P(x)$ should be in the units of the Y-test. I prefer reporting 100 RMSD(x) so that it is in the units of a *percentage of a standard deviation* of Y over **P**. This gives it a type of "effect size" interpretation and I use that in this chapter.

RMSD(x) is useful because it can be applied to any system of equating functions no matter how they are computed just as long there is an overall equating function and one function for each subpopulation of interest. There are, however, two additional measures discussed in Dorans and Holland (2000). The first reduces the function of x, RMSD(x), to a single average value, and is the REMSD or "root expected mean square difference." It is defined as

$$REMSD = \frac{\sqrt{\sum_j w_j E_P (e_{P_j}(\mathbf{X}) - e_P(\mathbf{X}))^2}}{\sigma_{YP}}, \tag{4}$$

where E_P denotes the "expected value" or average over the distribution of X-scores on **P**, that is, the random variable, **X**.

The second additional measure introduced in Dorans and Holland (2000) is the version of the REMSD that arises when a special system of the equating functions is used. This is the system that they call the "parallel-linear linking functions." These are all linear equating functions with the additional restriction that they are parallel and have a common slope, $(\sigma_{YP}/\sigma_{XP})$, rather than different slopes, $(\sigma_{YP_j} / \sigma_{XP_j})$. The benefit of using the parallel-linear system is that it shows how a seemingly different way of assessing population invariance of linking functions is the same as RMSD(x) or REMSD.

Dorans and Holland show that the following equation holds for a parallel-linear system of linking functions:

$$\text{RMSD}(x) = \text{REMSD} = \sqrt{\sum_j w_j \left[\left(\frac{\mu_{XP_j} - \mu_{XP}}{\sigma_{XP}} \right) - \left(\frac{\mu_{YP_j} - \mu_{YP}}{\sigma_{YP}} \right) \right]^2} \qquad (5)$$

The right-hand side of Equation 5 is the root mean square difference between the standardized mean differences for X and Y scores over the P_j. If X and Y line up the standardized mean scores for each P_j in exactly the same way, then the right-hand side of Equation 5 will be zero. This is another way of thinking about population invariance and the linkability of scores on two different tests. If X and Y line up the standardized scores for each of the subpopulations in very different ways, then we would suspect that they are not going to be linkable, and Equation 5 shows that REMSD will detect this. I point out that Equation 5 holds for any choice of weights.

The right-hand side of Equation 5 can be computed using data that are often available—means and standard deviations of subgroup and total-group scores on a common population. This fact makes the calculation of RMSD and REMSD for the parallel system of equating functions a useful tool for studying the effects of various sorts of test differences on equatability. Dorans and Holland (2000) propose that REMSD be used to give a quantitative measure to the various dimensions along which tests can differ in terms of their effects on population invariance and the linkability of tests. They give a few examples and here I augment those results with a few more. Clearly this work is in its infancy but some patterns are worth reporting at this point, if only for the questions they raise. As these computations come from a variety of sources I have suppressed the specifics of which tests are included, but Table 10.1 summarizes the results I could find so far. Most of the subgroups are gender based because these data are usually available. When given a choice I included only the computations using the parallel-linear formula, Equation 5, to avoid adding method differences to the mix. I have organized the 29 REMSD values I could find so that as we go down the rows of Table 10.1 we consider cases where test equating is viewed as more problematic. Thus, at the top I include the cases of equating parallel multiple-choice (MC) tests and at the bottom I include the cases of equating quantitative to language-based tests.

There are three immediate conclusions. The first is that the REMSD measures do reflect the trend as we move from more equatable tests to less equatable ones. The median values generally go up as we go down the rows of the table. Parallel tests have the smallest REMSD values, similar tests have intermediate values, and very dissimilar tests have the largest values.

TABLE 10.1
REMSD Values, as Percentages of a Standard Deviation,
for Different Types of Linkages Between Tests

Similarity of the Linked Tests	Range of REMSD Values (Number of REMSD Values)	Median REMSD Value
Parallel MC tests	0.6–1.7 (6)	1.45
Similar math tests		
Both MC	1.5–2.0 (2)	1.75
One non-MC	0.5–2.3 (2)	1.4
Similar nonmath tests		
Both MC	5.4–10.1 (6)	7.35
One non-MC	1.7–5.6 (5)	3.8
Linking quantitative to Language-based tests Both MC	13.3–20.3 (8)	14.1

This is gratifying. We also see two effects that are not necessarily expected. First, similar math tests have REMSD values close to those of parallel tests; this is true even if one of the tests involves some non-MC items and the other is all MC. In addition to these findings, we also see that for nonmath tests, the use of non-MC items in one of the tests does not appear to increase the REMSD values as one might have expected. In fact, the median REMSD for MC to MC for nonmath tests is about twice that of MC to some non-MC links. This may be an artifact of the sample of REMSD values I was able to find, but it is worth understanding.

Table 10.1 is suggestive of general trends and its format could be useful in related studies. However, statisticians working with testing programs are usually interested in the consequences of a given degree of population invariance for the scores reported in their programs. This is an additional topic beyond the work reported here. REMSD and related measures indicate how much the studied subpopulations affect the equating relationship between the two tests. They do not necessarily directly connect to what happens to reported scores. The consequences of these differences for reported scores are a next step and are affected by the types of scores and their uses. Work along these lines is reported in Dorans (2003).

In addition to their necessary focus on the consequence for reported scores, I encourage test program statisticians to use the various opportunities for studying linkages between nonparallel tests that arise in their tests to contribute to the study of how much various test factors influence REMSD values. Table 10.1 needs augmentation along many dimensions before we can respond quantitatively to the demand for linking the unlinkable. Every testing program has something to contribute to this enterprise, but some of these potential contributions may not directly relate to the reported scores of the program.

WEAKER FORMS OF TEST LINKING

In addition to test equating, there are other forms of test linking that are of interest. In this section I briefly indicate some work that Machteld Hoskens and I have published recently that bears on predicting scores from one test to another rather than equating them (Holland & Hoskens, 2003). This work is more theoretical in that it is based on classical test theory and involves the notion of the "true score" that lies behind the score that is actually observed for a given examinee. In our work we first showed how the usual form of classical test theory could be viewed as a first-order approximation to the more modern item response theory models. Then we applied these results to studying the predictions of true scores from observed scores and other examinee information. This type of *direct true-score prediction* has a long history and is an example of the "Kelley formula." The twist we considered was, what happens when you try to predict the true score of X but use the observed scores from Y, a possibly nonparallel test. This we called "indirect" prediction.

We were able to show that the usual linear regression function for predicting the observed score on X from the observed score on Y is the best linear predictor of the true score of X from the observed score on Y. There is, however, a reduction in prediction accuracy that must occur when nonparallel tests are linked in this way. The prediction error, a measure of how far on average the prediction is from the target, will be inflated by a factor, that we called H. To get a feel for H, if H = 1.5 then the prediction accuracy for indirect prediction is 50% larger than it is for direct prediction.

In an example that we used to illustrate our methods, a Science Performance Test predicted the true scores of a Science Multiple Choice Test with values of H ranging from 1.62 to 1.76, depending on which of three groups of examinees we considered. This suggests that linking very different *forms* of testing in the same subject can have quite large effects on degrading prediction accuracy. Although these results are interesting and suggestive, we are a long way from knowing how to use them in practice.

Measuring the sensitivity of equating functions to subpopulations and measuring the effect on inaccuracy of linking different types of tests are both areas of psychometrics that respond in part to the questions raised by

Uncommon Measures. Much more can and should be done on these topics to give us a quantitative assessment of what goes wrong and by how much it goes wrong when we try to link the scores on tests that were never meant to be linked. I encourage others to consider these problems and continue these lines of research. Linking the scores on two tests may never have been intended, but the impetus to do so may lead to its being done anyway. It is often only a matter of time.

REFERENCES

Angoff, W. H. (1971). Scales, norms and equivalent scores. In R. L. Thorndike (Ed.), *Educational measurement* (2nd ed., pp. 508–600). Washington, DC: American Council on Education.

Dorans, N. (Ed.). (2003). *Population invariance of score linking: Theory and applications to advanced placement program examinations* (Report No. RR-03-27). Princeton, NJ: Educational Testing Service.

Dorans, N., & Holland, P. W. (2000). Population invariance and the equatability of tests: Basic theory and the linear case. *Journal of Educational Measurement, 37,* 281–306.

Feuer, M. J. (2003, October). *E pluribus Unum: Linking tests and democratic education.* Paper presented at the ETS Invitational Conference: Measurement and Research Issues in a New Accountability Era, New York.

Feuer, M. J., Holland, P. W., Green, B. F., Bertenthal, M. W., & Hemphill, F. C. (1999). *Uncommon measures: Equivalence and linkage among educational tests.* Washington, DC: National Academy Press.

Holland, P. W., & Hoskens, M. (2003). Classical test theory as a first-order item response theory: Application to true-score prediction from a possibly nonparallel test. *Psychometrika, 68,* 123–149.

Koretz, D. M., Bertenthal, M. W., & Green, B. F. (1999). *Embedding questions: The pursuit of a common measure in uncommon tests.* Washington, DC: National Academy Press.

Linn, R. L. (1993). Linking results of distinct assessments. *Applied Measurement in Education, 6,* 83–102.

Mislevy, R. J. (1992). *Linking educational assessments: Concepts, issues, methods and prospects.* Princeton, NJ: Educational Testing Service.

Mislevy, R. J., & Braun, H. I. (2003, May 22). *Intuitive test theory.* Retrieved March 30, 2004, from http://www.education.umd.edu/EDMS/mislevy/papers/ITT09.pdf

von Davier, A. A., Holland, P. W., & Thayer, D. T. (2004). *The kernel method of test equating.* New York: Springer.

ACCOUNTABILITY ISSUES FOR ENGLISH-LANGUAGE LEARNERS

11

ELLs Caught in the Crossfire Between Good Intentions and Bad Instructional Choices

Lily Wong Fillmore
University of California–Berkeley

In this chapter, I discuss achievement issues related to English-language learners (ELLs). This is not a small matter, as you know. There are some (and this is very conservatively speaking) 4.6 million ELLs in our schools nationwide, a 32% increase over the past 5 years, adding up to 9.6% of the total U.S. school population (Kindler, 2002). More realistically, there are at least half again as many students who are not classified as ELLs, but whose command of English does not allow them to deal adequately with the academic work required of them in school. Among them are "former ELLs" who were reclassified as speakers of English well before they mastered English, and many others who are speakers of English only, but whose English does not support academic development. This has long been a problem, but the problem has been exacerbated considerably by recent changes in educational policy, and, unfortunately, practice. With the massive reforms mandated by the No Child Left Behind Act of 2001 (NCLB, 2002), ELLs like all children must be tested annually for educational progress, beginning in the third grade. Under NCLB, ELLs can be tested in their primary languages for up to 3 years, if tests in English do not reveal what they can do academically. Nevertheless, ELLs must also be assessed each year to determine whether or not they are making progress in learning English as a second language. These requirements for assessment are not in themselves a bad idea. We do need to know whether or not our schools are doing what they should be doing to enable students who enter school speaking little or no English to learn what they should be learning. The problem is in what happens when progress is less than it should be. The picture that is emerging is a dismal one. I briefly outline what is happening—you no doubt have been hearing about it already—but the dismal picture is *not* what this chapter is about. The real question is, why? To understand what is happening, we have to know what's missing from the basically good intentions of the policy and practice. This is actually a much more general problem affecting many students, but let's see how it affects ELLs specifically.

BRIEF DESCRIPTION OF WHAT'S HAPPENING—
THE DISMAL PICTURE

What is happening to ELLs, as schools across the country struggle to implement NCLB? How are schools dealing with the requirement that they show "adequate yearly progress" (AYP) in student scores? In the case of Title I–funded schools, the consequences of not showing adequate progress, at least for the first couple of years, is masked in "-isms"—optimism and euphemism alike—they are identified as schools in need of "program improvement," not such a bad thing because the school can then receive federal funds for staff development and "supplemental services." However, if after a couple of years of added support and teacher fix-ups, the school does not make progress in improving student test scores, then it is in serious trouble—kids can go hunting for a better school (assuming there are better ones to be found in the area), the school can be reconstituted, or it can be given to commercial companies to see if they can run it better and more effectively than public educators can.

So everything depends on how the students in a given school perform on tests. And no one is exempted—not even those who speak no English. Although for the most part they can be tested in their primary languages for the first 3 years, assuming there are tests, not only in Spanish and Chinese, but in Gujarati, Hakka, Somali, and Ilocano too, they must be assessed in English right from the beginning to determine whether or not they are making progress in acquiring it as a second language. In California, Arizona, and Massachusetts, ELLs have got to be included in statewide assessments of academic performance in English right from the start. There are no exemptions even for newcomers. As you might guess, these kids will not do as well in any test given in English as they would if they knew enough English to make sense of the test materials. If they do not perform well, their scores are going to drag down the school's overall performance rating, and that does make having ELLs in a school more difficult than not having ELLs. As I have said, the intention of NCLB is not the problem, exactly. How could it be a bad idea to hold schools accountable for all students, leaving no child behind, as it were? One would think that schools should be pleased at having a big enrollment of English learners, because they would lower the school's AYP sufficiently to trigger an infusion of funds for programmatic improvement and staff development (or at least the promise of funds)! The rationale is that such support should enable the school to do a better job educating ELLs, so test scores would go up in a short time, and that demonstrates that the children are getting a better education. But that is not how things have been playing out.

Instead, in many ways, getting an education from the public schools has become much more difficult since the passage of NCLB. Consider what is happening in many places: Because test performance is so crucial to a school's standing, enormous effort is put into improving it, especially for those students who are likely to have any difficulty doing well in tests. The phenomenon has been documented incisively by Linda McNeil and Angela Valenzuela (2001) in their recent study of how educators in Texas responded to the pressures to show gains in test scores or suffer the consequences of poor test scores in their schools. They found that aligning teachers' and administrators' job rewards to test scores resulted in a reduction in the quality and quantity of curricular instruction, with attention that might otherwise have been given to teaching, going into test preparation. They also found a single-minded concentration on teaching subjects and skills (i.e., low-level basic skills in reading, writing, and math) that were tested, and the neglect or abandonment of subjects that were not tested (e.g., science, social studies, art, etc.). They reported that ELLs were being relegated exclusively to ESL (English as a second language) classes where they got low-level English instruction and little other subject matter beyond that.

McNeil and Valenzuela (2001) argue that the much-vaunted success of the Texas testing program in raising the performance of low-performing schools has in fact had a harmful effect on education in that state. In their words, it has "widened the gap" between the education of children in Texas's poorest (historically low-performing) schools and that which is available to more privileged children. The children who have been most hurt by this effort to improve schools through testing have been ELLs, they found.

As one visits schools and listens to the reports of what is happening in schools across the country, it is evident that the Texas situation is hardly unique. Whereas in the past, schools might have devoted a couple of weeks or even a month to test preparation before achievement tests were given in the spring, these days normal instructional activities are set aside as early as January to prepare children for the tests they will be taking in May. Teachers report that the fear that ELLs are not going to do well in those tests is so great that they have no choice but to work exclusively on subjects, facts, words, and skills that are going to be tested. There is no time for anything else, they say—certainly not for frills like literature or social studies or field trips or anything that is not going to be on the annual academic tests children have to take. For ELLs, test preparation has become their primary curriculum, with children drilled on the facts and skills that are covered in the tests throughout the school year. Teachers who try to go beyond that regimen are called on the carpet, and are instructed by their supervisors to teach what they are supposed to be teaching.

In a large California school district (unidentified here), a first-year high school English teacher tried to give his 9th- and 10th-grade students some instructional substance—what he knew was included in the English curriculum for those grades: for example, the narrative analysis of different forms of dramatic literature—comedy, tragedy, drama, and dramatic monologue—and the way similar universal themes or topics are treated across genres, and so on.

His students, Chicano students from the barrio, were classified as low achieving and lacking in basic skills. In fact, most of them had performed poorly on the language arts part of the state's mandatory achievement test the year before. The English curriculum for such students in this unnamed school district is basic reading and writing—forget about literature and forget about the rest of the standards for high school students in the 9th and 10th grades. The district mandates a remedial phonics program using only simple decodable texts for low-achieving high school students, one that is so basic that it would be regarded as too low a level even for second graders.

The teacher—young, idealistic, and himself a Chicano from the same barrio—having informally assessed his students, had determined that they did not really need the low-level materials mandated by the district—it would kill what incentive they had left to learn. He believed that what they needed was a challenge and that they would be receptive to standard 9th- and 10th-grade materials as long as he gave them the instructional support they needed to make sense of them. He saw ways to develop English-literacy skills by using such materials, and he had ideas about how to make his students enthusiastic about learning. His ideas seemed to be working. In occasional e-mails to friends like myself, he reported that his students were coming to class, and they were getting really involved in the materials he was teaching—*Romeo and Juliet*! It had been a struggle, but he and his students were committed to understanding and getting everything they could from this timeless drama. One day, his friends received the following e-mail from him:

> It's a sad day today as I am told I must teach the XXX! program and discontinue teaching the stuff I enjoy and the kids enjoy. I was forced today to convince my students of this and I am feeling horrible. This program has been adopted by the district and many teachers seem to be buying into it. I teach

one block of this, 112 minutes every day. I also started teaching ZZZ. I feel very sad about this. I could have just gone to XXX! and ZZZ training and that's all I would've needed to be a teacher in—USD schools. I am really frustrated. I know you have heard my frustrations before, but this is the worst. The look on my kids' faces was too painful. I am in the middle of Romeo and Juliet and I was told to stop "and catch up" for the stuff I haven't done in the program. We will be getting "XXX! Police" in every school in the next 2 weeks and we must show proof of student progress through the rubrics given in the program. Okay, enough venting. This is what the biggest district in the state is doing, and others are continuing to join.

Was this teacher overdramatizing the situation? Let me share with you a passage from the texts he was told to teach in place of Shakespeare:

"The Van"

ﺍDad had a bad van.
Dad had a sad lad.
The sad lad had to nap.
The bad van had gas.
Dad had to pat the bad van.
Mad Dad had to rap the bad van. Mad Dad had to jab the bad van.
Mad Dad had to bam the bad van.
The bad van had to sag. The bad van had to lag.
A fat man had a cab.
The cab had gas.
Do Dad and the sad lad ban the van? Dad and the lad do ban the van.
The cab had the fat man, mad Dad and the sad lad. (Greene, 2000, Unit 3, Book 2)

To judge the appropriateness of these materials,[1] one has to keep in mind that the students who are getting 112 minutes of such instruction each day are 15- and 16-year-olds who will eventually have to pass California's High School Exit exam in order to graduate from high school. It's hard to see how "Mad Dad" is going to help.

---

[1]About the program from the California State Department of Education's Web site, http://www.cde.ca.gov/

This program was adopted as a partial reading/language arts program covering the standards of spelling, phonemic awareness, reading comprehension, and phonics. Materials include: two instructor's manuals, Sounds and Letters for Readers and Spellers Drill Book and cards, vocabulary card set, practice workbooks, and student books. This submission provides instruction in the standards in grades 1–12, although the State Board of Education only adopts materials for grades K–8. It begins at the student's remedial level and concludes with the student at grade level. It uses systematic, explicit decoding and other research based instructional techniques to enable below grade level readers to progress to grade level through an intensive model.

I get back to this vignette later when I discuss what is needed to make schools work better for English learners and for all those students who need help surviving in this new get-tough era of American educational policy and practice.

WHAT'S NEEDED?

As I said earlier, the NCLB legislation that has changed schooling so dramatically across the country is not, in itself, a bad idea. How could anyone argue that English and math literacy should not be promoted and well developed in all students in our schools? Or that the schools should not be held accountable for demonstrating that they are providing all students, including ELLs, with educational experiences that allow them to make academic progress each year in the subjects that are taught in school? And if the schools are not making progress, then what is so bad about making sure that they get some help to beef up their programs? Indeed, who would not agree that we want "highly qualified" teachers using methods that have been shown in research to be effective, scientifically speaking?

The problem is not what NCLB requires—the problem lies in its underlying assumption that all that's needed to make schools change is to mandate that they are going to change, or else. Change what? What do educators have to know, understand, believe, and do in order to improve what happens in schools? It is no secret that our schools have not served many children well—not just ELLs, but any child who comes from language or cultural backgrounds that differ much from the mainstream American background of the economically advantaged students in our schools. Our schools do a fine job educating children who are judged to be bright and promising; and they do well enough educating those who are thought to be average. The ones our schools do not serve well at all are those who are judged to be unpromising: children of color, the children of the poor, and especially those who do not speak English when they enter school. In fact, these children are often so poorly educated that one could make the case for educational malpractice just on the basis of the achievement gap alone. That's what has led policymakers to adopt the sweeping reforms in NCLB. But are we really clear about what's needed to improve our schools?

Yes, what has been mandated has not been supported with adequate funding—but that's *not* what I am going to talk about. What I would like to do is to offer my analysis of what I think is needed to improve the picture for ELLs—and perhaps for many other children on the wrong side of the achievement gap as well. Because I am a linguist who, over the past 35 years, has worked on issues related to language learning, language in learning, and language in teaching and testing, it is hardly surprising that my analysis focuses on language. It is certainly a critical issue for English learners, but I would argue that it is for many other students as well. English learners are not the only language learners in school. When children enter school at age 5 or 6, they speak whatever language or languages their caregivers have socialized them in, but they are hardly mature speakers of any of those languages. Over the next 12 or 13 years of schooling, they will be doing a lot more language learning—they have to master the register of English that is required for academic literacy and learning. The English learners have a bigger job—they too have to learn the register of English required for academic development, but they have to do it from scratch. It is clear to most people that these students need instructional help in English, although there is hardly any agreement on what kind of help would be most beneficial, or how much of it is needed. It is not at all clear that once they have learned enough English to get by in school, that they are going to need any more instructional help with language, any more than native speakers of English do, whether the English they speak is the standard variety used in school or is one of the many varieties of English that can differ substantially from the one used in school. The point here is that, aside from what gets covered in "Language Arts" in the elementary grades, there is little real attention given to language development in school.

I argue that for children who come to school already speaking Standard English, what they get from Language Arts may be all the help they need. Many of them—but not all—can extrapolate and acquire from the books they read most of the forms and structures that figure in academic English. For everyone else—former ELLs, speakers of varieties of English other than the standard (e.g., African American English, Puerto Rican English, Chicano English, Reservation English, Hawaiian Pidgin, Village English, and so on) this is not enough. They are going to need continuing instructional support for mastering the English used in school. But such help, generally speaking, is seldom provided in school, to the educational detriment of many students. Many students are on their own, fighting their way through the materials they are supposed to be learning from, materials that could be written in Elfish for all the clarity they impart. This I see as a fundamental problem in our schools. And why is help not provided? The reasons boil down to one fundamental problem: Few educators know enough about language and language learning to recognize the need for attention to language in teaching and learning.[2]

---

[2]This issue was examined in a monograph by Catherine Snow and me called "What Teachers Need to Know About Language" (Fillmore & Snow, 2002). We argued that in a society that is as diverse as ours, language is a critical factor in teaching and learning, and therefore, it is crucial that every teacher know enough about it to deal effectively with it in schools. An ironic note: I have been told that this article is being used to justify the use of the low-level, phonics-based "Mad Dad" program described earlier for high school students!

If we look at instruction, it appears that many educators assume that if children know English, and if they learn to read it, language is no longer a problem. They might need a little help with unfamiliar or technical vocabulary in school materials, but that's all the support that is needed. Consider, for example, the word *half*. When children first encounter it in a math activity, usually at the second grade, it is likely to be in the context of an activity such as the following: "Here is a circle that is divided into two parts. Color half of it red. Color the other half blue." At that point, *half* is treated as a math concept that must be carefully developed, to help children discover gradually how this term is used to describe a part of a whole, a division of a quantity that is expressible as the fraction "1/2," and so on. Its use as a "fuzzy" concept is even discussed in problems involving expressions such as "about or around a half," but once its use is established, it is assumed that children know what *half* means, and it does not need to be explicated further. That may be true most of the time—until somewhere along the line, they encounter the expression, "half again as many," as was used in the introductory remarks of this presentation: "More realistically, there are at least **half again as many** students who are not classified as ELLs, but whose command of English does not allow them to deal adequately with the academic work required of them in school." This was said in relation to the 4.6 million students in U.S. schools who are classified as ELLs. So what is the claim here? How many students am I saying lack the English-language skills required for academic development? How does anyone learn the meaning of expressions such as "half again as many" or "as much"? Is it by encountering texts such as the following one, where the reader has to do some mental computation based on the figures given to make sense of the relationships?

> Based on available data, in 2000, the Sonoran Desert human population was slightly less than 8 million. This number is nearly three and a half times the 1970 population of approximately 2.3 million, and nearly half again as much as the 5.5 million living in the region in 1995. (University of Arizona, 2002)

Here the population living in the Sonoran Desert in 1995 is given as 5.5 million, and to interpret "nearly half again as much," the reader has to see it as expressing the relationship between 5.5 million and "slightly less than 8 million" as meaning 5.5 million **times one and a half**, and not 5.5 million times **one half**. In other words, it means "times 150%" rather than "times 50%." "Half again" is not a bizarre usage, nor is it unique. One can go through any text materials at any grade level, in any subject area, and from any source one chooses and find endless examples of familiar words used in expressions that do not easily map onto the simple definitions of the constituent terms that children are taught in school—to the extent that any attention is even given to word meaning in schools. And notice that although an expression such as "half again as much" can be characterized as an idiomatic expression,[3] it is used not just in casual speech, but in academic texts too, as in the example just discussed.

What kind of help do ELLs need to learn English, and how much of it do they require? As I said, no one would question that some kind of instructional help is needed, but what should it consist in? Actually, ELLs do not always get much help learning English. Many teachers assume that when children don't know English, all they need is to be totally immersed in it, and as long as they are motivated, they will learn it as a second language. Moreover, the belief is that English is English. Thus, as long as ELLs are with classmates who speak English, they will learn it from them. I have spent a good many years studying the process by which children learn English—from English-speaking classmates, from other ELLs, and from teachers—and can testify that what children learn from one another is a far distance from the English they will need for academic learning.

When instructional help is provided these days, it is too often misguided. There is, these days, a belief that English can and should be taught through its writing system. The ESL field has well-developed instructional methods and materials based on theories of how languages are learned and thus, how they should be taught. But with the pressure to make ELLs measure up on English achievement tests as soon as possible, tried-and-tested ESL approaches have been sidelined, and ELLs are given heavy doses of phonics-based reading instruction because that's what gets tested not only in reading tests, but in tests of English proficiency that are being given in many states. Can students learn to read in a language they are just trying to learn? Though some can (as the evidence from immersion programs have shown), many others cannot. They can learn to decode, but are unlikely to make any sense of what they are "reading" until they have learned enough of the language to know what it means. On the other hand, what is there to understand when the materials are like the "Mad Dad" text? The idea is that such materials are so simple, anyone can "deal" with them, with or without much English. It is assumed that once kids have mastered the skills involved in decoding sentences such as "Mad Dad had to ban the bad van," they can make sense of any other sentence in English, such as, "What does the phrase disappear over the horizon mean in the following sentence: 'The

---

[3]Compare "half again as much" with idioms such as "not the half of it," which means "just a bit" or "a small part" or "hardly the whole story," or "by half" as in "He's too clever by half" meaning "by a considerable extent." These expressions tend to be used in more casual discourse, but notice that it would be hard to interpret them simply by knowing the meaning of the word *half.*

reward of working with a trained falcon is the companionship of creatures that can choose at any time to disappear over the horizon forever.' " This is from a released item used in the California High School Exam, one of the reasons why our English teacher had to teach the phonics program instead of *Romeo and Juliet* to his 9th- and 10th-grade students. His students were former ELLs, technically speaking. Most of them had been in the district's schools for as many as 8 or 9 years, and knew English, but performed poorly in the state's achievement tests, especially in the English language arts subtest. In fact, in that district, 87% of ELLs in the 9th grade and 86% of those in the 10th grade were scoring at levels "below basic" and "far below basic" in the English language arts part of the state's standards-based tests. Former ELLs were doing better, but not by much, with around 40% scoring "below basic" and "far below basic" on this test. In a district where overall, 54% of 9th graders and 48% of 10th graders are scoring below and far below basic in the English language arts subtest, one could argue that there was good reason for the district to take desperate measures to remediate the problem. The question that must be asked is this: Will what the district has decided to do enable these students, who make up a substantial proportion of the district's high school students, perform better in school and in the tests that everyone is worried about? Will "Mad Dad" help them use academic English more effectively, think better, be more enthusiastic about school and better prepared for the job market that is just 3 or 4 years down the road for many of them? There is no question that these students will have to learn to read well, and we can even be generous and suppose that "Mad Dad" will help them do that, but how do the students manage to vault from "Mad Dad" to grade-level-appropriate texts such as *Romeo and Juliet*?

So let's consider what is needed, and what might make a difference. In fact, let's be guided by the key mandates of NCLB, beginning with the requirement that all teachers after the enactment of Title I be "highly qualified." That's a start. It would be great if all teachers were highly qualified. But what does that mean? In NCLB, it means that teachers have to have at least a bachelor's degree, and be able to pass state-adopted subject-matter and pedagogy tests. That leaves a lot of room for interpretation, of course, and in fact, one finds districts finessing the requirement to such an extent that hardly anyone can be said *not* to be highly qualified.

What exactly does qualify a teacher to work with students in our diverse schools? What must a teacher know, believe, understand, and be able to do, as I have asked, to be at all qualified to improve what happens in our schools? Our young Chicano teacher certainly had it all when he was hired to teach. He had earned a B.A. in a prestigious "Big 10" university. He then went on to a 2-year rigorous teacher preparation program at another "Big 10" university where he earned a secondary teaching credential in English and an M.A. as well. In his program, he learned about language, language teaching and learning, how to teach literature and composition, and English as a second language. He is smart, committed, and talented. He was highly qualified when he stepped into his first classroom, despite being a freshly minted teacher. His students recognized his expertise, and they connected with him and with the literature he was so enthusiastic about. But the administrators in his school did not see that at all. They required that he and all the other teachers in schools like the one he was teaching in attend a week-long intensive training program in which he was drilled on the precise methods that were going to be used to teach high school students the "Mad Dad" program, and another just like it. When he wrote in his e-mail, "I could have just gone to XXX! and ZZZ training and that's all I would've needed to be a teacher in—USD schools," it was clear that he was feeling that there was no recognition on the part of the district administrators that his previous preparation as a teacher counted for anything.

That, to me, is something we must think about. Highly qualified teachers count for nothing if there aren't highly qualified administrators to support their efforts, and to trust them to do the right thing by their students. Not only do teachers need to know about subject matter, appropriate pedagogy, language, and language teaching and learning, but superintendents, principals, supervisors, and other administrators have to know about these matters too. In California, where one in every four students (25%) is extremely limited in English proficiency, there is so little confidence in teachers, qualified or not, being able to improve reading test scores, that the reading programs of choice are scripted ones, which require teachers to stick to a rigid format and schedule. In many schools, there are monitors hired to enforce strictest adherence to these programs, which are largely of the "Mad Dad" persuasion.

Next, let's consider reading and math, the two subjects that NCLB identifies as foundational skill areas. When we look at test scores, it is clear that these are subjects in which many students, not just ELLs, need help in mastering. But again, what kind of help and how much of it is needed? I have mentioned California's short-sighted approach to improving reading instruction. Math instruction could certainly use some help too. But what kind of help? I argue, that although language support is clearly needed in reading instruction, it is equally necessary in math instruction too. Can children handle the language of academic learning, whether in reading or math or science, without help? In my earlier discussion of language development, I alluded to children's need for support in acquiring the academic register of English used in school. This is something that gets mentioned here and there, but what does it entail? How is it acquired? It is not just Standard English, but a form of it, which, if it is learned at all, is learned in school.

There are precious few native speakers of academic English. Children who come from homes where there is a lot of book reading and elaborated speech used in everyday discourse have a head start on acquiring it, and indeed, some few children may have even acquired a young person's version of it before going to school. Everyone else learns, develops, and perfects it over the course of 12 and even 16 years of formal education, through reading, writing, thinking, explaining, and arguing. How to characterize it? It is the language of formal discourse, of texts, and of logical reasoning. It is more precise in expression, perhaps a bit more complex in structure, and makes use of vocabulary that is more often Latin and Greek in origin than Anglo-Saxon. If you want some examples, just open any formal text, narrative or expository, and you have it. Acquiring it involves something of a Catch-22 problem: It is most readily accessible through written texts, and it is through reading that most of us become familiar with its forms and structures. However, to make much sense of the texts we read, we have to be familiar enough already with the forms and structures used in those texts. So how do kids get access to it in the first place? I give one example of how this can be done, in a math program.

As I have said, language is a critical factor in math learning too, not just for ELLs but for most kids. This is not as obvious as one might think, especially to math teachers. The response one gets from math teachers (rather than grateful attention) is:

> Look math is itself a language—a universal language; that's all the language kids need to deal with it.

So why do ELLs and speakers of dialect have so much trouble learning math? Don't they need some help with the English you're using when you teach them about this universal language of numbers and concepts?

> Hey, I'm not an ESL teacher; my subject is algebra/geometry/calculus. English is someone else's problem.

Suzanne Chapin, a math educator, and Cathy O'Connor, an educational linguist, are engaged in some important research demonstrating that when attention is given to language development in math instruction, the payoff can be substantial (Boston University/Chelsea Partnership, 2003).[4] Over the past several years, this Boston University team has been working collaboratively with teachers, parents, and administrators in the Chelsea (Massa-

---

[4]*Project Challenge Year II Progress Report, 2001* and *Project Challenge Evaluation Summary, 1998–2001,* submitted to the Jacob K. Javits Gifted and Talented Students Education Program, U.S. Department of Education. Suzanne H. Chapin, Project Director, Boston University, Boston, MA.

chusetts) schools to explore ways to improve math teaching and learning
for students who are identified as disadvantaged. In fact, their goal was not
just to improve math instruction and thinking, but also to help kids discover that they were good, and perhaps even talented, in math learning.
How were they going to do that? The plan was to teach the children—mostly
minority, many of them ELLs, from diverse backgrounds—how to think,
solve problems, argue, and explain their math understandings the way
gifted kids would. The approach and methods were collaboratively designed by the classroom teachers and the university researchers. The project began in 1998, with Chapin and O'Connor recruiting approximately 100
fourth graders for their Project Challenge. The next year, they added a new
cohort of 100 fourth graders, with the first cohort moving up to the fifth
grade. The third year, they added still another cohort of 100 fourth graders,
with the earlier cohorts each moving up a grade. Nearly two thirds of the
children began the program as ELLs. By the end of the project's third year,
they had 283 students in the program, Grades 4 through 6. The curriculum
they followed was a rich and varied one. It went into "greater depth" and
was "more advanced" than the usual middle school math curriculum, based
on the assumption that any child would benefit from a program in which
the thinking and learning behaviors that are characteristic of gifted children are promoted and developed. The curriculum was aligned with the
Massachusetts Math Framework and the National Council of Teachers of
Mathematics Standards. Using problems that required team effort, the children learned to solve them, and to explain how they arrived at the solutions they got. Instructional activities supported the students' development
of more and more sophisticated understanding of the problem types they
were dealing with, and encouraged them to become more precise and
knowledgeable in their use of the academic discourse that was needed for
explaining their reasoning and strategies for solving the problems. Classroom discussions in which the children were guided and supported in explaining their reasoning in problem solving were not easy (O'Connor, 1999).
Chapin and O'Connor report that it took nearly a year and a half before
some of the students became confident enough to participate easily in such
discussions. Meanwhile, however, the children were encouraged to explain
in writing what they were thinking and why as they tackled the problems
they were working on, thereby developing their written language skills as
well as their mathematical reasoning. How did the children do as a result of
their participation in this program?

On every measurement used to track the children's progress and to
evaluate the effectiveness of the program—the Test of Mathematical Ability (TOMA–2), the mathematics computation, concepts, and applications
subtests of the California Achievement Test (CAT), and the Massachusetts
Comprehensive Assessment System (MCAS), which all public school stu-

dents take as well—Project Challenge students did extremely well, far exceeding the performance, not only of other students in the district, but of students in the entire state as well. Performance on the TOMA revealed that although Project Challenge students were pretty average in their math potential during the first year of the study, with 70% placing in the average ranks and 28% rated above average and superior, the next year the percentage of students rated as above average and superior had risen to 64%, as we see in Table 11.1, from their second-year project report. What we see here is evidence that a gifted program can actually dramatically increase math capability in students who would otherwise be pretty average or below that in math. Table 11.2 shows how well the first fourth-grade cohort performed on the MCAS math test after the first year of the program, compared to the other fourth graders in Chelsea schools, and in the state of Massachusetts (Boston University/Chelsea Partnership, 2003). After just 1 year, 61% of Project Challenge students were scoring at the proficient or advanced levels in this test, whereas only 18% of Chelsea students overall did as well in the fourth grade. The most striking finding was that by third year of the program, all but two of the Project Challenge students were scoring at the proficient or advanced level. In fact, all of the children in the Chelsea schools who scored at the advanced level on the sixth-grade MCAS math test were Project Challenge students. The students in this study were mostly minority, and largely limited in English

TABLE 11.1
Comparison of Rating of Cohort I Students on TOMA-2 in 1998 and 1999

Descriptive Ratings on TOMA-2 of 80 Project Challenge Participants	Number of Students	
	1998	1999
Very superior	1 (1%)	3 (4%)
Superior	3 (4%)	12 (15%)
Above average	18 (23%)	36 (45%)
Average	56 (70%)	29 (36%)
Below average	2 (2%)	0 (0%)

TABLE 11.2
1999 Grade 4 MCAS Mathematics Achievement Percentages

	Advanced	Proficient	In Need of Improvement	Failing	Absent	Number of Students
Chelsea	5%	13%	50%	30%	2%	473
Project Challenge students	21%	40%	37%	2%	0%	90
State	12%	24%	44%	19%		77,007

proficiency. What Project Challenge demonstrated was that good instruction and attention to language make a big difference educationally (O'Connor, Anderson, & Chapin, 2003). The teachers did an exceptional job, not just because they were exceptional people, but because they had faith in their students' ability to learn, and they were willing to do what it took to support their intellectual development. It was, I have been told, a lot of very hard work on the part of teachers and kids alike, but this project demonstrated, through careful and scientifically conducted research, that when economically disadvantaged students, minority-background students, and ELLs are given the instructional support they need, they can and do excel in school.

And in the final analysis, isn't that precisely what NCLB was hoping to achieve in its declaration that school improvement programs must use methods and instructional strategies that "scientifically based research" has shown to be effective? To that, one must say, YES! But there is no evidence that anyone has beaten a path to Chapin's and O'Connor's doors to ask how to do what they are doing. What Chapin and O'Connor have demonstrated is that there are no simple solutions to tough problems: Raising academic achievement for historically underachieving students requires faith in students' ability to learn, a lot of hard work from teachers and students, collaboration between researchers and front-line teachers, and knowledge about cognitive and language development, in addition to knowledge about math learning. Instead, what most educators seem to be looking for are magic bullets—fail-safe solutions that can be adopted and applied without much thought or effort, and strictly by fiat. The only thing that counts as "research based" instructional methods and strategies these days are programs that are reductionist in the extreme, reducing complex learning to mindless drilling on the most basic of skills, and cutting out the need for teacher or student thought and initiative. In California, for example, the only thing that anyone much cares about in reading is phonics. Oh, it is true, phonics is important, but it is not the be-all-end-all in the development of as complex a skill as reading. In math, yes, math facts like the times-tables are important, but they do not by themselves assure children that they will be able to solve problems and do math.

There is so little faith in teachers' being able to teach that the practice these days is to neutralize them and turn them into mere conveyers of the received and mandated curriculum, whether or not it is appropriate. Interestingly, NCLB may be providing the means to demonstrate eventually the short-sightedness and, indeed, the wrong-headedness of such approaches to educational reform. Magic bullets may be fine, as long as no one gets caught in the crossfire! In requiring that schools test children each year for academic progress, NCLB will reveal whether the reforms it has mandated are a boom or a bust for our kids and our schools.

REFERENCES

Boson University/Chelsea Partnership. (2003, September 1). *Twelfth report to the Legislature.* Retrieved March 29, 2004, from http://www.bu.edu/chelsea/pdfs/legreport2003.pdf

Fillmore, L. W., & Snow, C. E. (2002, September). What teachers need to know about language. In C. T. Adger, C. E. Snow, & D. Christian (Eds.), *What teachers need to know about language* (pp. 7–53). McHenry, IL: Delta Systems Co.

Greene, J. F. (2000). *Language! A literacy intervention curriculum program grades 1–12.* Longmont, CO: Sopris West Educational Services.

Kindler, A. L. (2002). *Survey of the states' limited English proficient students and available educational programs and services, 2000–2001 summary report.* Washington, DC: National Clearinghouse for English Language Acquisition & Language Instruction Educational Programs.

McNeil, L., & Valenzuela, A. (2001). The harmful impact of the TAAS system of testing in Texas: Beneath the accountability rhetoric. In G. Orfield & M. Kornhaber (Eds.), *Raising standards or raising barriers? Inequality and high stakes testing in public education* (pp. 127–150). Cambridge, MA: Harvard Civil Rights Project.

No Child Left Behind Act of 2001, Pub. L. No. 107-110, § 115 Stat. 1425 (2002).

O'Connor, C., Anderson, N., & Chapin, S. H. (2003). *Classroom discussions using math talk to help students learn, grades 1–6.* Sausalito, CA: Math Solutions Publications.

O'Connor, M. C. (1999). Language socialization in the mathematics classroom: Discourse practices and mathematical thinking. In M. Lampert & M. Blunk (Eds.), *Talking mathematics* (pp. 17–55). Cambridge, England: Cambridge University Press.

University of Arizona. (2002). *Sonoran Desert: A component of the drylands of the world portal.* Retrieved September 20, 2003, from http://alic.arid.arizona.edu/sonoran/index.html

12

Report on an Informal Survey of ELL Educators at the State and Local Levels

Julia Lara
Council of Chief State School Officers

There has recently been a great deal of visibility given to the challenges that the No Child Left Behind Act (NCLB) has presented to state-, district-, and school-level educators. The law has far-reaching accountability provisions that require states to move all students to the proficient level on statewide assessments of mathematics and English language arts within 12 years. Schools not meeting achievement targets are subject to a gradually increasing set of consequences that include school choice within the district, provision of supplemental educational services, development of a corrective action plan, and, ultimately, school restructuring. The costs of transferring low-income students from a low-performing school to a higher performing school and of supplemental services for these students are borne by the school district.

Though much has been written about the reactions of mainstream educators to NCLB, few articles have appeared in either the major newspapers or trade papers about the likely effect of the provision on the education of ELL (English-language learner) students. For example, a review of articles written in *Education Week* from January 2002 to October 2003 yielded fewer than five articles addressing the impact of NCLB on ELL students. During the same time period 34 articles focusing on NCLB implementation appeared in this newspaper.

This short chapter is intended to fill the void in current reporting of NCLB's perceived impact on ELL students. It reports the outcome of a short survey of state education agency ESOL/Bilingual Directors that was conducted in November 2003. The purpose of the survey was to elicit from state directors their views regarding the impact of the NCLB on both district-level ESOL (English for speakers of other languages) directors and general-education educators, who are now faced with an increasing number of ELL students in their classrooms. Local ESL (English as a second language) and mainstream educators were also surveyed but did not corroborate the statements provided by the state directors. However, a review of reports from the field as reported in education trade papers and newsletters supports the statements of local educators. A review of articles that have appeared in recent months regarding local educator's reactions to NCLB implementation provides evidence to this effect.

ELL students comprise approximately 10% of the total U.S. public schools enrollment (approximately 5 million students) and are the fastest-growing segment in public school enrollment. Since 1990–1991 there has been a 105% increase in total LEP enrollment growth (National Clearinghouse for English Language Acquisition [NCELA], 2002). It is important to understand the implementation challenges concerning ELL students as policymakers engage in discussion regarding potential refinements to the law.

In the fall of 2003, a total of 17 state directors of ESL/bilingual answered a four-item electronic survey that elicited information regarding (a) the reaction to NCLB by local ESOL/bilingual educators, (b) the reaction of general-education educators, (c) state specialists' own opinions regarding the impact of the law, and (d) the respondent's expectation of the long-term impact of the law on ELL students. The questions asked in this survey are listed in Table 12.1. Enrollments of ELL/LEP students in the states represented by the respondents are shown in Table 12.2. The importance of these figures becomes apparent when viewed from the perspective of the localities in which these students are enrolled. For example, an examination of jurisdictions in which LEP (limited English proficient) students comprise 1% to 5% of the total K–12 enrollment shows that LEP students comprise a significant percentage at the local level in cities such as Boston (20%), Des Moines (10%), Minneapolis (24%), and Newark (15%).

TABLE 12.1
NCLB and the Education of English Language Learners Survey

1. What are you hearing from local ESL/Bilingual educators about the impact of NCLB in their classrooms?
2. What are you hearing from general-education educators about the impact of NCLB in their classrooms?
3. What do **you** think the impact of NCLB is likely to be?
4. In your opinion, will NCLB lead to positive or negative results for ELLs? Why?

TABLE 12.2
Percentage of Limited English Proficiency Students
in Selected States, 2000–2001

Percent of LEP Enrollment	Number of States
0–1	2
>1–5	10
>5–10	2
>10–20	1
>20–30	2

Note. From *National Clearinghouse for English Language Acquisition,* October 2002, Washington, DC.

NCLB AND ELL/LEP STUDENTS

Though ELL students were expected to be included under the previous version of the Elementary and Secondary Schools Act (ESEA, 1994), NCLB added new requirements. For many educators, the most troublesome aspect of NCLB is the accountability provision under both Title I and Title III of the law. ELLs are one of the subgroups included in the accountability formula that requires that all students and subgroups show progress toward meeting the states' proficiency standards in mathematics and English language arts in 12 years. Specifically, under NCLB, states must develop English-language-proficiency standards; assessments that measure progress in learning English and are aligned to state standards; annual achievement targets for assessing movement from non-English-proficient to English-proficient status; and annual targets for moving students toward meeting the "proficient level" in the academic areas (mathematics, English language arts). In addition, states must include at least 95% of all ELL students (and other subgroups) in their state assessments. Moreover, ELL students must be tested after 1 year of instruction in English, but can be assessed with a non-English-language instrument for up to 3 years. After 3 years, students must be assessed in English unless there is special dispensation granted for a maximum of 2 years. Local educators must request this exemption.

Because ELL students must be tested after 1 year of instruction in English, and most states do not have subject matter assessments in a language other than English, ELL students are likely to be assessed in English. As soon as ELL students become relatively proficient in English they are "mainstreamed" and replaced by other students who are not yet proficient. Under these conditions, ELL students, when tested in English, are most likely to obtain scores that demonstrate lack of English proficiency, rather than lack of content mastery in the subject being tested. Consequently, it would be difficult if not impossible to draw valid inferences regarding ELL students' understanding of content. Under these conditions, the ELL subgroup included in the AYP (adequate yearly progress) formula for Title I purposes will most likely not meet the proficient standard and will consequently trigger schools into the school improvement status. In addition, failure to meet annual achievement goals could result in loss of Title III funds at the state level.

Recently the U.S. Department of Education (2004) issued policy guidance allowing states to exclude LEP students from the accountability calculation during their first year of enrollment in the United States. However, states must assess the English-language development of ELL students and assess in mathematics with accommodations, but the math scores and that of English language arts (should the state choose to administer this test) are not counted for accountability purposes. Although this new flexibility gives states some relief, it does not address the fundamental problem with the statute relative to Title I accountability: testing students in the content area (English language arts and mathematics) before students have the linguistic competence in English to show content knowledge.

RESPONSES OF LOCAL ESL EDUCATORS
AND GENERAL-EDUCATION EDUCATORS

A close examination of the survey responses received from state directors reveals that there is a great deal of unanimity between ESL teachers/specialists and mainstream educators regarding the challenges posed by NCLB at the local level. The most often occurring comment focused on inclusion of ELL students in the statewide content assessments and the AYP accountability formula under Title I. This provision of the law has become the most onerous for local and state educators. One director stated that this concern as follows: "Expectations of AYP in academics are unrealistic until ELLs have some concept of English language proficiency." Others objected to the additional testing required for all students, including ELLs: "There is not enough time to adequately prepare them in both acquisition of English and core content for the required assessments." A few ESL educators expressed concern about "backlash" against ELL students because they, as well as students with disabilities, are likely to trigger schools into school improvement status. Others reported that ESL teachers felt pressure to move students "too quickly," to "teach to the test," and to narrow the curriculum. Finally, there are local ESL educators that are not pleased with the inclusion of LEP students in statewide assessments and with the requirements for disaggregation of data. It is impossible to impute intent based on the responses received, given the format we used, limited (short-answer) statements.

Mainstream teachers seemed apprehensive about their ability to work effectively with ELL students. This is understandable, of course, because the requirement to test ELL students in the content areas at the end of Year 1 of English-language instruction might well drive schools to "transition" ELL students into mainstream classrooms earlier in their English-language development trajectory. State directors reported that these mainstream educators expressed the need for training in areas such as cultural diversity, English-language development, and appropriate instructional strategies for ELLs. In addition, they did not know how to balance the needs of ELL students with those of non-ELLs in their classroom. The concern regarding the lack of training to work with ELLs has been previously reported. The U.S. Department of Education's Schools and Staffing Survey (2002) reported that in the last 3 years, teachers have received a total of only 8 hours of training related to the education of ELL students. Another report noted that in the state of California, which enrolls the highest number of ELL students, only half of all teachers have received this type of training. It is therefore reasonable for local educators to have some level of anxiety regarding the increase of ELL (or recently mainstreamed) students in their general-education class without additional support.

Although few in number, local educators also expressed the belief that benefits were likely to accrue to ELL students as a result of increased attention to ELL students and the increase in funding that has accompanied it. For example, the following comment was typical of the few positive comments reported by the general educators and state bilingual/ESL specialists: "We are hearing very positive comments from the field about the new Title III accountability system ... for the first time ever there are statewide expectations for student growth and holding LEAs accountable for ensuring that students do not fall through the cracks." Two questions were asked in order to elicit responses regarding the "likely impact of NCLB," and expected results (negative or positive). The most positive comments regarding the likely impact of NCLB on ELL students came from the directors themselves. There were 35 statements provided in response to the question focusing on "likely impact." Responses to this question were wide-ranging with clustering on three to four issues related to impact on the quality of programs, data collection and use, attention to the needs of the ELL students, testing, and teachers. Six of the 35 statements anticipated that the law would have a negative impact; the remainder were mostly positive. This can be attributed to two factors. First, the respondents were ESL bilingual directors, many of whom view themselves as advocates of ESL students and programs. Second, these directors operate at the state level and do not foresee consequences falling directly on them, as would district- and school-level educators. Most positive comments from this group (7 out of 35) focused on the quality of the services and awareness of ELL student needs and the needs of the schools in which they are enrolled:

- I think NCLB will result in more and better (increased quality of) language acquisition programs and more intensive content-based instruction for ELLs.
- We will change programmatic laws related to ELL (for the better).
- Increased awareness of students ... more focus on low-performing schools.
- ELP standards will provide a tool to inform instruction.

The next set of positive comments most often cited by the directors focused on the benefits of the disaggregation requirements:

- There will be lots of data available, especially test data.
- We will have improved data capacities in our state—we will do a better job of tracking ELL and programmatic factors.
- We will have a better statistical picture of what is going on.

There was some disagreement among the directors about the impact on teachers and about whether there was sufficient funding to support the increased demand for services to ELL students. Though a few directors acknowledged the increase in Title I and Title III funding, others noted insufficient funding to "fix the problem." Comments related to impact on teachers were also mixed, with some stating that the law will aggravate the teacher shortage whereas others noted that it will increase the number of ESL teachers.

Finally, the state directors were asked whether NCLB would lead to negative or positive results. As was the case with the previous question, there was a range of responses, most of which anticipated positive outcomes (18 out of 27 comments) from the implementation of the new requirements. The following lengthy response by one director typifies the range of responses received on this question:

The positive results are:

- Attention is being focused on this population of students. LEP students are mentioned in NCLB more times than any of the previous authorizations of the Elementary and Secondary Education Act.
- State-level English-language proficiency (ELP) standards are good.
- Development of new standards-based ELP assessments is good.
- Formula-based Title III funding has allowed school districts that never had funding for LEP students before to develop programs and provide services.

- Scientifically based research requirement has caused educators to use methods for LEP/ELL students that have an appropriate research base.

The negative results are:

- School districts may be less inclined to identify LEP students because the low test scores of the identified students will push the district into school improvement status. Students that are not identified are averaged in with all students and may not impact the averaged scores.
- School districts are focusing so much on the single paper/pencil achievement test that other sorts of assessments are not being considered. LEP/ELL students often do better with other sorts of assessments.
- Title III was not funded to the level that provides support for all LEP students in a state. The confusion over some districts having Title III for LEP/ELLs and other districts not having funding creates a negativity that could impact student services in all districts.
- Many requirements for all students, including ELLs, is included in Title I. Title I has increased funding. Funding is good, but Title I personnel may not necessarily have the experience or training to work with ELLs.

SUMMARY

This brief essay was intended to provide policy thinkers and educators with an insight into early implementation of NCLB from the perspective of the local educators who are working with ELL students. They clearly share the same concerns that non-ELL educators have expressed, as reflected in the comments received through the CCSSO (Council of Chief State School Officers) survey. State specialists are more hopeful, however, that the new attention to ELL students will result in improved services to these students and greater alignment between the course of studies provided to ELL students and those of non-ELL students. Moreover, in spite of the challenges in assessing content knowledge of ELLs prior to their acquisition of English, the NCLB requirements relative to data collection and reporting are welcomed by most of the survey respondents.

REFERENCES

National Clearinghouse for English Language Acquisition. (2002, October). *Survey of states' limited English proficient students and available educational programs and services 2000–2001 summary report.* Washington, DC: Author.

U.S. Department of Education. National Center for Education Statistics. (2002). *Schools and staffing survey, 1999–2000: Overview of the data for public, private, public charter, and Bureau of Indian Affairs, elementary and secondary school.* Retrieved April 2, 2004, from http://nces.ed.gov/pubsearch/pubsinfo.asp?pubid=2003409

U.S. Department of Education. (2004, February 19). *Secretary Paige announces new policies to help English language learners.* Retrieved April 8, 2004, from http://www.ed.gov/news/pressreleases/2004/02/02192004.html

USING ECONOMETRIC MODES IN SCHOOL ACCOUNTABILITY

13

Have Assessment-Based School Accountability Reforms Affected the Career Decisions of Teachers?

Susanna Loeb
Felicia Estrada
Stanford University

Assessment-based school accountability reforms have swept through the states, often including new tests for students and repercussions for students, teachers, schools, and/or districts. A number of recent studies have looked at the effect of accountability on student outcomes. Carnoy and Loeb (2003), for example, find greater gains in student math scores in states that implemented stronger accountability programs, although no change in students' progression through high school. Yet, these reforms are likely to impact teachers, as well as students. Increased scrutiny of teachers, combined with a focus on student performance and direct consequences for school funding and management, can substantially change teachers' work life. These changes may, in turn, affect teachers' career decisions about whether to teach, where to teach, and, once teaching, whether to transfer to another school or to leave teaching. This chapter describes the approaches that economists have taken to understand the impact of these recent reforms on teachers' careers. It also contributes to the small literature in this area by comparing teachers' descriptions of their work life and their predictions for their future in teaching in states with and without strong accountability systems.

Clearly there are reasons that teachers may be dissatisfied with the recent changes. As districts and schools put more emphasis on test performance, teachers may not have as much flexibility in their classrooms. They may face pressures to teach topics that that they are less interested in or believe are less important for students, or they may need to teach in ways

225

that increase test scores but not other important skills. Teachers also may have more day-to-day distractions as parents and administrators scrutinize the details of their classrooms. In addition, teachers may worry about the security of their jobs, particularly if they teach in schools with low-performing students, which are more likely to encounter repercussions from the state.

The increased emphasis on accountability and rewards may not be all bad for teachers, however. Standards-based reforms can provide opportunities for schools to focus on student learning. Although a focus on learning was sure to have been the case in many schools prior to the recent reforms, there were other, poorly functioning, schools that were preoccupied in other ways. Administrators may use accountability policies as leverage with the district to get rid of ineffective or distracting teachers and simply may focus more on trying to create a school that benefits students. Teachers may prefer to teach in these environments rather than in environments that do not recognize success in the classroom.

Thus, it is unclear, a priori, how the recent reforms will affect teachers. They may dissuade potential teachers from entering the classroom or may increase the probability that teachers will quit. These effects may be greatest in low-performing schools that already have difficulty attracting and retaining well-qualified teachers. However, the effects may work in the exact opposite direction if testing and accountability have made teaching more satisfying, especially in schools that had been mismanaged prior to reform. In what follows, we start by reviewing the two studies that have used quantitative approaches to studying the response of teachers to accountability reforms. We then provide new analyses of national data on teachers to ask whether these reforms have changed teachers' career decisions. Although the estimates are not without problems, the results generally suggest that assessment-based reforms have not increased teacher turnover.

TWO PREVIOUS STUDIES

Two studies to date have looked at the effects of accountability on teachers' career choices, one looking at changes in teachers' career paths following the implementation of testing in New York State, and the other looking at the change in teachers' careers following North Carolina's accountability reform. Both studies use detailed state administrative data to estimate the impact of these assessment-based reforms on teachers. We review each of the studies in the next two sections.

New York

Boyd, Lankford, Loeb, and Wyckoff (2003) use data on New York State to study the response of teachers to the implementation of testing. In the 1998–1999 school year, the New York State Education Department implemented a revised assessment system that reflected higher learning standards and included mandatory tests in English language arts and mathematics in Grades 4 and 8. The content of the tests is tied to curriculum that is intended to lead to a high school exit exam. The results of the tests are publicly reported. This chapter compares changes in the quit and transfer behavior of fourth-grade teachers whose students were mandated to take the test, to changes in the quit and transfer behavior of other elementary school teachers. It also looks at differences in the characteristics of teachers new to the fourth grade relative the characteristics of new teachers in other elementary school grades. In this way, the approach utilizes the variation in the policy by grade and relies on differences across grades to identify the policy's effects.

The data for the New York study describe first- through sixth-grade teachers in the years surrounding the implementation of the test, 1994–1995 through 2001–2002. The data set includes information on every teacher who was a part of the New York State public schooling system at this time. It contains a range of information about the qualifications of teachers, as well as the environments in which these individuals make career decisions.[1] The 8-year record allows the researchers to track individual teachers across grades and schools over the course of their employment in any New York State public school, identifying the grade level a teacher taught both before and after the implementation of testing.

The chapter begins by asking whether or not the introduction of high-stakes testing in the fourth grade has increased the turnover of fourth-grade teachers relative to that of elementary school teachers in nontested grades. Other policies or economic changes may affect teachers' career decisions, but a differential change of fourth-grade teachers is likely due to policies that target these teachers in particular (namely, the tests). Logit models estimate the probability that a teacher will leave the grade in the following year, either to teach in another grade or to exit teaching alto-

---

[1] The core data come from the Personnel Master File (PMF), part of the Basic Education Data System of the New York State Education Department. The NYS Teacher Certification Database (TCERT) combined with the Barron's ranking of college selectivity gives a measure of college selectivity. The NYS Teacher Certification Exam History File (EHF) provides teacher certification exam scores of individual teachers and whether they passed the exams on their first attempts. A school-level data set adds information on the location, grade span, student composition, and student performance for each school.

TABLE 13.1
Logit Estimates of Teacher Leaving the Fourth Grade Relative
to Other Grades by Urbanicity and Quartile of Student Test
Performance, New York Teacher Study: Odds Ratios (Z-Stat)

Variable	All	Urban	Suburban	Rural
Fourth grade post-1998	0.91	0.89	0.92	0.91
	(4.25)	(3.64)	(2.47)	(1.69)
N	359,962	148,390	149,769	61,803
	Highest Quartile	Quart 2	Quart 3	Lowest Quartile
Fourth grade post-1998	0.91	0.93	0.94	0.88
	(2.21)	(1.74)	(1.36)	(3.32)
N	89,938	89,026	90,061	90,937

Note. Student test scores are the percentage of students scoring at the lowest levels, Level 1 or Level 2, on the fourth-grade math exam. The first quartile is the schools with the lowest proportion of these scores.

gether, as a function of: (a) teacher characteristics including teaching experience, the competitive level of their undergraduate institution attended, whether or not they failed a certification exam, and ethnicity; and (b) school characteristics including urbanicity, whether the school is in New York City, the percentage of Black and Hispanic students, the percentage of students eligible for free lunch, and the percentage of students who scored at the lowest level on the New York State English Language Arts Exam. In addition, the models include dummy variables for the year and the grade; and interactions of fourth grade with the posttest years. This final interaction captures the impact of test implementation on teachers' exit decision. The coefficient on the interaction of fourth grade with the posttest years provides an estimate of the extent to which these teachers were relatively more likely to leave in the years following reform.[2]

The study estimates these models separately for two different groupings of schools based on the geographical setting of the school (urban, suburban, or rural) and the quartile of student achievement based on the students' test scores. Table 13.1 gives the results. For instance, 0.91 in the first panel signifies that the teachers are 91% as likely to leave the fourth grade following the test as would be predicted if no test had been implemented. This estimate is strongly statistically significant. That is, following the test teachers are leaving the fourth grade *less.* This reduced turnover is particularly evident in urban schools and in schools with the lowest performing students (lowest fourth of schools).

---

[2]For details see Boyd et al. (2003).

The study also asks how the relative leaving behavior of fourth-grade teachers differs for teachers with different characteristics. To do this it expands the previous model to include interactions of teacher characteristics with the fourth grade by year interaction. The coefficients on these new interactions measure the differential effect of the test on teachers with different attributes. Table 13.2 summarizes the results. Teachers with more experience are more likely to leave than are new teachers (25% more likely for teachers with 6 to 19 years of experience and 35% more likely for teachers with 20 or more years of experience, compared with first-year teachers). However, this relatively greater leaving for more-experienced teachers is confined to suburban schools and to schools with high-achieving students. These same trends are not evident in schools with lower scoring students. Following reform, teachers from more competitive undergraduate institutions are relatively less likely to leave.

Finally, the analysis looks to see whether the attributes of teachers entering the fourth grade changed with the introduction of testing. Using a similar approach, the study estimates the likelihood that a new teacher has certain attributes, including whether they are a first-year teacher; whether they have 2 to 5 years of experience, 6 to 19 years of experience, or 20 or more years of experience; whether they attended a highly competitive undergraduate institution; and whether they failed a core certification exam. The model includes the school characteristics, controls for the years and grades, and an interaction term for fourth grade with the tested years. The coefficient on the interaction term measures the extent to which new teachers in the fourth grade are more or less likely to have a certain characteristic following reform. Table 13.3 gives these results. We see that teachers new to the fourth grade are less likely to be first-year teachers (8% less) or

TABLE 13.2
Logit Estimates of Leaving the Fourth Grade for Teachers With Different Characteristics by Urbanicity and Student Performance Quartile, New York Teacher Study: Odds Ratios (Z-Stats)

Variable	Exp = 2 to 5 Years	Exp = 6 to 19 Years	Exp = 20 Years +	Most Competitive	Failed Exam
Characteristic of Grade 4 post-1998	1.14	1.25	1.35	0.87	1.05
Urban schools					
Characteristic of Grade 4 post-1998	1.03	1.02	1.12	0.89	1.07
N = 148,390	(0.28)	(0.20)	(1.04)	(0.80)	(0.83)
Lowest test quartile					
Characteristic of Grade 4 post-1998	1.02	0.99	1.04	1.01	1.01
N = 90,937	(0.2)	(0.06)	(0.28)	(0.07)	(0.10)

TABLE 13.3
Logit Estimates of Teacher Characteristics for New Fourth-Grade Teachers by
Urbanicity and Student Performance Quartile: Odds Ratios (Z-Stats)

Variable	Exp = 0	Exp = 1–5	Exp = 6–19	Exp = 20+	Most Competitive	Failed Exam
Fourth grade post-1998	0.92	1.19	0.99	0.86	1.09	0.98
	(2.06)	(4.73)	(0.26)	(3.46)	(1.57)	(0.36)
N	110,296	110,296	110,296	110,296	84,713	63,249
Urban schools						
Fourth grade post-1998	0.86	1.17	0.98	0.96	1.14	0.97
	(2.75)	(2.12)	(0.26)	(0.56)	(1.37)	(0.45)
N	62,031	62,031	62,031	62,031	43,562	36,756
Lowest test quartile						
Fourth grade post-1998	0.79	1.13	1.05	1.05	1.30	0.93
	(3.66)	(2.05)	(0.88)	(0.7)	(2.50)	(0.99)
N	41,939	41,939	41,939	41,939	30,124	25,499

Note. Models include urbanicity, whether the school is in New York City, the percentage of Black and Hispanic students, the percentage of students eligible for free lunch, and the percentage of students who scored at the lowest level on the New York State Fourth Grade Mathematics Exam or on the English Language Arts Exam; and dummy variables for the year (Y) and the grade (G).

to have 20 or more years of experience (14% less). They are more likely to have 1 to 4 years of experience upon entry to the fourth grade. They are also more likely to come from more competitive undergraduate institutions although this estimate is statistically significant at traditional levels only for low-performing schools.

In summary, the results of Boyd et al. (2003) do not accord with the popularly held belief that teachers are leaving tested grades as result of the implementation of standardized tests. In fact, they find exit rates decreased in the fourth grade relative to other elementary grades after state-mandated fourth-grade exams were introduced in the 1998–1999 academic year. Fourth-grade teacher turnover decreased across urban, suburban, and rural schools and across schools with different levels of student achievement. It decreased most for teachers with less experience and for those with bachelor's degrees from more competitive institutions. In addition, new teachers to the fourth grade in the years surrounding the implementation of exams were, on average, less likely to be first-year teachers and, in low-performing schools, more likely to have attended highly competitive undergraduate institutions than new teachers in other grades and in other years.

New York State is a good example to use when asking the effect of testing on student behavior. It has excellent administrative data and a wide variety of schools and communities. In addition, the implementation of testing in just one elementary grade allows the comparison of this grade to other grades. Researchers are often limited to before- and after-implementation comparisons in which many other things could be changing at the same time. In order for the grade-comparison estimates to be biased, there must be something besides the reform in question that affects fourth grade differently than it affects the other elementary school grades. Most changes are likely to affect all elementary school teachers approximately equally.

However, although there are clearly benefits to this analysis, it alone cannot be definitive. In particular, assessment-based accountability reforms vary across states. New York's system does not have direct repercussions for teachers such as increased pay for higher performance. As such it may not illicit as strong reactions from teachers as do other states' systems. In addition, the effect of accountability may extend beyond the tested grades. In this case a comparison between the tested and nontested grades would miss some (and maybe all) of the effects of the reform on teachers' decisions. The North Carolina case provides an alternative approach and an alternative accountability system.

North Carolina

Like New York, North Carolina has exceptional data on teachers. North Carolina also has had a system of accountability since 1996–1997 for elementary and middle schools that includes direct incentives for teachers. The state's ABCs program (A for accountability, B for basic skills, and C for local control) tests students in each of the elementary school years (kindergarten through eighth grade). It uses a combination of the level of student achievement in school and the change in scores from year to year to rank schools as exemplary, no recognition, or low-performing. Low-performing schools fail to meet the standard for growth in test scores set by the state and have more than 50% of their students performing below grade level. Teachers in exemplary schools are each given a bonus of $1,500. Clotfelter, Ladd, Vigdor, and Diaz (2003) assess how this accountability system has changed the willingness of teachers to teach in low-performing schools. Unlike the New York study, which compares fourth-grade teachers to other elementary teachers, this study compares teachers in low-performing schools to those in higher performing schools, with the assumption that teachers in higher performing schools would be less affected by the implementation of this system.

The data for this study come from a microlevel data set from the North Carolina Department of Public Instruction. It follows teachers across schools over time and links teachers to the students in their classrooms. The data include the experience, gender, and race of all North Carolina elementary school teachers during the academic years 1994–1995 to 2000–2001 and the racial composition and test score performance of students in each of the schools in which the teachers work.

The study asks whether the accountability system has changed the decisions of teachers to exit low-performing schools. It uses a hazard model for the probability of leaving the school, which estimates whether teachers are more likely to quit low-performing schools, are more likely to quit postreform, and are more likely to quit low-performing schools differentially postreform. The model also adjusts for the teacher's gender and for whether the teacher is White. Table 13.4 gives the results of this analysis. For a typical teacher with 10 years of experience working in low-performing schools prior to the reform, the probability of leaving the school was approximately 17.6%. After the reform this increased to 19.1% (the change is significant at the .05 to .01 level in four of the five specifications reported in the chapter). This 1.5-percentage-point increase compares to a 0.5-percentage-point increase for teachers who were not in low-performing schools. For new teachers, the change was 5.1 percentage points for low-performing schools and 0.8 percentage points for those in other schools. The increase in the probability of leaving was even greater for those low-performing schools labeled as such by the state. Following reform, low-performing schools saw a substantially greater increase in the turnover rate of their teachers than did higher performing schools.

In another part of their analysis Clotfelter et al. (2003) assess whether the characteristics of teachers changed following reform, but find little difference between the changes in low-performing and higher performing schools. As shown in Table 13.5, they find that low-performing schools were more likely than other schools to have novice teachers prior to accountability (38% vs. 30%), but that this tendency did not increase following reform. However, the trends in the percentage of novice teachers did change. The 4 years prior to reform show a drop in novice teachers and teachers from noncompetitive colleges in low-performing schools. This trend did not continue in the years following reform. The change in trends before and after reform is not evident in higher performing schools, al-

TABLE 13.4

Estimated Probabilities of Departure From a School, Typical
Teachers With 10 Years of Experience and 1 Year of Experience

10 Years Experience		*1 Year Experience (New Teacher)*	
Typical individual	0.150	Typical individual	0.320
+ Post	0.155	+ Post	0.328
+ Low-performing	0.176	+ Low-performing	0.338
+ Low × Post	0.191	+ Low × Post	0.389
+ Label × Post	0.209	+ Label × Post	0.403

Note. Calculated by authors based on the coefficients of the model. Low-performing school is defined as a school in which more than half of its students are below grade level on math or reading test scores. Other definitions give similar results (Clotfelter et al., 2003).

TABLE 13.5
Proportions of Low-Quality Teachers by School Performance;
Levels and Trends, Pre- and Postaccountability

	Teachers With No Experience		Teachers From Uncompetitive Colleges	
	Lowest Tests Schools (20%)	Highest Tests Schools (20%)	Lowest Tests Schools (20%)	Highest Tests Schools (20%)
Fourth Grade				
Preaccountability[a]	0.380	0.304	0.268	0.196
Postaccountability[b]	0.363	0.293	0.260	0.215
Fourth-grade changes				
Preaccountability[a]	−0.048	0.011	−0.031	−0.003
Postaccountability[b]	0.006	−0.019	0.016	0.018
Seventh Grade				
Preaccountability[a]	0.376	0.308	0.290	0.221
Postaccountability[b]	0.363	0.305	0.290	0.225
Seventh-grade changes				
Preaccountability[a]	−0.042	−0.003	−0.070	0.021
Postaccountability[b]	0.031	0.002	0.050	−0.008

Note. None of the differences across periods is significant. Low-performing schools are the schools in the bottom 20% of the weighted distribution of schools ranked by the percentage of students below grade level; middle-performing schools are in the middle quintile (40% to 60%); and high-performing schools are in the top 20%, where the weights are the numbers of fourth or seventh graders in each school.

[a]The preaccountability period starts in 1995/1996 for teachers with no experience and in 1994/1995 for teachers from uncompetitive colleges; it ends in 1997/1998.

[b]The postaccountability period starts in 1997/1998 and ends in 2000/2001. Standard errors for the differences were calculated on the assumption that the errors of the pre- and postaccountability periods are independent.

though due to large standard errors the differences between school types are not statistically significant. This result is suggestive but not confirmatory of a negative effect of reform on the qualifications of teachers in low-performing schools.

North Carolina provides an excellent example for studying the effect of standards-based reforms on teachers' career paths because of the availability of detailed data and the sophistication of their accountability system, which includes both labeling of low-performing schools and direct financial incentives for teachers. Again, however, no single system or study can tell the whole story. Clotfelter et al. (2003) compare low-performing schools with higher performing schools. This comparison makes sense because the structure of the system increases the incentives for teachers to teach in high-performing schools; these are the schools more likely to receive an exemplary rating and less likely to be labeled as low-performing. However, there are drawbacks to this approach as well.

Low-performing schools face a greater difficulty in attracting and retaining teachers even without accountability reforms. As such, they are more susceptible to changes in the supply of and the demand for teachers. California's class-size reduction provides a vivid example of this phenomenon. When California dropped early elementary class size from 30 to 20 students, all elementary schools faced an increased demand for teachers. However, because high-performing schools are generally more attractive to teachers, these schools were able to pull teachers from lower performing schools. Thus, low-performing schools needed more new teachers, not only because of the decreased class size but because many of their teachers left to move to other schools. This reform created a highly visible problem for difficult-to-staff schools. Yet, less dramatic increases in the demand for teachers or decreases in the supply for teachers are likely to create similar disparities between high- and low-performing schools. Supply-and-demand changes magnify in low-performing schools. Thus, any change that might have been occurring in North Carolina concurrent with the reform could easily impact low-performing schools more than high-performing schools. We see that the probability of leaving other schools increased over the time period, although not as much as in low-performing schools. This magnification of the change in low-performing schools could be the result of any policy or economic force that influences the supply or demand of teachers, and not just policies that specifically target low-performing schools.[3]

In summary, to our knowledge only two studies have directly estimated the impact of standards-based reforms on teachers' career decisions. Boyd et al. (2003) find that teachers in tested grades are not more likely to leave the grade or teaching in general, and, in fact, are generally less likely to leave. This reduced exit behavior is particularly pronounced for less-experienced teachers and those from more-competitive colleges. When fourth-grade teachers do leave, they are replaced by experienced teachers, and, in low-performing schools, by teachers with stronger qualifications. This study uses data only on New York, however, so it is limited to a single policy environment and it does not look at changes in career decisions of all teachers as a result of reform, thus limiting its comparison to those in tested and nontested grades. As a result, the study may miss much of the overall impact of reform.

Clotfelter et al. (2003) also look at a single state, North Carolina, but this state has one of the most sophisticated accountability systems, including

---

[3]It is also not evident that testing should have stronger effects in low-performing schools because parents' groups tend to be stronger in high-performing schools and they can make teachers' lives difficult.

direct monetary incentives for teachers. They compare changes in the probability of leaving across school types instead of across grades and find that this probability increased more in low-performing schools. Although this differential is likely to be the result of the policy reform, low-performing schools are often more strongly impacted by changes in teacher supply and demand, and thus, the differential may not be the result of accountability but, instead, of concurrent policy or economic changes.

As these studies show, it is difficult to use a within-state comparison to estimate the effect of state-level reform. A national data set that allows comparisons across states with differing policy environments could provide useful additional evidence of the effects of standards-based reform on teachers' careers. Unfortunately, no national data set (to our knowledge) provides the information on teachers that is available at the state level in New York and North Carolina. The National Center for Education Statistics (2003) has collected the Schools and Staffing Surveys (SASS) in the 1993–1994 and the 1999–2000 academic years, which ask teachers about their plans for the future and their opinions about the benefits of teaching. In the remainder of this chapter we use these surveys to explore changes in teachers' responses across states that implemented different types of reforms.

DATA AND METHODS

Here we add to the previous studies by looking across states, comparing changes in teacher career decisions in states that instituted strong accountability with states that instituted weaker systems or no systems. The benefit of this approach relative to New York study is it allows the identification of effects on all grades, whereas the New York study could only find effects if they were specific to the tested grade. Similarly, it allows the identification of effects on all schools, whereas the North Carolina study could find effects only if they were specific to low-performing schools. The disadvantage of what follows is that national data do not provide nearly as good information on teachers' career paths. We rely on measures such as whether a teacher responds that she or he "definitely plans to leave teaching as soon as I can" or whether the teacher responds that she or he "certainly would become a teacher" when asked "If you could go back to your college days and start over again would you become a teacher or not?" We do not know the choices that teachers actually make.

To measure the policy environment we use a zero-to-five ranking of states based on the strength of their accountability systems as of the 1999–2000 academic year. We then compare the SASS responses of teachers in strong and weak accountability states. The accountability index comes from Carnoy and Loeb (2003), which used the index to assess the effect of accountability on student outcomes. Table 13.6 gives the index and the rele-

TABLE 13.6

Accountability Index, by State, 1999–2000

State	Grades With State Testing in 1999–2000	School Accountability 1999–2000	Repercussion for Schools 1999–2000	Strength of Repercussion for Schools 1999–2000	HS Exit Test in 2000	Grade HS Test First Given	First Grad Class	Index
Alabama	3–11	School report cards	Ratings, intervention	Strong	Yes	10	2001	4
Alaska	4–7	None	None	None	Yes	10	2002	1
Arizona	3, 5, 8, 10	Report cards	"Public shame"	Weak	Yes	10	2002	2
Arkansas	4, 6	None	None	None	No			1
California	2–11	Report cards	Ratings, awards, intervention	Strong	No	10	2004	4 (2)[a]
Colorado	3, literacy	None	None	None	No			1
Connecticut	4, 6, 8, 10	Reporting scores to state	Identify schools with needs	Weak	No			1
Delaware	3, 5, 8, 10, 11	None	None	None	No	10	2004	1
Florida	4, 5, 8, 10	Report cards	Ratings, subject to vouchers	Strong	Yes	10	1988	5
Georgia	3, 4, 5, 8, 11	School reports	None	None	Yes	11	1995	2
Hawaii	3, 5, 8, 10	None	None	None	No			1
Idaho	ITBS, 3–8	None	None	None	No			1
Illinois	3, 4, 5, 8, 10	Academic improvement	Watch lists, warnings, intervention	Moderate	No			2.5
Indiana	3, 6, 8, 10	Performance Assessment	Accreditation	Moderate	Yes	10	1999	3
Iowa	None	None	None	None	No			0
Kansas	3, 4, 5, 8, 10	School reports	Accreditation	Weak	No			1
Kentucky	4, 5, 7, 8, 10–12	Meeting state improvement goals	Monetary rewards, intervention	Strong	No			4
Louisiana	LEAP, 4, 8	Report cards, growth targets	Intervention	Moderate	Yes	10	1991	3
Maine	4, 8, 11	None	None	None	No			1
Maryland	3, 5, 8	School Performance Index	Monetary rewards, reconstitution	Strong	Yes	10, 11, 12	2001	4 (5)

State	Grades tested	Basis	Consequences	Strength	Has		Year	Rank
Massachusetts	4, 8, 10	Students only	Student promotions	Implicit only	Yes	10	2003	2
Michigan	4, 5, 7, 8	School rating	Accreditation	Weak	No			1
Minnesota	3, 5, 8, 10	School reports	None	None	Yes	8, 10		2
Mississippi	2–8	Only districts accountable, based on test scores	Public recognition, loss of accreditation	Moderate to strong at district level	Yes	11	1994	3
Missouri	3–11	School can be deemed academically deficient	Possible audit	Weak	No			1.5
Montana	4, 8, 11	None	None	None	No			1
Nebraska	None	None	None	None	No			0
Nevada	4, 8, 10	School reports	None	Weak	Yes	11	1999	1.5
New Hampshire	3, 6, 10	None	None	None	No			1
New Jersey	4, 5, 11	Mostly district level, 75% pass rate	Audits, possible state takeover	Strong	Yes	11		5
New Mexico	1–9	School ratings and district rankings	Some money rewards, probation	Moderate to strong	Yes	10	1990	4 (5)
New York	4, 5, 8, 11	State review of school performance	Freeze on pupil registration	Strong	Yes	10	1998	5 (2)
North Carolina	3–8	School ratings	Money rewards, intervention	Strong	Yes	9	1994	5
North Dakota	4, 8, 12	Improve student learning	Accreditation	Weak	No			1
Ohio	4, 6, 9, 12	Report cards, but mainly district level	Money for schools, sanctions for districts	Moderate	Yes	9		3
Oklahoma	5, 8	Reports to state	Accreditation	Weak	No			1
Oregon	3, 5, 8, 10	School performance ratings	Write school improvement plans	Weak to moderate	Yes	10	1991	2.5

(Continued)

TABLE 13.6
(Continued)

State	Grades With State Testing in 1999–2000	School Accountability 1999–2000	Repercussion for Schools 1999–2000	Strength of Repercussion for Schools 1999–2000	HS Exit Test in 2000	Grade HS Test First Given	First Grad Class	Index
Pennsylvania	5, 6, 8, 9, 11	High schools have ratings	Money for HS improvement	Weak	No			1
Rhode Island	3, 4, 7, 8, 10	Yearly progress on test results	Reconstitution	Weak implementation	No			1
South Carolina	3–8, 10	District only	District defined as impaired	Moderate	Yes	10	1990	3
South Dakota	2, 4, 5, 8, 9, 11	Test reports	None	None	No			1
Tennessee	3–8, 9	Test reports	Accreditation	Weak	Yes	9		1.5
Texas	3–8, 10	Report cards	School ratings, interventions	Strong	Yes	10	1991	5
Utah	3, 5, 8, 11	None	Accreditation	Weak	No	10	2007	1
Vermont	2, 4, 8, 10	School reports	Identify schools for assistance	Weak	No			1
Virginia	3, 4, 5, 6, 8, 9	Report tests, other data	Standards of Accreditation	Weak to moderate	No			2
Washington	2–10	School reports	Accreditation	Weak	No	10	2008	1
West Virginia	3–8	Performance audits	Intervention	Strong	No			3.5
Wisconsin	3, 4, 8, 10	Continuous Progress Indicator	Ratings of schools	Weak to moderate	No	11	2004	2
Wyoming	4, 8, 11	Only district	Accreditation	Weak	No			1

[a]Alternative specification of index, as per Margaret Goertz (personal communication), in parentheses. This alternative variable is used as a check on the models presented.

vant policy elements by state. Carnoy and Loeb constructed the table using the database developed by the Consortium for Policy Research in Education (CPRE), available on the CPRE Web site http://www.cpre.org/Publications/Publications_Accountability.htm.

The zero-to-five scale captures the degree of state external pressure on schools to improve student achievement according to state-defined performance criteria. States receiving a zero do not test students statewide or do not set any statewide standards for schools or districts. States that require state testing in the elementary and middle grades and the reporting of test results to the state but no school or district sanctions or rewards receive a 1. Those states that test at the elementary and middle school levels and have moderate school or district accountability sanctions/rewards or, alternatively, a high school exit test receive a 2. Those states that test at the lower and middle grades, have moderate accountability repercussions for schools and districts, and require an exit test in high school, receive a 3. Those that test and place strong pressure on schools or districts to improve student achievement (threat of reconstitution, principal transfer, loss of students) but do not require a high school exit test receive a 4. States receiving a 5 test students in primary and middle grades, strongly sanction and reward schools or districts based on improvement in student test scores, and require a high school minimum competency exit test for graduation. As examples, states such as Iowa and Nebraska, which do not have any state-level accountability requirements for schools or districts, are coded 0; and states with "maximum" state-level demands on schools and that require a high school competency exam for graduation, such as Texas, North Carolina, New Jersey, and Florida, are coded 5.

We combine these state-level policy data with teacher-level data from the SASS. The SASS is the largest sample survey of elementary and secondary schools in the United States. It includes surveys of teachers and administrators at the school and district levels and surveys in both public and private schools. For this study we use the surveys of teachers in noncharter public schools in 1993–1994 and 1999–2000 and the surveys of principals in these schools. SASS uses a stratified probability sample design both between and within schools. Because of this, all of our analyses are weighted so that the estimates are nationally representative.

Table 13.7 gives the descriptive statistics for the primary variables used in the analysis. Teachers have an average of 14 years of teaching experience, 9 in their current school. Three quarters are women and 87% are White. Schools, with an average enrollment of 781 students, have an average of 35% of children in poverty and 28% Black or Hispanic students.

Our analysis can be divided into two parts: the first, descriptive; and the second, seeking to estimate the causal effect of accountability. In the first section we use teacher reports from the SASS concerning their life in

TABLE 13.7
Descriptive Statistics for Variables

Variables	Obs	Mean	SD
Total full-time teaching experience (years)	89191	14.37	9.71
Experience in current school (years)	89191	9.40	8.32
Teacher's age	89191	42.64	10.13
Teacher's gender = Male	89191	0.26	
Teacher's race/ethnicity = Black	89191	0.07	
Teacher's race/ethnicity = Hispanic	89191	0.05	
Teacher's race/ethnicity = Asian	89191	0.01	
Elementary teacher	89191	0.35	
Math or science teacher	89191	0.13	
Teacher's college quality rating	84081	2.79	0.75
Total number of students enrolled in school	82777	781	569
Teacher's salary	89191	36717	12437
Percentage of children in poverty[a]	82777	35.28	28.87
Percentage of Black and Hispanic students in school	82777	27.98	31.06
Suburban	89191	0.41	
Rural	89191	0.31	
State accountability index score	88769	2.94	1.58
Year = 2000 (vs. 1994)	89191	0.54	
Certainly would teach again	89191	0.39	
Want to leave teaching	89191	0.14	

[a]Estimated by the number of students eligible for free or reduced lunch in school.

schools. For measures that are available only in the 1999–2000 SASS, we ask whether teacher responses differ in strong- and weak-accountability states. For measures that are available in both the 1993–1994 and the 1999–2000 SASS, we ask whether teacher responses have changed more in stronger accountability states.

The second half of the analysis focuses specifically on teachers' answers to the following two questions: "If you could go back to your college days and start over again, would you become a teacher or not," and "How long do you plan to remain in teaching?" From these we created two yes/no variables, one for "Certainly would become a teacher," and one for "Definitely plan to leave teaching" or "Will probably continue until something better comes along." Table 13.7 shows that 39% of teachers say that they would certainly become a teacher again, whereas 14% say that they want to leave teaching. We aim to ask whether states that implemented stronger accountability saw differential change in either of these measures following reform. To do this, we use an approach similar to that of Boyd et al. (2003). Logits at the teacher level include detailed controls for the characteristics of teachers and the schools in which they work. They include the state accountability index, a dummy variable for year, and an interaction of accountability and year. The coefficient on the interaction term tells us to what extent higher accountability states saw greater changes in the outcome in question. We cluster the analysis by state, so that the standard errors reflect the fact that accountability is measured at the state level. We run these analyses separately by school type and by teacher experience.

Using a similar approach, we also assess whether states that implemented stronger accountability systems saw differential changes in the characteristics of entering teachers. The teacher characteristic in question (the competitiveness of the teachers' undergraduate institution) is modeled as a function of school characteristics, the accountability index, year, and the year–accountability interaction. The interaction captures whether high-accountability states experienced a differential change in the characteristics of teachers post reform. The following section gives the results of these analyses.

RESULTS

Descriptive Results

First we look at two relevant measures of teachers' work lives that are available only for 1999–2000, after the states implemented their accountability reform described by the index. Figure 13.1 shows teachers' responses to how much influence they have on setting performance standards for students in their school. Teachers respond on a 5-point scale from "no influ-

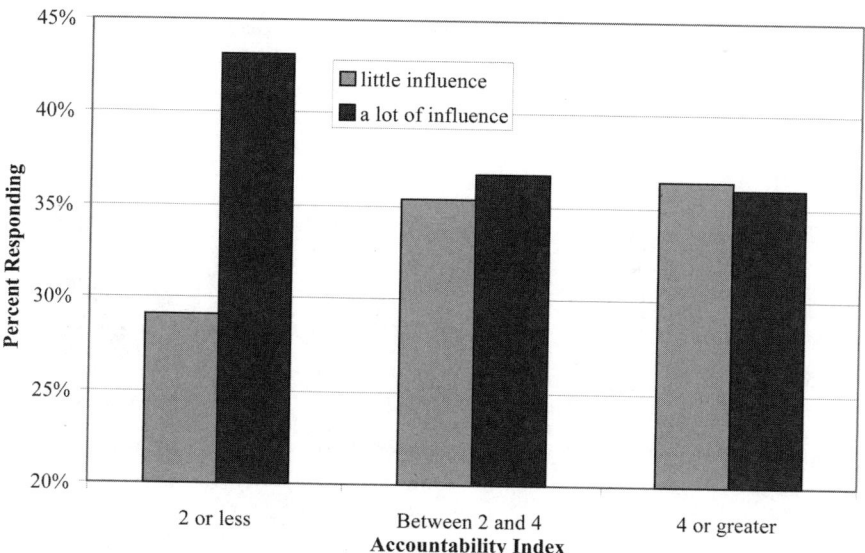

FIG. 13.1. Teacher influence on performance standards from the 1999–2000 schools and staffing survey.

ence" to "a great deal of influence." We have combined the two lowest responses for a measure of "little influence" and the two highest responses
for a measure of "a lot of influence." Teachers in states with weaker accountability systems are substantially more likely to report "a lot of influence" on performance standards. The correlation between state average of
influence and accountability index is −0.51 (p = .0002).

Teachers were also asked whether they worry about the security of their
job because of the performance of their students on state or local tests.
They ranked their answer on a 4-point scale from "strongly agree" to
"strongly disagree." Figure 13.2 gives these results. Again, the trend with accountability is evident. Teachers in states with stronger accountability are
more likely to strongly or somewhat agree with this statement and less
likely to strongly disagree. The correlation between state average of job security and the accountability index is −0.42 (p = .0023).

Although the questions addressing accountability directly are much
more likely to appear on the 1999–2000 SASS than on the 1993–1994 SASS,
there are a number of questions that appear on both that are relevant to
teachers' work lives. We find little relationship between accountability and
changes over time in these measures. There is no evident trend between accountability and the percentage of teachers that strongly agree with, "The
school administration's behavior toward the staff is supportive and encour-

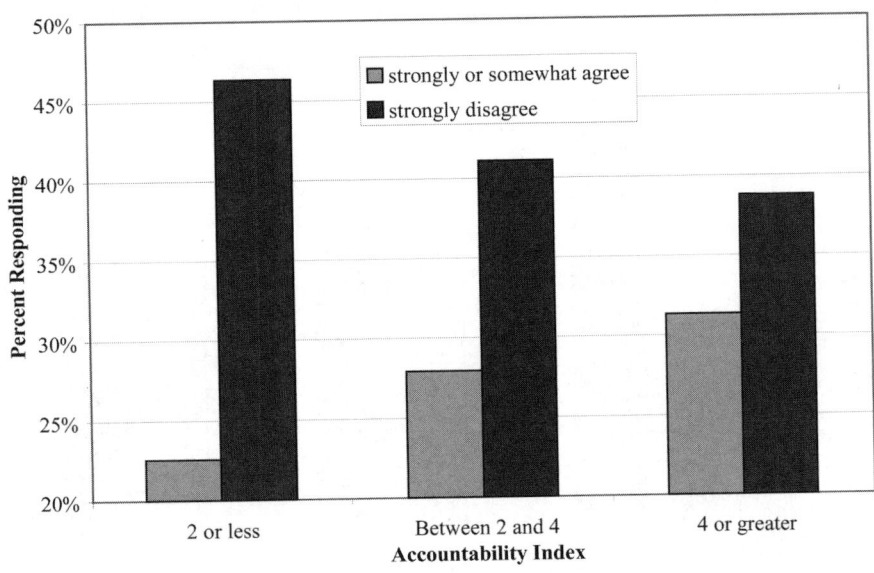

FIG. 13.2. "I worry about the security of my job because of the performance of
my students on state or local tests," from the 1999–2000 Schools and Staffing
Survey.

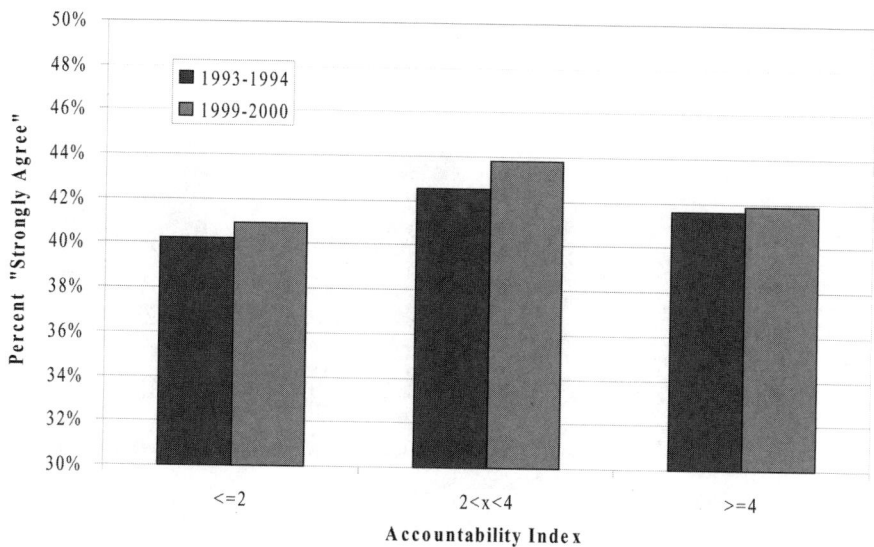

FIG. 13.3. Percentage of teachers that strongly agree with "The school administration's behavior toward the staff is supportive and encouraging," 1993–1994 and 1999–2000 SASS.

aging" (Fig. 13.3); the percentage of teachers that strongly agree with, "Most of my colleagues share my beliefs and values about what the central mission of the school should be" (Fig. 13.4); and the percentage of teachers that strongly agree with, "There is a great deal of cooperative effort among staff members" (Fig. 13.5). In each of these cases, the gains in low-accountability states tend to be greater than the gains in high-accountability states, but the mid-accountability states see the greatest gain. There is no significant correlation between accountability and teachers' responses to these questions in either year.

In both years SASS asks whether teachers sometimes feel that it is a waste of time to try to do their best as a teacher. The most evident trend, and a good one, is that the percentage of teachers strongly or somewhat agreeing dropped substantially from 1993–1994 to 1999–2000 (Fig. 13.6). However, although the drop is somewhat less in strong-accountability states, the differences are not large. The correlation between disagreeing with "Sometimes I feel it is a waste of time to try to do my best as a teacher," and the accountability index is -0.23 ($p = .11$) for 2000 whereas it is -0.35 ($p = .01$) for 1993; thus, it is negative but became somewhat more positive, not less, over time. The correlation between the change and accountability (0.22) is not statistically significant ($p = .13$).

Finally, there is a set of relevant questions that appear in both waves of SASS but where the responses are coded on a different scale in each year.

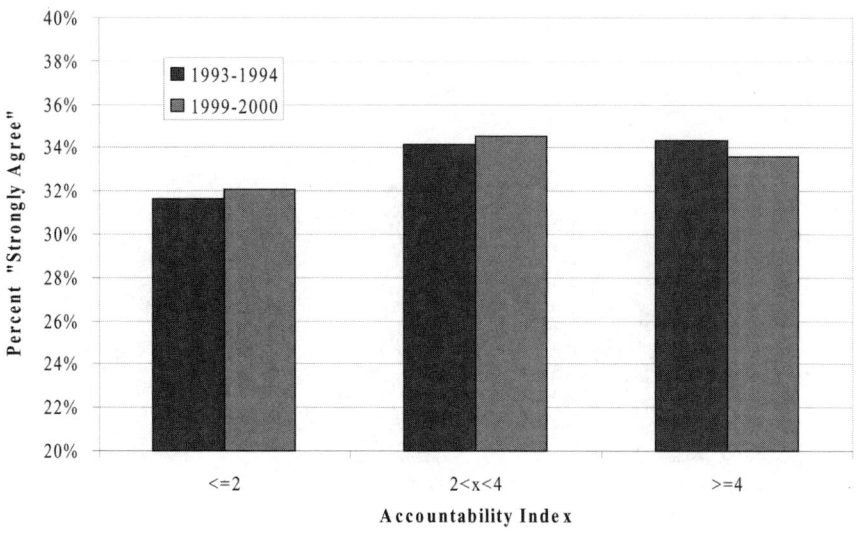

FIG. 13.4. Percentage of teachers that strongly agree with "Most of my colleagues share my beliefs and values about what the central mission of the school should be," 1993–1994 and 1999–2000 SASS.

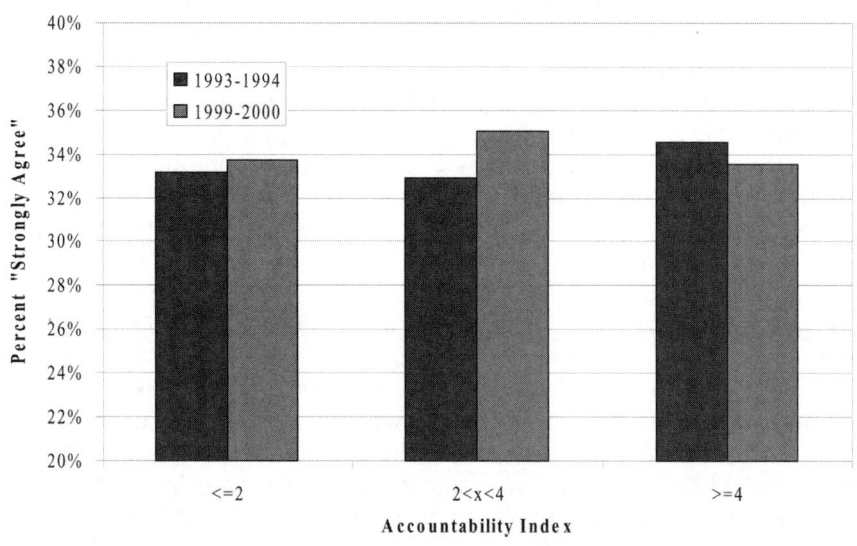

FIG. 13.5. Percentage of teachers that strongly agree with "There is a great deal of cooperative effort among staff members."

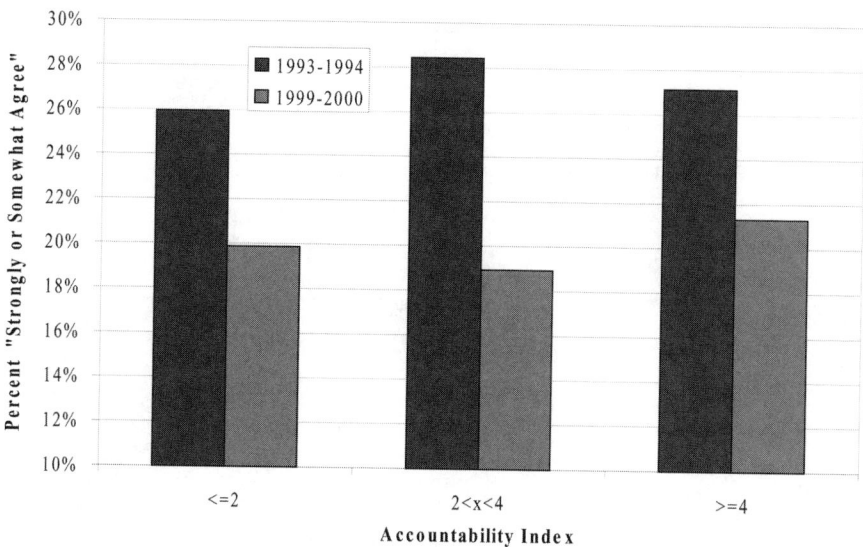

FIG. 13.6. Percentage of teachers that strongly or somewhat agree with "Sometimes I feel it is a waste of time to try to do my best as a teacher."

This change makes it difficult to compare across time. In order to compare the changes by accountability for these measures, we subtracted the year-specific mean and divided by the year-specific standard deviation. Thus, the new variables measure how far a teacher's response is from the average response in standard deviation units. This approach keeps us from looking at absolute changes over time, but allows us to compare changes in states grouped by the accountability index. Figure 13.7 plots teachers' responses to how much actual influence they think teachers have over establishing curriculum. Teachers in strong-accountability states perceived substantially less influence in both years, although no trend in the changes over time by accountability strength are evident. Figure 13.8 similarly illustrates teachers' responses to, "In your classroom, how much control do you think you have over selecting content, topics, and skills to be taught." Again, teachers in strong-accountability states have less control, although, in this case the differences across states by accountability level have actually decreased over time.

In summary, teachers believe that they have less control over performance standards, content, and curriculum in states with strong accountability, although this difference between the two groups of states does not seem to have increased over time. There is little evidence for differences in a teacher's work life as measured by the school administration's behavior (as supportive or encouraging), or by relationships with colleagues (as measured by shared beliefs and cooperative effort).

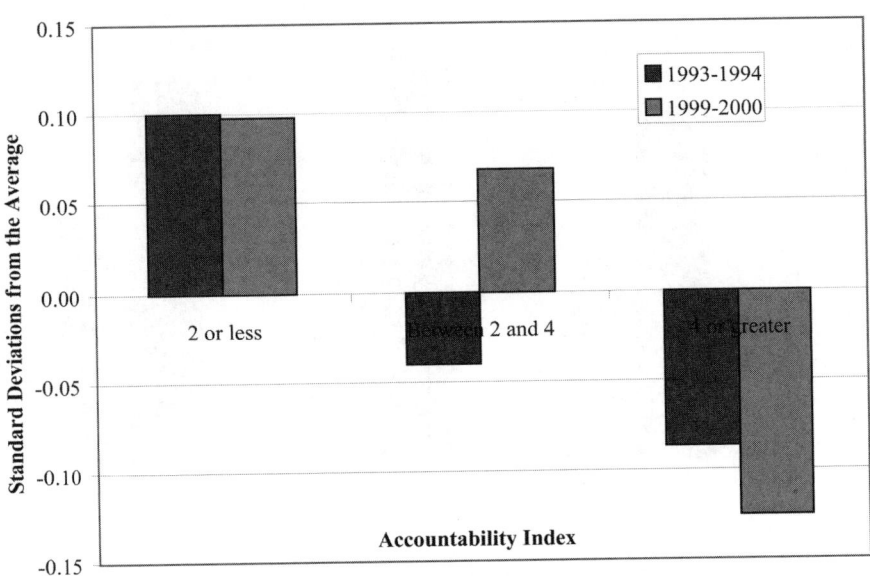

FIG. 13.7. Teachers' responses to how much actual influence they think teachers have over establishing curriculum, 1993–1994 and 1999–2000 SASS.

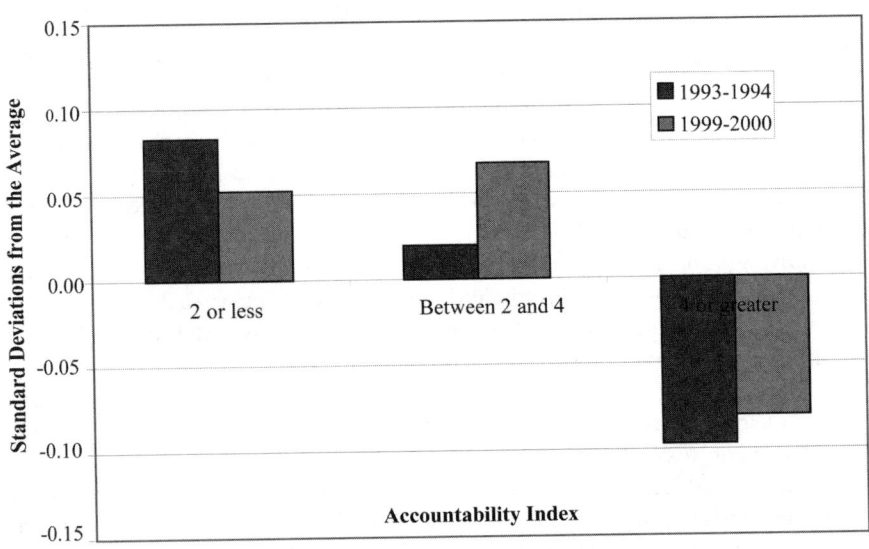

FIG. 13.8. Teachers' responses to, in your classroom, how much control do you think you have over selecting content, topics, and skills to be taught, 1993–1994 and 1999–2000 SASS.

Logit Results

Next we ask whether between 1993–1994 and 1999–2000 teachers in strong-accountability states became less likely to say that, if they had to do it over again, they would certainly become a teacher. Table 13.8 presents these results for all teachers. Teachers vary systematically in their response to this question. More-experienced and older teachers are less likely to say that they would certainly become a teacher, although the relationship is not linear. The decrease with age and experience dissipates with time. Men are also less likely to say that they would certainly become a teacher again; whereas Black and Hispanic teachers are more likely than White teachers to say that they would. Teachers who attended more-selective colleges are less likely to say that they would certainly become a teacher again.

Responses differed by school characteristics as well. Elementary school teachers are more likely than high school teachers and middle school

TABLE 13.8
Logit Results Predicting Whether the Teacher Says That She
or He "Certainly Would Become a Teacher" When Asked
"If You Could Go Back to Your College Days and Start Over
Again Would You Become a Teacher or Not?"[a]

Variables	Odds Ratio	Z-Stat
Total experience	0.931	(10.01)
Total experience squared	1.001	(6.15)
School experience	0.998	(0.37)
School experience squared	1.000	(0.75)
Age	0.945	(5.19)
Age 2	1.001	(5.68)
Male	0.848	(8.29)
Black	1.192	(2.64)
Hispanic	1.353	(4.54)
Asian	1.002	(0.02)
College quality	0.905	(3.63)
Elementary school	1.182	(6.92)
Middle school	0.788	(6.10)
Enrollment	1.000	(1.66)
Salary in thousands	1.015	(7.96)
Percentage students in poverty	1.000	(0.49)
Percentage Black or Hispanic students	0.998	(2.97)
Suburban	1.037	(0.68)
Rural	1.014	(0.22)
Accountability index	0.959	(1.57)
Year = 1999–2000	0.864	(2.76)
Accountability year interaction	1.031	(1.62)

[a]The alternative responses are "Probably," "Chances about even," "Probably would not," and "Certainly would not."

teachers are less likely than high school teachers to say that they would make the same choice again. Teachers in schools with a high proportion of Black and Hispanic students are less likely to say they would make the same choice, as are teachers in schools with lower salaries.

The year dummy variable shows that teachers are substantially less likely to report that they would certainly become a teacher again in 1999–2000 than they were in 1993–1994 (approximately 14% less). The point estimate of the odds ratio on the interaction term indicates that in this sample the drop in the percentage of teachers saying they would certainly become a teacher again is not as great in the high-accountability states. This difference is not significant at traditional levels, but it is similar in direction to the results in the New York study. This analysis provides no evidence that accountability has decreased teachers' willingness to teach.

In Table 13.9, we report the interaction terms of the same analysis, run separately for different types of schools and teachers. The interaction is significant and greater than one (indicating a more positive change for high-accountability states) in a number of the specifications including: (a) teachers with 5 or fewer years of experience in all schools, (b) teachers in urban schools, (c) teachers in rural schools, (d) teachers with 5 or fewer years of experience in schools with more than half Black and Hispanic students, and (e) teachers with 5 or fewer years of experience in schools with more than half of the students in poverty. Again, these results are consistent with the findings of Boyd et al. (2003) in that they show more positive labor market outcomes linked to accountability for teachers in low-performing schools.

We repeated the analysis using whether the teacher says that she or he "Definitely plans to leave teaching as soon as I can" or "Will probably continue unless something better comes along." The results are given in Tables 13.10 and 13.11. Teachers are more likely to say that they definitely plan to leave teaching when they are younger and less experienced (although first-year teachers are less likely than second-year teachers to express a desire to leave). Male teachers and Black teachers are also more likely to want to leave teaching, as are teachers from less-competitive colleges. Teachers in elementary school are less likely, and those in middle schools are more likely, to want to leave than are teachers in high schools. Teachers in schools offering higher salaries are less likely to want to leave, whereas those with a higher proportion of Black or Hispanic students are more likely to want to go. We find no evidence of a relationship between accountability and this measure, nor have teachers' responses to this question changed substantially between the surveys. This may be because accountability has not affected teachers' decisions or because the measure is not a particularly good one. We do not have a measure of actual attrition that is consistent between the 1993–1994 and 1999–2000 survey years.

TABLE 13.9
Logit Results by School Type Predicting Teacher Response "Certainly
Would Become a Teacher," When Asked "If You Could Go Back to Your
College Days and Start Over Again Would You Become a Teacher or Not?"

Model	Odds Ratio (Z-Stat)	Model	Odds Ratio (Z-Stat)
Full sample	1.031		
	(1.62)		
≤5 Years of experience	*1.078*		
	(1.95)		
6–10 Years of experience	1.012		
	(0.36)		
Urban	*1.046*	**Percent Black and Hispanic ≤50%**	1.032
	(1.93)		(1.56)
≤5 Years of experience	1.091	≤5 Years of experience	1.053
	(1.56)		(1.28)
6–10 Years of experience	1.061	6–10 Years of experience	0.976
	(1.12)		(0.58)
Suburban	1.006	**Percent in poverty ≤50%**	1.024
	(0.24)		(1.51)
≤5 Years of experience	1.050	≤5 Years of experience	1.040
	(0.98)		(0.95)
6–10 Years of experience	0.972	6–10 Years of experience	1.014
	(0.45)		(0.36)
Rural	*1.076*	**Percent Black and Hispanic >50%**	1.015
	(2.31)		(0.34)
≤5 Years of experience	*1.125*	≤5 Years of experience	*1.141*
	(1.99)		*(1.95)*
6–10 Years of experience	1.030	6–10 Years of experience	1.025
	(0.65)		(0.21)
Teach math or science	1.009	**Percent in poverty >50%**	1.048
	(0.25)		(1.32)
≤5 Years of experience	1.081	≤5 Years of experience	*1.121*
	(1.35)		*(2.02)*
6–10 Years of experience	0.869	6–10 Years of experience	0.991
	(1.28)		(0.12)

Finally, we look at the characteristics of new entrants to teaching. First
we ask whether the characteristics of teachers with 2 or fewer years of experience have changed differentially in states that have implemented stronger accountability reforms. We use as a measure of teacher characteristics
the five-level measure of undergraduate competitiveness. An ordered logit
with this variable as the outcome and a similar specification to the earlier

TABLE 13.10

Logit Results Predicting Whether the Teacher Says That She or He
"Definitely Plans to Leave Teaching as Soon as I Can" or "Will
Probably Continue Unless Something Better Comes Along"[a]

Variables	Odds Ratio	Z-Stat
Total experience	1.033	(3.37)
Total experience squared	0.999	(3.77)
School experience	0.999	(0.08)
School experience squared	1.000	(0.32)
Age	0.966	(2.88)
Age 2	1.000	(0.66)
Male	1.242	(6.50)
Black	1.208	(2.57)
Hispanic	0.989	(0.11)
Asian	1.040	(0.27)
Elementary school	0.799	(4.95)
Middle school	1.196	(2.88)
College quality	1.117	(3.50)
Enrollment	1.000	(0.60)
Salary in thousands	0.979	(6.20)
Percentage students in poverty	0.999	(1.51)
Percentage Black or Hispanic students	1.004	(4.27)
Suburban	0.950	(0.97)
Rural	0.964	(0.78)
Accountability index	1.011	(0.49)
Year = 1999–2000	0.979	(0.28)
Accountability year interaction	1.001	(0.04)

[a]The alternative responses are "As long as I am able," "Until I am eligible for retirement," and "Undecided at this time."

analyses gives the results. Again, the models are weighted and clustered to account for the state-level policy of interest. As shown in Table 13.12, higher salaries are associated with teachers from more-competitive colleges, whereas rural schools and those with a higher percentage of Black and Hispanic students are associated with fewer teachers from these institutions. There has been a decrease over the time period in the competitiveness of the colleges that new teachers attended; however, this trend has not been stronger in states with stronger accountability policies. Table 13.13 gives these results by school type. There is a tendency for strong accountability to be associated with a relative drop in college competitiveness, but none of the estimates is statistically significant.

Tables 13.12 and 13.13 give the estimates on the effects of accountability on novice teachers, but accountability might also be associated with the reallocation of teachers across schools. In Tables 13.14 and 13.15 we redo the

TABLE 13.11
Logit Results by School Type Predicting Teacher Response
"Definitely Plans to Leave Teaching as Soon as I Can" or "Will
Probably Continue Unless Something Better Comes Along"

Model	Odds Ratio (Z-Stat)	Model	Odds Ratio (Z-Stat)
Full sample	1.001		
	(0.04)		
≤5 Years of experience	0.988		
	(0.33)		
6–10 Years of experience	1.021		
	(0.41)		
Urban	1.038	**Percent Black and Hispanic ≤50%**	0.991
	(0.70)		(0.27)
≤5 Years of experience	1.065	≤5 Years of experience	0.982
	(1.14)		(0.43)
6–10 Years of experience	0.969	6–10 Years of experience	0.984
	(0.37)		(0.33)
Suburban	0.964	**Percent in poverty ≤50%**	0.982
	(0.84)		(0.70)
≤5 Years of experience	0.910	≤5 Years of experience	0.984
	(1.39)		(0.47)
6–10 Years of experience	1.017	6–10 Years of experience	0.966
	(0.18)		(0.68)
Rural	0.975	**Percent Black and Hispanic >50%**	1.018
	(0.80)		(0.24)
≤5 Years of experience	*0.904*	≤5 Years of experience	1.018
	(2.20)		(0.27)
6–10 Years of experience	1.005	6–10 Years of experience	1.169
	(0.08)		(1.56)
Teach math or science	1.009	**Percent in poverty >50%**	1.041
	(0.17)		(0.78)
≤5 Years of experience	0.935	≤5 Years of experience	1.023
	(0.62)		(0.35)
6–10 Years of experience	1.059	6–10 Years of experience	1.097
	(0.46)		(1.05)

preceding analyses for teachers with 2 or fewer years of experience *in the school* in each year. Because teachers new to a school may come with a variety of teaching experience, we run these analyses with years of experience as an outcome (linear regression), as well as college competitiveness (ordered logit). Again, we find a positive relationship between salary and both experience and college quality, but no evidence that accountability

TABLE 13.12
Ordered Logit Results Predicting a Five-Level Measure of the Competitiveness of Teachers' Undergraduate Institution

Variable	Coefficient	Z-Stat
Enrollment in hundreds	0.007	(1.15)
Salary in thousands	0.029	(4.32)
Percentage students in poverty	−0.007	(3.78)
Percentage Black or Hispanic students	−0.003	(1.26)
Suburban	0.052	(0.34)
Rural	−0.379	(3.23)
Accountability index	0.019	(0.28)
Year = 1999–2000	−0.210	(2.05)
Accountability year interaction	−0.056	(1.35)

TABLE 13.13
Ordered Logit Results Predicting a Five-Level Measure of the Competitiveness of Teachers' Undergraduate Institution by School Type

Variable	Coefficient on Interaction	Z-Stat
All	−0.056	(1.35)
Urban	−0.160	(1.83)
Suburban	−0.100	(1.33)
Rural	0.044	(1.06)
Percentage poverty ≤50	−0.033	(0.64)
Percentage poverty >50	−0.063	(0.85)
Percentage Black or Hispanic students ≤50	−0.018	(0.39)
Percentage Black or Hispanic students >50	−0.141	(1.38)

TABLE 13.14
Ordered Logit Results Predicting a Five-Level Measure of the Competitiveness of Teachers' Undergraduate Institution and Linear Regression Results Prediction Teaching Experience of New Teachers to the School (Experience ≤2 Years)

Variable	College Quality Coefficient	Z-Stat	Teaching Experience Coefficient	t-Stat
Enrollment in hundreds	0.010	(1.89)	−0.083	(4.16)
Salary in thousands	0.014	(3.85)	0.473	(16.05)
Percentage students in poverty	−0.0065	(3.83)	0.0047	(0.90)
Percentage Black or Hispanic students	−0.0030	(1.72)	−0.0051	(1.06)
Suburban	0.072	(0.53)	−0.890	(3.04)
Rural	−0.309	(2.95)	0.394	(1.33)
Accountability index	0.012	(0.21)	−0.198	(0.83)
Year = 1999–2000	−0.142	(1.66)	−2.491	(6.96)
Accountability year interaction	0.003	(0.08)	−0.033	(0.37)

TABLE 13.15
Ordered Logit Results Predicting a Five-Level Measure of the
Competitiveness of Teachers' Undergraduate Institution and
Linear Regression Results Prediction Teaching Experience of New
Teachers to the School (Experience ≤2 Years) by School Type

Variable	Coefficient on Interaction	Z/t-Stat
College Quality, Ordered Logit		
All	0.003	(0.08)
Urban	−0.059	(0.83)
Suburban	0.008	(0.16)
Rural	0.022	(0.48)
Percentage poverty ≤50	0.012	(0.30)
Percentage poverty >50	0.001	(0.01)
Percentage Black or Hispanic students ≤50	0.043	(1.68)
Percentage Black or Hispanic students >50	0.080	(0.98)
Teaching Experience, Linear Regression		
All	−0.033	(0.37)
Urban	−0.092	(0.73)
Suburban	0.335	(2.03)
Rural	−0.239	(1.79)
Percentage poverty ≤50	−0.077	(0.73)
Percentage poverty >50	0.005	(0.03)
Percentage Black or Hispanic students ≤50	−0.112	(1.00)
Percentage Black or Hispanic students >50	0.301	(1.38)

has affected the characteristics of new teachers. Only suburban schools show a significant coefficient on an accountability interaction, when teaching experience is the outcome. Given the number of models, the significance for suburban schools could be spurious.

In summary, the multivariate analyses suggest some positive effects of accountability on teachers' happiness with their choice to become a teacher. We find no evidence that accountability has affected teachers' decisions about whether to leave the profession, nor the characteristics of new entrants.

CONCLUSION

This chapter describes the approaches used by economists to estimate the effects of assessment-based accountability reforms on teachers' career decisions. Economists have sought to find ways of estimating the impact of reform that do more than simply look at teachers' behaviors before and after implementation. The problem with a before–after approach is that many things change over time that can influence teachers' decisions, and it is thus difficult to separate the effects of accountability from those of other concurrent policy or economic changes. To date, one study assesses reform effects by looking at a state that implemented testing in some grades (fourth and eighth) but not in others and by using differences in teachers' career decisions by grade level. Another study compares differences in teachers' career decisions in low-performing schools relative to higher performing schools before and after the implementation of an accountability system. The logic behind this approach is that low-performing schools are more likely to feel the effects of accountability because they are more likely to be labeled as low-performing and thus subject to repercussions.

The results of these studies are quite different. The grade comparison finds that teachers in tested grades are *less* likely to leave, especially those in suburban schools with less experience and those in low-performing schools who graduated from more-competitive undergraduate institutions. The school comparison study finds that teachers in low-performing schools are relatively *more* likely to leave following reform than those in high-performing schools. These results are difficult to align. It is possible that there are aspects of the reforms and the environments in which they are implemented that make one policy more detrimental than another. This is not out of the question, given the substantial differences in assessment-based policy between the two states. It is also possible that the grade analysis is capturing within-school movement whereas the school analysis is capturing across-school movement, and that these are different phenomena. There are also problems, however, with each approach for estimating the causal effect of reform. The grade-comparison study, for example, can find effects only if the impact of reform differs by grade. Testing may create a negative environment in schools that is detrimental to all grades. The grade-comparison study will not be able to identify such an effect. The school-comparison study also has drawbacks because, as discussed in more detail earlier, low-performing schools are more susceptible to changes in the supply of and the demand for teachers caused by economic or policy changes, even when these changes are not directed at low-performing schools. Thus the differences in teachers' behaviors found between low-performing and higher performing schools could be the result of other changes concurrent with the accountability reform.

In order to further our understanding of the effect of accountability on teachers, in this study we add to the previous literature by comparing changes in teachers' experiences and behaviors across states instead of across grades or schools. The advantage of this approach is that it can identify effects that are similar across grades and schools. There is also substantial variation in accountability strength across states, which makes this comparison feasible. However, national data on teacher career choices are quite weak. We rely on surveys that ask teachers about their plans for the future and their happiness with their decision to become a teacher. Lacking measures of actual behavior, we use these as proxies for career choices. The surveys do ask additional questions about teachers' work lives and we describe how their answers vary by the strength of the accountability system in the state in which they teach.

We find no support in the national data for the proposition that accountability has increased teachers' propensity to leave teaching, although the weakness of the available measures is an issue. Teachers in states with stronger accountability are *more* likely, in fact, to report that they would pursue teaching again if starting over, and this result is particularly strong for teachers with 5 years of experience or less, those in urban schools, and those in schools with more than 50% Black or Hispanic students or students in poverty. There is no evident relationship between teachers' plans to leave teaching and the strength of their state's accountability system.

The implementation of high-stakes testing brought with it substantial concern that teachers work lives would change for the worse and that schools would lose many of their best teachers. The research to date does not support this claim, although there are sure to have been some schools and districts whose effective teachers did leave in order to avoid the scrutiny of the administration or to move to higher-performing schools so as obtain the rewards promised by the recent reforms.

REFERENCES

Boyd, D., Lankford, H., Loeb, S., & Wyckoff, J. (2003). *Do mandatory tests affect teachers' exit and transfer decisions? The case of the 4th grade test in New York State.* Unpublished manuscript.

Carnoy, M., & Loeb, S. (2003). Does external accountability affect student outcomes? A cross-state analysis. *Education Evaluation and Policy Analysis, 25,* 305–332.

Clotfelter, C. T., Ladd, H. F., Vigdor, J. L., & Diaz, R. A. (2003, February). *Do school accountability systems make it more difficult for low performing schools to attract and retain high quality teachers?* Unpublished manuscript.

National Center for Education Statistics. (2003). *Schools and Staffing Surveys, 1993–1994 and 1999–2000.* Retrieved October 2003 from http://nces.ed.gov/surveys/sass/

14

Stricter Regulations or Additional Incentives? The Teacher Quality Policy Dilemma

Steven G. Rivkin

Amherst College, National Bureau of Economic Research
University of Texas–Dallas

As the following quote from the *Report on Education in the United States at the Eleventh Census, 1890* (Blodgett, 1893), shows the desire to improve the quality of instruction is far from new:

If the American school system is to successfully cope with the circumstances which confront it, and the still more trying circumstances which will confront it, it must be equipped with a more substantial teaching service. Perhaps one teacher in five or one in four is a professional. . . .

You tell me that the law regulates this thing; that it determines who may teach in the schools. It assumes to, but it does not. A law is good for nothing that does not operate effectually. What does the law do? Ordinarily it confers upon city boards of education and county or district commissioners' power to certify teachers. The members of the city board are not professional school men. How are they to intelligently determine who are qualified to teach school? But that is not all nor is it the worst of it, for if it was they could employ a competent person to determine for them. They have the authority to employ teachers. They have aunts and cousins and daughters and nieces who want employment. And they also have personal and political friends with retinues of relatives, friends and acquaintances. They are human. They like to please. Only the strongest of them dare confront the misunderstandings and enmities in which a refusal to aid their friends will involve them. The more honest and efficient [the county commissioner] is, the more people there will be to engage in the enterprise of taking off his official head. (p. 1163)

Moreover, the more stringent system of certification demanded in 1890 sounds quite familiar:

> Professional training must be insisted upon whenever practical, and where not, then at least a minimum standard of intellectual qualifications must be obtained at a public examination. The authority to certify and the power to employ must never be lodged in the same persons. The certificate must be gained before employment is legal. (Blodgett, 1893, p. 1163)

The belief that states must play an active role in the teacher selection process because districts and schools cannot be depended on to make hard choices and good decisions has persisted for a long time. Establishing a list of required courses, test score minimums, or other requirements for certification might succeed in raising the average skills of entering teachers. Yet it is unlikely that poorly managed schools would produce a high quality of education even if state policies were successful in weeding out unqualified applicants. Moreover, poorly run schools would likely discourage many potentially good teachers from entering or remaining in the profession.

In fact, those who demand more fundamental changes at the school and district levels seek to alter management practices in ways that would lead administrators and their teachers to produce a high-quality education. Though the details vary, these reformers argue that the evidence has shown that it is very difficult to regulate excellent teaching regardless of the amount of money spent. Rather school personnel must be given the appropriate incentives to provide a high-quality education.

The reality in many states is that standards are being tightened at the same time as incentives are being added to the system. Unfortunately, evidence is often not used extensively in the formulation of policy, likely leading to the adoption of policies that do not reap the advertised benefits and may even reduce the average quality of instruction, particularly for specific demographic groups. California's class-size reduction is a case in point: The need to hire so many additional teachers contributed to a dramatic increase in the share of teachers without full certification, particularly in schools serving a high proportion of disadvantaged students.[1]

This chapter develops a basic framework with which to examine the existing evidence on the determinants of teacher quality and the likely effects of various policy initiatives. Three distinct lines of research that relate in varying ways to teacher quality are discussed. The first traces changes over time in the salaries of teachers relative to those in other occupations,

---

[1]Jepsen and Rivkin (2002) describe the impact of class-size reduction in California on school quality.

focusing on the impact of the expansion of labor market opportunities for women. A second set of research investigates the relationship between pay and other characteristics of teaching jobs on the one hand and the characteristics of teachers in different schools and districts and teacher turnover on the other. Finally, the third line of research, closely related to the previous two, considers the determinants of teacher quality as measured by the contribution to student learning. This includes the evidence on merit pay, competition, and other incentive effects on teacher quality. Importantly, it is the failure to find a strong relationship between teacher effectiveness in raising performance one the hand and teacher education, experience, and salaries on the other that is crucial to understanding both the difficulty of designing policies that improve the quality of instruction and the potential for improved incentives to have a large impact on the quality of education.

This evidence on teachers in combination with a clearer understanding of behavioral responses to policy initiatives provides key information for policy development. The chapter considers a range of policies but focuses on initiatives that affect incentives. These include merit pay for teachers and schools and expanded school choice. Overall, it suggests that incentive-based policies are potentially much more cost-effective than regulations as a means to improve the quality of classroom instruction. The existing evidence is quite limited, however, and it is crucial to learn from the experiences of schools and districts across the country.

ANALYTICAL FRAMEWORK

A number of institutions and people combine to determine the quality of instruction in each district and school. Although there is some variation across states, most state systems contain these basic components: State legislatures establish the teacher-licensing process and determine state contributions to school budgets; districts and schools determine local contributions to schooling, pay scales, tenure guidelines, in-service training, mentoring, hiring criteria, and other factors, often in combination with unions or other teacher representatives; and potential teachers determine their willingness to work at schools throughout the state.

The following equations provide a simple framework with which to consider the key issues in the determination of teacher quality. Equation 1 represents average teacher quality in school s in district d as a function of teacher effort and a multidimensional set of skills.

$$\overline{TQ_{ds}} = f(effort_{sd}, skills_{sd}) \tag{1}$$

What determines the levels of skill and effort in a school? Equation 2 represents skills as a function of labor market supply and demand factors, personnel practices, and state regulations.

$$skills_{sd} = f(pay_{sd}, \ working \ conditions_{sd}, \ hiring \ and \ retention \ practices_{sd},$$
$$teaching \ opportunities_{sd}, \ other \ opportunities \mid state \ regulations) \qquad (2)$$

Higher pay and better working conditions tend to increase the number of job applicants, whereas higher compensation in other districts or other occupations tends to reduce the number of applicants. For example, the expansion of job opportunities for women has almost certainly hurt the public schools, whereas inner-city schools often have difficulties attracting and retaining teachers who have other opportunities.

Licensing regulations also require that teachers satisfy state requirements designed in part to remove incompetent teachers from the applicant pool. Both the preservice and in-service education requirements are intended to give teachers the skills needed to perform well in the classroom. Schools may also require or support continuing education above and beyond state requirements. Importantly, these requirements come at a cost of raising the amount of time and money it takes to become a teacher. Any additional hurdles will deter potential teachers from pursuing jobs in public education. Moreover, the requirements may also block some potentially competent teachers from the profession. As a result, the effect of licensing on teacher quality can be positive or negative, even if states succeed in using only fully licensed teachers (many states must hire teachers lacking full certification because of shortages in specific fields or districts).

Given the pool of applicants, districts determine which teachers receive job offers and whose contract is renewed. Perhaps the key question is whether administrators take the necessary steps to build the most effective teaching force available given other constraints. Many critics of public schools argue that the answer to this question is no, and there is some evidence to back up that claim (cf. Ballou, 1996). Regardless of distinct hiring practices, teaching is a complicated profession, and it is difficult to predict success as a teacher based on written records or brief interviews. Schools do have more information at the time of contract renewal.

The quotes at the beginning of this chapter focus solely on the characteristics of those hired, but today much more emphasis is placed on the behavior of teachers while at work. Research provides strong evidence that teachers respond to incentives regarding subject matter (cf. Deere & Strayer, 2003), and it is likely that work effort also depends in part on the rewards to hard work and penalties for not putting forth much effort. Equation 3 places some structure around this idea by representing effort of teachers as a function of incentives and other factors.

$$effort_{sd} = f(pay\ structure_{sd}, nonpecuniary\ incentives_{sd}, return\ to\ effort$$
$$outside\ of\ current\ school,\ pay,\ working\ conditions) \quad (3)$$

Stronger pecuniary and nonpecuniary incentives including decisions regarding contract renewal and tenure should elicit greater effort, although skeptics voice serious concerns about unintended consequences (e.g., little or no time allocated to subjects outside of any accountability system) and the potentially adverse impact on teacher cooperation. Effort also depends on the return to performance in the teacher labor market at large and in other occupations as well as on the degree to which teachers are motivated to do a good job regardless of any explicit set of rewards or sanctions. Higher compensation and better working conditions should enable schools to choose among a better pool of candidates along this dimension.

Substitution of Equations 2 and 3 into Equation 1 makes explicit the policy options available to raise the quality of instruction.

$$TQ_{ds} = f(pay_{sd}, working\ conditions_{sd}, return\ to\ effort\ outside\ of\ current$$
$$school,\ other\ teaching\ opportunities,\ nonteaching\ opportunities,$$
$$pay\ structure_{sd},\ nonpecuniary\ incentives_{sd},\ hiring\ practices_{sd}$$
$$|\ state\ regulations) \quad (4)$$

One important set of policy instruments relates to the size and quality of a district's pool of potential teachers. Districts can expand the pool of applicants by increasing compensation and improving working conditions. Evidence suggests that it would take large increases in salary to offset teacher labor market disadvantages to schools serving predominantly low-income, minority student bodies (Hanushek, Kain, & Rivkin, 2004). Therefore improvements in working conditions may have a large payoff. States can also affect the applicant pool through changes in the licensing process, acceptance of alternative certification programs, and other regulatory changes. The impact on the willingness to enter teaching should always be considered when reviewing any proposed changes to the certification process.

Notice that the competition among schools and between schools and other occupations is made explicit by Equation 4. Although there is little that policymakers can do in terms of nonteaching job opportunities, educators should be cognizant of the competition among schools. Policies such as class-size reduction in California appear to have inadvertently harmed schools (at least temporarily) serving disadvantaged students by creating large numbers of new teaching positions in suburban schools.

In addition to policies related to the applicant pool, policymakers can alter incentives faced by teachers and administrators. The two accountability terms in Equation 3, pay structure and nonpecuniary incentives (teacher retention practices are incorporated in the latter), potentially provide schools and districts with very cost-effective mechanisms for improving the quality of instruction. Unions have tended to oppose both the linkage of pay with performance and any relaxation of job security. This opposition has slowed the expansion of such programs.

Although some incentive structures focus specifically on individual teachers, most work through the school as a whole. In terms of the former, merit pay systems for teachers have been in existence for many years, although most programs typically last only a short period of time.[2] A number of states have implemented merit reward programs in recent years, although problems with program structure in some states threaten to undermine their validity.[3] Cheating and other perverse reactions to high-stakes testing have been documented, but there is far less evidence on their overall effect on the quality of instruction.[4]

Much more comprehensive than merit pay for individual teachers are the incentives for schools as a whole to perform at a higher level. One of Friedman and Friedman's (2002) main arguments against the public provision of education was that the lack of competition would lead to very inefficient and in many cases mediocre schools. The existence of the private school system, serving roughly 10% of elementary and secondary school students in the United States, does provide some degree of competition, as does the ability of families to select a public school district as part of their housing location decision (Tiebout, 1956). On the other hand, the growing state role in the financing and provision of education almost certainly dampens competition among public school districts.

Although these long-standing competitive forces have probably had some effect on the quality of public education, recent efforts have focused on expanding the choice of publicly funded schooling, providing much more information about school performance and making administrators much more accountable. Charter schools, vouchers, and public school choice (particularly across districts) potentially expand the school choice set for all families, even those with few resources. Movement away from poorly performing schools can have a direct impact on administrators and teachers in those schools. In some cases such as Florida, vouchers are given to students in public schools deemed to be failing. This both sanctions the poorly performing schools and provides some of the most needy students with alternative schooling opportunities. Other states simply

---

[2]Cohen and Murnane (1985, 1986) describe merit pay programs.

[3]Kane and Staiger (2001) discuss potential problems related to measurement error.

[4]Jacob and Levitt (2003) document cheating in the Chicago Public School System.

grade schools as a way to place increased pressure on educators and provide families with information.

RESEARCH ON TEACHER QUALITY

This section reviews four types of research on teacher labor markets and teacher quality. The first is a description of evidence on aggregate salary trends, the second is a discussion of the evidence on the determinants of teacher turnover and mobility, the third is a summary of findings on the variation of teacher quality as measured by student outcomes, and the fourth is a discussion of the evidence on the link between teacher quality and incentives.

Aggregate Salary Trends

Despite the fact that many emphasize the nonpecuniary rewards from teaching, there can be little doubt that money affects decisions about whether and where to teach. Because of the rapid expansion of employment opportunities for women, schools faced increased competition for teachers during the latter half of the 20th century. These changes almost certainly had a major impact on the composition of public school teachers.

Figure 14.1 traces the wages of teachers aged 20–29 compared to those of other young college graduates between 1940 and 1990. The calculations,

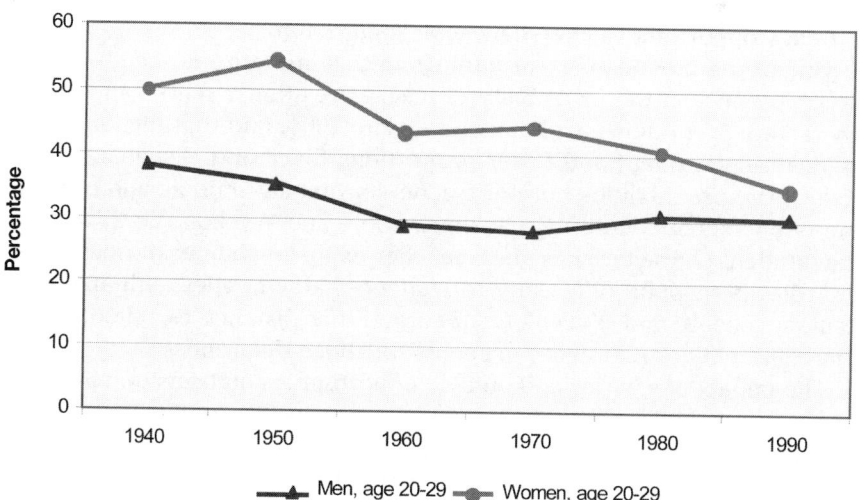

FIG. 14.1. Percentage college educated earning less than average teacher, by gender, age 20–29 from 1940 to 1990.

done separately by gender, give the proportion of nonteachers with a bachelor's degree or more who earn less than the average teacher.

Over the entire time period since World War II, teacher salaries fall relative to those for other occupations. However, the decline is more dramatic for women, particularly during the latter part of the 20th century. The changes are easiest to see for young teachers and college graduates, where the adjustment has been larger, but they also hold for teachers of all ages (see Hanushek & Rivkin, 1997).

It is important to recognize that expanded opportunities for women have not been the only factor putting upward pressure on teacher wages. Lakdawalla (2001, 2002) emphasizes the importance of increases in wages for highly educated workers due to technological change and other economic phenomena. Together these changes have sharply increased the price of teacher quality and almost certainly discouraged many potential teachers from entering the profession.

Entry, Exit, and School Switches

A substantial body of research examines the effects of salary and nonpecuniary factors on the flows into and out of teaching and on mobility among schools and districts. Nonpecuniary factors are often represented by various student demographic characteristics (explicit measures of working conditions are rarely found). One of the first such studies considers how the uniform pay structure in teaching leads to shortages in specific areas, such as mathematics and science teachers who have better outside earnings opportunities (Kershaw & McKean, 1962).

One of the most consistent findings in this literature is the strong relationship between the probability of teachers exiting a school and student characteristics. Hanushek, Kain, and Rivkin (2004) find that higher average student achievement and lower proportions Black and Hispanic students reduce the probabilities both of teachers switching schools and of exiting the public schools entirely. Lankford, Loeb, and Wyckoff (2002) also find that student characteristics affect teacher exit probabilities. It does appear that Blacks respond differently to student characteristics, although Boyd, Lankford, Loeb, and Wyckoff (2003) argue that distance to schools rather than differential preferences accounts for those differences.[5]

The impact of salaries and outside opportunities on transition probabilities is somewhat less clear, in large part because of the difficulty of controlling for differences in working conditions that can conceal the true effect of salaries.[6] There is, however, fairly consistent evidence that higher salaries

---

[5]The endogeneity of housing location complicates the interpretation of the results.

[6]Loeb and Page (2000) and Hanushek et al. (2004) discuss this issue.

reduce the probability of exit and that the effects appear to differ by experience; see, for example, Murnane and Olsen (1989, 1990), Dolton and van der Klaauw (1995, 1999), Brewer (1996), Stinebrickner (1999, 2001a, 2001b), Gritz and Theobald (1996), Murnane, Singer, Willett, Kemple, and Olsen (1991), and Scafidi, Sjoquist, and Stinebrickner (2002).[7]

Although there is strong evidence that teachers respond to working conditions and salaries, an important question is whether schools use higher salaries to buy better teachers. Most analyses of this question have considered entry into the teaching profession (Boyd et al., 2003; Hanushek & Pace, 1995; Murnane et al., 1991), and find that schools appear to favor teachers with better observable characteristics including certification, education, and test scores. Yet such characteristics may not be good predictors of job performance. Therefore, Hanushek, Kain, O'Brien, and Rivkin (2003) use estimates of the value added of teachers to student achievement growth to investigate both what types of teachers are most likely to transition out of a school and whether higher salaries attract more-effective teachers. There is little or no evidence that those who switch schools or districts, or who exit teaching entirely are systematically better than other teachers. There is, however, some indication that higher salaries enable districts to attract better teachers. Loeb and Page (2000) also find that higher salaries in a state raise the quality of education.

Measurement of Teacher Quality

One of the crucial issues for education policy is the identification of high-quality teachers. If it were the case that easily observable characteristics such as education, credential status, experience, or test scores explained the bulk of the variation in teacher effectiveness, the development of appropriate policies would be quite straightforward. The state would simply specify appropriate regulations and training criteria, and districts could then use readily available information in making personnel decisions. On the other hand, if such information does not explain much of the variation in teacher quality, performance evaluation at the local level takes on much greater importance.

A great deal of work investigates the relationship between student performance as measured by test score, years of schooling, future wages, or another outcome and teacher characteristics in an effort to identify those teacher characteristics that are systematically related to higher achievement. This type of empirical model, which is frequently referred to as an ed-

---

[7]Note that these conclusions are frequently implicit from an analysis of hazard functions for exiting teaching.

ucational production function, dates back to the "Coleman Report" (Coleman et al., 1996), an early study conducted under the auspices of the U.S. government. This body of research has failed to produce a consensus on the importance of a number of factors, primarily because of the difficulty involved in isolating the causal effect of different variables.

Recent studies using sophisticated econometric techniques or random-assignment experiments have produced more convincing results. There is quite strong evidence that teachers improve a great deal in their first and second years but not much in the subsequent years. Perhaps the most consistent finding in this literature is that a master's degree has little or no systematic relationship to teacher quality as measured by student outcomes.[8] These findings immediately raise a number of issues for policy, because additional experience and advanced degrees invariably lead to higher teacher salaries and because advanced degrees are required for full certification in a number of states. Indeed, over half of current teachers in the United States have a master's degree or more.

Standardized teacher tests are another component of many states' teacher certification processes, and the evidence suggests that tests are somewhat predictive of teacher quality (cf. Ferguson, 2000). The different focus and degree of difficulty of tests offered across the country make it difficult, however, to draw general conclusions about the value of tests. Even so, it is clear that these tests capture very little of the variation in teacher effectiveness.

Because teacher examinations and teacher educational attainment are two components of the certification process, it would be quite unlikely for certification to have a very strong link with quality, given the aforementioned results. In fact, the results for certification are somewhat mixed. Wayne and Youngs (2003) document the limitations of most studies of certification while reviewing some of the components of certification. Goldhaber and Brewer (2000) find, for example, that teachers with subject matter certification in mathematics perform better than other teachers of mathematics, whereas teachers with emergency certification perform no worse than teachers with standard certification. Darling-Hammond, Berry, and Thoreson (2001) dispute this interpretation; however Jepsen and Rivkin (2002) find small effects of certification on teacher value added to mathematics and reading achievement once the nonlinearities in the return to experience are adequately controlled.

All in all, the results show that observable characteristics of teachers explain little of the variation in student outcomes. This finding has often been cited as evidence that teachers do not have a major impact on academic

---

[8]See Hanushek (1997) and Rivkin, Hanushek, and Kain (2002) for evidence on both teacher education and experience.

progress. Yet this flies in the face of parental emphasis on school and particularly teacher quality in making housing choices and other decisions that may impact their children's education. An alternative explanation, much more consistent with the views of parents, educators, and the broader community, is that teachers do matter a great deal, and that the available research measures simply do a poor job of capturing actual differences in effectiveness.

A variety of studies (e.g., Armor et al., 1976; Hanushek, 1971, 1992; Murnane, 1975; Murnane & Phillips, 1981; Rivkin et al., 2002) have attempted to identify the total variation in the quality of teachers on the basis of student outcomes. Each of these studies attempts to estimate the portion of the variation in student outcomes that is due to teachers without the use of any differentiated measures of quality. Careful consideration of such work reveals the difficulties that must be overcome in order to estimate the variation of overall teacher effects. For example, teacher effects, school effects, and classroom peer effects are not separately identified if the estimates come from a single cross section of teachers.

Recent work on Texas public schools (Rivkin et al., 2002) uses the most comprehensive method for isolating the contribution of teachers and finds sizeable differences in teacher effectiveness. Specifically, the results show that the difference between having the median teacher and having one at the 85th percentile of teacher quality (i.e., moving up 1 standard deviation in teacher quality) is 4 percentile points in the annual gain in mathematics achievement. This is roughly equivalent to the effects of a 10-student (or roughly 50%) decrease in class size.

For a variety of reasons, these are lower-bound estimates of variations in teacher quality. The estimates rely on a series of conservative assumptions, all of which tend to lead to understatement of the effects of systematic teacher differences. Perhaps the most important is the reliance on solely quality variations within schools, for there is almost certainly systematic sorting of teachers across schools that would add to the total variation.

Incentives and Teacher Quality

The finding of substantial variation in teacher quality that is not captured by easily observable characteristics is consistent with an important role for effort and personnel decisions at the local level. A variety of programs and forms of competition currently exist whose purpose is to motivate teachers and administrators to produce high-quality schooling. These include but are not limited to state accountability systems, merit pay for teachers, and various types of school choice. Unfortunately, there is only limited research to date on the success of various types of incentive systems in raising the quality of instruction, primarily because most have not been in effect for very long.

The limited amount of evidence provides a mixed set of findings. In terms of merit pay, Cohen and Murnane (1985, 1986) find that programs typically last only a short period of time and do not have a substantial impact on teacher performance. Yet this does not provide an answer to the question of whether rigorous, permanent programs would have a substantial effect on both effort and the composition of teachers. In terms of state accountability systems, the evidence on overall program effects is mixed[9] and there is little direct evidence on the effects on teacher quality. The case is similar for most of the research on private and public school competition and school choice, with the exception of two studies. Hanushek and Rivkin (2003) find suggestive evidence that the greater choice of public schools leads to more systematic sorting by teacher quality; and Hoxby (2000) shows that choice leads schools to place greater value on teachers' effort, independence, quality of college education, and mathematics and science skills.

POLICY IMPLICATIONS

The previously discussed evidence on teacher quality brings information to bear on a number of aspects of education policy including the potential for additional incentives to improve the quality of instruction.

First, attention to teacher quality is warranted because it is an important determinant of student outcomes. There is substantial variation in teacher quality, even within schools, confirming both the importance of teachers in the education process and the potential for schools to do a much better job in selecting, mentoring, and retaining teachers.

Second, legislating "good teachers" is extraordinarily difficult, if not impossible. The currently available data give us little reason to believe that we know enough about good teachers to set appropriate training and hiring standards. For example, the lack of a systematic relationship between teacher quality and a master's degree is consistent with teachers' obtaining the least costly degree available, regardless of its quality, in order to move up the salary ladder or to comply with regulations. The idea behind most certification requirements is that we can ensure that nobody gets a really terrible teacher. In other words, the general idea is that we can put a floor under quality. But doing this requires knowledge of characteristics that sys-

---

[9]Deere and Strayer (2003) find that test scores improve much more in subjects that are part of the accountability system, and Koretz (1996) provides evidence that teachers may focus quite narrowly on tested material.

tematically affect performance. The current evidence does not indicate that we can do this with any certainty.

Perhaps even more troubling, additional requirements may actually reduce the quality of instruction, at least in some schools, for several reasons. First, some potentially good teachers may be unable to pass examinations; and second, certification requirements may discourage others from even attempting to enter the teaching profession by increasing the time and money cost (see, e.g., Murnane et al., 1991). The nature of this trade-off depends in large part on the objectives and skills of administrators who make teacher personnel decisions and on the specifics of the certification process.[10]

Third, higher salaries will likely raise teacher quality, at least over the longer term, but across the board raises would be very expensive and very inefficient. Certainly higher salaries would tend to increase the pool of potential teachers over time, but the impact of higher salaries on overall teacher quality depends on the ability of principals and human resource teams in districts to choose the better teachers among the types of teachers who choose not to exit teaching in response to the salary increase. Existing evidence, though not definitive, suggests that schools are not very effective at choosing the better teachers (Ballou, 1996; Ballou & Podgursky, 1997).

An alternative salary policy would be to raise both the level and variation in salaries in order to produce a closer link between compensation and job performance. This does not have to be mandated by the state, because district-initiated policies may be more likely to succeed. Strengthening the linkage between salaries and job performance could potentially affect the effort of existing teachers and also attract higher performing teachers into the profession.

Fourth, improved decision making at the local level has the potential to radically improve the quality of education. Certainly enhanced incentives and stricter regulations are not mutually exclusive policy options, but any constraints on local administrators necessarily limit the scope for decision making. If administrators are held accountable for school quality, why shouldn't they have a good deal of freedom in making personnel decisions? For example, why shouldn't districts have access to teacher test results but be free to hire regardless of the score?

Though state-run incentive programs for teachers may enjoy some success, the evidence suggests that policy reform should focus on local administrators. Given the fact that it is very hard to ensure high-quality instruction through regulations, local administrators must make decisions about teachers based on the evaluation of potential and actual effectiveness in

---

[10]I thank Dale Ballou for providing a clear description of this trade-off.

raising student performance, rather than on set of prior attributes. Although there is certainly room for improvement in hiring, it will always be an imperfect process. The other aspects of personnel management, on the other hand, including mentoring and support, tenure review, and the management of experienced teachers leave tremendous room for improvement.[11] A lack of serious incentives for administrators will inevitably lead many of them to take the path of least resistance and to avoid confrontations and difficult interactions with teachers. This is particularly true in districts with strong unions, and much more must be done to gather union support for innovations that link compensation and career advancement more closely to job performance.

Existing research demonstrates that principals do in fact know who the better teachers are.[12] Although the evidence is not as complete as one might like, the ability to identify teachers at the top and bottom of the quality distribution almost certainly goes further than this, particularly if good tests of student achievement are administered regularly. Unfortunately, little use is made of any such information in the current system, and we have little experience with the range of possible approaches.

As noted earlier, the measurement of teacher or administrator performance from student test score data is a complicated and often opaque process, and test scores are only one out of a number of important student outcomes. Nonetheless, much more needs to be learned about the effective use of test scores specifically, and about outcome information more generally, in the evaluation of teacher and administrator performance.

A variety of institutional structures may provide appropriate teacher incentives, and schools across the nation are experimenting with many organizational arrangements including charter schools, school report cards, merit schools, school vouchers, and public school choice. Although conceptually appealing, there is as yet little evidence upon which to judge the impact of these systems on the quality of instruction. In addition, the expansion of choice and accountability systems may have some costs. They may in some cases diminish the positive contribution schools make in terms of assimilation and the teaching of a common set of values. Communication and methodological flaws may undermine the validity of accountability systems and make it difficult for parents to make well-informed choices. Finally, students left behind in the public schools may be even more isolated and less well supported then before these systems were put in place. It is crucial that we learn more about the consequences of implementing dif-

---

[11]Though less studied, there is little evidence that the current requirements for administrator certification are closely related to the effectiveness of administrators. One relevant study is Ehrenberg, Ehrenberg, and Chaykowski (1988).

[12]See Armor et al. (1976) and Murnane (1975), who identify total teacher effects as discussed previously and relate them to principals' evaluations.

ferent types of choice and accountability programs in order to provide much better information for a policy debate that too often is driven by ideological considerations.

REFERENCES

Armor, D. J., Conry-Oseguera, P., Cox, M., King, N., McDonnell, L., Pascal, A., Pauly, E., & Zellman, G. (1976). *Analysis of the school preferred reading program in selected Los Angeles minority schools.* Santa Monica, CA: RAND Corporation.

Ballou, D. (1996, February). Do public schools hire the best applicants? *Quarterly Journal of Economics, 111*(1), 97–133.

Ballou, D., & Podgursky, M. (1997). *Teacher pay and teacher quality.* Kalamazoo, MI: W. E. Upjohn Institute for Employment Research.

Blodgett, J. H. (1893). *Report on education in the United States at the eleventh census, 1890.* Washington, DC: U.S. Government Printing Office.

Boyd, D., Lankford, H., Loeb, S., & Wyckoff, J. (2003). *Analyzing the determinants of the matching public school teachers to jobs: Estimating compensating differentials in imperfect labor markets* (Working Paper No. 9878). Cambridge, MA: National Bureau of Economic Research.

Brewer, D. J. (1996, April). Career paths and quit decisions: Evidence from teaching. *Journal of Labor Economics, 14*(2), 313–339.

Cohen, D. K., & Murnane, R. J. (1985). The merits of merit pay. *Public Interest, 80,* 3–30.

Cohen, D. K., & Murnane, R. J. (1986). Merit pay and the evaluation problem: Understanding why most merit pay plans fail and a few survive. *Harvard Educational Review,* (1), 1–17.

Coleman, J. S., Campbell, E. Q., Hobson, C. J., McPartland, J., Mood, A. M., Weinfeld, F. D., & York, R. L. (1966). *Equality of educational opportunity.* Washington, DC: U.S. Government Printing Office.

Darling-Hammond, L., Berry, B., & Thoreson, A. (2001). Does teacher certification matter? Evaluating the evidence. *Educational Evaluation and Policy Analysis, 23,* 57–77.

Deere, D., & Strayer, W. (2003). *Putting schools to the test: School accountability, incentives, and behavior* (Working Paper No. 0113). Unpublished manuscript, Texas A&M University, College Station.

Dolton, P., & van der Klaauw, W. (1995). Leaving teaching in the UK: A duration analysis. *The Economic Journal, 105,* 431–444.

Dolton, P. J., & van der Klaauw, W. (1999). The turnover of teachers: A competing risks explanation. *Review of Economics and Statistics, 81,* 543–552.

Ehrenberg, R. G., Ehrenberg, R. A., & Chaykowski, R. P. (1988). Are school superintendents rewarded for "performance"? In D. H. Monk & J. Underwood (Eds.), *Microlevel school finance: Issues and implications for policy* (pp. 337–364). Cambridge, MA: Ballinger.

Ferguson, R. F. (2000). Certification scores, teacher quality, and student achievement. In D. W. Grissmer & J. M. Ross (Eds.), *Analytic issues in the assessment of student achievement* (pp. 133–156). Washington, DC: U.S. Department of Education, National Center for Education Statistics.

Friedman, M., & Friedman, R. D. (2002). *Capitalism and freedom.* Chicago: University of Chicago Press.

Goldhaber, D. D., & Brewer, D. J. (2000). Does teacher certification matter? High school teacher certification status and student achievement. *Educational Evaluation and Policy Analysis, 22*(2), 129–145.

Gritz, R. M., & Theobald, N. D. (1996). The effects of school district spending priorities on length of stay in teaching. *Journal of Human Resources, 31,* 477–512.

Hanushek, E. A. (1971). Teacher characteristics and gains in student achievement: Estimation using micro data. *American Economic Review, 60*(2), 280–288.

Hanushek, E. A. (1992). The trade-off between child quantity and quality. *Journal of Political Economy, 100*(1), 84–117.

Hanushek, E. A. (1997). Assessing the effects of school resources on student performance: An update. *Educational Evaluation and Policy Analysis, 19,* 141–164.

Hanushek, E. A., Kain, J. F., O'Brien, D. M., & Rivkin, S. G. (2003, January). *The market for teacher quality.* Paper presented at the annual meeting of the American Economic Association, Washington, DC.

Hanushek, E. A., Kain, J. F., & Rivkin, S. G. (2004). Why public schools lose teachers. *Journal of Human Resources, 39*(2), 326–354.

Hanushek, E. A., & Pace, R. R. (1995). Who chooses to teach (and why)? *Economics of Education Review, 14*(2), 101–117.

Hanushek, E. A., & Rivkin, S. G. (1997). Understanding the twentieth-century growth in U.S. school spending. *Journal of Human Resources, 32*(1), 35–68.

Hanushek, E. A., & Rivkin, S. G. (2003). Does public school competition affect teacher quality? In C. Hoxby (Ed.), *The economics of school choice* (pp. 23–48). Chicago: University of Chicago Press.

Hoxby, C. M. (2000, August). *Would school choice change the teaching profession?* (Working Paper No. w7866). Cambridge, MA: National Bureau of Economic Research.

Jacob, B. J., & Levitt, S. D. (2003). *Catching cheating teachers: The results of an unusual experiment in implementing theory* (Working Paper No. 9414). Cambridge, MA: National Bureau of Economic Research.

Jepsen, C., & Rivkin, S. G. (2002). *What is the trade-off between smaller classes and teacher quality?* (Working Paper No. 9205). Cambridge, MA: National Bureau of Economic Research.

Kane, T. J., & Staiger, D. O. (2001). *Improving accountability measures?* (Working Paper No. 8156). Cambridge, MA: National Bureau of Economic Research.

Kershaw, J. A., & McKean, R. N. (1962). *Teacher shortages and salary schedules.* New York: McGraw-Hill.

Koretz, D. (1996). Using student assessment for educational accountability. In E. A. Hanushek & D. W. Jorgenson (Eds.), *Improving America's schools: The role of incentives* (pp. 171–195). Washington, DC: National Academy Press.

Lakdawalla, D. (2001). *The declining quality of teachers* (Working Paper No. 8263). Cambridge, MA: National Bureau of Economic Research.

Lakdawalla, D. (2002). Quantity over quality. *Education Next, 2*(3), 67–72.

Lankford, H., Loeb, S., & Wyckoff, J. (2002). Teacher sorting and the plight of urban schools: A descriptive analysis. *Educational Evaluation and Policy Analysis, 24,* 37–62.

Loeb, S., & Page, M. E. (2000). Examining the link between teacher wages and student outcomes: The importance of alternative labor market opportunities and non-pecuniary variation. *Review of Economics and Statistics, 82,* 393–408.

Murnane, R. J. (1975). *Impact of school resources on the learning of inner city children.* Cambridge, MA: Ballinger.

Murnane, R. J., & Olsen, R. (1989, May). The effects of salaries and opportunity costs on length of stay in teaching: Evidence from Michigan. *Review of Economics and Statistics, 71,* 347–352.

Murnane, R. J., & Olsen, R. (1990, Winter). The effects of salaries and opportunity costs on length of stay in teaching: Evidence from North Carolina. *Journal of Human Resources, 25*(1), 106–124.

Murnane, R. J., & Phillips, B. (1981, March). What do effective teachers of inner-city children have in common? *Social Science Research, 10*(1), 83–100.

Murnane, R. J., Singer, J. D., Willett, J. B., Kemple, J. J., & Olsen, R. J. (1991). *Who will teach?* Cambridge, MA: Harvard University Press.

Rivkin, S. G., Hanushek, E. A., & Kain, R. F. (2002). *Teachers, schools, and academic achievement* (Rev. ed.) (Working Paper No. 6691). Cambridge, MA: National Bureau of Economic Research.

Scafidi, B., Sjoquist, D. L., & Stinebrickner, T. R. (2002). *Where do teachers go?* Unpublished manuscript. Atlanta: Andrew Young School of Policy Studies, Georgia State University.

Stinebrickner, T. R. (1999). Estimation of a duration model in the presence of missing data. *Review of Economics and Statistics, 81,* 529–542.

Stinebrickner, T. R. (2001a). Compensation policies and teacher decisions. *International Economic Review, 42,* 751–779.

Stinebrickner, T. R. (2001b). A dynamic model of teacher labor supply. *Journal of Labor Economics, 19*(1), 196–230.

Tiebout, C. M. (1956). A pure theory of local expenditures. *Journal of Political Economy, 64,* 416–424.

Wayne, A. J., & Youngs, P. (2003). Teacher characteristics and student achievement gains: A review. *Review of Educational Research, 73*(1), 89–122.

15

Accounting for Schools: Econometric Issues in Measuring School Quality

Cecilia Elena Rouse

Princeton University and National Bureau of Economic Research

Believing that traditional forms of school improvement, such as class-size reduction and professional development, are expensive or ineffective, many policymakers have turned to methods of improving school perform-ance that focus on school incentives. These reforms fall under the general rubric of increased "accountability." Rather than increase funding for edu-cation or dictate particular interventions, these efforts are based on a belief that public schools are inefficient; schools can use the resources they cur-rently have more effectively, and the reform must simply provide the right incentive for them to improve. Accountability can appear at the district level (e.g., "report cards" for districts), the teacher level (e.g., monetary re-wards), or the student level (e.g., summer school or grade retention); in this chapter, I focus on accountability at the school level.

School accountability systems come in two basic flavors, although some systems include elements of both. The first, test-based accountability, relies on frequent student testing (which provides the metric of school perform-ance). Schools that do not attain certain predetermined goals are sanc-tioned by, for example, withholding funding. Schools that surpass goals are rewarded. The challenge of this approach is to devise a sensible, fair, and reliable way to assess school performance. Because there are so many in-puts to education, it is difficult to isolate the contribution of the school from the contributions of family, peers, and other external forces. Furthermore, one must devise a system of incentives that improve overall education without (too many) unintended consequences.

The second flavor relies on "market-based" accountability, or school choice. One of the arguments often made by supporters of school vouchers (and other forms of increasing parental choice) is that the forces of competition provide "market accountability" for schools without the need for elaborate data gathering and sophisticated analysis. Rather, schools that remain in operation must be "successful" as otherwise they would close for failure to attract students. In theory such a system should improve education without adverse consequences as there are few opportunities to "game" the system. However, if parents are not fully informed consumers, or if they choose schools on the basis of nonacademic characteristics, then there may not be a subsequent improvement in student (academic) outcomes.

The reauthorization of the federal *Elementary and Secondary Education Act,* called the *No Child Left Behind Act of 2001* (NCLB, 2002), contains elements of both kinds of accountability. NCLB governs the administration of funds targeted toward improving the academic achievement of disadvantaged students. A major innovation in NCLB is that it requires states to develop accountability systems for schools that serve primarily disadvantaged students (i.e., those receiving large amounts of federal funding). On the one hand, schools must meet prescribed outcome goals or face sanctions; on the other hand, many of the sanctions involve increased parental choice. Importantly, NCLB requires that the accountability system apply to all public primary and secondary schools. As a result, this piece of federal legislation is driving the creation of both kinds of school accountability systems in all 50 states.

In the first section of this chapter, I briefly describe some of the key provisions of NCLB and review the typical "economic" view of how to measure school quality. In the second section, I outline some of the important econometric issues in measuring school progress in a test-based accountability system, and in the third briefly discuss the market-based alternative. The fourth section reviews the evidence on whether either system appears to improve student outcomes, and the fifth section concludes.

ACCOUNTING FOR SCHOOLS

The No Child Left Behind Act of 2001 (NCLB)

NCLB is clearly fueling the development of school accountability systems throughout the United States. Though NCLB leaves specifics to state discretion, it does require that these systems have certain features. For example, by the 2005–2006 school year all students in Grades 3–8 and one high school grade must be tested annually in mathematics and reading or language arts.[1] Furthermore, NCLB requires states to identify "basic," "proficient," and "advanced" levels of achievement. Those scoring at proficient and advanced levels are viewed as having "high" levels of achievement. The goal is for all students to have high levels of achievement within 12 years (or by the 2013–2014 school year). Recognizing that this is a high hurdle, the statute allows states to specify a "starting point" that identifies an initial percentage of students who must be classified as high achieving. From this starting point, the passing rate is raised at predefined intervals (creating minimum proficiency rates) until it reaches 100%. NCLB requires that the starting point be defined as the maximum of either the percentage proficient of the state's lowest achieving subgroup or of the school at the 20th percentile in the state ranked by the percentage of students at the proficient level.[2]

A key requirement of NCLB is that states develop a road map for how schools will reach 100% proficiency for all subgroups. A school is considered to be making "adequate yearly progress" (AYP) if all subgroups of students are achieving at the predefined proficient or advanced levels of achievement. The subgroups include students from economically disadvantaged families, those from major racial and ethnic groups, disabled students, and students with limited English proficiency. If any subgroup does not meet at least the proficient level, the school must show that the percentage of students in that subgroup who did not meet the proficient level decreased by 10% from the preceding school year *and* that the group made progress on at least one other indicator of academic success;[3] this is known as the "safe harbor" provision. Because the hurdle that all subgroups meet or exceed the proficient level is extremely high, states and districts have been very focused on setting the level of proficiency and timeline for achieving 100% proficiency.[4]

Schools that fail to make AYP are subjected to increasingly stringent sanctions. If a school fails to make its AYP goals for 2 consecutive years,

---

[1]Beginning in 2007–2008, students must also be tested in science at least once during each of the grade spans: 3–5, 6–9, and 10–12.

[2]Note that this gives states an incentive to set the proficient level quite low so that the percentage of students achieving the benchmark is (easily) quite high. If the proficient level is low, however, then the starting point will be high (because so many students will reach the proficient level from the beginning), making it even more difficult for the lowest scoring schools and subgroups to make adequate yearly progress, as defined next.

[3]Most states appear to be choosing increased attendance for elementary schools and graduation rates for high schools.

[4]Some states require that the minimum proficiency level be increased at regular intervals throughout the 12 years; others use an "accelerating curve" in which more rapid gains are expected closer to the 2013–2014 school year.

then the school is identified for school improvement and the district must allow students to transfer to another public school (in the district) that has not been identified as failing. In addition, the school must adopt a plan to improve performance in core academic subjects and the district must provide technical assistance to aid the school. If the school fails to make AYP for 3 consecutive years, in addition to the previous remedies, the district must allow parents to choose supplementary education services from providers with a "demonstrated record of effectiveness." If a school fails to make AYP for 4 consecutive years, then in addition to the previous remedies, the district must take corrective action at the school by replacing staff, extending the school day or school year, instituting new curriculum, or restructuring the internal structure of the school. Finally, if a school fails to make AYP for 5 consecutive years, then in addition to the previous remedies the district must restructure the school by reopening it as a charter school, replacing all relevant staff, entering into a contract with a private company to operate the school, or initiating a state takeover of the school.

Thus, the goal is for all students to reach high levels of achievement. If not, the legislation attempts to assess the extent to which the failure is due to the effectiveness of schools. As a result, a key issue is how one measures school quality.

An Economic View of School Quality

Economists typically think of a school's performance as an "education production function." The school produces education using inputs and a production technology. One can then measure the effect of particular inputs on the output (education) and assess a school's efficiency. Specifically, one can think of a production function,

$$E_{ist} = f(NS_{it}, R_{ist}, X_{ist}, e_{ist})$$ (1)

where E_{ist} represents the output for student i in school s in year t; NS_{it} represents nonschool inputs into student i's educational attainment, such as her natural "ability," the extracurricular inputs provided by her parents (e.g., music lessons, extra tutoring in subjects), parental inputs (e.g., reading to their children, doing "educationally rich" activities at home), and her educational history (i.e., her achievement level in fourth grade is not only a function of her current school, but also of her schooling in kindergarten, first, second, and third grades); R_{ist} represents the resources under the control of school s in year t (e.g., class sizes, quality of teaching staff [to some extent], curriculum); X_{ist} represents the school inputs that are not typically under the control of public schools (e.g., the quality of a student's "peers"); and e_{ist} is an error term that represents all of the other "stuff" that is not otherwise represented (e.g., measurement error). The function, f, represents the "production function" or the educational practices that transform the inputs into what a student actually learns. Most researchers specify a linear production function (as this is amenable to multiple linear regression) but it is possible that the function is, in fact, nonlinear.

This formulation of the education production function highlights some of the issues that complicate the design of any accountability system: Few of the measures that one would ideally include are observable. Take, for example, E_{ist}—educational output. We rely on our schools to help children learn academic subjects as well as help them become full-functioning and happy adults by teaching democratic values, responsibility, cooperation, consideration, and other aspects of working well with others. Accountability systems that rely on test scores clearly reflect only one aspect of what we expect from schools. Furthermore, standardized tests do not fully reflect the academic achievement of students. They typically focus on only a few subjects, and in order to keep the testing affordable and not-too-intrusive, are relatively short and rely mostly on multiple-choice questions (that are less costly to score).

Second, when one considers whether a school is effective or not, one thinks of how well the school translates inputs within its control (represented by R_{ist}) into student learning. It can, however, be difficult to distinguish the factors that are within the school's control from those that are not, such as peer groups (X_{ist}). Several studies have estimated that peers can affect a student's achievement (e.g., Hanushek, Kain, Markman, & Rivkin, 2001; Sacerdote, 2000). And some (Bénabou, 1993) argue that the composition of the student body can affect the efficiency of the school's production function (with schools with "easier-to-educate" children appearing to be more productive for the same level of inputs). However, although the peer group forms a characteristic of a school, it is not necessarily an input that is under the control of school administrators, particularly in public schools that cannot select the students who attend. Furthermore, one cannot redistribute "good" peers, as they are (theoretically) in limited supply, in order to improve all schools.

Because of nonschool factors and inputs beyond the school's control, the average test scores in a school serving more disadvantaged students (School A) may be lower than the test scores of a school serving more advantaged students (School B), not because School A is worse than School B, but simply because of the nonschool inputs. The goal is to develop a system that adequately identifies the school's contribution to a student's educational outcomes.

ECONOMETRIC ISSUES IN TEST-BASED ACCOUNTABILITY

Adequate Yearly Progress (AYP)—Alternative Approaches

The Ideal Way to Measure School Progress. In order to distinguish the factors within a school's control from those that are not, it is useful to think of the ideal approach. Ideally, to measure whether a *school* is improving over time, one would begin with a group of students—randomly assigned to the school—and administer an assessment that perfectly reflects what the students know at the beginning of the school year. At the end of the year one would assess the *same* students (who would not have changed schools) and administer an appropriate follow-up test (that, again, perfectly reflects what the students know). The difference between what the students know at the beginning of the year and the end of the year can (mostly) be attributed to the school because the students are the same in each testing period. This would constitute the school's "value-added" in the first year. To assess the change in the school's value-added, one would conduct the same exercise the following year. The trick is that ideally one would keep the group of students constant—educating the same students in the same school as the previous year, in the same grade as the previous year, and with the same nonschool environment as the previous year (all as though the previous year did not occur).

Why is this the ideal design for measuring progress? First, the random assignment of students to schools initially controls for peer effects and levels the playing field in systems such as NCLB where schools much reach prespecified targets. That is, on average, all schools would have the same distribution of students and one can control for X_{ist}, school inputs usually beyond the school's control. This ideal design also controls for other nonschool inputs (NS_{ist}) by requiring that the students remain in the same school (so that one can difference out any "fixed" student characteristics, e.g., "natural ability"). Furthermore, by requiring that the second year the (same) students revert back to their first-year conditions, one controls for educational history and any other time-varying student characteristics (e.g., a divorce or other change in family situation). Finally, because the assessments perfectly reflect what students know, there is no measurement error. Because the students and their nonschool environments are held constant and there is no measurement error associated with the tests, one can isolate the influence of the school—the school's value-added.

This ideal evaluation is, of course, impossible to implement. A researcher (or educator) cannot require that students remain in the same school over the entire school year and, of course, one cannot turn back time to assess the same students under exactly the same conditions the following year. In addition, there has not been an assessment devised that *perfectly* reflects what students know. Rather, existing tests reflect only a part of what students know, and there are permanent confounding factors (such as different test-taking abilities) and random confounding factors (such as some students not feeling well on the day of the test or not getting enough sleep before the test). The policymaker's task is to implement a system that comes as close as possible to the ideal approach.

School Average Test Score Level. Before NCLB, many states simply assessed schools by average outcomes (e.g., test score levels, graduation rates) of the students attending the school. This approach is clearly not satisfactory, as a school may have low test scores not because of a low value-added, but because of nonschool inputs (NS_{ist}) and inputs beyond the school's control (X_{st}). After NCLB, states are only partially relying on the level of the school's test scores. Recall that according to NCLB a school is considered to be making AYP if all subgroups of students achieve at the proficient or advanced levels of achievement, without regard to the source of this achievement. Thus, the school may be deemed to be making AYP, *even if all of the student achievement can be attributed to inputs beyond the school's control.*[5]

Kane and Staiger (2003) highlight that, as a result, schools with minority subgroups will be disproportionately affected by NCLB's systems of sanctions for two reasons. First, the between-school variance in average test scores is quite low relative to the student-level variance in test scores. Second, the test score distribution for minority students has a mean quite a bit lower than the overall student mean. As a result, most minority students will not achieve the proficient level. Because a school is considered "failing" if *any* of the subgroups fail to achieve the minimum proficiency rate, Kane and Staiger estimate that the majority of schools with African American and Hispanic subgroups will likely fail on the basis of test score levels.[6]

Changes in School Average Test Scores. In an attempt to account for factors in test score levels that are beyond a school's control—for schools with low average test scores—most policymakers and researchers advocate

---

[5]This allowance clearly reflects the dual standards that are applied to schools. As long as the average test scores of a school are high, there is no further scrutiny as to whether the school itself is actually providing any value-added. The requirement that the school provide value-added is only applied to schools with low average test scores. In a sense it reflects ambivalence about what makes a school "good" (and conversely what makes a school "bad").

[6]Furthermore, they note there will likely be geographic variation in which schools fail as schools in racially and ethnically heterogenous states—that have more subgroups—will have a higher hurdle to clear than those in more homogenous states. And yet, it is not clear that this variation will be related to school quality.

some form of a "change" model. A simple form of this model involves measuring the change in the school's average test score (across all grades in the school) from one year to the next, as in the safe-harbor provision of NCLB. The approach comes closer to the ideal than that based on test score levels in that if the characteristics of students attending a school are the same from one year to the next, then by focusing on the change in test scores one controls for factors beyond a school's control that do not change over time. However, this approach does not control for the fact that the students attending a school change over time. For example, one cannot control student and family mobility (or other reasons for absenteeism on the dates of tests). In addition, students in the youngest grade (third grade in NCLB) in the second year would not have been tested the first year, and students in the highest grade in the first year would not be tested in the second year. As a result, the change in school average test scores is a function of the true change in a school's performance as well as changes in nonschool inputs.

If one assumes that the students who were tested in the second year are very similar to those tested in the first year—that the cohorts are similar—the contribution of the nonschool inputs should be relatively small. This is not likely to be the case, however. Hanushek, Kain, and Rivkin (2001) calculate that only about one half of students (one quarter of disadvantaged students) live in the same house for 3 consecutive years. As a result, the majority of students (particularly in the key subgroups for schools) are not in the same school from year to year.

Furthermore, Fig. 15.1 shows the percentage change in the average of some common student characteristics between the 1997–1998 and 1998–1999 school years; and between the 1998–1999 and 1999–2000 school years.[7] These data represent the racial/ethnic composition of students in Grades 3–12, and the percentage of students eligible for the National School Lunch Program (an indication of family income). Figure 15.1 shows the percentage change in each group along with the 95% confidence interval. If the 95% confidence interval includes zero (i.e., no change) then that estimated change in student characteristic cannot be considered statistically different from zero.

As is evident, schools in the United States experience large changes in the average characteristics of the students from one year to the next. For example, the average percentage of students in a school that were African American increased by 11% from 1998 to 1999 and by 8% from 1999 to 2000. Both changes are statistically different from zero. Furthermore, the average percentage of students in a school that were eligible for the National School Lunch Program increased annually by 5% to 8%. These observable charac-

---

[7]Author's calculations using the U.S. Department of Education's *Common Core of Data*.

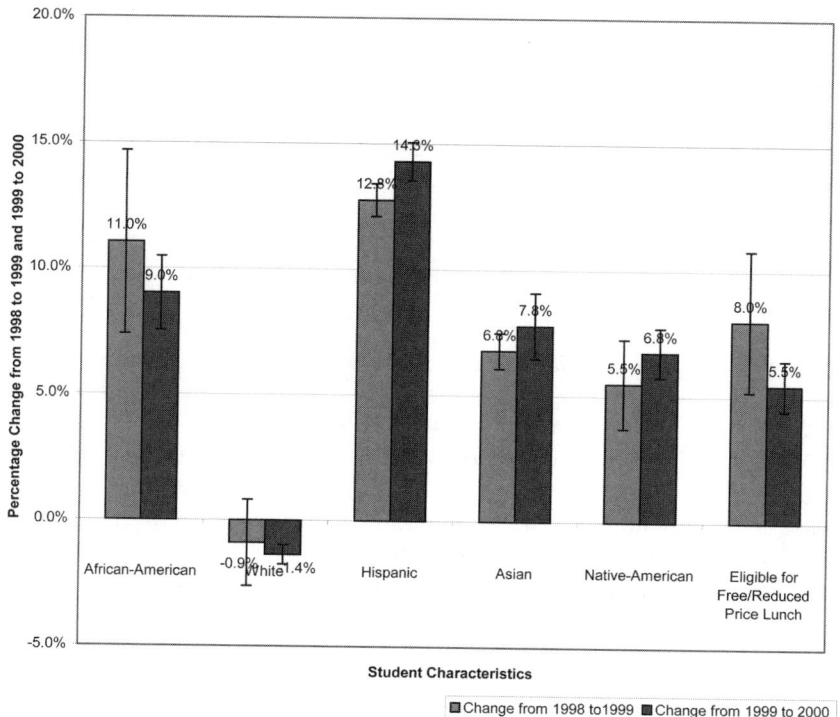

FIG. 15.1. Percentage change in school demographics from 1998 to 1999 and 1999 to 2000 (weighted by school enrollment). Author's calculations from *Common Core*.

teristics are correlated with test score outcomes, suggesting that these demographic changes would have generated a change in the school's average test scores without a change in the school's educational practices. In addition, Fig. 15.1 does not reflect unobservable characteristics of students (e.g., their motivation for learning) that also undoubtedly change over time. Clearly, some of the change in school average test scores from one year to the next actually reflects changes in nonschool inputs (as well as measurement error, as discussed later).

Many states attempt to address student mobility by requiring that the students included in the average have attended the school in question for the full year or a significant part of the year. Although these provisions protect schools from being held accountable for students the schools did not educate for long, they do not account for year-to-year changes in student body characteristics.

A variant on the model that compares school averages is to compute the AYP by *grade* level, or for different levels of schools. For example, the state may compare the outcomes of students in the fourth grade in Year 1 to the outcomes of students in the fourth grade in Year 2; or the state may compare the outcomes of students in the third grade in Year 1 to the outcomes of students in the fourth grade in Year 2; finally the state may track the progress of the elementary, middle, and high school–level students separately in schools that contain multiple levels of students. All of these approaches potentially confuse the contribution of nonschool factors with the school's contribution and are subject to problems with mobility, as the students at each grade level (or specific grade) change from year to year.

Individual Student Gain Scores. Short of the ideal design, most analysts agree that one should use data on individual students, over time, to measure changes in performance. At this point, Florida is the only state (that I could determine) that incorporates a measure of change for individual students. Even the Florida system mixes test score levels with student gains.[8] The primary advantage of longitudinal data on individual students is that one can compute the change in student achievement over time that perfectly controls for all student characteristics that do not change over time (whether one can observe them or not). That is, one can control for "time-invariant" factors such as parental educational attainment, race, ethnicity, gender, family dedication to education, and "innate student ability." One cannot address factors that may have changed over time, such as divorce (or other family disruptions) or health status.

Another disadvantage of such an approach is that one has to be very concerned about student mobility and other forms of attrition from the database. In order to compute a change in test scores for an individual student, one must have 2 years of data for that student. If the database does not allow one to obtain a prior test score for the student, then one cannot include the student in the analysis. Similarly, if the student changes schools (particularly by moving to another district), then the first district may not have the current test score for the student. If the students who move are different from those who do not *and* they would have had a slower educational trajectory than the students who remain, then by excluding the movers one will obtain an overly optimistic estimate of the school's performance. In addition, the problem of the enhanced role of measurement error remains in these models as well.

---

[8]Florida's system involves computing a "grade point average" for each school. The grade point average is the sum of six factors: the percentage of students attaining high standards in reading, mathematics, and writing; the percentage of students making "learning gains" in reading and mathematics; and the percentage of students in the school's bottom quartile who showed any yearly reading gains in scaled score points.

Another Statistical Challenge: Measurement Error

The fact that current assessments of student knowledge are imperfect raises another challenge for school accountability measures. In addition to the fact that it is impossible to design an assessment that perfectly measures what students know (i.e., there is measurement error at the individual level), school averages of test scores also do not perfectly reflect the performance of the school (i.e., there is also measurement error at the school level). School-level measurement error is composed of sampling variability (which decreases as the number of students tested increases) and random volatility (which is due to one-time factors such as a severe flu season or noisy construction, and does not decrease with an increase in the number of students). Next I discuss two implications of measurement error that pose a challenge for measures of AYP.

Mean Reversion. Given that AYP measures school test scores over time, a critical issue is how the measurement error evolves over time. If the measurement error is "mean reverting," then gains the following year by schools that score unusually low in one year are not likely to be normally distributed around the initial score; rather the schools are likely to experience larger than average gains the following year. This arises for two reasons. The first is that there is a minimum score a school can obtain on a test (a "floor effect") such that there is "nowhere to go but up." Similarly, due to "ceiling effects," schools that score highly on a test in one year are disproportionately likely to experience lower than average gains the following year. The second is that in order to be identified as low-performing, a school had to have low mean test scores in only one year. Therefore, it is possible that many of the low-performing schools in any one year had transitorily low test scores such that their scores would increase in subsequent years even in the absence of the accountability system.[9]

As an example, mean-reverting measurement error is one possible explanation for the seeming improvement of schools identified as "failing" under Florida's A+ Plan for Education, the accountability system that has been in place since 1999 and that was one of the models for NCLB. Under the A+ Plan, students are tested annually in Grades 3–10, and schools are given a grade, A through F, based largely on aggregate student test performance. High-performing and improving schools are given rewards and low-performing schools are subject to sanctions (as well as additional assistance). The most publicized sanction of the A+ Plan is the provision of pri-

---

[9]In the job-training literature, this phenomenon was first documented by Ashenfelter (1975, 1978) and has become known as the "Ashenfelter Dip."

vate school vouchers, called "Opportunity Scholarships," for students attending (or slated to attend) chronically failing schools (schools receiving a grade of "F" in 2 years out of 4, including the most recent year).

Greene (2001) analyzes changes in school average test scores in Florida from 1999 to 2000 and concludes that "the A-Plus Program has been successful at motivating failing schools to improve their academic performance" (p. 1). A major concern is that these gains are the result of mean reversion and do not reflect true improvement by the schools. It is possible that schools that scored unusually low enough to garner an "F" in 1999 may have improved simply because the low score in 1999 was a fluke; their scores in 2000 would have increased with or without the A+ Plan.

Figure 15.2 presents the deviation in average test scores for schools in Florida between the year in question and 1999, by the school's grade in 1999. Note the schools that received an "F" in 1999 had an unusually large decrease in reading test scores between 1998 and 1999 compared to higher rated schools, suggesting a preprogram "dip."[10] Greene (2001) attempts to assess the impact of mean reversion on his results and concludes that it does not explain the gains made by the F-rated schools. However, he uses only data from 1999 and 2000. Yet it is precisely the test score levels in 1999 that are potentially problematic. To assess the role of mean-reverting measurement error in the assessment of school improvement, one must have access to test scores from years prior to the one determining the school's classification. Thus, in Florida, one would need access to data prior to 1999.

The potential for mean reversion to complicate inference is present whenever the outcome under consideration is the same metric used to determine whether a school is considered to be low-performing. Within the context of NCLB, a disproportionate share of schools that fail to make AYP in 1 year will appear to make unusually large gains the following year. Though some of this improvement may reflect genuine changes in educational practice, some of it would likely have occurred anyway.

Small Samples. Another problem with measurement error that arises under NCLB is that the number of students over which school averages are computed may be rather small. Although the national average number of students in a school is 510, the average number of students in any grade is about 120, and the average number of students in any elementary grade level (3–5) is about 70. Furthermore, recall that one of the innovations of NCLB is that it imposes high standards, even for subgroups of students. However, in many schools the number of students in these subgroups may be very small. For

---

[10]Author's calculations using data available on the Florida Department of Education's Web site (http://www.firn.edu/doe/sas/fcat/fcinfopg.htm). The difference between the decrease by the F-rated schools and higher rated schools is statistically significant at the 5% level.

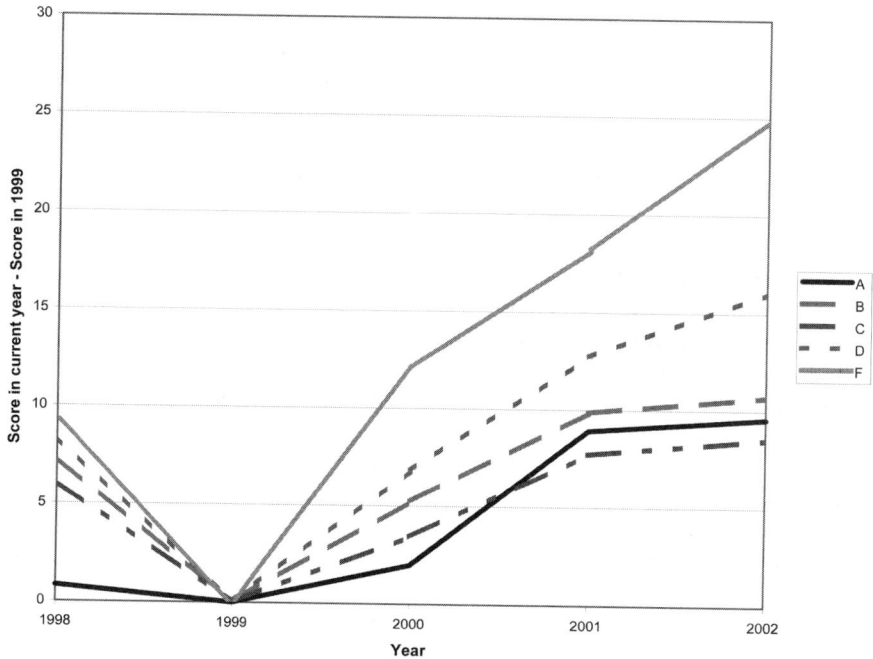

FIG. 15.2. Deviation in fourth-grade FCAT reading scores from 1999 level, by school grade in 1999. Author's calculations from Florida State data.

example, in U.S. schools in 2000 the median number of students in Grades 3–12 in the following subgroups was: 20 African American students, 14 Hispanic students, 6 Asian students, and 3 Native American students.[11] Thus, 50% of schools that had any African American students had fewer than 20 African American students (in Grades 3–12) and 50% of schools with any Hispanic students (in Grades 3–12) had fewer than 14 Hispanic students. At issue is whether one can derive a reliable measure of a school's performance for different groups of students given the small numbers.

In an insightful paper on measurement error in school-level test scores, Kane and Staiger (2001) argue that school-level measures are quite imprecise. And that this imprecision makes measures of school performance that rely on changes in test scores extremely unreliable. The problem is that if the random error is large relative to the contribution of the school to the test score level, by taking the differences (i.e., using test score gains) a higher proportion of the random error remains than of the contribution of the school.

---

[11]These figures are for students in Grades 3–12 in 2000 from the *Common Core*. Only schools with any students belonging to the subgroup in question are included in the calculations.

Using data from North Carolina, Kane and Staiger (2001) estimate that nearly 40% of the variance in fifth-grade reading scores is due to sampling variation and transitory sources (e.g., a severe flu season). Furthermore, they estimate that less than one half of the variance in the mean test score gain between fourth and fifth grade is due to persistent differences between schools (i.e., what *might* be considered differences in school quality).

Figure 15.3 further illustrates their main point—that there is much more noise in test score measures than previously appreciated. The figure shows the distribution of the number of times that schools would rank in the top 10% of schools between 1994 and 1999 using test score gains (adjusted for student characteristics) for math and reading. Note that nearly 40% of schools would have ranked in the top 10% at some point in the 6 years. However, only 15% to 18% would have ranked in the top 10% more than once. No school would have been ranked in the top 10% for all 6 years based on reading scores. Kane and Staiger (2001) compare these distributions to what one would expect if a school's ranking were determined by a random lottery held each year ("Annual Lottery"). The distributions are disturbingly similar. They estimate that test scores are so variable that school

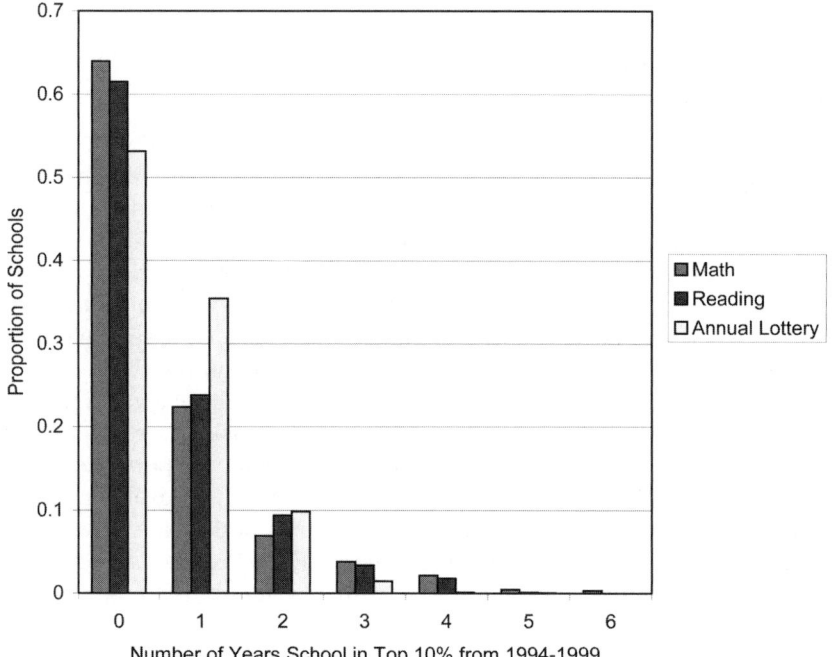

FIG. 15.3. Proportion of schools ranking in the top 10% on fifth-grade test scores in North Carolina, 1994–1999. Data from Kane and Staiger (2001).

rankings (based on either test score levels or gains) more closely resemble the distribution that one would expect from an annual lottery, where rankings were determined at random, than from persistent differences between schools. This problem is exacerbated in schools where sampling variability is greater—smaller schools. Thus they argue that small schools (or small subgroups) are much more likely to experience large test score gains or losses, and that these changes are largely the result of statistical variability. As a result, small schools (or schools with small subgroups) will be more likely to receive rewards and sanctions, and that these will be based on factors largely beyond their control.

In theory, two provisions of NCLB help to mitigate the problem of volatile test score gains. First, a school is not subject to sanctions unless the school fails to make AYP *in consecutive years.* If a school performs poorly simply because of measurement error, it is unlikely to perform poorly in consecutive years; rather performance will be poor in one year and not poor the next. Schools that perform poorly in consecutive years, in contrast, may be truly poor-performing. Second, NCLB states that AYP "shall not be required in a case in which the number of students in a category is insufficient to yield statistically reliable information." However, the minimum number of students required for the AYP to be calculated is left to each state's discretion. The modal minimum currently being proposed by states is 30 students; only nine states require more than 40 students. Unfortunately, the analysis by Kane and Staiger (2001) suggests that these minimums may not provide much protection against spurious volatility in test score changes by schools. In their data the average elementary school had 60 students per grade level, and yet there was much volatility in test scores, as discussed previously.

One must also keep the subgroup requirement in NCLB in mind. Schools in which there are small numbers of students in the subgroups will be more likely to experience large yearly swings in test scores because of measurement error. As a result, it will be difficult to distinguish whether these changes are due to true educational changes at the school level or simply due to measurement error. Volatility in test scores will provide another mechanism by which integrated schools serving large numbers of subgroups are disproportionately likely to be considered failing: The odds that at least one of the subgroups will have an unusually low test score in any one year are relatively high.

Behavioral Changes

Suppose one could reliably identify a school's value-added and there were no measurement error problems. There would still remain the question of whether any observed changes in school performance were due to productive behavioral changes (such as reallocating resources to their most productive uses) or to unproductive changes (that create the appearance of improved school performance when there has been little or no underlying improvement in education production).

There is some evidence that school administrators make changes that are intended to genuinely improve student outcomes. For example, Ladd and Zelli (2001) report that principals in North Carolina were more likely to focus on low-performing students and most reported an increased ability to improve the effectiveness of their teachers in response to the imposition of a school accountability system. Furthermore, Ladd and Zelli report that principals say they attempted to raise student achievement by developing extracurricular activities focused on math and reading, and by encouraging a greater focus on math and reading in the teaching of other subjects.

At the same time, researchers have documented several unintended consequences of increased accountability. One of the best known of these potential consequences is efforts to improve student achievement on the specific test required by the accountability system; that is, "teaching to the test." Teaching to the test is not necessarily a bad outcome of a school reform, if the test is well designed and measures what educators believe students should know. If, however, "teaching to the test" involves teaching test-taking skills (such as whether or not one should guess or how to properly fill in the circles) or that improve a student's outcome on a particular test but not on more general tests of the same subject(s), then any observed increases in student achievement should be viewed with caution. And many believe that teaching to the test is prevalent. For example, Jacob (2002) finds a much larger improvement in the high-stakes test than in the low-stakes test following the introduction of Chicago's school accountability system.

Another obvious way to artificially increase test scores is simply to cheat. Jacob and Levitt (2003) estimate that cheating occurs in 4% to 5% of elementary school classrooms annually in Chicago, and they provide evidence that suggests cheating increases when teachers have an incentive to do so (such as with high-stakes tests).

Furthermore, Cullen and Reback (2003) and Figlio and Getzler (2002) find that administrators reclassify low-achieving students as learning disabled so that the (presumably low) scores of these students will not be included in the school's average test score calculation. Similarly, Figlio (2003) reports that schools are more likely to suspend students during the testing cycle in an apparent attempt to alter the composition of the testing pool. NCLB attempts to minimize this type of "gaming" by requiring that at least 95% of the students in each of the subgroups be included in the assessments, nevertheless administrators have a large incentive to work around this requirement.

It is worth noting that although these unintended consequences may have the short-run effect of increasing a school's average test score, it is unclear that any of them would persist when measuring school test score changes, particularly in the long run. The reason is that if a school increases its average test scores by, for example, reclassifying students, it is unclear that the school will continue to experience large gains in the future, as it can only gain by reclassifying new students. Similarly, once students have learned test-taking skills, then it is unclear that there will be much more gain from further instruction in the future. That said, if the effect of teaching to the test is to substantially narrow the curriculum (as Ladd & Zelli, 2001, found in North Carolina), there may continue to be gains in the tested subjects (perhaps geared to the specific test instrument), but there may not be improvements in student achievement more broadly conceived.

SCHOOL VOUCHERS—MARKET-BASED ACCOUNTABILITY

Advocates of vouchers argue that one of the theoretical advantages of a voucher program is that it shifts the burden of standards and accountability to the marketplace. If a school is not performing to the standards demanded by parents (the consumers), then the schools will not attract students. Thus, the government does not need to assess, through an elaborate bureaucracy, whether or not a school or district has reached its academic goals and the government does not have to find itself in the awkward position of having to sanction "failing" schools. Many voucher proponents would further argue that private schools need not be part of a publicly instituted accountability system because the market provides the discipline.

The reason that increased school choice has the potential to improve student outcomes, advocates argue, is that because children are required to attend their neighborhood school, schools have little incentive to improve (Chubb & Moe, 1990; Friedman, 1962). Whereas wealthier parents can voice dissatisfaction with their residential school by moving to another neighborhood or enrolling their child in a private school, poorer parents cannot. Vouchers would, at a minimum, provide disadvantaged children with more educational options. If, in addition, they were to receive a better education in the private schools, the program may offer a cost-effective way to improve student achievement, at least for those students who use the vouchers. Some argue that a large voucher program would also improve the schooling of all children. In the most unrestricted program, all (or a substantial fraction) of the students in the public schools would be eligible to attend a private school. Because state funding would be tied to student enrollments, the public schools would have to "compete" for students, as in the marketplace, which would give the public schools an incentive to improve.

Though vouchers have many supporters, others question the validity of applying the economic model to the education market (e.g., Bagley, Woods, & Glatter, 1996; Frey, 1992; Garner & Hannaway, 1982). Because public schools are not "profit maximizing" enterprises, the nature and extent of their responses to competitive pressures is not obvious. Opponents also worry that vouchers would lead to a widening of the achievement gap between various groups of students because family resources, including information about school quality, are unequal (e.g., Schneider, 1999). Similarly, vouchers could lead to reduced public support for public schools, in terms of both desire to fund the public sector as well as volunteer efforts in the public sector (particularly if the most motivated parents leave for the private sector). All of these factors could lead to increased inequality in student outcomes, and reduced student outcomes for those "left behind" in the public schools.

There are also reasons why school vouchers may not lead to increased educational productivity. First, choice requires that parents choose schools based on their value-added. If, instead, parents choose schools based on the characteristics of schools that are not in the school's control—such as those with desirable peers—then increased school choice will not generate improvements in educational outcomes because peer groups are in limited supply and cannot be replicated in schools that must serve students who are less desirable peers. Rothstein (2002) finds little evidence that parents choose schools based on the effectiveness with which they translate inputs (in their control) into student achievement; parents appear to focus on the characteristics of the other students in a school. Second, some argue that there is already ample competition within the public school system arising from "residential choice," or the fact that many families choose the neighborhood in which they live based on the quality of the local schools (Barrow & Rouse, 2004; Hoxby, 2000). In this case, there may not be a large improvement in school performance with further parental choice. Finally, Levin (1998) has argued that any large-scale voucher program would also eventually need a structure by which to hold schools accountable, eventually leading to a new bureaucracy and entailing substantial cost.

DOES EITHER SYSTEM WORK?

Ideal Evaluation Designs

A key issue is whether either approach to accountability is more effective than the status quo. To assess whether a reform improves the way a school (or district) operates, one would ideally compare the outcomes of the school under the new reform to outcomes of the same school under another reform or the status quo. Again, by comparing the treatment schools or districts to themselves, one perfectly controls for nonschool inputs. But, this counterfactual is impossible to observe.

Unfortunately (state-level) test-based accountability systems and school choice are also difficult to evaluate experimentally. In theory one should be able to evaluate the effectiveness of school vouchers experimentally. There have already been experiments addressing the question of whether the achievement of students who use school vouchers improves (discussed later). However, to learn whether vouchers provide incentives for public schools to improve, one would need to randomly choose to provide or deny vouchers to entire districts.[12] Given that there are more than 15,000 school districts in the United States, such an experiment is theoretically possible. In practice, however, it will be difficult to implement due to political opposition from some groups. In addition, the time-limited nature of any evaluation may generate different behavior from educators than would be elicited in a true change in education policy.

Test-based accountability systems would be much more difficult (if not impossible) to evaluate experimentally. The reason is that there are only 50 states and the assignment to treatment or control status may represent such a radical change in a state's education policy that it is not feasible to implement. Therefore, one straightforward nonexperimental assessment of legislated accountability (at the state level) is to compare the outcomes of students in one state that has, for example, an accountability system in place to those in another state where there is no such system. The problem with this approach is that one cannot be assured that the schools in the "treatment" states are truly comparable to those in the "control" states, before the imposition of the reform. In other words, there may be other factors that explain any outcome differences between the two groups of students or schools. A second strategy would involve comparing the outcomes of students before the accountability system was put into place to their outcomes afterward. One cannot be assured, however, that student outcomes did not change for another reason (that would have affected the students in the absence of the accountability system). Again, there may be other factors that explain any change. Despite the design limitations, in this section I review what we know about both types of accountability systems, in practice.

---

[12]Entire districts need to be involved because (a) theoretically the public schools should respond so one could not simply compare the outcomes of students in the status-quo public schools to those in voucher-eligible public schools—over time the outcomes of the students in the two should converge; (b) the public schools need to potentially lose enough students to ensure that they respond to the market "threat"; and (c) many administrative decisions are made at the district (not the school) level.

Evidence on Test-Based Accountability Systems

The evidence on test-based accountability systems is thin and the results mixed. Recent nationwide studies by Carnoy and Loeb (2002) and Hanushek and Raymond (2002) find significant improvement in student outcomes as a result of standards-based accountability. The results from specific state systems have been less positive, however. For example, Koretz and Barron (1998) and Clark (2003) examine the effect of Kentucky's school reform (known as KERA) in the early 1990s on student achievement. Although there is evidence that KERA may have improved the scores of some students, there is not much evidence of improvement overall, or among, for example, the lowest scoring schools. Furthermore, Haney (2000) questions the perceived achievement gains made in Texas after the institution of its test-based school accountability system in the mid-1990s. He argues that any perceived improvements were due to changes in the population of students taking the state test (the Texas Assessment of Academic Skills or TAAS) and teaching-to-the-test, and that trends in data not collected by the state of Texas (such as the SAT or the National Assessment of Education Progress [NAEP]) do not show such improvement. In addition, Kane and Staiger (2003) do not find evidence that holding schools accountable for the achievement of racial and ethnic subgroups (in California and Texas) improves the performance of these traditionally lower achieving students.

The Evidence on School Vouchers

The best evidence to date on private school vouchers comes from experiments in which one group of students is randomly allocated a voucher (the "treatment" group) and a second group of students is (randomly) denied a voucher (the "control" group). This experiment was conducted in three cities around the country and the data were analyzed by Howell et al. (2002). They report that, overall, after 3 years there was no effect among all students or among non–African American students of attending a private school (in fact, the point estimates for non–African Americans are negative). In contrast, they find that among African American students who actually attended a private school there was a significant increase in student test scores. This result is entirely driven by the results in New York City, however, as there was no effect of switching to a private school found in Washington, DC, and they collected data in Dayton, Ohio for only 2 years. However, a reanalysis of the data from New York City by Krueger and Zhu (in press) suggests that these initial results are not robust to alternative decisions in the analysis. Specifically, when they include students missing baseline test scores in the analysis[13] and broaden the identification of African Americans, they no longer find that there was an improvement in the achievement of African American students who were offered a voucher or who attended a private school. Thus, results from the voucher experiments suggest *at most* a small effect for African American students (although even this result is not robust to alternative research decisions).[14] It is important to keep in mind these programs were too small to provide insight into the potential student achievement benefits of a larger voucher program. They did not provide evidence on whether providing vouchers would also improve the schooling of students who remain enrolled in the public schools.[15]

CONCLUSION

Many policymakers and educators are well-intentioned when they attempt to improve school accountability. And both test- and market-based accountability systems have potential to improve schools without large additional expenditures, at least in theory. Unfortunately, both systems also have potential pitfalls that may limit their effectiveness. The main problem with test-based accountability systems is that they require analytical methods for assessing both student and school performance. And though most researchers would agree that one should use data on individual students to make such judgments, it is difficult for states to implement such systems because of complicated data requirements and the fact that the results may not be transparent to the public. Furthermore, though one would want to assess student test score changes over time (to isolate better the effect of the school), such strategies enhance the role of measurement error, leaving one with few analytical options. Finally, because administrators and teachers may respond in a variety of ways to the incentives of any particular pro-

---

[13]Because in a randomized evaluation one randomly assigns students to receive a voucher or not, in principle one does not need to control for baseline characteristics (including test scores) because, on average, there are no differences between the students who were offered vouchers and those who were not.

[14]Evidence from the Milwaukee Parental Choice Program, the oldest publicly funded voucher program in the nation, also suggests mixed effects on student achievement. Specifically, students selected to attend a voucher school experienced significantly faster gains in math scores, but showed no differential gains in reading (Rouse, 1998a, 1998b). These results also held for African Americans, although Hispanic students who attended a voucher school also showed significantly faster gains in their reading test scores (Rouse, 2004).

[15]There is a small literature that attempts to judge (indirectly) whether the achievement of students improves when schools face more competitive pressure (e.g., Hoxby, 2000, 2001).

gram, test-based accountability systems are more likely to suffer from unintended behavioral responses.

In contrast, market-based accountability should theoretically lead to school improvement without explicit approaches to measuring school and student performance. Rather, the invisible hand of the marketplace should lead to the most-productive (and efficient) schools remaining open and the least-productive schools closing. Although the theory is elegant, the most unrestricted version of this approach has not been tried on a large scale such that we do not know if it ultimately would lead to better schools or not.

NCLB, the federal legislation that is forcing test-based accountability to take center stage, contains elements of both models of accountability. Schools are measured based on annual standardized tests and the sanctions include greater parental choice (which should generate more competitive pressure for the schools to improve). Schools that already serve high-achieving students will be regarded as performing well, whereas those serving lower achieving students will face tougher hurdles. Importantly, schools serving heterogeneous populations (i.e., integrated schools) will face the toughest hurdles, as they must show that all of their students are making adequate yearly progress or be considered "failing." Yet, these schools will be less likely to make AYP based on the test score levels of many of the subgroups of students, and they will be less likely to achieve AYP based on test score gains because of measurement error, which is exacerbated for the subgroups. (Even without the volatility in test scores, the gains that schools will be expected to make are quite large and not realistic.) The likelihood that many schools will fail also weakens the potential for increased parental choice to lead to genuine school improvement—students in districts with a high proportion of failing schools will not have many alternative schooling options. Overall, although the intention of NCLB to raise achievement for all children in the U.S. through a system of rewards and sanctions for schools is well-intentioned, it is unlikely to do so because it primarily holds schools accountable for factors beyond their control.

ACKNOWLEDGMENTS

I would like to thank David Figlio, Tom Kane, and Lisa Markman for helpful conversations, and Nina Badgaiyan and Benjamin Kaplan for expert research assistance. Any errors in fact or interpretation are mine.

REFERENCES

Ashenfelter, O. (1975). The effect of manpower training on earnings: Preliminary results. In *Proceedings of the twenty-seventh annual winter meeting of the Industrial Relations Research Association* (pp. 252–260). Madison, WI: Industrial Relations Research Association.

Ashenfelter, O. (1978). Estimating the effect of training programs on earnings. *The Review of Economics and Statistics, 60,* 47–57.

Bagley, C., Woods, P., & Glatter, R. (1996). Barriers to school responsiveness in the education quasi-market. *School Organisation, 16*(1), 45–58.

Barrow, L., & Rouse, C. E. (2004). Using market valuation to assess public school spending. *Journal of Public Economics, 88*(9–10), 1747–1769.

Bénabou, R. (1993). Workings of a city: Location, education, and production. *Quarterly Journal of Economics, 108*(3), 619–652.

Carnoy, M., & Loeb, S. (2002). Does external accountability affect student outcomes? A cross-state analysis. *Education Evaluation and Policy Analysis, 24*(4), 305–331.

Chubb, J. E., & Moe, T. M. (1990). *Politics, markets, and America's schools.* Washington, DC: Brookings Institution Press.

Clark, M. A. (2003). *Education reform, redistribution, and student achievement: Evidence from the Kentucky Education Reform Act* [Mimeo]. Princeton, NJ: Princeton University.

Cullen, J. B., & Reback, R. (2003). *Tinkering towards accolades: School gaming under a performance accountability system* [Mimeo]. Dearborn: University of Michigan.

Figlio, D. (2003). *Testing, crime, and punishment* [Mimeo]. Gainesville: University of Florida.

Figlio, D., & Getzler, D. (2002). *Accountability, ability, and disability: Gaming the system?* (Working Paper No. 9307). Cambridge, MA: National Bureau of Economic Research.

Frey, D. E. (1992). Can privatizing education really improve achievement? An essay review. *Economics of Education Review, 11*(4), 427–438.

Friedman, M. (1962). *Capitalism and freedom.* Chicago: University of Chicago Press.

Garner, W. T., & Hannaway, J. (1982). Private schools: The client connection. In M. E. Manley-Casimir (Ed.), *Family choice in schooling* (pp. 119–133). Lexington, MA: Heath.

Greene, J. P. (2001). *An evaluation of the Florida A-Plus accountability and school choice program.* Davie, FL: The Education Research Office, Center for Civic Innovation at the Manhattan Institute for Policy Research.

Haney, W. (2000). The myth of the Texas miracle in education. *Education Policy Analysis Archives, 8*(41).

Hanushek, E. A., Kain, J. F., Markman, J. M., & Rivkin, S. G. (2001). *Does peer ability affect student achievement?* (Working Paper No. 8502). Cambridge, MA: National Bureau of Economic Research.

Hanushek, E. A., Kain, J. F., & Rivkin, S. G. (2001). *Disruption versus Tiebout improvement: The costs and benefits of switching schools* (Working Paper No. 8479). Cambridge, MA: National Bureau of Economic Research.

Hanushek, E. A., & Raymond, M. E. (2002). *Improving educational quality: How best to evaluate our schools* [Mimeo]. Stanford, CA: Stanford University, Hoover Institution.

Howell, W. G., Peterson, P. E., Wolf, P. J., & Campbell, D. E. (2002). *The education gap: Vouchers and urban schools.* Washington, DC: Brookings Institution Press.

Hoxby, C. M. (2000). Does competition among public schools benefit students and taxpayers? Evidence from national variation in school districting. *American Economic Review, 90*(5), 1209–1238.

Hoxby, C. M. (2001). Rising tide. *Education Next, 1*(4), 68–75.

Jacob, B. A. (2002). *Accountability, incentives and behavior: The impact of high-stakes testing in the Chicago Public Schools* (Working Paper No. 8968). Cambridge, MA: National Bureau of Economic Research.

Jacob, B. A., & Levitt, S. D. (2003). Rotten apples: An investigation of the prevalence and predictors of teacher cheating. *Quarterly Journal of Economics, 118*(3), 843–877.

Kane, T. J., & Staiger, D. O. (2001). *Improving school accountability measures* (Working Paper No. 8156). Cambridge, MA: National Bureau of Economic Research.

Kane, T. J., & Staiger, D. O. (2003). Racial subgroup rules in school accountability systems. In P. E. Peterson & M. R. West (Eds.), *No child left behind? The politics and practice of accountability* (pp. 152–176). Washington, DC: Brookings Institution Press.

Koretz, D. M., & Barron, S. I. (1998). *The validity of gains on the Kentucky Instructional Results Information System (KIRIS)* (Report No. MR-1014-EDU). Santa Monica, CA: RAND Corporation.

Krueger, A. B., & Zhu, P. (in press). Another look at the New York City voucher experiment. *American Behavioral Scientist.*

Ladd, H. F., & Zelli, A. (2001). *School-based accountability in North Carolina: The responses of school principals* [Mimeo]. Durham, NC: Duke University.

Levin, H. M. (1998). Educational vouchers: Effectiveness, choice, and costs. *Journal of Policy Analysis and Management, 17*(3), 373–418.

No Child Left Behind Act of 2001, Pub. L. No. 107-110, § 115 Stat. 1425 (2002).

Rothstein, J. M. (2002). *Good principals or good peers? Parental valuation of school characteristics, Tiebout equilibrium, and the incentive effects of competition among jurisdictions* [Mimeo]. Berkeley: University of California.

Rouse, C. E. (1998a). Private school vouchers and student achievement: An evaluation of the Milwaukee Parental Choice Program. *Quarterly Journal of Economics, 113*(2), 553–602.

Rouse, C. E. (1998b). Schools and student achievement: More on the Milwaukee Parental Choice Program. *Economic Policy Review, 4*(1), 61–78.

Rouse, C. E. (2004). School reform in the 21st century: The effect of class size and school vouchers on minority achievement. In C. A. Conrad (Ed.), *Building skills for Black workers: Preparing for the future labor market* (pp. 15–50). Lanham, MD: University Press of America.

Sacerdote, B. (2000). *Peer effects with random assignment: Results for Dartmouth roommates* (Working Paper No. 7469). Cambridge, MA: National Bureau of Economic Research.

Schneider, M. (1999). *The role of information in school choice.* Unpublished manuscript.

VII

ALIGNING THE ELEMENTS OF ACCOUNTABILITY SYSTEMS

16

Improving Preparation for Nonselective Postsecondary Education: Assessment and Accountability Issues

Michael W. Kirst
Stanford University

The biggest student preparation problems are evidenced in the approximately 80% of the students who go to minimal or nonselective 4-year institutions and community colleges (American Council on Education, 2002; Carnevale & Rose, 2003). These students are accepted because they are 18 years old or have passed the required high school courses to be admitted. These "broad access" institutions may require the SAT, but rarely use it for admissions decisions (Barrons Educational Series, 1998; Carnegie Foundation, 2001). More than 50% of their students are in remediation, and their completion rates are very low (American Council on Education, 2002).[1] The students who attend broad-access postsecondary institutions face many obstacles. High school counseling resources are minimal, parents know little about higher education, and high school teachers in the middle- and lower ability groups do not provide much knowledge about college. Because admission is virtually certain, these students' initial hurdle, and de facto key academic standard, is a placement test once they enroll at postsecondary education.

Baltimore City Community Colleges (BCCC) provides an extreme example (Abell Foundation, 2002). Of 1,350 first-time students who entered BCCC in fall 1996, only 13 had received a vocational certificate, a two-year associate's degree, or transferred to a bachelor's degree–granting college 4 years later. Ninety-five percent needed remediation, and 45% required three math

---

[1]See also Bridge Project Web site at http://www.stanford.edu/group/bridgeproject/.

courses to reach the credit level. Their math placement test, Accuplacer™, was not matched to Maryland state high school math standards that emphasized "authentic problem solving" (e.g., word problems with applications to real-life scenarios). The BCCC placement exam included Algebra 2 content.

Improvements in the K–16 system require simultaneously looking down from higher education to secondary schools as well up the pipeline. For example, the most relevant 4-year schools for Baltimore high schools are Coppin State, Morgan State, and the University of Baltimore, not the selective schools that receive most of the media attention. What signals do these types of schools send secondary school students about what they need to know and be able to do for completion of their college programs? The Bridge Project at Stanford University studied these issues through surveys and interviews of educators, students, and parents in six states plus a review of literature. Bridge focused upon what college readiness signals that postsecondary education sent, and what signals were received at secondary schools (Kirst & Venezia, 2004).

Although the reality for students is that more than 70% will likely continue their education beyond the secondary years, federal, state, and institutional policies continue to reflect a significant separation between K–12 and postsecondary education. The current organization of secondary schools and postsecondary institutions is such that communication and information dissemination between levels is difficult, especially for those students headed to broad access postsecondary education. For instance, students—particularly those who are economically disadvantaged, or whose parents did not attend college—often do not know what colleges expect of them for admission or placement requirements (Haycock, 2003). Many students believe that nonselective 4-year institutions and community colleges do not have high academic standards. This is not the case, as is evidenced by the widespread use of placement tests for access to first-year credit-level courses. Also, policies across the segments—particularly those concerning the transition from high school graduation to college admission—are fragmented and confusing. Students who attend broad access institutions usually work part-time, and many have family responsibilities so they reside at home.

Education standards have swept across the United States, engulfing almost every state. Forty-nine states (all but Iowa) have created K–12 academic content standards in most academic subjects. At the state level, there is substantial progress in clarifying: (a) what students must be able to know and to do in the K–12 grades, and (b) how to align standards, assessments, textbook selection, and accountability measures at the K–12 level. A gaping hole in this reform strategy, however, is the lack of coherence in content and assessment standards between higher education institutions and systems and K–12 systems. Unless we close this standards gap and align K–16 policies, students and secondary schools will continue to receive a confusing array of signals and will not be able to prepare adequately for higher education. The current K–16 scene is a Babel of standards, rather than a coherent strategy.

The roots of this problem go very deep in the history of American education standards policy. The United States created two separate mass-education systems (K–12; and universities and colleges) that rarely collaborated to establish consistent standards. Universities provide some good reasons why they pay little attention to K–12 standards or assessments. Universities and college emphasize that they were not involved in the process of creating or refining K–12 standards. Moreover, universities and colleges are concerned that state K–12 standards keep changing because of political or technical problems. The K–12 assessments are not evaluated to see how well they predict freshman grades (although this is not difficult to do). Postsecondary leaders hope that the SAT and ACT (American College Test) will make adjustments to accommodate these new K–12 standards, and feel more comfortable with these two assessments that they know and can influence.

These disjunctures will be hard to fix unless there is an institutional center for K–16 reform. For example, very few states have any policy mechanism that can deal with K–16 standards alignment. Higher education coordinating bodies do not include K–16 standards alignment within their purview. In short, there are few regular opportunities for K–12 educators to discuss standards issues with college and university faculty or policymakers. The professional lives of K–12 and higher education proceed in separate orbits. In some states, the governor's office is the most logical place to put these fractured standards systems together, but higher education leaders want to guard their political independence from gubernatorial and legislative specification of admissions criteria. Because each state has a distinctive K–12 standards and assessment system, it is not clear what can be done nationally. President Clinton's advocacy of a national voluntary test died after protests about states' rights and local control of K–12 education.

IMPROVING SIGNALS AND INCENTIVES

Signaling theory suggests that streamlined and aligned high-quality and appropriate content messages have a positive impact on students' learning and achievement, and that mixed signals—the current state of affairs—have the opposite effect (Rosenbaum, 2001). Crucial aspects of appropriate signals and incentives are simplicity, clarity, and consistency (Henry &

Rubenstein, 2002). Consistency is enhanced when signals, incentives, and institutional policies are aligned—for example, the alignment of format and content of state and local student assessments with SAT I. Incoherent and vague signals and incentives sent to secondary school students cause inadequate student preparation for postsecondary. Minority students are often placed in lower level academic high school courses and tracks that decrease both motivation and preparation (Oakes, 1992).

Rosenbaum (2001) found that in the Chicago area counselors do not want to give low-achieving students negative information about their future prospects, so they advocate college for all without stressing necessary academic preparation. Because it is easy to enter so many 4-year and 2-year schools, there are scant incentives to work hard in high school (Conley, 1996). Once students enroll in broad-access institutions they face challenging placement exams, faculty expectations, and general-education/graduation requirements that they often did not know about in high school. They end up taking remedial noncredit courses that better signals may have prevented, such as the 60% failure rate of placement exams by first-year students entering the 19-campus California State University system from high school.

A key issue is whether K–12 exit-level and postsecondary entrance-level signals and incentives are delivered to students in isolation from one another, or through interaction and reinforcement. Three possible scenarios for signal delivery are: (a) postsecondary education drives policy, (b) K–12 drives policy, and (c) combined efforts of K–12 and postsecondary education drive policy. The preferred delivery is Option c.

Combined efforts by postsecondary education and K–12 will improve college knowledge that is essential for student aspiration and preparation. College knowledge is acquired and possessed unequally among students and families of different social classes and racial/ethnic backgrounds. College knowledge by secondary school students and parents includes knowledge of tuition, curricular requirements, placement tests, and admission procedures and selection criteria. A high school's collegiate-preparation culture cannot be fully measured via simple, visible, or discrete indices such as standardized test scores; honors and Advanced Placement™ (AP) courses; and postsecondary placement. Collegiate culture also encompasses the less tangible, more elusive qualities that can best be described through narratives that reveal the sustaining values or ethos of a high school.

Signals and incentives sent along through either a separate postsecondary education or K–12 system will result in less student preparation, college knowledge, and postsecondary outcomes. Strong signals have positive impacts on desirable outcomes, whereas confusing or weak signals provide a negative influence. Combined efforts between K–12 and postsecondary especially help disadvantaged students, whereas honors and AP students can succeed with less K–16 cooperation. Teachers can be a crucial source of college knowledge, but students in nonhonors courses receive less communication about college (Kirst, Venezia, & Antonio, 2003). Clear and consistent signals are related to positive outcomes such as less remediation and more completion of a student's desired postsecondary program (Henry & Rubenstein, 2002). Joint efforts between postsecondary and lower education are crucial in creating positive outcomes for more students, particularly those from economically disadvantaged families, families in which a parent did not attend college, and those students who face stigmatization and racism as they proceed through school. If there is no K–16 interaction and reinforcement of signals, the more-advantaged students will receive ample signals and incentives to prepare for postsecondary education. But the more educationally disadvantaged high school graduates will enroll at lower rates, require more remediation, and experience lower postsecondary completion rates.

IMPROVING K–16 TRANSITIONS

There are no organized groups that lobby for improved K–16 linkages, even though state capitals are overflowing with education interest groups. K–16 is on the margins of concern of all education levels, so no one loses a job for poor K–16 linkages. Rarely do states or localities provide accountability systems or data on how students fare in postsecondary education once they leave high school.[2] This is despite a recent flurry of state and federal K–12 accountability policies.

Federal K–16 efforts and funding are overwhelmingly focused on student financial aid, not on postsecondary persistence and completion. Federal programs such as GEAR UP and Trio are some of the numerous fragmented outreach programs that help some students, but suffer participant attrition, impact a small number of students, and know little about long-term outcomes for students (National Center on Postsecondary Improvement, 2001). Many outreach programs focus on selective institutions, rather than on broad-access institutions where the greatest problems exist (Adelman, 2001.) It is unlikely that outreach programs can create systemic reform across K–16 sectors, but they can and do help some qualified students gain access to higher education. In sum, public policy needs to move from a fo-

---

[2]For an exception, see Southern Regional Education Board, "Reporting on College Readiness."

cus on patching up and ameliorating the effects of the current system to a fundamental K–16 systemic overhaul.

CRUCIAL POLICY QUESTIONS FOR K–16 REFORM

A first strategy should be for K–16 educators and policymakers to understand their own policies and needs by asking themselves some fundamental questions. These questions are congruent with the Bridge Project framework, which has better student results when higher education and K–12 are sending similar reinforcing signals as early as middle school. Moreover, educators and policymakers should conduct a K–16 policy audit in order to understand the scope and alignment of their current policies. These key questions include:

- Are the K–12 academic content standards similar or dissimilar to the academic content taught in the first-year courses at the college and university level?
- Do your state K–12 assessment standards ask students to know and do the same things that are required by your state's public universities for admission and placement?
- Does your state have a statewide higher education placement examination? If not, how do individual colleges' tests relate to each other or the content of the state's K–12 assessment? How can your state consistently assess its needs regarding student remediation?
- Do your schools have a sufficient number of counselors whose main role is to advise students about college options and help them navigate through broad-access institutions that serve mostly part-time students?
- Do all students have early, repeated access to college preparation information? One effective process for examining these issues is the Standards for Success Project (S4S), which compares expectations of college freshman teachers with state K–12 standards and assessments. The S4S Director, David Conley (Conley & Brown, 2003), describes their process:

> Standards for Success convened a series of meetings at research universities throughout the country to gain input from faculty who teach first-year courses. The faculty were asked to identify the knowledge and skills necessary for success in those courses, to submit examples of student work that meets that standard, to annotate the work to illustrate how the work meets the standard, and to contribute course outlines and assignments that identify more clearly what students are expected to do in those classes. This information was analyzed and synthesized. From it, a brochure and CD-ROM were assembled and distributed to every

high school in the nation. The goal of the project is to create standards statements that for the first time express the expectations of university faculty in language that parallels that of state high school standards. Standards for Success also analyzed state high school assessments to ascertain the degree to which they yield results that might be of use in the college admissions process. (p. 124)

Conley found major differences between college faculty expectations and the standards in many statewide secondary school exams (Conley & Brown, 2003).

One way to enhance preparation is to enroll *all* students in Algebra I and II and other college preparation courses that predict postsecondary persistence and degree of completion. Such a policy would allow parents to remove students from a required college preparation curriculum through a parent permission form. If no action is taken by the parents, the student continues in a college preparation curriculum during all years of secondary school. Texas has implemented this college preparation policy, called the "default curriculum." This recommendation, however, should be accompanied by high schools and postsecondary education working together to develop a broader array of college preparation courses. One example would be a physics option that is integrated into an applied mechanics course. The "default curriculum" in Texas merits careful evaluation of its impact and unintended consequences.

Teachers can be a key source of college information, and have been found to be as helpful as counselors in postsecondary education planning (Noeth & Wimberly, 2002; Kirst & Venezia, 2004). Counselors are not available to work intensively with students who do not go to selective postsecondary institutions. Consequently, teachers need to be provided with the knowledge *and the time* to play a larger role in disseminating postsecondary information. Counselors and teachers should work out a collaborative relationship concerning imparting college knowledge.

Outreach programs can be a useful college knowledge component, but several basic questions arise:

- Do outreach programs connect universities and community colleges with local schools and districts? Are these outreach programs coordinated with national, state, and nonprofit outreach programs? Are these outreach programs evaluated using comparison groups of students who did not participate in outreach? Do these outreach programs focus on broad access postsecondary education?
- Do dual-enrollment and early college programs in high schools include more students than those on a path for selective postsecondary education? Can blended institutions like early college high schools enhance college knowledge?

Higher education data systems contain crucial gaps because they cannot follow students on a longitudinal basis. For example, California does not have individual student identifiers, so it cannot track college enrollment trends, evaluate progress in college, or relate college success to secondary preparation patterns. States need to ask questions such as:

- Can your state agencies (K–12, community colleges, and higher education) link their databases in order to assess needs throughout the K–16 continuum?
  - Can policymakers and researchers tell whether there are inequalities in terms of who enters and graduates from college?
  - Can they address issues of college preparation by tracking student success in higher education by district or by school?
  - Can your state measure persistence rates among different types of students, and determine which students drop out of college and when they do so?

These data elements need to be an integral part of a comprehensive K–16 accountability system that includes such concerns as:

- Do you have a statewide K–16 accountability system? Does it hold high schools accountable for offering college preparatory work, including AP courses? Does it hold higher education institutions accountable for graduating its students, and working with K–12 to prevent the need for remediation?
- Is there a stable/permanent entity or mechanism that will allow K–12 and higher education stakeholders to work together and overcome fragmentation concerning policy alignment, faculty interaction, and K–12 information systems?

These questions should be deliberated through long-term state and regional institutional structures that overcome the traditional separation of education governance into a K–12 governing board and one or more higher education boards. State funds are needed to allow activities, deliberation, and projects that cut across K–16 boundaries. K–16 education policymakers and practitioners from formerly separate higher and K–12 departments can use the questions and issues raised earlier to work together for policies and common goals. This K–16 process must move beyond administrators and policymakers, so that the divide between high school teachers and postsecondary faculty can be broken down. In large states, implementation could be enhanced if there is a regional basis for K–16 policy linkage (Suggs, 2001).

THE SENIOR-YEAR PROBLEM

Students who slack off during their senior year of high school are so common in the United States that this phenomenon has become known as "senior slump" or "senioritis." But most of these students are merely playing the hand that's been dealt them. High school seniors who take a break from tough academic courses are reacting rationally to a K–12 system and a college admissions process that provide few incentives for students to work hard during their senior year. Neither K–12 nor postsecondary education has an academic purpose for the senior year other than AP.

In effect, the education standards reform movement has written off the senior year, and so have our colleges and universities. For instance:

- The K–12 accountability movement has no strategy for assessment in the senior year. Only New York's statewide K–12 assessment includes subject matter from the senior year; most other state assessments extend only to the 10th-grade level. Grade 11 state tests are most useful for postsecondary purposes.
- The college admissions calendar encourages students to excel in their sophomore and junior years, but provides few incentives for them to study hard during their senior year.
- Because the content of K–12 state tests differs significantly from the content of college placement tests, many students learn only after enrolling in college that their senior year in high school did not prepare them adequately for college-level work.

Senior slump appears to be unique to the United States, or nearly so. In many other countries (e.g., England, France, Germany, Australia), students in their senior year of high school must pass crucial final examinations. For the 70% of high school students who will be moving directly into postsecondary education, senior year should be reconceptualized to improve academic preparation for college placement exams and college-level coursework, with emphasis on the skills and knowledge that are components of a general or liberal arts education. Students should understand that access to higher education—college admission—is only one aspect of their senior year, not the sole goal. Moreover, high schools should link their senior-year curriculum to the general-education requirements for the first year of college or university, or the technical requirements of a community college vocational certificate. Colleges should set explicit standards for senior-year performance in all courses and withdraw admissions offers if those standards are not met. Students should be required to take a specific number of academic credits during each semester of their senior year. Because students often forget math taken during their junior year of high school, colleges that require math proficiency for graduation should include a high school senior-year math course in their admissions requirements. (Many states require only 2 years of math for high school graduation.)

The federal government's 12th Grade National Assessment of Educational Progress (NAEP) assessment should focus on college readiness including the skills and knowledge needed to succeed in postsecondary education. NAEP performance levels for senior year should be set at levels above and below postsecondary remediation to indicate clearly the extent of preparation problems.

RECOMMENDATIONS FOR CHANGE IN COLLEGE ADMISSIONS AND PLACEMENT POLICIES

Colleges and universities should make sure that recommended courses for high school students provide adequate preparation. The TIMSS study of course-taking patterns for math, physics, chemistry, and biology found that college preparation students had 70 different patterns, and no pattern was taken by more than 15% of the students. The most common course pattern for general-education students includes no chemistry or physics. Only a fourth of the general-education students took biology and algebra II. TIMSS found a "bewildering array" of course titles for eighth-grade mathematics (Schmidt, 2002). This may be a particular problem for community colleges.

Colleges and high schools should cooperate in setting formulas for how the high schools are to calculate grade point averages and class rankings. (Currently, high schools in some states can elect to include or exclude grades from nonacademic courses in their computations.) Colleges should accord appropriate weight for honors and AP courses, and performance in senior-year academic courses should be an important component in computing class rank.

Some new statewide secondary-school assessments provide useful information for college admissions and placement. Because postsecondary education was not involved or interested in these K–12 exams, they have paid little attention to them. Many southern states use end-of-course exams that are, or could be, aligned with postsecondary preparation. The California State University will use the 11th-grade state tests for English language arts and mathematics for its own placement exam. New York postsecondary education has made the Regents' Exams an admission consideration for decades. Secondary students need to see some stakes from the current statewide tests. College admissions and placement could provide these consequences, and stimulate K–16 deliberations on academic standards and articulation (Kirst, 2004). If the congruence with state content standards is sufficient, states should consider whether the revised SAT-I in 2005, and the ACT exam including the writing sample, could be part of their 11th-grade assessment programs. At present, Illinois and Colorado include the ACT in their 11th-grade exams for all students, and it provides some useful feedback to schools and students about their college preparation.

RETHINKING SECONDARY AND POSTSECONDARY CURRICULUM

More fundamental curricular reform could be stimulated by reconceptualizing general education as a curriculum that spans the last 2 years of high school and the first 2 years of college. A common problem faced by those involved in initiatives to align standards of college admission and placement with performance-based K–12 standards is that the crucial years of school-to-college transition, Grades 11–14, are devoid of clear and sequential standards for student learning (Orrill, 2000). Most state standards for high school graduation are anchored in 10th grade (or lower) level content. Some students spend the first 2 years of college fulfilling a smorgasbord of general-education requirements, and may not confront challenging college standards until they begin work in their majors. In order for secondary schools to improve student preparation, postsecondary institutions should collaborate with K–12 to reach mutual goals. For example, community colleges need to send clearer signals to high school students about their standards for placement in nonremedial core courses.

Another idea is to design accountability systems for both K–12 and higher education to include outcomes that each system cannot possibly deliver on its own. Higher education could be held accountable for decreasing the number of first-year students requiring remediation. Haycock (2001) points out that if postsecondary mathematics departments taught only the mathematics *not also* taught in high school, 80% of the credit hours of postsecondary mathematics departments would be lost. There are powerful disincentives in terms of budgets and students for postsecondary mathematics departments to reduce remediation. But there are some promising practices as well. For example, in Oklahoma, 8th graders take ACT/Explore and 10th graders take the PLAN assessment, which tests English and mathematics. Feedback was provided to students, and some enhanced their preparation. Oklahoma has reduced its need for postsecondary remediation, increased postsecondary persistence, and reduced the time to obtain degrees (Mize, 2000).

PUBLIC OPINION SUPPORTS THE STATUS QUO

Any of the changes recommended in this chapter, however, confront the public's high approval rating for the current performance of postsecondary education, and satisfaction with status quo arrangements. Colleges and universities earned a respectable "B" in a 2001 nationwide random sample, whereas secondary schools were a full grade or more lower (Immerwahr, 1999). The public's collective advice is that colleges and universities continue to focus on what they do best. According to public opinion, college students themselves as adults bear a considerable share of responsibility for succeeding in higher education. The public feels generally assured about the performance and academic quality of higher education. Only 12% of the public would raise entrance standards to postsecondary education.

Although the public believes that college students are less prepared in 2001 than were the college students of a decade ago, only 11% hold postsecondary institutions responsible for students' failure to persist. Half of a national sample thinks that students are to blame, and another 40% think that it is a failure of high schools to prepare students for college-level study that causes them to drop out. Very few respondents think the presence or absence of K–16 services such as better counseling or higher education working with public schools is a primary cause of student success or failure. Moreover, a majority of the public thinks students of color have about the same opportunities as White, non-Latino students. This public opinion poll concluded that there is no mandate for change—or even a suggestion of what kind of [higher education] change would prove necessary (Immerwahr, 1999). The public message seems to be stay the course. A major public information campaign is needed to highlight the lack of persistence and completion in broad-access postsecondary education.

TOWARD IMPROVED PUBLIC POLICY

There are some powerful currents pushing for K–16 policy changes. Some governors and business leaders are already in the forefront, but the fear of state-level control of higher education limits their capacity for acting alone to improve policy. A broad coalition is needed that includes university and college staff, trustees, civil rights groups, teachers unions, and higher education faculty. A national policy issue network similar to the one developed in the 1970s by the Ford Foundation for school finance is part of the solution (Kirst, Meister, & Rowley, 1984). Such a network needs to include added components such as students, faculty, administrators, advocacy groups, policy analysts, and politicians. It can utilize the K–16 accountability information system recommended earlier as a starting point.

K–16 reform and students' successful completion of postsecondary education need to be part of the social charter of the American people. That charter must emphasize the public purposes of postsecondary education, rather than just the private benefits from higher education. In return for financial support of postsecondary education, the public has expected postsecondary institutions to provide widespread and affordable access, and academic results that enhance an educated citizenry, assist the disadvantaged, and contribute to economic development. But the social charter is a two-way street where postsecondary expects societal support for academic values such as freedom of inquiry (Gumport, 2001). The public, however, has every right to expect improvement of higher education's inadequate persistence and completion rates (U.S. Department of Education, 2001). The preceding recommendations will help improve postsecondary outcomes and buttress the social charter. The long-term support of higher education may rely upon the continuation of a two-way agreement with public support of higher education, in return for better student outcomes. The aspirations of students and parents are moving beyond access to a seat in higher education, to completion of a community college program or a 4-year degree.

REFERENCES

Abell Foundation. (2002). *Baltimore City Community College at the crossroads.* Baltimore: Author.

Adelman, C. (2001). Putting on the glitz: How tales from a few elite institutions form America's impressions about higher education. *Connection: New England's Journal of Higher Education and Economic Development, 15*(3), 24–30.

American Council on Education. (2002). *Access and persistence.* Washington, DC: Author.

Barrons Educational Series & Barron's Publishing. (Eds.). (1998). *Barron's profiles of American colleges* (23rd ed.). Hauppauge, NY: Author.

Carnegie Foundation for the Advancement of Teaching. (2001). *The Carnegie classification of institutions of higher education.* Menlo Park, CA: Author.

Carnevale, A. P., & Rose, S. J. (2003). *Socioeconomic status, race/ethnicity, and selective college admissions.* New York: Century Foundation.

Conley, D. T. (1996). Where's Waldo: The conspicuous absence of higher education from school reform and one state's response. *Phi Delta Kappan, 78*(4), 309–315.

Conley, D. T., & Brown, R. (2003). *Comparing state high school assessments to standards for success.* Eugene, OR: Center for Education Policy Research.

Gumport, P. J. (2001). Built to serve: The enduring legacy of public higher education. In P. G. Altbach, P. J. Gumport, & D. B. Johnstone (Eds.), *In defense of American higher education* (pp. 85–109). Baltimore: Johns Hopkins University Press.

Haycock, K. (2001). *Why is K–16 collaboration essential to education equity?* Washington, DC: Educational Trust.

Haycock, K. (2003). A new core curriculum for all. *Thinking K–16, 7*(1), 1–2.

Henry, G. T., & Rubenstein, R. (2002). Paying for grades: Impact of merit-based financial aid on education quality. *Journal of Policy Analysis and Management, 21*(1), 93–110.

Immerwahr, J. (1999). *Doing comparatively well: Why the public loves higher education.* San Jose, CA: National Center for Pubic Policy and Higher Education.

Kirst, M. (2004). Rethinking admission and placement in an era of new K–12 standards. In W. J. Camara & E. W. Kimmel (Eds.), *Choosing students: Higher education for the 21st century.* Mahwah, NJ: Lawrence Erlbaum Associates.

Kirst, M., & Venezia, A. (2004). *From high school to college.* San Francisco: Jossey Bass.

Kirst, M. W., Meister, G., & Rowley, S. (1984). Policy issue networks. *Policy Studies Journal, 13*(2), 247–264.

Kirst, M. W., Venezia, A., & Antonio, A. (2004). *From high school to college.* San Francisco: Jossey-Bass.

Mize, D. (2000, November). *Oklahoma education planning and assessment system.* Paper presented at the annual meeting of The Educational Trust, Washington, DC.

National Center on Postsecondary Improvement. (2001). A report to stakeholders on the condition and effectiveness of postsecondary education part two: The public. *Change, 33*(5), 23–38.

Noeth, R. J., & Wimberly, G. L. (2002). *Creating seamless educational transitions for urban African American and Hispanic students.* Iowa City, IA: ACT.

Oakes, J. (1992). Can tracking research inform practice? Technical, normative and political considerations. *Educational Researcher, 21*(4), 12–21.

Orrill, R. (2000). *Grades 11–14: The heartland or wasteland of American education.* Washington, DC: Woodrow Wilson Institute.

Rosenbaum, J. (2001). *Beyond college for all.* New York: Russell Sage Foundation.

Schmidt, W. H. (2002, April). Too little, too late: American high schools in an international context. In D. Ravitch (Ed.), *Education policy* (pp. 268–276). Washington, DC: Brookings Institution Press.

Suggs, E. (2001, January). Georgia's Placement K–16 Initiative. In G. Maeroff, P. Callan, & M. Usdan (Eds.), *The learning connection: New partnerships between schools and colleges* (pp. 78–86). New York: Teachers College Press.

U.S. Department of Education. (2001). *Conditions of education.* Washington, DC: National Center for Education Statistics.

Venezia, A., Kirst, M., & Antonio, A. (2003). *Betraying the college dream: How disconnected K–12 and postsecondary education systems undermine student aspirations.* Stanford, CA: Stanford Institute for Higher Education Research.

17

Aligning Curriculum, Standards, and Assessments: Fulfilling the Promise of School Reform

Eva L. Baker
University of California, Los Angeles
National Center for Research on Evaluation,
Standards, and Student Testing (CRESST)

Throughout the last 40 years, educational policymakers have designed educational interventions for the purpose of improving the learning of disadvantaged students and of children with special needs, beginning with the Elementary and Secondary Education Act of 1965 (ESEA). More than 20 years ago, with the publication of *A Nation At Risk* (National Commission on Excellence in Education, 1983), American educational policy widened its focus to include the learning and achievement of all children, in part as a reaction to U.S. students' mediocre performance rank in international achievement comparisons. In the current climate, educational improvement is no less important an end. The recent version of reform, standards-based education, grew out of several linked events: (a) the action of governors interested in their state's economic competitiveness in the United States (National Governors Association, 1991); (b) the report of a congressionally appointed national panel on standards and assessment (*Raising Standards for American Schools*, National Council on Education Standards and Testing, 1992); (c) the National Education Goals Panel's (1991a, 1991b, 1991c, 1992, 1993) recommendations on goals and reporting; and (d) successively enacted legislation, including America 2000 (1991), Goals 2000 (1994), and the Improving America's Schools Act of 1994. The most recent and expansive legislation, the renewal of the ESEA, articulated in the language and policies supporting the No Child Left Behind Act of 2001 (NCLB, 2002), emphasizes the importance of the measured achievement of all students. It has raised the consequences of test score results while at the same time requiring more grade levels to be tested and more detailed reporting on the performance of groups within schools. Although there are numerous other provisions, involving requirements for teacher quality, the use of evidence in making decisions, and so on, NCLB early became known for its emphasis on testing and accountability. As the dominant, legislated form of educational improvement, NCLB enjoins states to rely on student test results as the primary information source to assess progress and to guide the improvement of learning. In a framework that emphasizes accountability as the path to growth, NCLB archetypically demands a system where responsibility for outcomes is located and sanctions (or rewards) are assigned. For the purpose of this chapter and for brevity, let's call this amalgamated set of strategies results-based reform (RBR).

How should RBR work? The rhetorically preferred sequence of RBR begins with the specification of standards, or educational goals, operationally states performance standards, not unlike behavioral objectives of my youth (Baker & Popham, 1973), applies interventions (instruction, teacher development, motivation, and/or other resources), and publicizes the results of tests or other measures of performance of relevant groups (typically, but not always, students). It is planned that the first set of findings triggers an iterative cycle of (wise) inferences and (effective) actions inspired by successive and useful reports of accurate results. In the articulated plan, this system works, focusing each year on those who might be left behind, until after a 12-year cycle, all children meet explicit levels of proficiency—that is, first graders need to be proficient in first-grade standards, seventh graders in seventh-grade standards, and so on. It isn't just the 12th-grade students who will reach the achievement nirvana. In reality, it is likely that this approach will end somewhat sooner than planned, perhaps when asymptote is reached, a new test is brought in, the rules change, or new policy goals are posited. On the surface, the logical framework of the reform is straightforward: To be most effective, there needs to be quality and coherence in the array of stated goals or standards—they should combine to enable the student to exemplify the compleat learner, or something close. Furthermore, there must be a known relationship among standards, benchmarks or targets, tests, information received by teachers, their interpretation, and the generation of new, improved approaches. For the system to work right, the iterations should occur within a school year, or better still, within a unit or academic segment, rather than among years. Thus, measurement of results, a glowing signal for need of improvement, could take place many times in a term and would occur as close to the relevant instruction as possible. Once-a-year, formal measurement offers lean hope of fixing the system, except by extrapolation—teachers may redesign their year-long course in hopes of remedying performance yet to be exhibited by a new cohort of students. The students who already have been left behind will have to catch up in the next course. How will these students, who have done poorly, make faster progress? Evidence about retention in a grade level (another model based on a "whole year" unit of analysis) confirms that this approach, as a remedy for social promotion, has neither breadth nor depth of scientific base (Hauser, 2004).

Among the assumptions of this general system, or what is now called a theory of action (Baker & Linn, 2004), are that goals can be usefully described, and instructional options are available and can be carefully selected and applied to improve outcomes that relate operationally to the standards. Over the years, this model has made multiple appearances on the education policy stage, in modest and lavish costume and in different roles. The star components of RBR have been subject to different interpretations.

For example, among the variations have been the optimal degree of specificity of learning goals, the details of description (or not) of curriculum, the unit of analysis chosen for improvement, and the forms and frequency of measurements and assessments. In addition, the clarity of expectations, the audiences for reports, and the consequences of following the process and achieving ends have toggled back and forth. Some changes are simple, lexical preferences—for instance, standard, goal, objective—and may presage (should we have them) the verbal analogies on tests in years to come: *goals : standards* as *behavioral objectives : performance standards.*

Yet, the underlying steps are always the same, whether inferred from the rationalism of Aristotle or the more explicit procedures of the curriculum *rationale* articulated by Tyler (1949). The system has a logical set of requirements and both chronological and looped sequences. Figure out what should be taught, be prepared to teach it, help students learn it, measure their learning, and continue the cycle until desired improvement is met. As my grandfather often said at his persuasive heights, "So what could be bad?"

Continuing on a personal level, the general RBR approach early on made sense to me, despite my strong reservations about what and how much can or should be engineered in learning. Looking back on my own work, RBR has pervaded much of what I taught, how I tried to conduct my own teaching, and my choice of research and development (R&D) strategies in instructional design, measurement, and teacher education. It had nothing at all to do with my private life or my parenting. As a graduate student, I saw the RBR logic made concrete, albeit imperfectly and in micro form, in teacher education (Popham & Baker, 1970) and in the procedures and products of programmed instruction (Holland & Skinner, 1961; Lumsdaine & Glaser, 1960; Markle, 1967). More important, I saw it used to produce reliably important learning. Without a doubt, I am an ancient partisan. In the broader scheme of things, the enterprise of instructional systems design

(ISD), as practiced in military and business training, was not incidentally built on the identical paradigm (Baker, 1972, 1973), accounting, perhaps in part, for the almost uniform faith accorded RBR by leaders in business and industry. Even common, small R&D strategies, like pilot tests in research studies and the practice of formative evaluation, use the same syntax—focused empiricism: Conduct trial, review data, revise, and when warranted, expand. As we all can attest, RBR has moved rapidly across the rhetorical and policy horizons to its present ascendance, in tractor-beam with accountability.

At a more earthly level, the theory of action of RBR in an accountability framework requires an ever-greater number of particular steps. When broad-based reform is the goal (as opposed to, let's say, a functioning instructional program), the components of RBR consist of (a) the announced benefits or sanctions associated with accomplishment; (b) goals or standards; (c) intended beneficiaries; (d) the desired level of operational attainment equivalent to targets; (e) the rate of progress of these attainments, usually expressed in percentages of the population reaching certain levels of competence, or adequate yearly progress in NCLB-speak; (f) the inputs; (g) the resources; (h) the operations; (i) the measures; and (j) the obtained results, reported as required. The results trigger another series of events: (a) External inferences are made from the data (good, improving, disastrous, weak at occasional points), followed by (b) the invoking of consequences associated with accountability, (c) retargeting goals for all or subsets of students, (d) redesign of the reform implementation, (e) reallocation of resources, and (f) fielding the revised effort, ad infinitum, or until the individuals or institutions meet the goal, or it disappears, or the accountability system is revised.

A key part of the theory underlying this set of events assumes that there is adequate knowledge of the components and alternative courses of action by participants in the system, the wherewithal to implement them, and an acceptance of the power of the incentives and sanctions attendant to results.

Alignment

The focus of this piece is alignment. Alignment is the ether in which float the component parts of RBR. The logic of actions, the accuracy of inferences, and at the core, any reason at all to believe that systematic action will achieve positive results in an RBR framework depend on alignment. So what is the present state of the concept of alignment, who wants it, how is it variously conceived, how has it been measured, and in what ways may it be given added utility—or reconceived?

Much discussion of alignment occurs as a general proposition—a system is either aligned in whole or it is not. Yet, even a cursory analysis of the number of required pair-wise relationships of the aforementioned list of components suggests that alignment is a massive undertaking. Even for one subject matter at one grade level, true alignment, or the explicit relationships leading to the management of instruction and testing, is beyond the capacity of most school programs. If required to document the logical or empirical (let alone scientific) evidence of relationships, we find the number of separate links is in the thousands. If the relationships, or the links among components, are further multiplied by the number of improvement cycles, the number and backgrounds of students, and the range of different organizational contexts of classrooms, schools and regions, personnel capabilities, and resources, we are swamped by the overwhelmingly large number of relationships that are required for effectiveness and efficiency.

The Quandary

Without a semblance of alignment, nothing hangs together. Goals may or may not be exemplified in practice, children may or may not learn what is expected, and test scores could represent standards or miss their mark entirely. Inferences about results could rarely be tightly justified, and subsequent findings may not respond to deliberate actions by students and educators. In an unaligned system, audiences can be misled by reports and may attribute change in results, or the lack of it, to inappropriate sources, a not unknown error in causal inferences. Deficiencies in alignment result in ambiguity that may affect some or all parts of the system, like an incubating virus—dangerous but not that obvious. In accountability contexts, we choose ways to improve performance, invoke sanctions with real-world consequences, and, over time, desire to help more students reach a full range of goals. Without adequate alignment evidence, we are left with luck and magical thinking as our tools of choice to improve education.

If alignment probably cannot be taken literally, even at the level of planning, what is the midpoint between tightly matched processes and hocus-pocus? Where are the critical places for alignment to operate? Are there complementary or alternative formulations that will attain the wanted outcomes—that complex learning becomes a clear and unequivocal result of schooling and the attendant preparations of teachers and students?

Grasping Alignment

In the olden days, in an analytic presentation or article, it was common to start the exposition with a definition. This appeal to authority usually cited *Webster's Dictionary* or the *Oxford English Dictionary*. The practice has changed. The equivalent, in the electronic era, is to rely on the Internet. Its authority comes not from precision but from sheer numbers. So, in preparation for this discussion, I Googled *alignment*. The search engine spit out a list of 2,800,000 hits for the exact word *alignment,* so I decided not to vary form class, for instance, the verb *align*. I sampled, as you might imagine, the list, exploring what seemed to be common and where very different interpretations were exhibited. In the most literal interpretation of alignment, components are *lined* up, arranged in a straight line. Like the Rockettes or the University of Iowa marching band, either of which is a sight to behold. How is such alignment achieved? As a precocious child, I had the honor of assuring the alignment of the Hollywood High School marching drill team. Each young woman was required to arrange her shoulders so that they were at even in the horizontal with those of her colleague to her left. I monitored each line, to assure that every marcher, undistracted by pompoms or the cheers of the spectators at football games and the Hollywood Christmas parade, maintained her relative position with the girl on her left, whether walking on sidewalks, turf, or, on occasion, up a flight of stairs. Alignment was managed by making sure each link was positioned in space as planned. Yet, we have already disclaimed the likelihood of success of such an approach in the complexity of educational reform.

Discounting the lining up in alignment, and eschewing the acknowledgment of magical thinking as the only alternative, I believe that my Google search helped me understand a reasonable midpoint for thinking about alignment—the various metaphors that can be used to interpret the term.

Here are some Googled (and non-Googled) examples:

Chiropractic is the metaphor here (see Fig. 17.1). This sweet dog, apparently aging, needs to have its spine aligned. Alignment of the spine does not mean the same thing at the cervical or lumbar regions. Thus, adjustments

FIG. 17.1. Max (copyright 2004 DK Cavanaugh). Reprinted with permission of DK Cavanaugh.

FIG. 17.2. http://www.fly-ford.com/StepByStep-Front-Series.html. Reprinted with permission of Marlo's Frame & Alignment, http://www.fly-ford.com.

are made to reduce, on the one hand, pain and perhaps to provide, on the other hand, a sense of well-being. In this picture, the bed (or the framework) is intended to be central, and to prevent the dog from falling out of alignment.

In this very frequent example of alignment (see Fig. 17.2), we have more than one feature needing to be adjusted—all four wheels must work together, and because of the variations in tires, cars, weight distribution, and wear and tear, alignment means not only that the wheels will go in the direction one wants, but also that they will proceed in a balanced way (wheel balancing is usually a component of alignment). Thus, linked relationships and balance represent two criteria of alignment.

In this version of alignment (see Fig. 17.3), we extend the notion of balance to the extreme. But in order to achieve such a balance, the practitioner must be aligned not only in the corporeal sense, but in other ways as well. Achieving some of the more difficult positions or *asanas* occurs only when the practitioner is more deeply aligned—mind (intentions), body, and spirit (a calm, a centering) working together. This kind of alignment comes from inside out rather than from a surface analysis.

One of the most common uses of the term alignment, and one of the most ancient, comes from the study of the heavens (see Fig. 17.4). Both astronomy and astrology, documenting regularities, calculating relationships and drawing inferences about the cosmos, depend on understanding how relationships are formed, how long they last, and when they may be ex-

FIG. 17.3. http://www.powerofyoga.com/. Reprinted with permission of Sherri
Baptiste Freeman, Baptiste Power of Yoga.

pected to occur again. In the astrological interpretation, alignments of certain types—which planets, moon, time, and place—portend different futures.

In the astrological version of alignment, one finds some common ground
with educational practice—that is, the more general the prediction (you will
feel angry at someone today, but your future is bright), the better. Thus,
alignment in education has been claimed for instruction when it has been

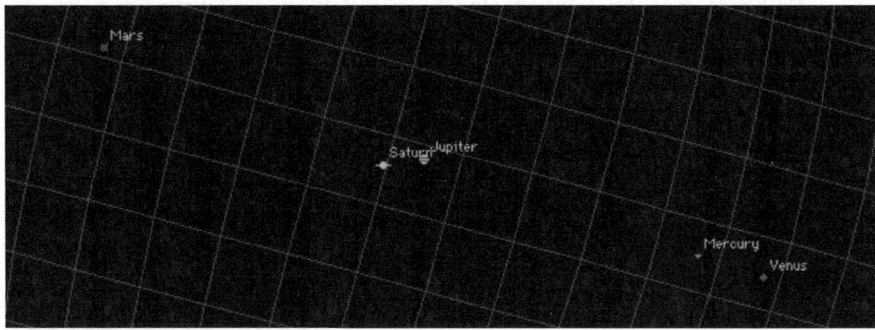

FIG. 17.4. http://www.carinasoft.com. Created with Voyager II software. Reprinted with permission of Carina Software.

documented by survey that teachers have seen and read the content standards for which they are to be accountable,[1] or that one item of many performance standards is related to an overarching content standard, to wit, "The area of this square is _____" for a content standard that says "to demonstrate a deep understanding of geometric principles."[1] These examples illustrate that the general use of a term such as alignment, for instruction or testing purposes, encourages the most minimalist interpretations to be allowable. This minimalism developed from imprecision is exactly where policy has placed the world of practice. If, for instance, the law says a system will be aligned (and leaves alignment, as it should, to the state or local authority), and the state requires of its test vendor, for instance, tests aligned to standards, any evidence of the positive will count. The test will be aligned.

But the most important idea, a deeper truth, can be learned from this planetary type of alignment. It is that alignment is not forever. Planets fall in and out of alignment. The idea of "aligned system" then is only a temporal one and will change with changing emphases, resources, and, like the stars, time. The changes in educational alignment will be far less predictable, but change there will be. This suggests to me that the range of alignment (acceptable parameters) should be articulated, rather than imagining alignment to be, first, an on–off principle, and second, something stable, unchanging, and good for all time.

There were many other examples of alignment, one of which was the DNA coils (see Fig. 17.5). Some of you know that at UCLA, we began a study of alignment that was modeled on this metaphor. Instead of the Genome, we called it the LEARNOME (Baker, Sawaki, & Stoker, 2002), and it derived from a paper given at ETS (Educational Testing Service) on the occasion of the Angoff lecture (November 1998). The idea was to find the smallest usable primitives that could characterize tests and instruction. The domains to be "mapped" involved content knowledge and skills, cognitive demands, linguistic requirements, tasks, and situational demands. There were other features that could be studied, for instance, the range of developmental trajectories through the space, and the way individual and institutional artifacts could be represented. In our preliminary work, really an illustration of how to take the linkages of alignment most literally, we were most advantaged by the work of linguists (e.g., Sawaki, Xi, Stoker, & Lord, 2004) and stymied by the complexity of the cognitive requirements. This experience, although now in part translated into part of the 10-year plan for the Federation of Behavioral, Psychological, and Cognitive Sciences (Kelly, 2004), has led me to look at different approaches to alignment in educational reform as a set of metaphors that might be expanded, discarded, or adopted.

---

[1]References are omitted as a kindness.

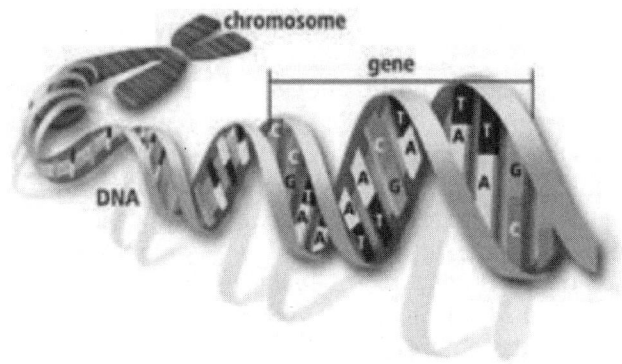

FIG. 17.5. http://www.ornl.gov/hgmis. Reprinted with permission of the United States Department of Energy Human Genome Program.

METAPHORS FOR ALIGNMENT

Alignment as Congruence

Congruence is the easiest state of alignment to describe and the hardest to achieve acceptably. It means that each and every goal in the system is clearly specified and is measured completely and without added irrelevance. It means that instruction matches both the goals and the measures, and covers their intentions completely. It implies that deliberate action (i.e., instruction) explains a large proportion of increased performance. Congruent states of alignment can be achieved in highly focused systems. For example, as part of the qualification to be certified as a Navy SEAL, one of the elite forces in the military, the candidate must swim underwater for 50 meters on one breath. The goal is clear, the criterion or performance standard is set, the instruction involves practicing the behavior, with the subcomponents of controlling anxiety, keeping oxygen consumption low, and swimming at a reasonable rate. Congruence of the goal, instruction, and measurement is achieved. Note that there are metacognitive and emotional skills, as well as psychomotor skills, involved. Even here, congruence of alignment is difficult because of the important issue of transfer; that is, under what other conditions, physical, geographical, and emotional, will the SEAL need to be able to perform this task?

Congruence is especially difficult in two common cases in education: (a) where the goals are broad and generally stated, and/or (b) where there are too many goals to be adequately taught and measured. In those cases, the logical course of action is to focus on something other than the goals or standards as the basis for alignment. In practice, because the test or set of measures is seen as an operational definition of the domain of interest rather than a sample of it, the test is used as the guide, somewhat like the shoulder of the girl to the left in a drill team.

At best, this approach simulates system congruence by matching instruction to a subset of what is intended—the specific measures rather than the goals. Students are then given practice on the form and specific content of the tests used for accountability. Trivial modifications in wording of the examination are included in test practice materials, for instance, performing calculations on sets of oranges instead of apples. Pejoratively called teaching to the test, or teaching the test, this approach can be very effective in raising the scores on the particular measures in use. It is eminently rational, particularly if there are no clearer guidelines. It is true that alignment of a sort is attained. I first thought that if the claim was made that students were proficient at the standards, then the price was inappropriate inferences about student performance and institutional quality. After more thought, it seemed that the price might be small if the public persists in believing that raised test performance is in fact the goal of education, and that the standards are merely documents for communicating in common language.

The real cost, however, is the learning that students are supposed to apply outside of school: transfer or application to new settings and conditions, with varied pieces of knowledge, help, time pressures, and criteria. It is possible, by examining tests of the same domain, or transfer tasks, to assess in part the degree to which any identified test is adequately substituting for the standards or goals, and thereby actually supports transfer (Koretz, 2003a, 2003b). One expects that students' performance will be lower on tests or measures differing in format or content examples, unless the measured test requirements include the content addressed by the alternative tests. For example, if students were expected on the official examination to solve equations with more than one unknown and the alternative examination included conceptually easier items (i.e., one unknown only), then it is likely that performance would be comparable. But for instruction to approach anything like efficiency, the number of standards prescribed and the clarity with which they are described must be limited, both so that instruction can be focused on them and so that the standards may be adequately measured (Commission on Instructionally Supportive Assessment, 2001). Congruence is partially inferred from results, but we allude to the knotty problem of measuring indicators of alignment in a later section. Note that accountability systems with short intervals before imposed consequences assume a degree of congruence rarely realized in complex systems. So if congruence were adopted as the model of alignment what would be the summary risks and mitigations?

Risks of Congruence.

- Unknown level of real learning.
- Limits on domain learning and transfer.
- Ethical questions.
- Boredom and disengagement of students.

Mitigations.

- Systematic, breadth-and-depth sampling strategies.
- Rotating constructs.
- Publication of test items.
- Evidence of rising test scores, thus political protection.

New Metaphors

To stimulate thinking, and in no way to present fully worked out options, consider some conceptions or metaphors for alignment that may provide a usable approach to addressing the relationships among educational processes, results, and inferences.

Alignment as a Set of Correspondences. Correspondence is the state of being "in agreement, harmony" (Morris, 1981, p. 299). Correspondence permits analogies, functional rather than literal agreement, and a table of equivalences. For example, in the area of reading comprehension, it is possible to describe and illustrate the types of text and sorts of answers an individual is expected to provide to meet different levels of a standard, to make progress, and so on. One excellent example is the recently published volume from Equipped for the Future (EFF), *EFF Standards* (EFF Assessment Consortium, 2004), where standards, performance levels, and assessment tasks are admirably related and illustrated, essentially at the level of what goes with what. The benefit of a correspondence model of alignment is that it is at heart based on illustrations. The limitation of this approach, of course, is that it requires some sophisticated extrapolation about other examples that would serve the same function for common standards and tasks. This correspondence approach, however, is bolstered by its explication of elements that can be readily specified, for instance, the types of rubrics and exemplar papers that can be used to illustrate a performance level. Most examples in educational reform at best approach the correspondence rather than the congruency level, although few are as thorough as they might be. As to the "harmony" implied in the definition, we are on weaker ground. Harmony within a discipline at a single grade, or up and down the grades, is rarely achieved. Harmony among the disciplines is rarely considered. Only in theory might we imagine the degree to which disciplines and areas of inquiry complement, support, or contrast with one another, or the extent of transfer of learning to be attained by the study of structured or discursive knowledge. Yet, finding the explicit points of relationship in the form of corresponding illustration may be an attainable strategy for educational alignment.

What are the consequences of this approach?

Risks of Correspondence.

- Distance between "correspondences" is too far or not intuitive.
- Few examples will be widely accepted.
- Generalization by teachers and students will be difficult.
- Nonaligned components will be obvious.
- Relationships are exaggerated.
- Trajectories are difficult to map out.

Mitigations.

- A partial solution based on examples.
- Relatively easy to develop additional examples, varying by only a few variables.

Alignment as a Bridge. Correspondence specifies how x relates to y. A bridge as a metaphor for alignment suggests connection of another type. A bridge is a pathway that provides the connector from one location to another. What is the bridge from standards to assessment tasks? It is typically agreed to be the performance standards (or operational objectives describing accomplishments of students at various levels of proficiency). What is the bridge between measures and instruction? In traditional practice, it is the general specifications used to design the test, describing a general content and skill matrix. With assessments of constructed performance, it is the scoring rubric. The scoring rubric, with its description of needed prior knowledge, criteria for expression and analysis, and levels of expertise demonstrated for the award of particular points, presents an operational set of guidelines for the designer of instruction or the teachers themselves. By no means specifying chronology, the rubric lays out an explicit set of requirements to be met. The risk of this approach to instructional design is that the rubric design is arbitrary and does not represent useful or general conceptions of performance in the domain of interest. This is much the same complaint that was accorded early efforts to form a bridge from objectives to instruction using task analysis. Gagné (1965) and his followers used a question as a device (what does the learner need to be able to do in order to perform . . .) to understand the prerequisites of tasks. The risk of this approach was that the analysis was dependent upon idiosyncratic views of the tasks or goals by the analyst, or that he or she held close a particularly comfortable instructional strategy. In other words, what a learner needs to be able to do depends on your preferred sequence of teaching. Although the myriad task analyses generated in the last 40 years and the cognitive task analyses in the last two decades have rarely been subjected to empirical verification, they nonetheless have the benefit of being explicit and understood by many, and have the potential to be generalized to other similar tasks. In the ideal world, rubrics would be subjected to rigorous validity studies (see Baker, Freeman, & Clayton, 1991) or minimally to criteria promulgated to support high-quality measurement (see Linn, Baker, & Dunbar, 1991). Their great benefit as a bridge is that empirical data can be obtained to support their use.

Other key bridges need to be built, or at least reinforced. For example, one major weakness in the entire RBR edifice is the lack of good measures of classroom practice. If learning is the key condition, then how do we reconcile a system that uses second- or third-order indicators as means to understand what is occurring in classrooms? One approach developed at CRESST (National Center for Research on Evaluation, Standards, and Student Testing) and empirically validated in LAUSD (Los Angeles Unified School District; Matsumura, Garnier, Pascal, & Valdés, 2002) is the analysis of assignments teachers give to students as a measure of the teachers' understanding simultaneously of the standards they are expected to teach, the levels of performance their students are expected to achieve, and their understanding of external measures. Looking at teacher assignments (validating them with student performance and work) is an excellent proxy for measuring instructional process, but our collective efforts in that realm are not yet convincing.

Obviously the strongest bridge possible, and one we hope to see more of, is a coherent curriculum, that is, one that exemplifies both broadly and concretely the intentions of the standards, and the content and skills to be taught and learned. Depending on its development, the curriculum itself may be closer to a correspondence approach than a congruence model. But most important, it presents, even in syllabus form, an analytical and chronological support for instructional practice, classroom assessment design, and external measure development.

Risks of Bridges.

- Weak in description and logical and empirical relationships.

- Inadequate professional development to encourage use.
- Weak prioritization.

Mitigations.

- Documented guidance against which progress can be measured.

Alignment as Gravitational Pull. The Google search generated many examples of alignment related to scientific processes, most frequently astronomical phenomena. One metaphor provoked by this array of cosmic geometry is the idea of alignment as gravitational pull. Gravity, its force a product of mass moderated by distance, enables us to make precise predictions about the location of objects in time and space. Alignment of educational outcomes, processes, and goals could well be specified by looking at the centripetal forces that hold disparate activities together. For example, if standards, instruction, and assessments are designed to focus on a set of cross-curricular skills, such as problem solving, knowledge acquisition and understanding, communication, and metacognition (Baker, 2003), then these common underpinnings, made explicit by definitions and examples, could be used to hold together otherwise disparate pieces of content. The elements, at their best, should be general across more than one (but certainly not every) subject matter domain. These elements, for instance, of problem solving, then can be reused again and again, permitting both the efficient and effective design of learning. Each of the sets of cognitive demands, acting as the core features of reform, would have characteristics that delimit optimal teaching strategies, learning experiences, and measurement design and scoring. How change would occur depends on answers to the following questions:

- Into what content or subject matters are the domain-independent requirements embedded? For example, what does problem identification (a key element in problem solving) look like in algebra word problems, in prose analysis of novellas, or in determining unknown substances in chemistry?
- What features of the domain-independent problem-solving model (or that of knowledge understanding, etc.) are appropriate to create a developmental path of greater expertise? How do these features vary explicitly by grade level? (For example, how complex is the masking or conflicting information provided to obscure the identification of the problem?)
- What elements of scientifically based content models (of learning or of pedagogy) should be included in the subject matter goals, instruction,

and outcome measurement, that is, in domain-specific models (Pellegrino, Chudowsky, & Glaser, 2001).

The alignment, in this case, would be based on a common set of elements at the center of the reform, rather than the analysis of superficial features.

A second important source of gravitational pull, or the holding together of a system, is something outside the typical discussion of achievement-based educational reform. The development of social capital at the institutional (school) or organizational (district) levels can provide another axis on which the system can rotate. Social capital (see Hargreaves, 2003) involves a recognition of the shared priorities of a group, their beliefs in collective efficacy, trust, networking, and transparency (Baker, 2003). Even in an environment with partial academic alignment, the alignment of motives and efforts will exert a powerful force on the local educational system. Such social alignment among individuals in an institution will give rise to the pursuit of the details that may be missed in a more bureaucratic approach to educational alignment.

The second notable attribute of the gravitational pull model is that relationships are dynamic. Systems move in and out of alignment based on instructional emphases, staff capability, and policy decisions. This approach should smooth out the differences and permit the system to be less volatile.

Risks of Gravitational Pull.

- Requires sophisticated understanding of cognition and subject matter.
- Changing priorities in subject matter may be viewed as a weakness.

Mitigations.

- Deep relationships can persist, supporting teaching and learning.
- Transfer can be incorporated as a goal of learning.
- Recognizes the dynamic and changing relationships in educational reform rather than imagining a steady state.

I believe that the practice in educational reform does not need to exhibit a lockstep progression through these different metaphors, albeit that for now, we are locked into the congruency concept with occasional bows to correspondence processes. Rather, the notion of common cognitive demands would allow the inevitable changes to be made in the topical content of the instruction without disturbing the fundamental relationships of the reform elements. This approach also presages the measurement and, if luck holds, the teaching of transfer, for accomplishment of the cognitive tasks can be implemented in examples that might share the same content standard (e.g., understanding the role of the frontier in American history), but vary greatly in context, format, and specific topic.

Measuring Alignment

An excellent article analyzing alignment by Bhola, Impara, and Buckendahl (2003) describes the processes to date used to characterize, document, and quantify alignment. The authors discuss levels of complexity of alignment, and focus for the most part on the alignment of standards to measures (or the reverse). They describe the important work of Webb, Porter and others (e.g., Porter, 2002; Webb, 1997, 1999). They reference research by Herman, Webb, and Zuniga (2002) that used linguistic criteria as well as content, cognition, and task requirements in their study of alignment. Almost all of these studies flow from a congruency model, although Porter's work, emphasizing the theoretical sampling of a standard's domain, may have something of the correspondence metaphor in it.

R&D Priorities

Where do we go from here in the measurement, or at least the solid documentation, of alignment? Clearly the area that needs most attention is the measurement of instructional and learning processes. We need to know what is actually happening in classrooms, what work students are being given, and how teaching and learning are taking place. The current approaches, involving questionnaires answered by students and teachers, observations by experts or peers, and logs or other chronological records, suffer from many limitations. Accuracy, reliability, validity, feasibility, and cost are just a few, but total to the claim that we have no scalable approaches for understanding what is happening in instructional practice. A black box for the key active component of schooling is unacceptable, especially if direct practice of test items or itemlike events is to be avoided. Approaches to documenting alignment in a regular, scalable, and accurate way will undoubtedly require a switch in our general strategy of declaring alignment as a proportion of all or nothing.

Rather, close-up studies must be continued that address the extent to which different instructional strategies have differential effects on measures, or to shift the focus, the extent to which different measures have known propensities to respond to instructional treatments (see Niemi, Baker, Steinberg, & Chen, 2004).

Once there is evidence of instructional approaches that work, there can be research undertaken to target the measurement of those processes in classroom settings. Such a state of affairs would be far more satisfying than a census listing of what had been "covered" in content. Moving from measures of coverage to engagement to learning should be our goal.

Among the vast number of unresolved problems, which might we emphasize and select for first priorities?

Earlier I made reference to the LEARNOME as a research approach, and I expand only briefly. Whatever its components—linguistic requirements, explicit maps of prior and to-be-learned content knowledge, families of cognitive demands, task sequences—investigations into such an area will force the development of missing parts of our reform goals. First, what language (lexicon) can we use to identify the pieces that we casually describe using our own implicit definitions? Can we develop a common language to describe educational processes and outcomes? Second, at what level of granularity should we engage—how micro should the relationships be between learning and measurement? If the research is to be trusted at all, the relationships need to be made at very detailed levels. Third, how can we predict performance based on these relationships? For whom and with what accuracy? How can these relationships, at a system or curriculum level, or even as the learning of a particular child, be represented? How can a test or instructional segment be characterized so that its shared and disparate elements are obvious? Can technology provide us with an automated analysis of the relationships among performance standards, tests, classroom assessments, texts, and student activities?

Can we conduct validity studies of "power" goals or standards, those outcomes that either provide underpinnings for a wide range of outcomes or require a known set of steps to be achieved prior to accomplishment? If we can identify these power standards, we can vastly simplify the process of alignment and move to a more focused set of standards as recommended by Popham and his colleagues on the Commission on Instructionally Supportive Assessment (2001).

Given the turbulence in policy, a desirable goal would be to find a way to simulate what would happen if student learning were stable over time, sheared of annual policy accoutrements. As of now, we have only a vague idea of what continuity of learning content and method would feel like from the child's eye up.

On the development side of R&D, we can support alignment by creating assessment design tools for use by classroom teachers and by external assessment developers. If based on common constructs and operational definitions, teachers' classroom analyses could make a deeper contribution to the view of educational effectiveness we have developed.

SUMMARY

Now to state the obvious. Useful metaphors are rarely made operational. Alignment should be treated as a goal rather than as a bureaucratic requirement to be checked off. If it is the latter, we will never attain it. And should we believe we have "aligned" our system, we must remember that the world moves, and alignment strengthens and weakens with change. In addition, we need more powerful conceptual analyses and tools to achieve reform ends. Let us find the centripetal elements that hold systems together—cognitive demands that can be taught, learned, measured, and transferred, and the social capital that motivates and energizes effort—or identifiable shared experience. Only a system that is held together from the inside can stimulate the deep and useful learning of all children.

ACKNOWLEDGMENTS

The work reported herein was partially supported by Educational Testing Service and under the Educational Research and Development Centers Program, PR/Award Number R305B960002, as administered by the Institute of Education Sciences, U.S. Department of Education.

The findings and opinions expressed in this report do not reflect the positions or policies of Educational Testing Service, the National Center for Education Research, the Institute of Education Sciences, or the U.S. Department of Education.

REFERENCES

America 2000 Excellence in Education Act. (1991). Proposed legislation (H.R. 2460), 102d Cong. 1st Sess. (ERIC Document Reproduction Service No. ED341115)

Baker, E. L. (1972). *Preparing instructional materials* (Report to the Department of Health, Education, and Welfare, Office of Education, Project No. 1-0027, Grant OEG-0-71-0645). Los Angeles: University of California, Graduate School of Education. (ERIC Document Reproduction Service No. ED 068458)

Baker, E. L. (1973). The technology of instructional development. In R. M. W. Travers (Ed.), *Second handbook of research on teaching* (pp. 245–285). Chicago: Rand McNally.

Baker, E. L. (2003). *From usable to useful assessment knowledge: A design problem* (CSE Rep. No. 612). Los Angeles: University of California, National Center for Research on Evaluation, Standards, and Student Testing (CRESST).

Baker, E. L. (2003). Multiple measures: Toward tiered systems. *Educational Measurement: Issues & Practice, 22*(2), 13–17.

Baker, E. L., Freeman, M., & Clayton, S. (1991). Cognitive assessment of history for large-scale testing. In M. C. Wittrock & E. L. Baker (Eds.), *Testing and cognition* (pp. 131–153). Englewood Cliffs, NJ: Prentice-Hall.

Baker, E. L., & Linn, R. L. (2004). Validity issues for accountability systems. In S. Fuhrman & R. Elmore (Eds.), *Redesigning accountability systems for education* (pp. 47–72). New York: Teachers College Press.

Baker, E. L., & Popham, W. J. (1973). *Expanding dimensions of instructional objectives.* Englewood Cliffs, NJ: Prentice-Hall.

Baker, E. L., Sawaki, Y., & Stoker, G. (2002, April). *The LEARNOME: A descriptive model to map and predict functional relationships among tests and educational system components.* Paper presented at the annual meeting of the American Educational Research Association, New Orleans, LA.

Bhola, D. S., Impara, J. C., & Buckendahl, C. W. (2003). Aligning tests with states' content standards: Methods and issues. *Educational Measurement: Issues and Practice, 22*(3), 21–29.

Commission on Instructionally Supportive Assessment (W. J. Popham, Chair). (2001, October). *Building tests to support instruction and accountability: A guide for policymakers.* Convened by: American Association of School Administrators, National Association of Elementary School Principals, National Association of Secondary School Principals, National Education Association, National Middle School Association. Retrieved April 2, 2004, from http://www.aasa.org/issues_and_insights/assessment/Building_Tests.pdf

EFF Assessment Consortium: SRI International and Center for Literacy Studies. (2004, January). *Equipped for the Future. EFF standards and performance level descriptors for: Reading, writing, math, speaking, and listening* (Prepared for the National Institute for Literacy). Knoxville: University of Tennessee, Center for Literacy Studies. (See also National Institute for Literacy, Washington, DC, http://www.nifl.gov/lincs/collections/eff/eff.html)

Elementary and Secondary Education Act of 1965, Pub. L. No. 89-10, 79 Stat. 27 (1965).

Gagné, R. M. (1965). *The conditions of learning.* New York: Rinehart & Winston.

Goals 2000: Educate America Act, Pub. L. No. 103-227, 108 Stat. 125 (1994).

Hargreaves, D. (2003, January). *From improvement to transformation.* Keynote address to the International Congress for School Effectiveness and Improvement 2003 conference "Schooling the Knowledge Society," Sydney, Australia.

Hauser, R. (2004, March). High stakes. In *Old lessons for a new decade: Reflections on BOTA projects.* Presentation at the meeting of the Board on Testing and Assessment, National Research Council, Washington, DC.

Herman, J. L., Webb, N., & Zuniga, S. (2002). *Alignment and college admissions: The match of expectations, assessments, and educator perspectives.* Paper presented at the annual meeting of the American Educational Research Association, New Orleans, LA.

Holland, J. G., & Skinner, B. F. (1961). *The analysis of behavior: A program for self-instruction.* New York: McGraw-Hill.

Improving America's Schools Act of 1994, Pub. L. No. 103-382, 108 Stat. 3518 (1994).

Kelly, H. (2004, February). *Integrating technology with cognitive science to improve assessment and learning.* Presentation at the American Association for the Advancement of Science Annual Meeting, Seattle, WA.

Koretz, D. (2003a). *Teachers' responses to high-stakes testing and the validity of gains: A pilot study* (Draft deliverable to the National Center for Research on Evaluation, Standards, and Student Testing). Cambridge, MA: Harvard Graduate School of Education.

Koretz, D. (2003b, April). Using multiple measures to address perverse incentives and score inflation. In *Multiple perspectives on multiple measures.* Symposium presented at the annual meeting of the National Council on Measurement in Education, New Orleans, LA.

Linn, R. L., Baker, E. L., & Dunbar, S. B. (1991). Complex, performance-based assessment: Expectations and validation criteria. *Educational Researcher, 20*(8), 15–21. (ERIC Document Reproduction Service No. EJ 436999)

Lumsdaine, A. A., & Glaser, R. (Eds.). (1960). *Teaching machines and programmed learning: A source book.* Washington, DC: National Education Association of the United States.

Markle, S. M. (1967). Empirical testing of programs. In P. C. Lange (Ed.), *Programmed instruction. Sixty-sixth yearbook of the National Society for the Study of Education, Part II* (pp. 104–140). Chicago: University of Chicago Press.

Matsumura, L. C., Garnier, H., Pascal, J., & Valdés, R. (2002, April). *Classroom assignments as indicators of instructional quality.* Presentation at the annual meeting of the American Educational Research Association, New Orleans, LA.

Morris, W. (Ed.). (1981). *American heritage dictionary of the English language.* Boston: Houghton Mifflin.

National Commission on Excellence in Education. (1983). *A nation at risk: The imperative for educational reform.* A report to the nation and the Secretary of Education. Washington, DC: U.S. Government Printing Office.

National Council on Education Standards and Testing. (1992). *Raising standards for American education. A report to Congress, the Secretary of Education, the National Education Goals Panel, and the American people.* Washington, DC: U.S. Government Printing Office.

National Education Goals Panel. (1991a). *Measuring progress toward the national education goals: Potential indicators and measurement strategies* (Compendium of interim resource group reports). Washington, DC: Author.

National Education Goals Panel. (1991b). *The National Education Goals report, 1991: Building a nation of learners.* Washington, DC: Author.

National Education Goals Panel. (1991c). *Potential strategies for long-term indicator development: Reports of the technical planning subgroups.* Washington, DC: Author.

National Education Goals Panel. (1992). *The National Education Goals report, 1992: Building a nation of leaders.* Washington, DC: U.S. Government Printing Office.

National Education Goals Panel. (1993). *Report of goals 3 and 4, Technical Planning Group on the Review of Education Standards.* Washington, DC: Author.

National Governors Association. (1991). *Results in education, 1989: The governors' 1991 report on education.* Washington, DC: Author. (ERIC Document Reproduction Service No. ED 313338)

Niemi, D., Baker, E. L., Steinberg, D. H., & Chen, E. (2004, April). Validating a large-scale performance assessment development effort. In J. Evans (Chair), *Applying research-based performance assessment models in routine practice in a large urban school district: The pleasure–pain principle.* Symposium presented at the annual meeting of the American Educational Research Association, San Diego.

No Child Left Behind Act of 2001, Pub. L. No. 107-110, 115 Stat. 1425 (2002).

Pellegrino, J., Chudowsky, N., & Glaser, R. (Eds.). (2001). *Knowing what students know: The science and design of educational assessments* (Committee on the Foundations of Assessment; Board on Testing and Assessment, Center for Education. Division on Behavioral and Social Sciences and Education). Washington, DC: National Academy Press.

Popham, W. J., & Baker, E. L. (1970). *Systematic instruction.* Englewood Cliffs, NJ: Prentice-Hall.

Porter, A. C. (2002). Measuring the content of instruction: Uses in research and practice. *Educational Researcher, 31*(7), 3–14.

Sawaki, Y., Xi, X., Stoker, G., & Lord, C. (2004). *The effects of linguistic features of NAEP Math Items on test scores and test-taking processes* (Draft deliverable to U.S. Department of Education). Los Angeles: University of California, National Center for Research on Evaluation, Standards, and Student Testing (CRESST).

Tyler, R. W. (1949). *Basic principles of curriculum and instruction.* Chicago: University of Chicago Press.

Webb, N. L. (1997). *Research Monograph No. 6: Criteria for alignment of expectations and assessments in mathematics and science education.* Washington, DC: Council of Chief State School Officers.

Webb, N. L. (1999). *Research Monograph No. 18: Alignment of science and mathematics standards and assessments in four states.* Madison, WI: National Institute for Science Education.

Author Index

A

Aaron, H. J., 43, 54
Abell Foundation, 301, 313
Achilles, C. M., 83, 94, 95
Ackerman, M., 42, 55
ACT & Council of the Great City Schools, 33, 35, 38
Adelman, C., 305, 313
Alexander, K. L., 79, 81, 92
Allen, B. A., 82, 92
Allensworth, E., 87, 94
Alt, M., 116, 138
America 2000 Excellence in Education Act, 315, 333
American Council on Education, 131, 137, 301, 313
American Educational Research Association, American Psychological Association, & National Council on Measurement in Education, 175, 181
Anastasi, A., 7, 18
Anderson, N., 213, 214
Angoff, W. H., 186, 195
Ansell, S. E., 146, 161
Antonio, A., 302, 305, 307, 314
Appleton, H., 60, 92

Armor, D. J., 267, 270, 271
Arrow, K., 179, 181
Ashenfelter, O., 285, 296, 297

B

Bagley, C., 292, 297
Bain, H. P., 83, 95
Baker, E. L., 61, 93, 100, 111, 316–318, 323, 328–331, 333–335
Ball, D. L., 12, 13, 18
Ballou, D., 260, 269, 271
Bandeira de Mello, V., 114, 137
Barnett, W. S., 80, 92
Baron, R. M., 144, 161
Barrons Educational Series & Barron's Publishing, 301, 313
Barron, S. I., 294, 297
Barrow, L., 292, 297
Bartfai, N., 114, 139
Bassey, M., 104, 110
Baum, C., 42, 54
BBC Education, 104, 110
Bell, D., 158, 161
Bénabou, R., 279, 297
Berliner, D., 167, 181

Berry, B., 151, 162, 266, 271
Bertenthal, M. W., 185, 195
Betebenner, D. W., 100, 111
Bhola, D. S., 331, 334
Biddle, B., 167, 181
Bidwell, C., 119, 137
Bielaczyc, K., 14, 18
Birman, B. F., 90, 93
Black, P., 109, 110
Blackstone, T., 100, 110
Blair, J., 32, 38
Blodgett, J. H., 257, 258, 271
Bobbitt, S., 114, 116, 137, 138
Boruch, R., 45, 54
Boston, K., 102, 110
Boston University/Chelsea Partnership, 210,
    212, 214
Boyd, D., 227, 228, 230, 234, 240, 248, 255, 264,
    265, 271
Boyd-Zaharias, J., 83, 94
Boykin, A. W., 82, 92
Braswell, J. S., 27, 30
Braun, H. I., 187, 195
Breda, C., 83, 95
Brewer, D. J., 81, 92, 265, 266, 271
Brice-Heath, S., 82, 92
Bristol, J., 35
Broadfoot, P., 105, 111
Brophy, J. E., 143, 144, 161
Broughman, S., 114, 137
Brown, M., 100, 106, 110
Brown, R., 306, 307, 313
Bryk, A. S., 87, 88, 94, 127, 138
Buckendahl, C. W., 331, 334

C

Campbell, D. E., 294, 297
Campbell, E. Q., 266, 271
Carey, N., 114, 139
Carlson, D., 21, 30
Carnegie Forum on Education and the
    Economy, 147, 161
Carnegie Foundation for the Advancement
    of Teaching, 301, 313
Carnevale, A. P., 301, 313
Carnoy, M., 225, 235, 239, 255, 294, 297
Carroll, J. B., 61, 92
Center on Education Policy, 50, 54
Chaney, B., 120, 138

Chaplin, S. H., 213, 214
Charlton, K., 78, 92
Chaykowski, R. P., 270, 271
Chen, E., 331, 335
Chen, X., 116, 138
Cheong, Y., 118, 139
Choy, S., 116, 138
Chubb, J. E., 167, 181, 291, 297
Chudowsky, N., 330, 335
Clark, M. A., 294, 297
Clayton, S., 328, 334
Clotfelter, C. T., 231–234, 255
Clune, W. H., 85, 92
Coalition for Evidence-Based Policy, 49, 54
Cobb, C., 117, 139
Cohen, B. A., 114, 139
Cohen, D. K., 12, 13, 18, 46, 54, 165, 181, 262,
    268, 271
Cohen, E., 145, 161
Coleman, A., 118, 140
Coleman, J. S., 12, 266, 271
Coley, R., 118, 140
Collins, A., 14, 18
Commission on Instructionally Supportive
    Assessment, 325, 332, 334
Committee for Economic Development, 131,
    138
Conant, J., 114, 138
Conley, D. T., 304, 306, 307, 313
Connor, R., 60, 92
Conry-Oseguera, P., 267, 270, 271
Cook, T. D., 60, 92
Cooper, H. M., 10, 18, 78, 92, 144, 161
Cox, M., 267, 270, 271
Cremin, L., 165, 166, 168, 181
Cronbach, L., 172, 181
Crossen, C., 176, 181
Crouse, J., 77, 78, 94
Cuban, L., 166, 183
Cullen, J. B., 290, 297
Currie, J., 80, 92
Cutspec, P. A., 47, 54

D

Darling-Hammond, L., 116, 117, 126, 131, 138,
    151, 162, 266, 271
David, I. P., 177, 181
Davis, L. H., 82, 92
Deere, D., 260, 268, 271

Delany, B., 133, 138
Delpit, L., 158, 161
DeMoya, D., 45, 54
Denton, K., 143, 162
Department for Education and Skills, 110
DePascale, C. A., 22, 30
Desimone, L., 90, 93
de Tocqueville, A., 168, 181
Dianda, M., 82, 95
Diaz, R. A., 231–234, 255
Dillon, S., 176, 181
Dolan, L. J., 82, 95
Dolton, P., 265, 271
Donovan, M. S., 15, 18
Dorans, N., 188, 189, 191, 192, 195
Dunbar, S. B., 61, 93, 328, 334
Dunst, C. J., 47, 54

E

Earl, L., 105, 110
Easton, J. Q., 87, 94
Eccles, J., 81, 93
Education Commission of the States, 31, 39
Education Sciences Reform Act of 2002, 43, 54
Education Trust, 115, 138
Education Trust West, 32, 39
Education Week, 115, 134, 138, 146, 161
EFF Assessment Consortium: SRI International and Center for Literacy Studies, 326, 334
Ehrenberg, R. A., 270, 271
Ehrenberg, R. G., 81, 92, 270, 271
Eisenhart, M., 45, 54
Elementary and Secondary Education Act of 1965, 315, 334
Emergency Student Loan Consolidation Act, 173, 181
Entwisle, D. R., 79, 81, 92
Erickson, F., 10, 18, 49, 54
Erpenbach, W. J., 21, 30, 37, 38
Etzioni, A., 136, 138

F

Farris, E., 114, 139
Feinberg, L., 61, 92
Feldman, M., 46, 54

Ferguson, R. F., 79–84, 92, 266, 271
Feuer, M. J., 21, 30, 52, 54, 172, 175, 179, 181, 185, 187, 195
Figlio, D., 290, 297
Fillmore, L. W., 205, 214
Fineout-Overholt, E., 42, 55
Fink, C. M., 87, 93
Folger, J., 83, 95
Forte-Fast, E., 37, 38
Fotiu, R., 118, 139
Freeman, M., 328, 334
Frey, D. E., 292, 297
Friedman, M., 167, 181, 262, 271, 291, 297
Friedman, R. D., 262, 271
Fullan, M., 105, 110
Fulton, B. D., 83, 94, 95

G

Gagné, R. M., 328, 334
Gakidou, E., 177, 183
Galper, A., 143, 162
Gambrill, E., 42, 54
Gamoran, A., 84–86, 92, 93, 95
Gampert, R. A., 87, 93
Garet, M. S., 90, 93, 165, 181
Garner, W. T., 292, 297
Garnier, H., 328, 335
Geis, S., 116, 138
Geppert, J., 22, 30
Getzler, D., 290, 297
Gewertz, C., 146, 161
Gipps, C., 100, 106, 109, 110
Glaser, R., 317, 330, 335
Glatter, R., 292, 297
Gleick, J., 11, 18
Goals 2000: Educate America Act, 315, 334
Goertz, M., 238, 255
Goldhaber, D. D., 266, 271
Good, T. L., 143, 144, 161
Gottfredson, D. C., 87, 93
Graham, N., 87, 93
Grant, C. A., 143, 161
Graue, M. E., 144, 161
Greathouse, S., 78, 92
Green, B. F., 185, 195
Greenberg, E., 118, 138
Greene, B., 114, 139
Greene, J. F., 203, 214
Greene, J. P., 286, 297

Greenwald, R., 80, 93, 118, 138
Grigg, W. S., 27, 30
Grissmer, D., 42, 54, 116, 117, 138
Grissom, J. B., 87, 93
Gritz, R. M., 265, 271
Gruber, K., 114, 139
Gumport, P. J., 313
Guskey, T. R., 81, 93
Gutierrez, K., 10, 18, 49, 54

H

Haberman, M., 155, 156, 161
Haggstrom, G. W., 116, 117, 138
Haller, E. J., 81, 93
Haney, W., 294, 297
Hannaway, J., 292, 297
Hanushek, E. A., 261, 264–268, 272, 273, 279, 282, 294, 297
Hargreaves, D. H., 109, 110, 330, 334
Hart, P. D., 2, 3
Haug, C., 22, 30
Hauser, R., 317, 334
Haycock, K., 126, 138, 302, 311, 313
Haynes, R. B., 48, 55
Hedges, L. V., 10, 18, 63, 76, 80, 83, 84, 93, 94, 118, 138
Hemphill, F. C., 185, 195
Henke, R., 114, 116, 138, 139
Henry, G. T., 303–305, 313
Herman, J. L., 331, 334
Herrnstein, R. J., 32, 39, 60, 93
Hill, R. K., 22, 30
Hirsch, E., 115, 138
Hirschman, A., 175, 179, 181
Hobson, C. J., 266, 271
Hochschild, J. L., 77, 95
Holland, J. G., 317, 334
Holland, P. W., 175, 177–179, 181, 185, 188–192, 194, 195
Holmes, E., 106, 110
Holmes Group, 147, 161
Horn, L., 116, 138
Hoskens, M., 194, 195
Howe, K. R., 44, 54
Howell, W. G., 294, 297
Hoxby, C. M., 268, 272, 292, 295, 297
Hutchings, M., 104, 111
Hutchins, E., 82, 93

I

Immerwahr, J., 312, 313
Impara, J. C., 331, 334
Improving America's Schools Act of 1994, 315, 334
Ingersoll, R., 114, 120, 133, 136–139, 150, 161
Institute of Medicine, 42, 54

J

Jacob, B. A., 87, 88, 94, 290, 297
Jacob, B. J., 262, 272
Jencks, C., 59, 77, 93
Jepsen, C., 258, 266, 272
Johnson, M. S., 27, 30
Johnston, J., 83, 95
Jonsson, P., 158, 161
Joseph, D., 14, 18
Jussim, L., 81, 93

K

Kaestle, C., 43, 54, 166, 169, 181
Kain, J. F., 261, 264, 265, 272, 279, 282, 297
Kain, R. F., 266, 267, 273
Kane, T. J., 22, 30, 262, 272, 281, 287–289, 294, 297, 298
Karweit, N. L., 82, 95
Katz, M., 166, 181
Kelly, H., 323, 334
Kemple, J. J., 265, 269, 272
Kershaw, J. A., 264, 272
Kindler, A. L., 199, 214
King, N., 267, 270, 271
Kirst, M. W., 85, 94, 134, 139, 302, 305, 307, 310, 312–314
Knapp, M., 115, 138
Kohn, M., 119, 139
Konstantopoulos, S., 83, 84, 94
Koppich, J., 115, 138
Koretz, D. M., 175, 185, 195, 268, 272, 294, 298, 325, 334
Kosters, M. H., 62, 89, 93
Kozol, J., 126, 139, 157, 161
Krueger, A. B., 294, 298
Kulik, C. L., 84, 93
Kulik, J. A., 84, 93

L

Ladd, H. F., 81, 92, 231–234, 255, 290, 291, 298
Ladson-Billings, G., 143, 154, 156, 161
Lagemann, E. C., 7, 11, 19, 52, 54
Laine, R. D., 80, 93, 118, 138
Lakdawalla, D., 264, 272
Lankford, H., 227, 228, 230, 234, 240, 248, 255, 264, 265, 271, 272
Law, M., 42, 54
Lee, V., 127, 138
Leithwood, K., 105, 110
Levin, B., 105, 110
Levin, H. M., 292, 298
Levine, D. L., 82, 93
Levitt, S. D., 262, 272, 290, 297
Lewis, L., 114, 139
Lieberman, J., 116, 138
Lindblom, C. E., 46, 54
Lindsay, J., 78, 92
Linn, R. L., 22, 25, 27, 30, 61, 93, 100, 110, 176, 180–182, 186, 195, 317, 328, 334
Lintz, M. N., 83, 95
Loeb, S., 225, 227, 228, 230, 234, 235, 239, 240, 248, 255, 264, 265, 271, 272, 294, 297
Lord, C., 323, 335
Lortie, D., 119, 136, 139
Lumsdaine, A. A., 317, 335
Lutkus, A. D., 27, 30
Luxembourg Income Study, 177, 182

M

Madden, N. A., 82, 95
Madon, S., 81, 93
Manzo, K. K., 48, 54
March, J. G., 46, 54
Mare, R. G., 84, 92
Marion, S., 21, 30
Markle, S. M., 317, 335
Markman, J. M., 279, 297
Mast, B. D., 62, 89, 93
Mathews, J., 176, 182
Matsumura, L. C., 328, 335
McAlister, S., 100, 106, 110
McCabe, M., 146, 161
McCallum, B., 100, 106, 110
McDonnell, L., 267, 270, 271
McGrath, D., 114, 139

McIntire, W., 117, 139
McKean, R. N., 264, 272
McLaughlin, D., 175, 182
McMillen, M., 114, 137, 139
McNeil, L., 201, 214
McNess, E., 105, 111
McPartland, J., 266, 271
MDRC & Council of the Great City Schools, 34, 37, 39
Medrich, E., 116, 138
Meister, G., 312, 313
Melnyk, B. M., 42, 55
Mencken, H. L., 1, 3
Messick, S., 9
Mislevy, R. J., 186, 187, 195
Mize, D., 311, 314
Moe, T. M., 167, 181, 291, 297
Moirs, K., 117, 139
Monk, D., 127, 139
Mood, A. M., 266, 271
Morrill, W., 53, 55
Morris, J., 99, 111
Morris, W., 326, 335
Mosteller, F., 83, 93
Murnane, R. J., 81, 93, 262, 265, 267–272
Murray, C. J. L., 32, 39, 60, 93, 177, 183

N

National Academy of Sciences, 171, 182
National Association of State Directors of Teacher Education and Certification, 132, 139
National Center for Education Statistics, 61, 62, 76, 85, 93, 235, 255
National Center on Postsecondary Improvement, 305, 314
National Clearinghouse for English Language Acquisition, 216, 217, 221
National Commission on Excellence in Education, 85, 88, 94, 166, 182, 315, 335
National Commission on Teaching and America's Future, 115, 133, 139, 143, 152–155, 161
National Commission on the Reform of Secondary Education, 166, 182
National Council for Education Statistics, 33, 36, 39

National Council of Teachers of Mathematics, 86, 94, 170, 182
National Council on Education Standards and Testing, 315, 335
National Education Goals Panel, 315, 335
National Governors Association, 315, 335
National Panel on High School and Adolescent Education, 166, 182
National Reading Panel, 42, 55
National Research Council, 42, 45, 47, 50, 52, 55, 170, 172, 173, 175, 177, 179, 180, 182
National Research Council, Committee on Learning Research and Educational Practice, 82, 94
National Science Board, 85, 94
National Science Foundation, 89, 94
Nelson, J. E., 27, 30
Niemi, D., 331, 335
Nisbet, J., 107, 111
Nisbett, R. E., 60, 94
No Child Left Behind Act of 2001, 2, 3, 21, 23, 24, 30, 32, 39, 41, 55, 89, 94, 142, 161, 171, 182, 199, 214, 276, 298, 315, 335
Noeth, R. J., 307, 314
Norris, N. A., 27, 30
North Central Regional Educational Laboratory, 51, 55
Nowell, A., 63, 76, 93
Nye, B. A., 78, 83, 84, 92, 94

O

Oakes, J., 84, 94, 126, 139, 304, 314
O'Brien, D. M., 265, 272
O'Connor, C., 213, 214
O'Connor, M. C., 211, 214
O'Day, J., 89, 95
Office for Standards in Education, 103, 111
Ogbu, J. U., 91, 94
Olsen, D. R., 14, 19
Olsen, R. J., 265, 269, 272
Olson, L. S., 25, 30, 79, 92
Organisation for Economic Co-operation and Development, 103, 109, 111
Orrill, R., 311, 314
Osborn, M., 105, 111
Osthoff, E. J., 85, 94

P–Q

Pace, R. R., 265, 272
Page, M. E., 264, 265, 272
Pajares, M. F., 143, 161
Panel on Youth of the President's Science Advisory Committee, 166, 182
PA News, 105, 111
Parker, W., 159, 162
Parsad, B., 114, 139
Pascal, A., 267, 270, 271
Pascal, J., 328, 335
Pascarella, E., 119, 139
Pauly, E., 267, 270, 271
Pellegrino, J., 330, 335
Peterson, P. E., 294, 297
Pettigrew, T. F., 43, 55
Phelps, R., 118, 140
Phillips, B., 267, 272
Phillips, M., 59, 77, 78, 93, 94
Podgursky, M., 269, 271
Pollard, A., 111
Popham, W. J., 316, 317, 334, 335
Porter, A. C., 85, 86, 90, 93–95, 331, 335
Potts, A., 37, 38
President's Committee of Advisors on Science and Technology, 53, 55
Qualifications and Curriculum Authority, 105, 111

R

Rabinowitz, S., 21, 30
Ralph, J., 77, 78, 94
Raudenbush, S. W., 12, 13, 18, 50, 55, 118, 139
Ravitch, D., 169, 182
Raymond, M. E., 294, 297
Reback, R., 290, 297
Redfield, D. L., 47, 51, 55
Reynolds, A. J., 87, 94
Rhodes, D., 118, 138
Richards, J. S., 37, 39
Richardson, S. R., 48, 55
Rist, R., 144, 162
Rivkin, S. G., 258, 261, 264–268, 272, 273, 279, 282, 297
Robinson, V., 117, 134, 139
Roderick, M., 87, 88, 94
Rogers, E. M., 46, 55
Rose, S. J., 301, 313

Rosenbaum, J., 303, 304, 314
Rosenberg, W., 48, 55
Rosenholtz, S., 152, 161
Ross, A., 104, 111
Ross, S., 82, 95
Rothstein, J. M., 292, 298
Rouse, C. E., 292, 295, 297, 298
Routitsky, A., 61, 94
Rowan, B., 12
Rowley, S., 312, 313
Royal Swedish Academy of Sciences, 179, 182
Rubenstein, R., 303–305, 313
Rubin, H. G., 34, 39
Ruby, A., 133, 139

S

Sacerdote, B., 279, 298
Sackett, D. L., 48, 55
Sacks, P., 31, 39
Santapau, S. L., 27, 30
Sawaki, Y., 323, 334, 335
Scafidi, B., 265, 273
Schmidt, W. H., 310, 314
Schneider, M., 292, 298
Schneider, S. A., 85, 94
Schooler, C., 119, 139
Scovronick, N., 77, 95
Seefeldt, C., 143, 162
Sen, A. K., 179, 183
Senior, A. M., 82, 92
Seppänen, R., 109, 111
Shaffer, A., 60, 92
Shanker, A., 114, 139
Shaughnessy, C. A., 27, 30
Shavelson, R. J., 9, 19, 21, 30, 52, 54, 179, 181
Shaw, M., 103, 111
Sheinker, J., 21, 30
Shepard, L. A., 87, 93
Shulman, L., 123, 139
Silberman, C. E., 18, 19
Simon, H., 178, 183
Singer, J. D., 11, 19, 265, 269, 272
Sivin-Kachala, J., 47, 51, 55
Sjoquist, D. L., 265, 273
Skinner, B. F., 317, 334
Slater, J., 104, 109, 111
Slavin, R. E., 82, 95
Smerdon, B., 114, 139

Smith, J., 127, 138
Smith, L., 82, 95
Smith, M. S., 89, 95
Smithson, J. S., 85, 86, 93–95
Snow, C. E., 15, 18, 205, 214
Snyder, B., 45, 54
Soler, S., 131, 139
Sousa, A., 177, 183
Staigler, D. O., 22, 30, 262, 272, 281, 287–289, 294, 297, 298
Stancavage, F., 118, 138
Stanovich, K. E., 47, 51, 55
Stanovich, P. J., 47, 51, 55
Steadman, S., 100, 110
Steinberg, D. H., 331, 335
Stierer, B., 100, 110
Stinebrickner, T. R., 265, 273
Stoker, G., 323, 334, 335
Stokes, D. E., 9, 19
Stone, P., 42, 55
Strayer, W., 260, 268, 271
Suggs, E., 308, 314
Sweet, R., 43

T

Tamkin, G., 60, 92
Tandon, A., 177, 183
Tay-lim, B. S. H., 27, 30
Teeter, R. M., 2, 3
Terenzini, P., 119, 139
Thayer, D. T., 190, 195
Theobald, N. D., 265, 271
Thomas, D., 80, 92
Thompson, M. S., 81, 92
Thoreson, A., 266, 271
Thornton, K., 104, 111
Tiebout, C. M., 262, 273
Tilly, C., 91, 95
Toch, T., 131, 139
Tom, D. Y. H., 144, 161
Torrance, H., 104, 111
Towne, L., 9, 19, 21, 30, 45, 52, 54, 179, 181
Townsend, R., 117, 139
Travers, R. M. W., 107, 108, 111
Triggs, P., 111
Trivette, C. M., 47, 54
Tryneski, J., 120, 140
Turner, R., 61, 94
Tyack, D., 136, 140, 166, 173, 183

Tyler, R. W., 317, 335

U

University of Arizona, 206, 214
U.S. Congress, Office of Technology
  Assessment, 172, 173, 176, 180, 183
U.S. Department of Education, 22, 24, 30, 42,
  45, 47, 49, 51, 55, 56, 88, 95, 143, 162,
  218, 222, 313, 314
U.S. Department of Education. National
  Center for Education Statistics, 219,
  222

V

Valdés, R., 328, 335
Valenzuela, A., 201, 214
van der Klaauw, W., 265, 271
Venezia, A., 302, 307, 305, 314
Vigdor, J. L., 231–234, 255
von Davier, A. A., 190, 195

W

Wainer, H., 181
Wallenhorst, M. P., 83, 94
Wang, A., 118, 140
Ward, H., 105, 111
Wasik, B. A., 82, 95
Watson, N., 105, 110
Watts, D. J., 11, 19
Wayne, A. J., 266, 273
Webb, N. L., 331, 334, 335
Weber, S. J., 60, 92
Weinfeld, F. D., 266, 271

Weiss, C. H., 46, 56
Wenger, E., 15, 19
White, C., 21, 30
White, K. R., 76, 95
White, P. A., 85, 86, 92, 93, 95
Whitehurst, G., 41, 48, 56
Whitty, G., 100, 111
Wigdor, A. K., 15, 18
Wigfield, A., 143, 162
Wiliam, D., 109, 110
Williams, S., 99, 111
Williamson, O., 167, 183
Willett, J. B., 11, 19, 265, 269, 272
Wimberly, G. L., 307, 314
Wise, A., 151, 162
Wolf, A., 108, 111
Wolf, P. J., 294, 297
Woods, B. D., 7, 19
Woods, P., 292, 297
Word, E., 83, 95
Wyckoff, J., 227, 228, 230, 234, 240, 248, 255,
  264, 265, 271, 272

X–Y

Xi, X., 323, 335
Ye, X., 118, 138
Yoon, K., 90, 93
Youngs, P., 266, 273
York, R. L., 266, 271

Z

Zaharias, J. B., 83, 94, 95
Zelli, A., 290, 291, 298
Zellman, G., 267, 270, 271
Zhu, P., 294, 298
Zuniga, S., 331, 334

Subject Index

A

ability grouping, 79, 84, 90, 144, *see also* tracking
accommodation, 188, 218, 303
accountability, 7, 173, 262, 301, 302, 318, 319
  and education research, 8, 9, 14
  and No Child Left Behind, 21, 22, 29, 35–37, 90, 115, 135, 142, 176, 200, 215, 217–219, 316
  and schools, 87, 89, 99, 103, 166, 200, 234, 269, 275, 276, 283, 285, 292
  and student achievement, 42, 87, 89, 225, 309, 325
  and teachers, 104–106, 108–110, 135, 136, 225, 226, 231–235, 241–255, 323
  and the public, 43, 100, 103, 167, 169
  state by state, 236–246
  system, 1–3, 13, 22, 24, 29, 37, 178, 232, 261, 267–271, 279, 290–296, 305, 308, 311, 312
achievement gap, 2, 3, 32, 35, 38, 59–63, 75–92, 201, 204, 292
achievement test, 86, 201, 202, 207, 208, 211, 221
adequate yearly progress (AYP), 21–30, 36, 37, 89, 176, 200, 201, 218, 277, 278, 280, 281, 283, 285, 286, 289, 296, 318

Advanced Placement (AP), 304, 305, 308–310
after-school program, 8, 15, 87, 88
A-level, 102, 103
alignment, 3, 89, 90, 178, 201, 211, 217, 221, 254, 302–304, 306, 308, 310, 311, 315, 318–333
all students, educating, 1–3, 8, 14, 16, 18, 21–23, 32, 34, 36, 38, 48, 59, 82, 83, 89, 135, 142, 159, 166, 167, 215, 296, 307, 315, 333
American College Test (ACT), 303, 310, 311
Ashenfelter Dip, 285
assessment, 185, 186, 220, 225, 301, 311, 317
  aligned, 89, 90, 217, 302, 304, 315, 326–329, 332
  and No Child Left Behind, 21, 32, 290
  and teachers, 149, 150, 154, 155, 159
  data use, 31, 32, 35, 126, 144, 157, 170, 180, 188, 195, 199, 286, 303
  design, 187, 189, 221, 280, 281, 285
  NAEP, 27, 170, 173, 174, 310, *see also* NAEP
  national, 100, 101, 104–106, 109, 110
  performance, 61, 100, 187
  statewide, 25, 26, 29, 32, 173, 174, 200, 211, 215, 227, 231, 254, 293, 306–309
  United Kingdom, 99–106, 109, 110
Assessment for Learning, 109
at-risk students, 2, 22, 29, 79, 82, 166, 167
audit, 306

B

benchmark, 26, 27, 172, 175, 176, 277, 316
bridge model, 327, 328
broad-access institutions, 301–307, 312
budget cuts, 8, 53, 133, *see also* funding

C

Campbell Collaboration, 9, 42
causation, 10, 11, 43, 45, 91, 239, 254, 266, 319
ceiling effect, 285
certification, 81, 115–126, 131, 132, 134–136,
    145–150, 159, 227–229, 257–261,
    265–270, 301, 309, 324
change (research on), 11, 12, 50, 282
chaos theory, 11
charter schools, 262, 270, 278
cheating, 105, 262, 290
class, *see* socioeconomic status
class-size reduction, 42, 79, 82–84, 91, 133,
    134, 142, 160, 234, 258, 261, 267, 275
clinical trials, 44
college knowledge, 304, 305, 307
college readiness, 302, 305, 310
communities of practice, 15, 16
community college, 301, 302, 307–311, 313
comparability, 178
comparing schools, 27–29, 102, 133, 141, 176,
    254, 293
congruence model, 324–326, 328, 330, 331
consensus, 49, 117, 119, 191, 266
constructed-response items, 174, 187
correspondence model, 326–328, 330, 331
counselors, 304, 306, 307, 312
course placement, 34, 37, 38, 85, 304, *see also*
    tracking
criterion referencing, 100
cross-national comparisons, 177
culture, 13, 16, 17, 48, 52, 82, 151–154, 166,
    171, 179, 188, 204, 219
curriculum, 12, 108, 152, 157, 168, 304, 311,
    317, 332
  aligned, 89, 227, 315, 328
  developing, 154, 155, 159, 173, 202, 213,
    245, 246, 278, 291
  for disadvantaged students, 37, 61, 84, 218
  national, 99–106, 109, 172
  strengthening, 85, 86, 165, 211, 307, 309
  teacher education, 16, 17
cut scores, 188

D

decentralization, 167, 168, 173
default curriculum, 307
descriptive data, 13
design experiments, 14
differential item functioning, 177
direct true-score prediction, 194
disability, 2, 22, 32, 42, 89, 149, 170, 218, 277,
    290
disaggregating data, 31–38, 62, 83, 89, 90, 218,
    220
distributed leadership, 136
diversity, 32, 127, 143, 149, 159, 168, 172, 175,
    205, 208, 211, 219
drilling, 213
dropping out, 8, 34, 85, 87, 104 (teachers)
dumbing down classes, 85, 86

E

economic downturn, 8, 142
education production function, 266, 278, 279
Education Reform Act of 1988 (in UK), 100
education research methods, 8–14, 18, 42, 52
Education Sciences Reform Act of 2002, 42,
    43
effect size, 77, 82, 84, 191
embedding, 177, 185, 188
empiricism, 318
end-of-grade test, 34, 87
English language learners (ELL), 2, 22, 32, 35,
    37, 60, 89, 188, 199–213, 215–221, 277
enrichment, 84
equal opportunity, 12, 34, 168, 308, *see also*
    opportunity to learn
equating function, 189–194
equity in education, 8, 34, 90, 141–143,
    146–150, 153, 157–159, 166, 189
essay questions, 174
ethnicity, 190, 294, 295
  and achievement gap, 59–63, 75–81, 83–85,
    90, 91, 158, 204
  and expectations, 144, 145, 155–159, 204,
    211–213, 304, 312
  and NCLB requirements, 22, 23, 32, 35, 89,
    277, 281–284, 287
  and teacher quality, 141, 142, 146–150, 153,
    154, 228–232, 240, 247–253, 255, 261,
    264

ethnographies, 13
evidence report, 46
Examination Board, 101
exit exam, 31, 203, 227, 236–239
expected value, 191

F

federalism, 167–169, 174
feedback, 110, 311
floor effect, 285
financial aid, 305
funding
　accountability, 21, 225, 275, 291
　federal, 41, 53, 108, 167, 172, 200, 218
　inadequate, 8, 50, 133, 204, 220, 221, 292
　No Child Left Behind, 21, 41, 200, 201, 215,
　　218–221, 276
　property-tax based, 157, 158, 169
　state-level, 34, 50, 218, 259, 262, 291,
　　308
　teacher, 8, 160, 201, 220, 258, 259, 262

G

gender, 32, 144, 145, 159, 169, 189, 190, 192,
　　231, 232, 240, 247–250, 264, 284
gifted, 31, 34, 145, 211, 212
goal, 106, 178, 211, 275, 308, 311, 315–319, 324,
　　325, 328–330, 333
　instructional, 12, 48, 49, 52, 53, 88, 89, 166,
　　278, 291, 309, 316, 332
　national, 168–171
　No Child Left Behind, 23, 26–30, 115, 130,
　　176, 218, 236, 276
　of high-quality teachers, 135
grade-level equivalents, 78
graphing theory, 11
gravity model, 329, 330

H

hazard model, 232
Head Start, 80
higher order skills, 103, 110
high-stakes testing, 7, 34, 88, 142, 156, 159,
　　160, 173, 180, 188, 227, 255, 262, 290
history of ETS, 7

I

immersion, 207
incentive, 1, 303, 304, 311, 318
　No Child Left Behind, 176, 277
　researcher, 17, 52
　school, 275, 291, 293
　student, 202, 305, 309
　teacher, 12, 231, 233, 235, 257–263, 267–270,
　　290, 295
incremental increase, 24
in-field teaching, *see* out-of-field teaching
inquiry, 44, 45, 82
Institute of Education Sciences (IES), 9, 42,
　　43, 46, 48, 53
instructional regime, 13
instructional systems design (ISD), 317, 318
intermediate goals, 23–27
internships, 8, 149
intervention, 2, 16, 38, 60, 79–82, 91, 100, 169,
　　236, 238, 275, 315, 316
intuitive test theory, 187

J

jargon, 46
joint degree program, 17

K

Kelley formula, 194

L

league tables, 100, 105, 107
LEARNOME, 323, 332
linear regression, 194, 251–253, 279
linking education theory and practice, 8, 9,
　　16
local control, 13, 14, 48, 142, 168–171, 174,
　　231, 269, 303, 323
local needs, 48, 49, 52, 100, 145, 168–170, 259
longitudinal data analysis, 11, 12
lottery, 288, 289

M

market, 100, 158, 159, 167, 169, 208, 248,
    259–261, 263, 276, 291–293, 295,
    296
mean score (μ), 190, 192, 240, 245, 281, 285,
    286, 288
measurement error, 174, 262, 279, 280,
    283–287, 289, 295, 296
measurement research, 3, 22, 180, 317, 331,
    332
mentoring, 8, 153, 156
merit pay, 259, 262, 267–270
metacognition, 82, 91, 329
minimalism, 323
minority, *see* ethnicity
monitor, 209
multiple-choice questions, 61, 174, 187, 192,
    193, 279
multiple measures, 175, 176, 178

N

national assessment in UK, 100, 101, 104, 105,
    109
National Assessment of Educational
    Progress (NAEP), 26–29, 35, 61, 62, 76,
    77, 86, 90, 118, 167, 170, 173, 174, 176,
    294, 310
national testing, 171, 172, 303, *see also*
    voluntary national test
nature-nurture controversy, 60
network, 11, 15, 330
No Child Left Behind Act, 2, 167, 171, 209,
    216, 282, 285, 318
    and teachers, 2, 47, 113–117, 120, 121, 126,
        128, 134, 135, 141, 142, 208, 213, 316
    criticized, 36, 135, 176, 201, 204, 213, 218,
        221, 281, 286
    described, 21, 22, 41, 43, 89, 142, 199, 215,
        276, 289, 296, 315
    implementation, 3, 47, 49, 50, 200, 221, 289,
        290
    praised, 37, 219, 220
    requirements, 21, 22, 26–29, 32, 35, 47, 89,
        121, 130, 142, 176, 199, 208, 213–217,
        276–281, 289, 315, 316
norm, 12, 13, 16–18, 43, 82, 152, 156, 158, 167,
    168

O

open-ended questions, 174
Opportunity Scholarships, 286
opportunity to learn, 61, 80, 90, 91, 143, 166,
    312
outcomes, 12, 235, 263, 266–268, 270, 276, 279,
    281, 284, 290–294, 304, 305, 313,
    316–319, 330, 332
out-of-field teaching, 113–121, 123–128,
    130–137, 146
outreach programs, 305, 307

P

parallel-linear linking function, 191, 192
parents, 12, 47, 144, 153, 155, 158, 168, 172,
    226, 234, 267, 270, 276, 278, 284, 291,
    292, 295, 296, 301–307, 313, 317
participation rate, 62
payment by results, 106
pedagogical content knowledge, 123
pedagogy of poverty, 155, 156
peers, 279, 280, 292, 331
performance assessment, 100, 187, 236
performance level, 76, 77, 109, 110, 170, 310,
    316, 326, 328
permission to fail, 156
persistence, 308, 311–313
phonics, 207, 208, 213
placement test, 301, 302, 304, 306, 309, 310
population invariance, 189, 191–193
portfolio, 150
positivism, 9
poverty, *see* socioeconomic status
practicum, 17, 147
prediction, 194
preschool, 79, 80, 90, 91
principals, 133–135, 142, 151, 166, 209, 239,
    269, 270, 290
private school, 127, 239, 262, 268, 286, 291,
    294, 295
privatization, 158, 167, 278
probation, 87, 160, 237
procedural rationality, 175, 178–180
professional development, 18, 110, 117, 143,
    152, 158, 275, 316, 329
    aligning, 89, 90
    funding, 8, 154, 200, 201
    improving, 37, 52, 115, 153, 160

in-service, 31, 115, 132, 135, 219, 259
preservice, 115, 119–121, 131–136, 146–150, 208, 209, 258, 265, 268
proficiency, 21, 23–29, 37, 89, 118, 207, 209, 212, 213, 215, 217, 218, 220, 277, 281, 310, 316, 325, 327
programmed instruction, 317
promotion, 87, 88, 91, 173, 317
property taxes, 157, 169
psychometrics, 171–174, 177, 185–187, 189, 194
public opinion, 2, 42, 50, 99, 100, 145, 153, 155, 172, 180, 267, 292, 295, 311, 312, 315

Q–R

Qualifications and Curriculum Authority (QCA), 101, 105
race, *see* ethnicity
racism, 157, 158, 160, 169, 305
randomized trials, 10, 43–46, 49, 80, 83
ranking, 188, 227, 231, 233, 235, 237, 288, 289, 310
rationalism, 317
reductionism, 9, 11, 213
reflective practice, 159
reform, 46, 48, 142, 165, 171, 302–306, 311, 312, 317, 320, 323, 326
 and accountability, 1, 225, 234, 240, 241, 253, 275
 and achievement gap, 59, 60, 79–82, 91
 and teachers, 109, 113, 128, 130, 143, 148, 229, 232–235, 241, 253, 290
 data use, 38, 116, 180, 231, 254, 292–294, 318, 328–333
 funding, 53, 157
 legislation, 42, 89, 115, 170, 213
 program, 41, 49, 51
 standards-based, 47, 88–90, 145, 166, 226, 234, 235, 309, 315, 316
register, 205, 209
regression effect, 78, 189
reliability, 22, 23, 29, 41, 43, 171, 174, 175, 178, 180, 186, 187, 189, 287, 289, 317, 331
religion in education, 169
remedial courses, 301, 304–306, 308, 310, 311
replicable evidence, 10, 23, 41, 43, 45, 52, 82, 114
research synthesis, 10, 52

research training, 16–18
resources
 and student outcomes, 12, 104, 144, 160, 278
 constraints, 13, 47, 53, 83, 133, 134, 152, 154, 160, 301
 funding, 53, 157, 158
 increasing, 87, 91, 167, 316, 318, 319
 reallocating, 142, 275, 290
restructuring, 28, 91, 165, 215, 278
results-based reform (RBR), 316–318, 328
retention (in grade level), 87, 91, 160, 275, 317
role model, 91
root mean square, 191, 192
rubric, 326–328

S

safe harbor, 277, 282
sample bias, 62, 187
sample coverage, *see* test content
sanctions, 28, 29, 237, 239, 261, 262, 275–277, 281, 285, 289, 291, 296, 316, 318, 319
satisficing, 178, 179
scale differences, 191
schadenfreude, 175
Scholastic Aptitude Test (SAT), 301, 303, 304, 310
school
 -based management, 136
 choice, 142, 167, 215, 259, 262, 267, 268, 270, 276, 291–293
 environment, 13, 82, 89, 104–106, 152, 153, 156, 226, 227, 234, 235, 254, 330
 improvement, 28, 29, 105, 200, 213, 218, 221
 inspection, 102
 leadership, 12, 133, 158
 -leaving examination, 99, 100, *see also* exit exam
 performance tables, 100, 102, 236, 237
 report card, 236–238, 270, 275
 size, 127, 136, 286, 289
Schools and Staffing Survey (SASS), 113–117, 120, 131, 133, 146, 235, 239–243, 246
scientific evidence, 21, 29, 41
scientifically based research (SBR), 21, 22, 28, 29, 41–53, 143
self-identification, 75
senioritis, 309

Sesame Street, 60, 61
signals, 303–306, 311, 316
social capital, 330, 333
socioeconomic status (SES)
    and achievement gap, 60–62, 76, 78–80, 84,
        90, 91
    and college preparation, 302, 304, 305
    and No Child Left Behind, 32, 277, 282, 283
    and teachers, 126, 127, 132, 141–150,
        153–160, 228, 230, 240, 249–253, 255
    and testing, 61, 81, 82
special education, 31, 34–37
special-needs students, 315, *see also*
    disability
standard deviation (σ), 190–193, 240, 245, 267
Standard English, 205, 209
standardized effect sizes, 76
standards, 171, 227, 281, 312, 318, 319
    academic, 35, 146, 301
    -based reform, 3, 47, 88–91, 150, 173, 226,
        233–235, 309, 315
    content, 86, 90, 166, 169, 170, 203, 208, 211,
        217, 218, 220, 302, 303, 306, 307, 310,
        315, 323, 325–331
    performance, 103–108, 110, 167, 170, 231,
        239, 241, 242, 245, 291, 294, 309, 311,
        316, 317, 323, 324, 327, 332
    research, 8, 13–18, 43, 44, 52
    student achievement, 2, 22, 25, 48, 99, 154,
        165, 167, 176, 202, 286, 306
    teacher, 124, 132, 133, 136, 137, 143–146,
        159, 165, 258, 266, 268
Standards for Success (S4S), 306, 307
states' rights, 169
statistical research, 11, 12, 179, 186, 193
stereotyping, 32, 38
Strategic Education Research Partnership
    (SERP), 15, 16, 47, 50
stress, 103
student achievement
    and educational resources, 12, 42, 166, 292
    and incentives, 12, 231, 277
    and No Child Left Behind, 21–25, 28–30,
        32, 37, 276, 277, 281
    and teachers, 81, 118, 119, 143, 144,
        228–231, 264, 265, 270
    and testing, 101, 105, 172, 173, 270, 279,
        284, 290
    gap, 59–62, 77–91
    improving, 35, 59–62, 80, 83, 86, 88, 91, 143,
        166, 213, 239, 276, 290–295, 303
student knowledge, 12, 144, 285

subject-matter knowledge, 115, 117, 120, 121,
    208, 209, 266, 309, 329, 330
Success For All, 82
summer, 78, 79, 87–91, 275
surveys, 13
symmetry requirement, 189, 190
systemic reform, 88, 89

T

target population, 190, 191
target setting, 102–106, 108, 109, 217, 236,
    280, 316, 318
task analysis, 328
teacher-deficit perspective, 135
teacher
    dropout, 104, 136, 146, 150–152, 225–230,
        232–235, 240, 248, 253, 255, 264, 265,
        269
    effort, 259–261, 267–269
    expectations, 81, 91, 143–145, 156, 213, 304,
        307
    knowledge, 12, 80, 81, 117–120, 123, 135,
        153, 208
    morale, 104–108, 154, 176, 202, 203, 225,
        226, 243, 245, 253
    pay, 160, 231, 240, 247, 248, 250–252,
        258–269, 275
    quality, 2, 34, 36, 47, 80–84, 90, 99, 109, 110,
        113–121, 123–128, 130–137, 141–143,
        146, 147, 149, 151–153, 158–160, 204,
        208, 209, 226, 227, 233, 234, 257–260,
        263–270, 316
    recruitment, 104, 115, 133–136, 143, 146,
        150–154, 226, 234, 258, 260, 265
    shortage, 132, 133, 148, 149, 151, 159, 220,
        234, 260, 264
    training, *see* professional development
teaching to the test, 202, 218, 290, 291, 294,
    325
technical language, 46, 206
technology, 136, 148, 264, 278, 332
tenure, 17, 52, 259, 261, 270
test
    content, 187, 227, 304, 309, 325, 327
    design, 174, 327
    equating, 188, 189
    format, 174, 187, 304, 325
    linking, 172–178, 180, 185–189, 192–195
    preparation, 201, 202

security, 188
theory, 187, 194
testing services, 7, 169, 174, 323
testing students, 2, 7, 8, 24, 31, 87, 99–103,
    171–173, 275, 310, 316, 328
test-score changes, 11, 103, 188, 201, 282–284,
    288–291, 294–296, 326
textbooks, 169, 302
theory of action, 176, 317, 318
TIMSS, 310
Title I, 21, 41, 59, 89, 170, 200, 208, 217, 218,
    220, 221
tracking, 84, 90, 304, 308, *see also* ability
    grouping and course placement
true score, 194
tutoring, 8

U

unions, 259, 262, 270, 312
unit of analysis, 317
usable knowledge, 8
U.S. Department of Education, 45, 47–49, 51,
    53, 114, 143, 146, 218, 219, 282
use-oriented basic research, 9

V

validity
    of inferences, 22, 23, 29, 30, 144, 174, 217
    of No Child Left Behind, 22, 23, 27–30
    of research standards, 43, 117, 171, 262,
        270, 292, 328, 331, 332
    of testing, 9, 22, 23, 27–30, 32, 102, 171,
        174–180, 185–189
value-added, 280, 281, 289, 292
values, 13, 304, 313
vocational examination, 102, 103
voluntary national test (VNT), 172, 173, 176,
    185, 303
vouchers, 167, 172, 236, 262, 270, 276, 286,
    291–295

W

war on poverty, 59
weighted tests, 190–192, 233, 239, 250, 310
What Works Clearinghouse, 9, 46, 51, 53
workload, 104, 105